UPPER
CANADA

THE FORMATIVE YEARS

GERALD M. CRAIG

UPPER CANADA

THE
FORMATIVE
YEARS
1784-1841

The Canadian Centenary Series

McClelland and Stewart

Reprinted 1966, 1968, 1972, 1977, 1979

0-7710-2311-1

DESIGN: FRANK NEWFELD

The Canadian Publishers
McClelland and Stewart Limited
25 Hollinger Road, Toronto   M4B 3G2

Manufactured in Canada by Webcom Limited

THE
CANADIAN
CENTENARY
SERIES

A History of Canada

W. L. Morton, EXECUTIVE EDITOR

D. G. Creighton, ADVISORY EDITOR

VOLUMES STARRED ARE PUBLISHED

†ALSO AVAILABLE IN PAPERBACK

CONTENTS

Upper Canada: The Formative Years

The Canadian Centenary Series
xi

PREFACE
xiii

MAPS

Courtney C. J. Bond, CARTOGRAPHER

———————

The Canadian Cenetnary Series

Half a century has elapsed since *Canada and Its Provinces*, the first large-scale co-operative history of Canada, was published. During that time, new historical materials have been made available in archives and libraries; new research has been carried out, and its results published; new interpretations have been advanced and tested. In these same years Canada itself has greatly grown and changed. These facts, together with the centenary of Confederation, justify the publication of a new co-operative history of Canada.

The form chosen for this enterprise was that of a series of volumes. The series was planned by the editors, but each volume will be designed and executed by a single author. The general theme of the work is the development of those regional communities which have for the past century made up the Canadian nation; and the series will be composed of a number of volumes sufficiently large to permit an adequate treatment of all the phases of the theme in the light of modern knowledge.

The Centenary History, then, was planned as a series to have a certain common character and to follow a common method but to be written by individual authors, specialists in their fields. As a whole it will be a work of specialized knowledge, the great advantage of scholarly co-operation, and at the same time each volume will have the unity and distinctive character of individual authorship. It was agreed that a general narrative treatment was necessary and that each author should deal in a balanced way with economic, political, and social history. The result, it is hoped, will be an interpretive, varied, and comprehensive account, at once useful to the student and interesting to the general reader.

The difficulties of organizing and executing such a series are apparent: the overlapping of separate narratives, the risk of omissions, the imposition of divisions which are relevant to some themes but not to others. Not so apparent, but quite as troublesome, are problems of scale, perspective, and scope, problems which perplex the writer of a one-volume history and are magnified in a series. It is by deliberate choice that certain parts of the history are told twice, in different volumes from different points of view, in the belief that the benefits gained outweigh the unavoidable disadvantages.

The editors present G. M. Craig's volume, the first to be published in the series, as a distinguished example of the character and quality they sought to have realized in the individual volumes. Professor Craig's theme is the development of the colony of Upper Canada from its beginning in 1784 to its re-union with Lower Canada in 1841. In this half-century was formed the character of that part of Canada which became the Province of Ontario in 1867. In it the great issues of Canadian history, the adjustment of French and English institutions, the relations of church and state, the claims of imperial unity and colonial responsible government, were raised and debated. These issues Professor Craig presents with scholarly skill in the context of contemporary events and personalities. He carries the narrative to the Canadian Union of 1841, itself the prelude to the British American Union of 1867.

W. L. MORTON,
Executive Editor.
D. G. CREIGHTON,
Advisory Editor.

PREFACE

Upper Canada : The Formative Years

During its first half-century Upper Canada grew from a few scattered
pioneer settlements into a relatively complex and mature community – the
base from which English-speaking civilization developed in central and
western Canada. On this ground British and American settlers, ideas, and
ways of doing things both clashed and joined, and the result eventually was
a people who were Canadian with a Canadian point of view. Inevitably, it
was a quarrelsome and tense process, highlighted by the dramatic events
of 1812 and 1837. But the deeper and more lasting story is of the hard work
done by many thousands of plain people to clear the land, to build farms
and towns, to improve communications, to adapt political, religious, and
educational institutions to their own needs, and to find satisfactory relationships with their American neighbours and with their fellow subjects in the
mother country. On all these fronts notable advances had been made by
1841.

The work of research was lightened by kind and scholarly people at
various libraries and archives, especially Dr G. W. Spragge, the Archivist
of Ontario, and his staff at the Ontario Department of Public Records and
Archives, Mr W. G. Ormsby at the Public Archives of Canada, and Miss
Edith Firth at the Toronto Public Library. I am grateful to Major C. C. J.
Bond who drew the maps and who also caught several mistakes in the
manuscript. I wish to thank three of my colleagues at the University of
Toronto, Professor D. G. Creighton, the Advisory Editor of the Series, and
Professor J. M. S. Careless, who read through the entire manuscript, and
Colonel C. P. Stacey, who read it in part. My thanks also go to Professor
J. J. Talman, of the University of Western Ontario for a careful reading
of the manuscript. My most profound and pervasive indebtedness is to that
master-historian, Professor A. L. Burt, of the University of Minnesota,
under whom I first began to study the history of Upper Canada, and who

read most of the manuscript. I have no words to describe my gratitude to the Executive Editor, Professor W. L. Morton, of the University of Manitoba, for his patient and skilful advice and editing. All of these people saved me from many errors; they have no responsibility for those that remain. My wife shared in the research at an earlier stage and cheerfully responded to cries for help at all times.

G. M. CRAIG.

UPPER CANADA

CANADA

THE FORMATIVE YEARS

CHAPTER 1

Loyalists Make a New Province

After more than a century and a half of European colonizing activity in eastern North America, one of its fairest and most accessible regions still lay almost untouched by civilization at the end of the 1770's. There were many reasons why this land, which was to become Upper Canada, then Ontario, was nearly empty of settlers, and not the least of these was its island-like situation. Along its northern side flowed the Ottawa River, which was easily ascended by fur-traders on their way from Montreal via the Mattawa, Lake Nipissing, and the French River into Lake Huron and to the western country. Or, if the explorer and trader from Montreal decided not to use the waters of the St Lawrence's mightiest tributary, he could journey up the great river itself, reaching at Lake St Francis the bounds of the last Canadian seigniory, the western limits of effective settlement in the days of the French régime. Another hundred miles, many of them through the white water of treacherous rapids, brought the traveller into the maze of islands that heralded the entrance into Lake Ontario. Once in the lake he could reach Lake Simcoe, and so Lake Huron, either through the Trent River system or along the Toronto portage. But if his curiosity, his business, or his duty led him to follow the sequence of the world's most stupendous chain of lakes, he must get round the mammoth cataract in the Niagara River, and traverse the often dangerous waters of Lake Erie, before entering the Detroit River, which would bring him to Lake Huron by way of the Lake and River St Clair.

Frenchmen and Canadians of the seventeenth and eighteenth centuries had come to know well this country enclosed by the Ottawa, the St Lawrence, and the lower Lakes. It was penetrated by Champlain and his young men within a few years of the founding of Quebec. Missionaries followed on the heels of the explorers, or were themselves explorers. In the 1630's and 1640's the Jesuits lived out their epic among the Hurons south of Georgian Bay. Within half a century the French dreamers and organizers of North American empire were already looking well beyond the lower lakes, drawn ever west, to the Mississippi and then to the Saskatchewan. Behind them they left armed posts at Fort Frontenac, at the eastern end of Lake Ontario, at Niagara, at Detroit, and at Michilimackinac. From these and other bases the French fought desperately against the growing strength of their English rivals for the trade and empire of the interior. It was a bold, a prolonged, but inevitably an unequal contest, in which the French went down before their richer and more numerous foes. With the surrender of Fort Niagara to Sir William Johnson in 1759 the country north of Lakes Ontario and Erie lay open to the English. After the capitulation at Montreal in the following year, the Massachusetts-born Robert Rogers travelled west to take formal possession of it in the name of the young King George III, newly acceded to the British throne.

The land beyond the Ottawa was now British, but for a time the transfer of sovereignty did little to disturb the fur-trading empire. Indeed in 1763, the British government closed off the whole region to settlement, in an effort to calm the Indians, who had been alarmed by the defeat of their French allies. There were, to be sure, a few farmers on either side of the Detroit River who had been brought up from the lower St Lawrence in the last decade of the French régime; those who took up land across the river from the fort at Detroit were the first white men to make lasting settlements in what is now Ontario.[1] Otherwise, the land belonged to the Indians, the fur-traders, the soldiers, and a handful of merchants. In 1774 the peninsula between the upper St Lawrence and Lake Huron was included within the greatly extended boundaries of the province of Quebec, which now reached to the Ohio and the Mississippi, but there was still no expectation of an early settlement of this inland country.

Already, however, Britain's American empire had begun to quiver and quake under the impact of resistance in the old colonies along the Atlantic seaboard to the new policies emanating from London. In the spring of 1775 resistance culminated in open rebellion, with the outbreak of fighting at Lexington and Concord, in Massachusetts. In July of the following year the Thirteen Colonies declared their independence of Great Britain.

For half a dozen years North America was once again the scene of widespread and bitter warfare, as troops under General Washington's command, with invaluable financial and military help from France, battled the armies raised by the British government. But the colonists did not rise as one man to defend the standard raised by the Continental Congress. On the contrary, a large and varied group opposed the resort to force against British authority. Some made this decision willingly, immediately, and inevitably. Others were driven to it after that heart-searching and travail of spirit which only a civil war can bring. Some sprang quickly to arms to support the Crown.

others did so when forced to take a stand one way or the other, while still others tried to the last to stay in the shadows. The Tories, as their enemies contemptuously dubbed them, or the Loyalists, as they proudly called themselves, were to be found in every level of society, from the wealthy merchant to the struggling backwoods farmer, and in every colony, from the province of Maine to the recently established settlements in Georgia. Their numbers can never be certainly known, for there were almost infinite degrees of positive and passive loyalism, but those who hoped and worked and fought for the defeat of the rebellion made up perhaps a quarter of the nearly two million residents in the Thirteen Colonies.

As it gradually became apparent that the rebellion was to become a successful revolution many of these Loyalists decided that they could not live within the new republic being formed out of the old empire. Some in fact left very early, notably when General Howe evacuated Boston in 1776, while others did not make the fateful decision until after the peace treaty of 1783 when His Britannic Majesty formally acknowledged the independence of the United States of America. Some left indignantly and scornfully, others reluctantly, to avoid persecution by their successful rivals. Most of the people of loyalist inclination did not leave at all, but silently made what peace they could with the new order. Of those who left, a fair number drifted back in later months and years. All told the exodus amounted to about fifty thousand persons. Some of them went to the West Indies, to Bermuda, to Britain (and it was a cheerless home for many of these Americans), while about thirty thousand went to Nova Scotia and just under seven thousand to the province of Quebec.[2]

The movement to the north and west got under way as the fighting went on. In 1776 Sir John Johnson, Sir William's son, escaped from his estate west of Albany, and with many of his followers reached Montreal for the purpose of joining the king's standard. Presently, the King's Royal Regiment of New York was formed. Other New York and Pennsylvania Loyalists joined Colonel John Butler's Rangers, with their headquarters at Niagara. These and other units, in conjunction with those of the Six Nations Indians who stayed with the royal cause, engaged vigorously in the bitter partisan campaigning which marked the war in the central regions of New York. After the surrender of the British army under Burgoyne at Saratoga in 1777 and after the foray into western New York in 1779 by American troops under General John Sullivan, the fighting Loyalists of the north had to fall back to the river and the lakes. By 1780 they were being received into camps near Three Rivers and at Sorel, where the governor of the province of Quebec, General Frederick Haldimand, was making arrangements to feed and clothe them. At Niagara several hundred of Butler's Rangers were established on either side of the river, and some of them were beginning to till the soil for the purpose of supplying the garrison with food. These refugees from New York and Pennsylvania, many of them of German or Huguenot origin, formed the first permanent settlements made since the arrival of the French Canadians at the opposite end of Lake Erie a generation earlier.[3]

When all hopes of preserving imperial unity were dashed by the peace treaty in 1783 the movement out of New York State into the old province of Quebec swelled, as weary exiles toiled northward, to emerge on Lake Ontario either at Oswego or Sackets Harbor, with a crossing in open boats needed to complete the journey. Some came out on the upper St Lawrence, at the present town of Ogdensburg, or opposite what is now Cornwall.[4] Two parties, led by Captain Michael Grass and Major Peter Van Alstine, sailed from New York when Sir Guy Carleton evacuated the city in November 1783, and they went directly up the river to the concentration points for the Loyalists near Montreal. As well, the loyal Six Nations Indians under Joseph Brant's leadership had fallen back across the lake. Haldimand had on his hands the formidable task of caring for several thousand refugees, to whom the faith of the British government was pledged. Most of the adult men were members of provincial regiments, but there were some civilians and the women and children of their families. Fortunately, the right man was in the right place, for the somewhat aloof Swiss professional soldier proved to be a good friend to the Loyalists in their predicament. With a mixture of firmness and sympathy, of high executive ability and willingness to cut red tape, he saw the Loyalists established in their new homes.

While he was caring for the Loyalists in the camps, Haldimand was considering how to settle them on the land. His first inclination was to look east, not west, and to relocate the refugees of European origin in the maritime regions, particularly Cape Breton Island, for he believed that the Western country should be reserved to the Indians, whose loyalty to Britain was being sorely tried by reports of the peace treaty with the United States. The Indians felt betrayed and deserted by the boundary arrangements of the treaty, which left their traditional hunting-grounds within the new republic. Assurance of a home in the country north of the lower lakes should go a long way toward convincing them of British concern for their welfare. Accordingly, when Haldimand sent the Surveyor General, Major Samuel Holland, up the St Lawrence at the end of May 1783, to begin surveys, it was with the purpose of providing for the Indian rather than the white Loyalists.

The pressure of events in the summer and autumn of 1783, however, caused Haldimand to change his mind. In the first place he was much impressed by the favourable tone of the surveyors' reports on the quality of land from the Long Sault to the Bay of Quinte. Although some of it was "broken land" (where the Precambrian Shield reaches down across the St Lawrence), most of it was so fair that "I think the Loyalists may be the happiest people in America by settling this country."[5] It would be hard to deny such land to loyal subjects whose leaders already knew about it. Moreover, Haldimand's hand was forced by the decision of Sir Guy Carleton at New York to send the party of two hundred families led by Captain Grass to Cataraqui, at the eastern end of Lake Ontario. Finally, the Governor learned that the Indians would not regard the Loyalists as unwelcome invaders. There was plenty of land for all, and old comrades-in-arms, red and white alike, would feel a greater security from their enemies to the south by living near one another in their new homes. In short, Haldimand soon came to see many advantages in encouraging this "respectable body" of settlers, who would be "attached to the interests of Great Britain and capable of being useful upon many occasions,"[6] and he began to plan for the introduction of as many settlers into the upper country as wished to come.

As he was thus assuming, somewhat involuntarily, his mantle as the father of Upper Canada, Haldimand had to secure the Crown's title of land to be made available to the newcomers, and then to arrange for its disposition.

It was an established and wise policy of the British government to forbid all private purchases of land from the Indians. Instead, the procedure was to make formal treaties with the Indians, who regarded themselves as the allies, not the subjects, of the British king. In October 1783 land was purchased from the Missisaugas, extending from Cataraqui to the Trent, and in May 1784 an area west of Niagara and the head of Lake Ontario was acquired, out of which a home for the Six Nations Indians was to be carved.[7] Other Indian purchases were made in subsequent years as land was needed for settlement. Unlike the nearby American states, Upper Canada never had an angry Indian frontier.

With Crown land becoming available, Haldimand turned to the tasks of surveying it and allocating it to Loyalists and to intending settlers among the soldiers who might be demobilized in British North America. On these matters he had definite instructions from the British government.[8] Surveyed lands were to be incorporated into the existing seigniorial system: "distinct Seigneuries or Fiefs" were to be formed, and lots within them were to be held of the king on the same terms as in the old sections of the province. A church glebe of 300 to 500 acres was to be reserved in each seigniory. Lands were to be allotted to settlers according to status and rank. The head of a family would receive 100 acres, with an additional 50 acres for each member of the family. A single man was entitled to 50 acres. Non-commissioned officers were to get 200 acres, and privates 100 acres, again with 50 acres for each member of the individual's family. By supplementary instructions of August 7, the promises to officers were laid out, ranging from 1000 acres for field officers to 700 acres for captains and 500 acres for subalterns, staff officers and warrant officers. All these grants were to be free, with the expenses involved in surveying and granting the land to be borne by the government.

In the spring of 1784 surveying was resumed in earnest. Two ranges of townships were laid out: the first (the Royal Townships), running westward from the seigniory of Longueuil, consisted of nine townships, and the second (the Cataraqui Townships) running westward from the fort of that name, contained five townships, and reached into the eastern portions of the Bay of Quinte region. The townships were numbered rather than named, since the whole scheme was intended to fit into the seigniorial system, and were thus to be thought of as numbered fiefs. Another feature of Haldimand's plan was that the men of disbanded army units were to be kept together in the townships. The first five of the Royal Townships went to the first battalion of Sir John Johnson's Royal Yorkers, the settlers being divided, at their own request, according to race and religion. Catholic Highlanders, Scottish Presbyterians, German Calvinists, German Lutherans, and Anglicans accordingly occupied these townships in that order. The next three townships were allotted to Major Jessup's corps. No. 1 of the Cataraqui Townships went to Captain Grass's party from New York, No. 2 to remaining members of Major Jessup's corps, No. 3 and No. 4 to members of Johnson's second battalion, to whom were joined men from Major Rogers's Corps and the other party from New York city led by Major Van Alstine. The last township in the Cataraqui series, the present Marysburg, was settled by detachments of disbanded regulars, including some Germans. In July 1784 Sir John Johnson, who had been given the superintendence of the movement, reported that 1,568 men, 626 women, 1,492 children, and 90 servants had been distributed in these townships.[9]

To the west, the settlers in the Niagara peninsula were steadily increasing in numbers, while some scores of Loyalists were finding homes among the earlier French-speaking settlers in the southwestern tip of the province, across from Detroit. And at the same time the loyal Six Nations Indians moved onto the lands made available to them. These consisted of nearly three million acres stretching six miles on either side of the Grand River from its mouth on Lake Erie back to its source.

The exodus of the Loyalists into the western peninsula of the old province of Quebec has been rightly seen as an epic in Canadian history. These people were refugees, touched with the forlornness and the bitterness and the tragedy which that word evokes. Having made a good start in life, or indeed become well established, on their pleasant and fertile holdings in

New York, Pennsylvania, and some other colonies, they had then been caught up in what was for them a desperate and cruel civil war. Now they must start over again in a new and strange country. Whatever they had owned of worldly possessions, whether of real or sentimental value, had for the most part been left behind, with little or no prospect of redress from the revolutionary governments that viewed them as public enemies. A large proportion of the men had spent long years in the field or the camp with their regiments and their hands were now more used to the musket than to the plough. They had to make a new start in a country where great virgin forests came everywhere down to the water's edge, defying the settler to find space to plant his seeds or even for his cabin. The sheer back-breaking toil facing the Loyalists was appalling, all the more so since many of them were no longer in the vigorous strength of early manhood and had had their fill of pioneer life in their old homes.

The hardships of the Loyalists should not be forgotten; certainly there is little danger of this happening in Canada. Yet these refugees experienced a kinder fate than have most exiles in the long sad tale of humanity uprooted. (And perhaps few tears should be shed for men who would certainly have wreaked a stern vengeance of their own had they been on the winning side.) They came to a new country, but it was not a far country; sometimes they went back to their old homes to visit friends and relatives, and occasionally they even quietly remained there. Much of the bitterness died down with the passing years, and it was not equally intense among all the Loyalists. It took later events, especially the War of 1812, to revive the old memories, and it was not until the rising Canadian nationalism of the mid-nineteenth century that a Loyalist cult began to form.

Moreover, the tasks awaiting the Loyalists, although burdensome and, for many of them, depressing to contemplate, were by no means unfamiliar. Nearly all of those who came into Upper Canada had been farmers in the old colonies. The accidents of war and revolution had thrown into the northern province just the kind of people needed for its development. The ability to attack and conquer the North American wilderness, to reduce it to orderly farms and settled communities, was a hard-earned skill, but it was one the Loyalists possessed. And they did not face the wilderness unaided. Apart from the free land grants promised to them by the British government, and the prospect of compensation for losses of property suffered through loyalty to the king's cause, they were also assured of the food, tools, and other supplies needed for beginning their new life. On January 31, 1785, Sir John Johnson prepared a list of articles that would be needed by the Loyalists, comprising the following items: "Nails, hammers, gimlets, plains, chizzels, gouges, hinges, iron rimmed locks, padlocks, handsaws, X cut saws, broad axes, adzes, rub stones, whipsaws, window glass, carpenter tools, blacksmiths tools, carpenter squares and compasses, hoes, spades, pick axes, plow shares, twine."[10] Haldimand undertook to meet their needs in these and other matters, even before he had specific government authorization and when there was the possibility that he might have to meet the cost out of his own pocket. The required supplies were not always available, despite the willingness of the government to supply them, but unquestionably the rigours of pioneer life were alleviated by this bounty. When Haldimand left the province in 1784, he reported that 6,152 refugees had been settled, of whom 5,576 were drawing full rations.

Provisions were supplied until after the crop of 1786 was harvested, but remarkable advances were to be seen in the first summer after the main settlement. A young Englishman travelling up the St Lawrence in June of 1785 wrote that "you see abundance of fine wheat, Indian corn, and pota- toes wherever you go," and in general he found the settlers to be "very happy," although sometimes sad at having had "to leave one of the sweetest countries in the world."[11] Later on that same year Lieutenant-Governor Hope reported that his agents had found the Loyalists to be "in general highly satisfied with the prospects before them and all grateful for the bounty and indulgence Government has so liberally bestowed." They were making such rapid improvements as to promise them "a permanent pros- perity." Rations were being supplemented by "quantities of wild Pidgeons and fish."[12] Some three months later Hope summarized the conditions of the Loyalists in these "promising Settlements" when writing to the Com- missioners of American Claims who had been appointed by the British government. The Commissioners at first proposed to hear all claims in Halifax, but Hope pointed out that with few exceptions the Loyalists in the province of Quebec were not "Persons of great Property or conse- quence." "They are chiefly Landholders, Farmers and others from Inland parts of the Continent," whose claims to compensation cannot singly be considerable," certainly not worth a trip to Halifax.[13] When the Commis- sioners did come to the upper country, they soon confirmed the points made by Hope. One of them, Colonel Dundas, wrote that the claims were numerous – 1,100 to 1,200 – but small in amount. The settlers were "mostly farmers from the back parts of New York and Pennsylvania," who were now thriving to the extent that they could "supply the King's posts with bread." They were a "happy, flourishing people" living on land as good as might be found in "any part of America."[14]

The official mind probably exaggerated the bucolic bliss being enjoyed in the new settlement. The "Hungry Year" or the "Starving Time" of 1789, when a variety of circumstances led to a famine, showed how closely the settlers were living to the edge of subsistence. The hard work, the drudgery, and the frequent heartache of the first stages of pioneer existence were not as real to touring officers as they were to the people in the tiny clearings.

Occupied with their daily round of tree-cutting, cabin-building, ploughing, and sowing, the settlers had little time or inclination to think about large problems of government. Haldimand, indeed, had firmly believed that people who had suffered so much "by Committees and Houses of Assembly" would be very well satisfied to live under the non-representative form of government established by the Quebec Act.[15] Yet, there was another feature of that Act that irritated the Loyalists from the beginning, and that was its provision for seigniorial tenures. On this subject they voiced increasingly loud complaints.

As early as April 11, 1785, Sir John Johnson and a group of officers petitioned the King on behalf of the Loyalists whom they had led into the province.[16] They stressed that these people were unfamiliar with the "rigorous Rules, Homages and Reservations, and Restrictions of the French Laws and Customs, which are so different from the mild Tenures to which they had ever been accustomed." They proposed that a new district be established to comprehend the Loyalist settlements. This district, although subordinate to the Governor and Council of Quebec, could have British laws and tenures introduced into it without disturbing the French Canadians in the old sections of the province. This request was but asking for the same treatment that their "Fellow Sufferers" in Nova Scotia and New Brunswick were receiving: the enjoyment of British laws and customs, for which they had fought and courted exile. Without "the Establishment of a liberal system of Tenure, Law, and Government," they had little hope that the new settlements would flourish.

This petition, and the many others that followed, intensified a controversy that was as old as the province of Quebec, for the place of British laws and institutions in that province had been the subject of debate since 1763. A small group of English-speaking residents, mainly merchants, had fought a lonely and losing battle against a government which was usually concerned mainly to protect French-Canadian sensibilities. But these people now smelled success, as they viewed the growing strength of the Loyalists in the light of added weight to be used in waging the old struggle.

The fact of several thousand Loyalist settlers along the north shore of the river and Lake Ontario was indeed a momentous one. It required a whole new approach to the problem of maintaining British authority in the remaining provinces of North America. Over a dozen years before, the governor of the province, Guy Carleton, had argued that it was of prime importance to ensure the fidelity of the French Canadians: his views had been embodied in the Quebec Act of 1774. Following his successful defence of the province against American invasion in 1775-76, for which he had

been knighted, Carleton had left Canada in 1778, involved in bitter disagreements with Lord George Germain, the Secretary of State. Four years
later, he returned to America as commander-in-chief with the unpleasant
task of winding up the war and supervising the evacuation of the Loyalists
from New York. Back in England in the middle of the 1780's, it was now
clear to Sir Guy that a policy framed with only the French Canadians in
mind was no longer adequate; the active co-operation of the Loyalists must
be won if the vital inland regions were to be held. He warned the home
government that these British subjects, who were outnumbered ten or
fifteen to one by the Americans to the south, must be convinced that it
was clearly in their interest to cleave to the mother country, that the
rewards of loyalty were greater than those of rebellion. In particular, "all
burdens on land which [might] serve to excite animosities against the
Crown should be taken off." In general, the British government must willingly make concessions to the loyal provinces that they had grudgingly proposed to make to the old colonies under the pressure of rebellion.[17] Such was
the advice of the man who returned to Canada as governor in 1786 under
his new title, Lord Dorchester. His task was to advise whether and in what
respects the Quebec Act should be altered and whether the province should
be divided.[18] Obviously, a change was in the air.

It was, however, easier for conscientious officials, either in London or
Quebec, to agree that a change should be made in the arrangements for
governing the province than it was to determine what should replace the
Quebec Act. The "French Party," which included some men not of French-
Canadian origin, stood out adamantly against change. They pointed out
that the French Canadians still made up ninety-five per cent of the population, and that they had received assurances for their way of life in the
capitulations of 1760 and specific guarantees in the Quebec Act. The system
of laws and government in force in the province had been well known to
the Loyalists. If the latter were not prepared to accept this system, they
should go to other British colonies. Moreover, the country did not depend
upon the new settlers for its advancement. The French Canadians had
nearly doubled their numbers since 1760, and would presently be able to
take up lands now vacant. British dominion would thereby be assured, for
the French Canadians would never coalesce with nor fall under the influence
of the Americans.[19]

Sir John Johnson vigorously opposed this view. He called attention to
the sufferings and losses of the Loyalists, which ought to be redressed by
restoring them to the "Blessings" of life under the British Constitution,
blessings which their fellow-Loyalists in Nova Scotia and New Brunswick
were in fact enjoying. Johnson wanted to see a policy adopted that would
have the effect of "assimilating this to the other of his Majesty's Colonies

in America." Loyalists in Great Britain and loyal subjects in the United States would then flock into the province.[20] Johnson's hand was strengthened by petitions in the same vein from magistrates in the new settlements.[21]

In this situation Lord Dorchester confessed himself to be baffled. He could think of no form of government that would be equally fair and satisfactory both to the English and to the French. He did recommend, however, that freehold tenures be immediately adopted, and that quit-rents be abolished. Such rents had never been collected with any effectiveness in the old colonies, where they had caused discontent without strengthening the Crown. It was important that British subjects enjoy "a situation at least as eligible, as that of their neighbours."[22]

The mood of the Loyalists was very much on Dorchester's mind at this time. Reports of unrest in the new settlements had caused him to appoint, only a few days before, a committee of two (W. D. Powell and John Collins) to seek out the reasons for the unrest, and the two investigators had also been authorized to announce the Governor's intention of forming these settlements into a new district. (Hitherto they had been part of the District of Montreal.) Dorchester was particularly anxious to satisfy all legitimate grievances before there was any appearance of bowing to popular demand.

Some two months later Powell and Collins submitted their report to the Governor, and it threw an interesting light on the infant community of Loyalists along the St Lawrence and the eastern end of Lake Ontario. There was apparently "a very dangerous Jealousy and want of Confidence" subsisting "between the Majority of the settlers, and their late Officers." The officers wished to retain the position of authority which they had held in time of war. They were secretive about the nature and extent of the King's bounty, in the hope of keeping the settlers dependent upon them. And when the officers had arranged the preparation of an address of welcome to the newly arrived Governor, their mysterious comings and goings had raised clouds of suspicion among a population that was "more illiterate than is the General character of the Northern Loyalists." They were a reliable people, ready to accept authority, grateful for the help given by the government, but inclined to resist any "caprice and partiality" on the part of those in authority.[23] They would need careful handling.

This little storm blew itself out, but it helped to convince Dorchester that the whole policy of the government must be aimed at demonstrating to these people the superior advantages of life under British dominion. They would soon have neighbours just across the river and the lakes who could acquire land cheaply and without quit-rents. Under these circumstances, "the Provincials must have nothing to gain by a separation," for whatever the sentiments of "the present generation of Loyalists . . . their posterity [would] never draw their swords to perpetuate a burthen, with which the subjects of the states, their near neighbours, are not encumbered, and without the support of their swords Great Britain cannot maintain her dominion for a long time. . . ."[24] This theme, with almost innumerable variations, would sound through the history of Upper Canada until it received its fullest orchestration at the hands of Lord Durham. Dorchester himself returned to it on several occasions during the following year.

Any major constitutional change would have to wait upon the British parliament; besides, it was clear by now that Dorchester had no plan to offer. But it was within his power, and in accord with his views, to grant a larger element of autonomy to the new settlements. On July 24th, 1788, it was announced that four new districts had been created: Luneburg, extending to the Gananoque river, Mecklenburg, reaching to the Trent, Nassau, comprising the country from the Trent to Long Point, and Hesse, made up of the western regions. One of the most frequently expressed grievances had been the inadequate arrangements for dispensing justice. Each of the new districts was to have a court of common pleas made up of three judges. Some months later four Land Boards were also set up, one for each of the new districts, to expedite and fufil the government's promises.

Land being uppermost in the settlers' minds, Dorchester had already gone far to satisfy the desire for larger grants. On June 2, 1787, he had increased the bounty by an additional 200 acres to heads of families who had already improved their lands. The Land Boards took this order to mean that all those who had borne arms would be entitled to 300 acres or more, according to their rank, and other Loyalists would receive an initial grant of 200 acres.[25] As a further boon the council, at Dorchester's behest, ordered, first, that a registry of the names of Loyalists be kept in order that their posterity be distinguished from future settlers, and second, that the Land Boards grant 200 acres to the sons of Loyalists, when they came of age, and also to their daughters at that time, or at their marriage. It is clear that these grants were intended for the children of Loyalists already in the province, that the children were expected to occupy and improve the grants, and that such grants would be made only if there were "no Default in the due Cultivation and Improvement of the Lands already assigned to the Head of the Family, of which they were members."[26] These conditions were soon forgotten, or ignored.

On October 22, 1788, Dorchester also ended a discrepancy which had caused much dissatisfaction. By a long standing promise going back to 1775 the officers of the 84th Regiment had been assured grants of 5,000 acres for field officers, 3,000 acres for captains, and 2,000 acres for subalterns, a bounty which was three to five times as high as that held out to officers of other regiments. All grants were now raised to the level promised to the officers of the 84th. Just before taking this step, Dorchester had visited the new settlements, which he found to be flourishing. He reported that the majority of the Loyalists declared themselves to be "better circumstanced and happier than before the rebellion," although still very anxious on the question of tenure. He expected that this contentment among the Loyalists would "have an extensive influence" on nearby American settlers, who contrasted their lot with that of the Loyalists who had "persevered in their duty."[27]

By now the British government, pushed on by the parliamentary opposition, was reluctantly coming to grips with the constitutional question in Canada. On September 3, 1788, Sydney, the Secretary of State, asked Dorchester for information and advice on which the government's plan might be based. The Governor was requested to give his opinion on a contemplated division of the province west of the seigniory of Longueuil, and was informed that, whether or not the division took place, the new settlers were to be given tenure in free and common socage. Could the western settlements support an assembly, and if so, what should be done about the French Canadians at Detroit? Dorchester replied on November 8 with some general remarks about the nature and location of the population, and by casting doubt on the proposals for division and for an assembly. The province was too strung out for an assembly, while the new settlements were not yet sufficiently advanced to support one. His recent establishment of districts in the west satisfied the present needs of the Loyalists, but he did think that they should receive a lieutenant-governor, who could "bring their concerns with dispatch to the knowledge" of the governor at Quebec. If, however, the British government should nevertheless decide upon a division, the Governor saw "no reason" why the western settlers should not have an assembly and English laws.[28]

The tone of this dispatch was not likely to encourage the government to take quick action, and Sydney had no such inclination.[29] But in June 1789 William Grenville succeeded to Sydney's post, and soon prepared a plan which was put before Dorchester in a draft bill sent from Whitehall on October 20, 1789.[30] The Governor also received both a private and a public dispatch, as well as a memorandum explaining the reasoning behind the bill. From these various documents, and particularly from the memorandum, it is possible to understand the British government's motives and objectives in providing a new Constitution for this "most considerable of the King's remaining provinces in America."[31]

The long debate over whether or not there should be a representative assembly under the new constitution was easily decided in the affirmative. Of the many arguments that had been advanced on the two sides of this question, one was decisive: the new government must possess the power to levy internal taxes in the province. As matters stood now, Canada was costing Britain about £100,000 a year, "exclusive of the pay of the troops, kept up there," a burden which the British taxpayer could not fairly go on bearing. It was, of course, impossible for the home government to raise a revenue within the colony, or any British colony, because this power had been abandoned forever in an Act of Parliament passed in 1778, as an attempt to conciliate the thirteen rebellious colonies. It was clear, further, that Parliament would not vest the taxing power in any local legislature unless it followed the British model. In short, it must have a representative element.

But it had been quite properly objected that one assembly for the province of Quebec would be unworkable. "Dissensions & animosities," racial in origin, would hideously disfigure such a body. Moreover, the distances in a colony, stretched across more than 1,100 miles, made efficient organization impossible. Fortunately, these and other problems were readily disposed of by the simple device of dividing the province in two. Such a division was naturally and easily made, as indeed spokesmen for the Loyalists had often pointed out. Nearly all the French Canadians lived in the older sections down the river from Lake St Francis, while the new settlers were established to the west. Each group had distinctive customs and a distinctive outlook; each could safely be allowed a preponderant voice in its own district. This solution suffered from one glaring defect: it left the English-speaking minority in the prospective lower province adrift in a French-Canadian sea; Grenville, however, did not address himself to this problem, beyond holding out the hope that the commercial code might be changed to safeguard the interests of this predominantly mercantile group. It could also be assumed that the English element would find protection and security in the non-representative parts of the government. An additional by-product of this solution that would raise many difficulties in the future was that the western province would be the Empire's first inland colony, without an ocean port, since ocean navigation stopped at Montreal.

Was it intended, then, simply to establish two new royal provinces on the model offered by the former provinces, such as Virginia or New York? By no means. British political leaders were convinced that the American Revolution had revealed certain obvious weaknesses in the constitutions under the old empire; democratic elements in these constitutions had been allowed to grow strong at the expense of the monarchical and aristocratic elements. A truly British system kept the balance even among all three. Hence, provision must be made for strengthening the position of the king's representative, the governor, by freeing him from abject dependence upon the Assembly from which the governors in the old colonies had suffered. The aristocratic branch of government stood in even greater need of strengthening than did the monarchical, for the constitution of the council had been the "most defective" feature of the old colonial governments. It was therefore intended to provide for a separate legislative council, and to assimilate it "more nearly to the Upper House in England."

By these arrangements the new provinces would receive as close an approximation to the British Constitution as colonial conditions permitted. In all this there was no assurance that they would remain loyal and faithful dependencies of the mother country, for it seemed to be the fate of "so great & distant a dominion" to fall away eventually. This process was undoubtedly accelerated by the existence of local legislatures, however constituted. If complete control of colonies was the only imperial objective no legislature of any sort would be permitted, an approach that was neither desirable nor possible. Grenville did believe that the proposed constitution would "promote the prosperity" of Canada, and by avoiding the errors found in the governments of the "antient Colonies," prevent "the growth of a republican or independent spirit." In any case, there was no alternative, no possible hope that a more arbitrary system, such as existed under the Quebec Act, could long prevail. British subjects living beside the self-governing American states and not far from the Maritime Provinces would not remain contented under an autocratic government. Moreover, there was no likelihood that Parliament would agree to the continuance of an unrepresentative system. It was the mark both of wisdom and of prudence to make a free grant of concessions before these were extorted by force.

The draft bill embodying this scheme was forwarded to Dorchester for his advice upon particulars. With the assistance of the Chief Justice, William Smith, he answered specific questions relating to the boundaries of the new provinces and the size of the legislative houses, and made a few observations based upon local information. He added some clarifying language to the plans for converting seigniorial to socage tenure, and suggested a few further changes in detail. More important, the Chief Justice, with the Governor's full concurrence, proposed that all the provinces of British North America be brought together into one general government, under a Governor General, with a bicameral legislature to be drawn from the several provinces. Smith, who had carefully observed the government of New York and of the other former provinces, stated categorically that such a federal union would prevent the northern colonies from developing those dangerous tendencies which had produced rebellion in the old colonies to the south. This proposal fell upon deaf ears in London.

Dorchester's dispatch did not reach England until April 18, 1790, too late for the bill to be introduced into the session of Parliament then well advanced. Despite Fox's complaints of procrastination, the government did not feel able to give notice of the measure until February 25, 1791, when it was announced that the King intended to divide the province as soon as

Parliament should establish a suitable constitutional framework. A week later, on March 4, Pitt moved that the bill be brought in. A committee was named to hear petitions, and debate began on April 8, continuing intermittently until the bill passed the House on May 18. The government agreed to make only two changes in the measure, one reducing the maximum term of an assembly from seven to four years, and the other increasing the minimum size of the Lower Canada assembly from thirty to fifty. Attempts by members speaking for the English-speaking mercantile interests of Lower Canada to prevent the division of the province were easily defeated.

Although the bill emerged almost unchanged, it had been severely criticized by the opposition during the debate. Charles James Fox strongly objected to a group of clauses, which had not appeared in Grenville's earlier draft but to which the government now gave much prominence. The first of these clauses made "a permanent Appropriation of Lands . . . for the Support and Maintenance of a Protestant clergy," the amount to be "equal in Value to the Seventh Part" of the lands granted in every township. Another clause stated that it would be lawful to authorize the governor or lieutenant-governor of each province, with the advice of the Executive Council, "to constitute and erect, within every township . . . one or more Parsonage or Rectory . . . according to the Establishment of the Church of *England*" and "to endow every such Parsonage or Rectory with so much or such Part of the Lands so allotted and appropriated" as might be deemed expedient.[32]

Fox disagreed with the whole of the scheme on the twin grounds that one-seventh was too large a proportion of the land to be put at the disposal of the clergy, and that a stronger argument could be made for establishing either the Roman Catholic Church or the Church of Scotland, in the light of the population currently in the province. On the other hand, Pitt believed that it was desirable to give a permanent encouragement to the "Protestant clergy of the established church."[33] But what did these words mean? Obviously, only the Church of England could receive clergy lands for the endowment of rectories, but could the clergy of the established Church of Scotland also receive some of the proceeds coming from lands that were not used to endow rectories? Apparently the government intended to leave open this possibility, but the matter was not openly discussed.[34] Moreover, the Act itself, in the first clause mentioned above, spoke only of "a Protestant clergy." Did this clause include, or exclude, Protestant denominations other than the two established churches in Great Britain? Further, the Act contemplated the *endowment* of rectories according to the "Establishment of the Church of England." It did not specifically state that the Church of England was to be *established* in the Canadas, yet zealous adherents of that communion might easily draw this conclusion. Thus, what proved to be the Pandora's Box of Upper Canada's politics lay ready to be opened.

During the debate over the Bill, however, Fox centred his main attack on the structure of the legislative council. He urged that the government of Canada had to be constructed on very different foundations from those that might be suitable in other colonies, such as the West Indian islands. This government had to serve a growing European population, living next door to the independent American states. Under these circumstances nothing must be done to make the inhabitants of Canada feel that their situation was worse than their neighbours'; all possible causes of envy must be avoided. Fox believed that a hereditary Council, setting up artificial distinctions, would lead to an "unfavourable comparison" with the situation across the line, where such distinctions were unknown. Elected councils chosen on a restricted franchise from the propertied men of the two provinces would provide a truer aristocracy; if this were not acceptable, it would be better to give councillors seats for life, without the hereditary element. Pitt would have nothing to do with these suggestions, repeating that the whole purpose of the new constitution was to provide a close approximation to the British model, with the legislative council answering as nearly as possible to the House of Lords. Both men agreed that Anglicizing the French should be a main object of legislation, Fox believing this end would be attained by leaving the province undivided and Pitt arguing the opposite.[35]

When the Bill passed through the Lords at the end of May, its original author, now Lord Grenville, looked upon his child and found it handsome. He explained to his fellow-peers that the Quebec Act had to be replaced because Canada now had a population which was not only well acquainted with "British privileges," but "which had retired to that country for the express purpose of enjoying them in greater perfection than they could elsewhere." These people deserved "the blessings of the English constitution . . . the best in the world." In other words, the division of the province, which had been opposed by the mercantile element of Montreal and Quebec, and the grant of an assembly, which had been opposed by the French party, had both been dictated in large part by the need to give satisfaction to the Loyalists. Thus the small English-speaking population in what was to become the heartland of the later Dominion had won its first victory. It now had a base on which it could proceed to build what would be the most populous and the richest section of the North American nation to come.

The Constitutional Act (often called the Canada Act), given the royal assent on June 19, 1791, provided the basis of government for Upper and Lower Canada during the next half-century.[36] The Act itself did not effect a complete repeal of the Quebec Act, nor did it divide the province. Only those parts of the Quebec Act related to the appointment and powers of the Council were superseded, while the Act noted that division would be accomplished by executive action. The latter course was adopted in order to avoid public discussion of the exact boundaries of the two provinces, a subject which could be embarrassing as long as Great Britain retained the posts on the American side of the Great Lakes.

Each province was given a bicameral legislature. The legislative council was to be appointed by the governor (or as it would be in the case of Upper Canada, the lieutenant-governor), and was to consist of at least seven members in the upper province. They would hold their seats for life, unless they left the province without permission for periods of more than two to four years, or gave up their allegiance to the King. The Act also authorized the King to issue hereditary titles of honour, to which might be annexed "an Hereditary Right of being summoned to the Legislative Council." This provision, which figured so prominently in the preliminary discussions of the Bill, and in the parliamentary debates, required several clauses in the Act to receive its full definition, but since the idea was never implemented, these clauses need no discussion. Finally, it was provided that the Speaker of the legislative council would be named by the Governor.

The Assembly was to consist of at least sixteen members, in the case of Upper Canada, and to sit for a maximum term of four years. The governor or lieutenant-governor was authorized to divide his province into "Districts, or Counties, or Circles, and Towns or Townships," and to declare the number of representatives to be chosen from each. Voters in rural areas must be possessed of a freehold worth at least forty shillings annually, and town voters must own property with a yearly value of at least five pounds, or have paid rent for at least a year at the rate of ten pounds *per annum*. There were no property qualifications for sitting in the Assembly, but clergymen were excluded.

The governor was given an important part in the legislative process. Within the limits of an annual meeting, and the four-year term, mentioned above, he had the usual responsibility for calling, proroguing, and dissolving the legislature. He had the power to withhold the royal assent from a bill which came to him after passing through both Houses of the legislature; he could also reserve a Bill for consideration by the home government. Yet the governor himself might be overruled: after he had approved a bill, it might still be disallowed in London within two years of its passage. The powers of the legislature were especially circumscribed in the matter of the Clergy Reserves. These provisions could be varied or repealed by the local legislature, but only under carefully defined restrictions. Any bill revising the arrangements for the Clergy Reserves must be clearly labelled as such;

it must be laid before both Houses of the British parliament for thirty days, and receive their approval, before the King might sign it. In other words, any such legislation would have to undergo the careful scrutiny of the bishops in the House of Lords.

Three other features of the Act should be briefly noted. The boon of free and common socage tenures, long requested, was granted to Upper Canada, with provision for retiring existing seigniorial grants. In the matter of taxation, the self-denying Act of 1778 was recited, but so was its qualifying section, that the British parliament would continue to regulate commerce by means of the Navigation Laws. The net proceeds from the duties levied by these Acts would be spent in the provinces with the concurrence of the Assemblies. Lastly, in light of the future history of the two provinces, it is of interest that the Act did not define the nature or the duties of the executive council, or indicate its relationship to the governor or to the two legislative bodies. There were only a few passing references to this body, although it would be well understood, by anyone acquainted with British colonial government, that the executive council was intended to be an advisory body, answerable to the governor and not to the legislature. But just as the wording of the Clergy Reserves clauses contained trouble for the future, so did these references: in the obscure and uncertain character of the executive council lay the germ of the second great issue of Upper Canada's politics, responsible government.

CHAPTER 2

The Simcoe Years

While the Loyalist settlers were attacking the virgin forests of the newly emerging province of Upper Canada, the man who was to inaugurate its government was busy making his plans. He was Lieutenant-Colonel John Graves Simcoe, at present a Member of Parliament, but a soldier rather than a politician. As a young subaltern he had been posted to America at the outbreak of the Revolutionary War, where he soon developed an immense admiration for those Americans who were opposing the rebellion. In 1777 at his own request he received the command of the Queen's Rangers Regiment, formed from Loyalists of the New York and Connecticut region, and he saw much hard service with them until his return to England in 1781. At loose ends after the return of peace, Simcoe sought eagerly for a fresh field of activity, and none could have seemed more attractive to him than this new province being formed by faithful Loyalists of the kind that he had known so well a decade earlier and with whom he had never lost contact.

As the first lieutenant-governor of Upper Canada, Simcoe inevitably has a distinctive place in its history, but that place is enhanced by his own character and temperament and by the contrast between him and his successors over the following half-century. Those who came after him, with the calamitous exception of Sir Francis Bond Head, were for the most part orthodox, correct, rather frozen-faced individuals who did not come very much alive either for their contemporaries or for posterity. Simcoe, on the other hand, although deeply conservative in outlook, was filled with bubbling vigour and with an intense if at times naïve enthusiasm for the work to be done. Spurred on both by personal ambition and by the sense of a singular opportunity, he was determined to do all in his power to make the new province a home fit for Loyalist heroes and a bastion of British power in North America. His mind was filled with projects for accomplishing these ends.

At the centre of Simcoe's plans for Upper Canada was his belief that the American Revolution had been a conspiracy instigated by a minority, and that many people in the new republic remained actively loyal to Great Britain, while a great many more could easily be won back to their old allegiance. He reasoned that these people must be dissatisfied with a government, which he scornfully dismissed as unstable and corrupt, and he argued that if he could establish on their border, indeed almost in their midst, "a free, honourable British Government," marked by the "pure Administration of its Laws," he could rally the sound element in the American population to the British standard.[1] The new colony, with "a Superior, more happy, and more polished form of Government" than that presided over by George Washington, would be a standing reminder of what had been lost in leaving the Empire and of the benefits awaiting those who would come back into the fold. It would obviously be of the utmost importance to "inculcate British Customs, Manners, & Principles in the most trivial, as well as serious matters" in order "to assimilate the colony with the parent State."[2]

Simcoe's plans for securing and prospering the colony touched on nearly every facet of its present and future life. In its military aspect he argued that in no sense should Upper Canada be regarded as "on a Peace Establishment." With dangerous neighbours, the new province must be given sufficient troops to deter possible invaders. Adequate force on the scene was the only sure way of ensuring peace alongside such restless people. But troops would also have a vital and positive role to play, in furthering "civil purposes," such as the construction of public works and improving communications; he built many of his plans around the idea of a corps of part-time soldiers, who would speed the opening up of the country.[3] In its economic aspect, Simcoe saw Upper Canada as a favoured land, bound to prove attractive to farmers. Moreover, its strategically located peninsula, jutting into the American interior, would draw the trade of the trans-Appalachian country out through a British funnel, the incomparable St Lawrence route.

Simcoe was a rigid and uncompromising churchman. He believed that the Church of England was established in Upper Canada, and he asked that a bishop be immediately appointed. From a political point of view, this step was essential to stem the influence of "enthusiastic & fanatick Teachers." The avowed aim of these sectaries was to destroy the national form of church government; an Anglican establishment, headed by a bishop, was the "best security that Government can have for its own internal preservation."[4] And the bishop must superintend the creation of schools and seminaries, if "The Levelling Spirit" were to be discouraged. Finally, Simcoe urged that great care be taken in selecting men to fill offices of trust in the new government. Capable, zealous, and active men, free of sinecure mentality, would be needed, and they would be best found among the American Loyalists. He was pleased, however, that a respectable English lawyer in the person of William Osgoode had been appointed as Chief Justice; the "pure Administration of Justice" would discourage the carrying of appeals to Great Britain, which were not only burdensome in themselves, but would "appear to the Inhabitants of the United States as Badges of inconvenient Subjection."[5]

Thus did Simcoe, in letters of tedious length, urge upon Whitehall officials the need for "vigorous and systematic Support" of the infant province which would be "the Rival, for public Estimation & preference, of the American Governments near to which it is situated." Without such support, the colony might "starve into a petty Factory for the accommodation of the Fur Traders"; with it, Upper Canada would "become the means of preserving all the transatlantic Dominions of Great Britain by exemplifying the Felicities of its Laws & Government." More than that, Simcoe indulged the hope that a colony so conceived would open up the possibility of reuniting the Empire, since it was in the interest of North America and Great Britain once again to be joined together.[6]

As Simcoe was preparing to leave England, the documents necessary to start the wheels of government turning were drawn up and issued. On August 21, 1791, an Order in Council effected the formal division of the old province of Quebec. On September 12 and 16, instructions and commissions were issued to Lord Dorchester as Governor-in-Chief and to Sir Alured Clark and Simcoe as Lieutenant-Governors.[7] A few days before, Simcoe had received assurance that the much desired Corps of Infantry, of some 425 officers and men, would be raised for service in Upper Canada, but he was disappointed to learn that his military rank would be raised only to that of colonel, and that his command would extend only to the new corps. All other troops in his province would be under the direction of the governor at Quebec, who had been appointed commander-in-chief of all the forces in British North America.[8] On September 26 he sailed from Weymouth, arriving at Quebec on November 11. A week later Clarke, in the absence of Dorchester, issued a proclamation ordering that the Constitutional Act was to go into effect on December 26, 1791.[9]

For the first half-year of its existence, however, the new province of Upper Canada was without the government provided for it. The lieutenant-governor could enter upon his duties only after he had taken the oath of office before a quorum of the executive council, and only one out of its four members so far appointed was then in Canada. Simcoe had perforce to wait in Quebec until the Chief Justice, William Osgoode, and the Receiver General, Peter Russell, arrived during the following June. At first there was some doubt whether the orderly administration of justice could proceed in the western settlements, but it presently became apparent that judges and law officers appointed under the old régime could carry on in the interim.

Although chafing at this enforced inaction, Simcoe was soon in busy correspondence with men in Britain, Canada, and the United States about plans for Upper Canada, and about its problems and prospects. He was, to begin with, quickly plunged into the delicate yet crucial difficulties surrounding the British retention of the posts, notably Oswego, Niagara, Detroit, and Michilimackinac. These fortified positions on the American side of the boundary line were still in the hands of British garrisons nearly ten years after the ratification of the Treaty of 1783, and would so continue until 1796. An excuse for this action was found in the non-fulfilment of the treaty by the United States in the matter of redress and compensation to the Loyalists and the non-payment of debts, but the main reason for holding on to the posts lay in the need for pacifying and reassuring the Indians of the Ohio region who had felt abandoned and betrayed when the British ceded everything south of the lakes to their hated foes, the Americans or "Long Knives." Now Americans were clamouring for British withdrawal at the same time that the armies of the republic were seeking to humble the Indians between the Ohio and Lake Erie, and so make the American paper title to the region a real one. If the Indians were defeated, they might turn in anger upon a nearly defenceless Upper Canada; victory by American troops would bring them into dangerous proximity to the isolated British garrisons.[10]

During the next four years this potentially explosive problem would occupy much of Simcoe's attention as well as that of the governments in London and Philadelphia. For the moment, Simcoe, and British authorities generally, had been given some time to work out a policy as a result of the Indian repulses of American armies sent into the Ohio country in 1790 and 1791 under Generals Harmar and St Clair. Simcoe was also made sharply aware of the powerful interests which demanded a favourable solution of this matter when he received a communication in December 1791, from a group of the leading merchants of Montreal. These men had been shocked by the concessions made to the United States in 1783, and still refused to accept the definition of the boundary in that treaty as final. They warned Simcoe that nothing "would give so fatal a Stab to the growing prosperity and importance of these Provinces as the Surrender of the Posts."[11] High British policy saw the retention of the posts as a means to peace and tranquillity in the interior, but the fur-trading magnates saw the posts as a weapon for forcing a more sensible redrawing of the boundary line, one that would afford adequate scope for their western operations.[12]

Neither then nor later did Simcoe formulate policies in order to protect the interests of the fur trade: that trade played little part in his plans for Upper Canada, since it would hold back settlement and debase the morals of those who did come.[13] But he nevertheless believed strongly that the posts must be retained and the Indian enemies of the United States supported. His concern was for the safety and security of Upper Canada. It must be safe-guarded and protected during its infancy, and this meant keeping those restless and dangerous Americans, who were loyal to the Congress, as far as possible from its borders. It meant maintaining a strong force in Upper Canada as a deterrent against invasions or forays across the frontier: mili-tary power, Simcoe believed, was the only argument expansionist Ameri-cans would understand. Moreover, he fell in heartily with the British government's plan to offer to mediate the dispute between the Indians and the Americans, with the attendant possibility of an Indian buffer state between the Ohio and the lakes. Simcoe was to follow this will-o'-the-wisp for two years until it was finally lost to sight in the smoke rising from the battlefield of Fallen Timbers.

Although Simcoe was determined to keep hostile Americans away from the territory of Upper Canada, he felt very differently about that vast popu-lation in the States which was, he felt certain, still actively or at least pas-sively loyal to King and Empire. In response to the home government's in-structions[14] to make public the terms of land-granting in the province and the advantages which they held for settlers, he anticipated the formal in-auguration of his administration by issuing a proclamation, dated February 7, 1792, addressed to "such as are desirous to settle on the Lands of the Crown in the Province of Upper Canada."[15]

This proclamation set forth the basic features of the Provincial land-granting system. Surveyors were to mark off townships, which were to be ten miles square in the interior, or nine by twelve miles along navigable waters. Within a township, the size of a farm lot was fixed at 200 acres, but at the discretion of the government any person might be granted an addi-tional amount up to 1,000 acres. Petitioners for land must give assurances that they would cultivate and improve their grants, and must take an oath of loyalty to the King. Lands were not to be sold; they were to be granted free of all expenses, except for fees payable to officials concerned in passing and recording the patents. Grants were to be made only after the surveyors had reserved one-seventh of the township for the support of a Protestant clergy and an additional one-seventh "for the future disposition of the Crown." This latter provision – the origin of the Crown Reserves – had not been mentioned in the Constitutional Act, but had resulted from an execu-tive decision of the British government aimed at providing the governors of the new colonies with an additional revenue. Thus, it was hoped, they would be freed from that excessive dependence on the assemblies which had so marred the government of the lost colonies. The two-sevenths of reserved land were to be interspersed among the other lots and to be of "like Value" with them.

How these provisions would be interpreted, and how they would be administered, were matters for the future. At the moment Simcoe was mainly concerned to make them widely known, in order that prospective settlers would be kept out of the clutches of American land-speculators and attracted into his province. These speculators would never allow his proclamation to be brought in from Canada and published in the United States, but he hoped that publication in English and West Indian newspapers would soon cause its contents to be known by interested people in the States. As it turned out, the proclamation did find "its way into the States in sufficient numbers."[16] He also wrote a long letter to the British consul in Philadelphia stating the advantages of Upper Canada for emigrants from Pennsylvania, and in particular, stressing that adherents of the Society of Friends would be welcomed and exempted from bearing arms.[17]

Before he ever set foot in Upper Canada Simcoe had determined upon those points in the province most suitable for advancing defensive and political purposes. He would build the capital at the head of navigation on the Thames River, that is, at the site of the later town of London. This site would be relatively safe from attack, and would afford ready access to Detroit and to Lake Erie. Toronto was the "natural arsenal" of the province, for the concentration of naval and military strength. For the present he would assemble the legislature at the mouth of the Niagara River, easily reached by water, with some public buildings, and a small concentration of settlement.[18]

Finally, the Lieutenant-Governor tried to impress upon the government at home the necessity of making immediate provision for "the education of the superior classes of the country." There was no need for early concern about "people in the lower degrees of life" whose limited requirements could be cheaply met, but schools for the "higher classes" could be provided only through the "liberality of the British Government," since there was no revenue in sight by which the province could establish them. If schools were not provided, "the Gentlemen of Upper Canada" would be forced to send their children to the United States, where the British principles of the Loyalists, at present the strongest bulwark of the province, would be "totally undermined and subverted." Simcoe therefore asked that the British parliament vote a thousand pounds a year for a few years to support two school-masters at Kingston and Niagara and a university at the capital. The staff of the latter should all be members of the Church of England "and, the medical professor perhaps excepted, clergymen." In his reply to these suggestions the Secretary of State, Henry Dundas, threw cold water on any talk of a university at this time, although he indicated that there might be assistance for a first-class preparatory school when the province had taken the initiative.[19] Simcoe had nevertheless touched on a theme which would sound down the years for a half-century to come.

Early in June 1792 Simcoe was at long last able to set out up the river to breathe life into the government of the new province. After a few days' stop at Montreal, where he was pleased to learn of the arrival of the first section of the Queen's Rangers, giving him the rank of colonel and some troops to command,[20] he and his party continued on their way until Kingston was reached on July 1. Here, in the largest community within the boundaries of the province – it contained fifty houses[21] – the leading officials of the new government were assembling. On July 8 the Lieutenant-Governor took his oaths of office, and on the following day the three executive councillors present took theirs. On the sixteenth, two important proclamations were issued. The first divided the province into nineteen counties, extending from Glengarry on the east to Essex on the west, and then went on to allocate representation in the Legislative Assembly, to a total of sixteen, on the basis of existing settlement as gauged by the militia returns. The second proclamation ordered elections to be held in these electoral districts. At the same time nine men were summoned to the legislative council, and some other appointments were made.[22] After these arrangements, Simcoe set sail on a government schooner on the twenty-third, reached Niagara three days later, and took up residence at Navy Hall.

Here, at Newark, the name which Simcoe now gave to the little settlement on the left bank, where the Niagara River emptied into Lake Ontario, the Lieutenant-Governor met his first legislature on September 17. With a full consciousness of the occasion and with such military pomp as he could muster, he sought to impress the members of the two Houses with the "great and momentous Trusts and Duties" placed in their hands. They and their constituents had shown their loyalty to the British Constitution; they had now been rewarded by having its benefits secured to themselves and their descendants. With this boon, with the "natural advantages" of the province, and aided by the generosity of the British government, it needed only the "fostering care" of the members to ensure the rise of "a numerous and Agricultural people." This speech was apparently heard with high approval; the formal parliamentary history of Upper Canada had begun in a mood of unity, enthusiasm, and anticipation.

On the whole, this mood was sustained during the work of the first session, as steps were taken to fashion Upper Canada into the truly British province envisaged by Simcoe. In fact, the first statute introduced "the English law as the rule of decision in all matters of controversy, relative to property and civil rights," on the ground that the province had "become inhabited principally by British subjects, born and educated in countries where the English laws were established." Accordingly, those parts of the

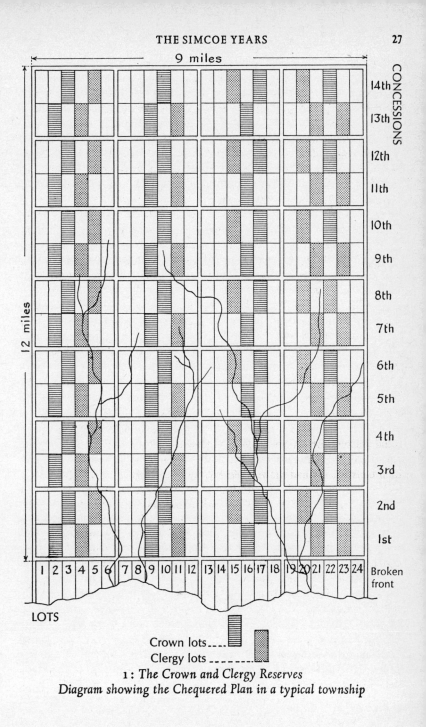

1: *The Crown and Clergy Reserves*
Diagram showing the Chequered Plan in a typical township

Quebec Act establishing French civil law were repealed.[23] It followed naturally that the second statute provided that all issues of fact before the courts of justice in the province should be "determined by the unanimous verdict of twelve jurors, which jurors shall be summoned and taken conformably to the law and custom of England."[24] Among other statutes of this first session was one renaming the Districts[25] (Eastern, Midland, Home, and Western in place of Luneberg, Mecklenburg, Nassau, and Hesse), and providing for the establishing of jails and court houses in each. The English system of weights and measures was established. The essential machinery of law and government was being set up.

The first session was, however, not without its mild warnings of disagreements and differences to come, as topics were broached that would bear a more ominous face in the future. The troublesome marriage question, which would disturb the province for more than a generation, now appeared in a simple form, with the attempt by Richard Cartwright, a leading merchant in the legislative council, to secure the validation of his and other marriages performed irregularly at a time when clergymen were almost non-existent in the province.[26] Simcoe managed to postpone the matter temporarily. The House of Assembly early showed a cheerful propensity for appropriating funds, as in providing salaries for officers of the legislature, but a marked coolness to proposals for raising money that might come out of their own or their constituents' pockets. An attempt to impose a small land tax was negatived by those holding grants with the hope of selling them to prospective settlers. On the other hand, the landholders in the Assembly were very ready to put a duty on wines and spirits coming into the province (mainly for the purpose of the fur trade in the northwest), but the merchants in the Council killed this bill, fearing that it would cause trouble with Lower Canada: the problem of dividing import duties with Lower Canada was one that would have to be settled in the future. Finally, some members of the House, accustomed to town meetings in the old colonies, proposed their introduction into Upper Canada, but this suggestion apparently smacked too much of the "Elective principle,"[27] which was thought to have brought on the American Revolution, and was deferred.

Simcoe felt that the first session had passed off well enough, considering the materials of which the Assembly was composed. (He had noted a distressing desire on the part of the voters to choose men "of a Lower Order, who kept but one Table, that is who dined in Common with their Servants.") The members of the Assembly were the leading figures of the several counties, but they were men of limited experience, and "newly acquainted with power"; fortunately, the legislative council had proved to be an effective check upon the more "precipitate" measures of the House, making unnecessary his use of the veto.[28] In his speech proroguing the session, on October 15, 1792, he complimented the two Houses on the results of their labours, and sent them back to their homes with the urging that they explain to the inhabitants that "this province is singularly blessed, not with a mutilated Constitution, but with a Constitution which has stood the test of experience, and is the very image and transcript of that of Great Britain, by which she has long established and secured to her subjects as much freedom and happiness as it is possible to be enjoyed under the subordination necessary to civilized Society."[29] In thus implying a contrast between the fledgling Constitution of the United States and the ancient British Constitution the Lieutenant-Governor doubtless had no intention of asserting that a distant colony would enjoy all the practices of the latter exactly as at home; but, all unwittingly, he had uttered words that would echo through the political debates of the next half-century.

This little legislature met four more times in annual session at the mouth of the Niagara River before the first parliament of Upper Canada was dissolved. Working sometimes at the behest of the executive and sometimes on bills proposed by private members, the two houses attempted to solve immediate problems and to encourage future growth. There was, to begin with, the fact of war with France, the news of which reached Newark early in May 1793. The seat of war might be remote from the province, but it was well to be prepared, especially since the neighbouring states were still in alliance with the country that was now an enemy. Accordingly, it was thought proper to strengthen the militia. Simcoe had already appointed county lieutenants, and now the legislature passed a bill placing each lieutenant at the head of the militia in his county, and providing that male inhabitants from 16 to 50 were liable for service anywhere in the province. Many statutes followed this first one in an attempt to bring efficiency to the militia, but a start at least had been made.[30]

Inevitably, financial questions occupied much of the time of the legislators. They did not have to find money to pay the salaries of the leading executive and judicial appointees, for these were paid by the British parliament in annual grants of the order of £6,000 to £7,000 for this period, but funds were needed for minor officials, including the officers of the legislature, and for various local purposes. After the failure of the first session, the members were now able to agree on some expedients for raising money. Local rates were levied, duties imposed upon stills, and licences were to be required of tavern-keepers. The thorny question of Upper Canada's share of the duties collected in Lower Canada was approached by the appointment of three commissioners empowered to meet with the officials of the lower province and reach an agreement. Subsequent negotiations resulted in a decision giving Upper Canada one-eighth of all customs revenue collected down the St Lawrence, an arrangement which lasted for only two years.

The administration of justice also received further attention in the successive sessions of the first parliament. In particular, Simcoe secured the passage in 1794 of a judicature act setting up the Court of King's Bench as a superior court of civil and criminal jurisdiction. This measure represented a deliberate and conscious attempt by Simcoe and Chief Justice Osgoode to assimilate the judicial structure of the province more closely to that of the mother country, and provoked vigorous opposition from leading residents, especially the merchants Richard Cartwright and Robert Hamilton, as being quite unsuited to a new province with a small and scattered population.[31] District surrogate courts and a provincial court of probate were also established. On a lower level, but of greater import to most residents, was the regulation of the time and place of meetings for the courts of quarter sessions, presided over by the justices of the peace. The J.P.'s, as we shall see later, exercised a great range of powers, administrative as well as judicial; they were the real basis of local government throughout the history of the province.[32] In an attempt, however, to satisfy the still persistent demand for town meetings, the legislature in 1793 provided that the J.P.'s might issue warrants for the election of parish or township officers (clerks, assessors, collectors, overseers of highways, pathmasters, and fence-viewers, and so on) on an annual basis. This device was a very pale replica of the New England town meetings, for the meetings had almost no authority beyond that of the annual elections and real local power continued to be in the hands of the J.P.'s. The settlers had won a small concession, but it was never to be significantly enlarged.[33]

The first parliament was busy with several other matters important to a new and pioneer community. Arrangements for the registering of deeds, regulations for the practice of law and medicine, the fixing of millers' tolls, definition of who might sit in the Assembly, and provision for paying the members: these were all subjects of legislation. Wild and domestic animals were never far from the minds of these forest legislators and their constituents, as was evidenced by acts to encourage the destruction of wolves and bears and "to restrain the custom of permitting horned cattle, horses, sheep, and swine to run at large." The first two of a long series of statutes aimed at encouraging the building and maintenance of "public highways and roads" were also passed; responsibility was placed in the hands of local authorities, a system "which kept the roads of this Province a disgrace to civilization for a century."[34]

Despite Simcoe's continuing opposition the second session carried through a bill on the marriage question, which the Lieutenant-Governor reluctantly approved. It validated existing marriages performed by magistrates and military officers in a period when clergymen were not available, and it provided for the future that justices of the peace might solemnize marriages, according to the form of the Church of England, when the parties lived more than eighteen miles from an Anglican clergyman in a District containing fewer than five such clergymen. When, however, five or more Anglican clergymen were resident in a District, the J.P.'s would lose this power. So limited a measure, passed only because Simcoe would have vetoed a more liberal one, inevitably excited much objection in a province with a non-Anglican majority. Petitions were received from both Presbyterians and Baptists, asking for their clergy the right to perform marriages, but Simcoe denounced these as disloyal and wicked.[35] This incident strengthened Simcoe's belief that Anglican clergymen must be attracted to the province as rapidly as possible. The next claim on the part of the Dissenters, he warned prophetically, would be for a share of "the sevenths set apart for the National Clergy."[36]

One further act of this parliament, passed in the second session, provided for the gradual abolition of slavery in the province. In contrast to the marriage bill, this measure was strongly pressed by Simcoe and accepted with some reluctance by several members of the legislature. Many of the Loyalist settlers had brought Negro slaves with them, and expected to go on using them. The high cost and scarcity of labour were stressed by those defending the use of slaves. After Simcoe's measure was moderated, however, the members agreed to pass it. Slaves already in the province would continue in that state to the end of their lives, but no new slaves would be admitted. Children born to female slaves in the province were to become free upon reaching the age of twenty-five years.

Thus the province had seen the work of its first parliament under its first lieutenant-governor. As a rule the members had been ready to follow the lead of the executive, with the result that much useful and necessary if perhaps unexciting legislation had followed from this co-operation. Occasionally the houses had insisted on measures opposed by Simcoe, but usually he had been able at least to water down and limit these. Sometimes he could take advantage of disagreements between the Houses to ensure the defeat of what he thought to be unsound or unwise proposals. He bemoaned his lack of influence on the legislature, yet usually managed to get his way. On the whole he was satisfied with the Assembly, which he thought had proved to be a loyal and well-disposed body, more so in all probability than its successors would be.[37] As for the legislative council, on which he had always pinned such high hopes, it had proved to be generally reliable, except for the occasional opposition of the two prominent merchants, Cartwright and Hamilton. This opposition infuriated Simcoe. He called Hamilton "an avowed Republican," and he accused Cartwright of "vanity & sordidness." He wished that he had fuller control over the army commissariat in the province, in order to deprive such merchants of government contracts when they did not support executive measures.[38] Cartwright, on the other hand, felt that Simcoe had already gone too far in the direction of weakening the independence of the legislative council by appointing so many of its members to the executive council and to government offices "dependent for their salaries on the good pleasure of the Governor."[39] In short, the great majority of the settlers were too busy with immediate tasks, too little informed on public matters, and too scattered about the province to be able to question Simcoe's measures with any closeness, but some of the leading men who were nearer to the centre of affairs were far from pleased with all features of the Lieutenant-Governor's design for the province.

For Simcoe and his associates in the executive government the short annual meetings of the legislature were, however, only part of a constant round of activities looking to the growth and protection of the province. And of all their concerns none was more immediate than that of fostering settlement. This was a many-sided enterprise: it meant encouraging people to come into Upper Canada, trying to locate them in the most suitable places from the point of view of the imperial interest, improving communications, especially roads, and developing an effective land policy. Simcoe turned early to the enterprise, with enthusiasm and with optimism. He believed that his province could quickly attract a considerable population which would be, or would soon become, loyal to the British Crown, and that this population would be the basis of present security and of future prosperity. In his sanguine, or as one critic[40] thought, utopian visions, he saw Upper Canada dominating the interior of the continent and the base for winning back some or all of the lost colonies to British allegiance. But first, every effort must be bent to the acquiring of a population.

For attaining this goal Simcoe believed that, apart from the natural attractions of the province, he had at hand a powerful weapon in the arrangements for granting the vacant lands of the Crown. These lands were extensive, they were readily accessible, and they were, as already noted, to be granted free to the settlers except for the payment of fees to certain government officials. Above all, they were to be granted under the wise and generous supervision of a benevolent government, not put in the hands of grasping land jobbers, as in the United States. In addition, he believed that the plan for Crown Reserves would be agreeably received, since the revenue derived from them would exempt the residents from the taxation imposed upon settlers in the states across the lakes.[41] Accordingly, Simcoe was certain that Upper Canada had substantial advantages over competing regions, such as the Genesee tract of northern New York. Indeed, such tracts benefited the province, because they drew migrants to the interior, where they might hear about the superior qualities of Upper Canada and so decide to enter it.

Simcoe had, as we have seen, set out to advertise the lands of the province even before he had arrived in it, by his proclamation of February 7, 1792. Almost át once he began to get nibbles, and by the time he and the executive council inaugurated the government at Kingston in the summer of that year, there were several claimants for land. Many of these claimants, however, were asking not for a mere couple of hundred acres but for a whole township on behalf of themselves and their associates. The spokesmen assured the government that back in their communities in the United States there lived a number of people who were loyal or potentially loyal to British interests and who wanted to live together in Upper Canada. (By contrast, one applicant, William Willcocks, proposed to bring settlers from Ireland.) In the hope of speeding up settlement, the council granted some twenty-five townships to such leaders during the following year, but the hope was disappointed. The leaders placed few actual settlers on the land, and after 1796 many of their claims were declared forfeited. Some of these men were simply speculators, but others were the victims of unfortunate circumstances. In any event this device of using middlemen to assist in the work of colonization proved to be premature.[42]

While this experiment was running its course, other practices were being established which stored up trouble for the future. One of these, derived from earlier colonial precedent, was the system of allowing officials of the government, such as the Attorney General, the Secretary of the Province and the Clerk of the Executive Council, through whose hands a patent passed before it was completed, to supplement their rather meagre incomes by charging fees for their services.[43] In relation to the number of acres granted these fees were fairly low, but they nevertheless posed difficulties to persons with little ready money, and they amounted to considerable sums for individuals who were able to accumulate extensive holdings for future sale. As a result, a great many people did not complete the formalities which would entitle them to their deeds; instead, they simply relied on their "location ticket," which did not give legal title. Yet land transactions began to take place, based only on the location tickets, and before fees had been paid. Apparently soldiers, "roving Yankees," "Canadian Battoe men," and others who had no serious intention of becoming farmers received locations, which they then "sold for a trifle" to men who were building up large holdings for future speculation.[44] After 1794, when Simcoe abolished the Land Boards which had been established in 1788 and left recommendations for land in the hands of the magistrates, there was even less careful screening of applicants than before.

Further, Simcoe took the view that members of the executive and legislative councils and other leading citizens should receive grants of equivalent generosity to those being given to military officers. The practice was estab-

c

lished, at the end of Simcoe's period, of giving such people some 3,000 to 5,000 acres, and usually their children, sometimes very numerous, could count on each receiving 1,200 acres. Thus Simcoe hoped to build up the aristocracy that was central to all his plans for Upper Canada. The recipients, however, had no intention of becoming country gentlemen on their broad acres, which were in any case often rather scattered, but instead expected to sell them profitably in the future. These practices did not slow up settlement in this early period, for there was plenty of land for everyone, but they did cause settlement to be widely dispersed, and they locked up land which would one day be in demand.

Another factor which contributed to the dispersion of settlement was the arrangement for laying out the Crown and Clergy Reserves. For his guidance in this matter Simcoe could refer to the clause in the Constitutional Act of 1791 requiring that the Clergy Reserves, and by analogy the Crown Reserves, be allotted within each township when other lands were being granted, and that the Reserves be of "like Quality" with such other lands;[45] but these phrases left open for decision the precise manner of allocation. During his residence in Lower Canada in 1791-92 Simcoe learned that officials there favoured lumping the Reserves all together in one large block in each township. After he and his Acting Surveyor General, D. W. Smith, had given more thought to the subject, however, they agreed that the Reserves must be scattered in individual two-hundred-acre lots all through each township. Only in respect to townships surveyed before the Act of 1791 went into effect would block reserves be made, necessarily in adjacent townships. Smith set to work on a scheme for future surveys, which Simcoe reported to the Secretary of State on November 4, 1792, as having been approved by the Council and put into operation.[46]

This bald announcement on a subject of much interest to the home government brought a demand for more information, which was provided in Smith's report, sent to Whitehall on September 16, 1793.[47] Thus was produced the "Chequered Plan," which played so fateful a part in the subsequent history of Upper Canada. The normal township was to be 9 miles along the front and 12 miles in depth. There would be 14 rows of 200-acre lots, each row separated from the next by a concession road. This made 24 lots in each row and 336 lots in the whole townships. Two-sevenths of the whole came to 96 and two-sevenths of each row came to 6 and six-sevenths. To avoid the fraction, however, it was decided to reserve seven lots in each concession, making two lots reserved in each township beyond the required two-sevenths, to be used for the general purposes of the government. There were other details, and some exceptions, especially that settlement along important roads was to be unbroken (that is, reserves would be made away from the roads), but these were the essentials of the scheme.[48] No grants of land could be made in any township until the "sevenths" had been reserved. There was no intention of selling the Reserves until they would bring an adequate revenue to the clergy and Crown, but in the meantime, Simcoe suggested that some return could be realized by a leasing policy. Simcoe also reserved land for more immediate purposes: "such as to remunerate the expenses of opening the *Military Roads* by the Soldiers, building *Inns* or Posts necessary for Communication, and the erection of a *Wharf* at York," these, too, to be held until they would bring a good return.[49]

The improvement of communications was, in fact, a leading preoccupation with Simcoe. In order to base his plans upon personal observation, he early seized opportunities to make tours of inspection about the province. In February and March of 1793 he went westward to Detroit, and on the way confirmed his earlier impression that the permanent capital of the province ought to be at the "confluence of the main Branches of the Thames." The site was not immediately practicable, however, and as a first step to the securing of the western regions he decided to build a military road from Burlington Bay to the Thames. In the early summer of 1793 a contingent of the Queen's Rangers was put to work building this road, which was named Dundas Street, after the Secretary of State. If Niagara should be taken, it would still be possible to hold the western regions by means of this road. In May, Simcoe went across the lake to Toronto, which he renamed York, and concluded that here would be the best location for an "Arsenal," military and naval, since it was more readily defensible than either Kingston or Niagara.[50] In August he returned to York, with the intention of transferring the seat of government temporarily to that place. A town site was laid out, with soldiers of the Queen's Rangers again being used for the work.

He then journeyed northward to Lake Aux Claies, renamed Lake Simcoe in honour of his father,[51] and then out to Georgian Bay by way of the Severn River, coming back to York by the same route. This trip further convinced Simcoe that a military road should be opened from York to Lake Simcoe to ensure rapid communication with the upper lakes. Work on portions of a road along this route had already been started by a surveying party and by the settlers brought in by William Berczy; in 1796 another party of Queen's Rangers was also detailed to this project, now called Yonge Street after the Secretary at War. Although military purposes were uppermost in the planning of Dundas and Yonge Streets, they proved to be of great assistance in furthering the settlement of the province.

It was more than routine professional interest that led Simcoe to plan these military highways. The state of Upper Canada's relations with the United States throughout most of his four years in the colony caused him to consider every subject from its military aspect. The province must be kept in a posture of readiness and defence if it was to play its part successfully in the complicated struggle going on for the control of the American Northwest, that is, the regions south and west of the lower Great Lakes. The waging of this contest was ever in the forefront of Simcoe's mind. He did not want the contest to end in war, despite his expressed wish to meet the Americans again on the field of battle, because he knew that the infant province was not ready for it. Yet he would accept war if it came, and he made what dispositions for it that he could. Essentially, however, his purpose was to skirt the edge of war, to bluff the Americans, to manœuvre them into acceptance of a neutral zone south of the lakes reserved to the Indians. Thus would he safeguard Upper Canada, and put it on the road to eventual predominance in internal America.

It will be recalled that the Lieutenant-Governor, even before he reached Upper Canada, had entered eagerly into plans to take advantage of the weakness of the United States revealed and deepened by St Clair's defeat in the autumn of 1791. He corresponded with George Hammond, the British minister at Philadelphia, about the possibility of British mediation in the fighting between the Americans and the Indians, and he conferred with Alexander McKee, of the Indian Department,[52] on the best means for bringing this about. It was agreed that McKee should attend a meeting of the Indian confederacy, in September 1792, and inspire the tribes to make a spontaneous and unanimous request for British mediation.[53] The Indians did ask, unsuccessfully, for Simcoe's presence at their forthcoming meeting with American commissioners planned for the summer of 1793, but the debates in September disclosed a fact which weakened Simcoe's program. This fact was disagreement between the Western Indians on the one hand, who demanded that a stand be taken for the Ohio boundary, and the Six Nations tribes, led by Joseph Brant, on the other hand, who counselled a compromise boundary giving the Americans much of the region north of the Ohio. Simcoe's plans called for a determined and unyielding united front on the part of all the Indians as a means of forcing the Americans to accept a large buffer zone south of Lake Erie and even reaching east to some of the territory south of Lake Ontario. He became very bitter against Brant, who believed that now was the time to make peace with the United States.[54]

But the United States was now too strong in the West for Simcoe's plans to have any hope of success. When the western Indians reiterated their demand, during the summer conference of 1793, that the Americans remain south of the Ohio, the negotiations broke off in failure, and a well-trained army under Anthony Wayne prepared for another campaign. Since a successful outcome would allow Wayne to menace Detroit, the governor at Quebec, Lord Dorchester, who had recently returned from England, ordered Simcoe, on February 17, 1794, to occupy positions near the mouth of the

Maumee River as a means of protecting communications around the western end of Lake Erie. The result was the erection of Fort Miami a few weeks later.

Tension mounted in the spring and summer of 1794. Simcoe believed that Wayne's advance would either bring him into collision with British forces or would so menace the province's borders that retaliation would be essential. Events reached a climax on August 20 when Wayne's troops met and defeated the Indians at the Battle of Fallen Timbers, in the near vicinity of the still uncompleted Fort Miami. For a few days British America and the United States stood poised perilously on the brink of war as Wayne approached within gunshot of the new fort, and tried to overawe its commander, Major Campbell. The latter stood firm against the American general's verbal attempts to dislodge him, but in no way joined his cause to that of the Indians. Wayne, in turn, stopped just short of provoking Campbell into the retaliation which Simcoe had thought to be inevitable; satisfied with his victory and with having flaunted his strength before the British flag, he retired from the area. For their part the Indians drew the necessary moral: although they had been joined in the recent battle by some militia men acting as volunteers, it was obvious that they were not going to receive assistance from responsible British officers.

Meanwhile, on the larger scene, successful efforts were under way to settle Anglo-American differences, of which the ones mentioned here were only a part. Chief Justice John Jay, President Washington's special envoy, had reached London in the middle of June, and it was soon apparent that he had arrived at a time when he and the British foreign secretary could do business together, since the dangers raised by the war with France made the British government ready to seek an easing of tension with the United States. As an important stage in this process it was necessary to avoid provocation in the interior of North America, and it was accordingly agreed to maintain the *status quo* there until an agreement was reached between the two governments. By November 1 the treaty was signed, and its contents were known in the west in the early summer of 1795. Among several articles covering relations between the United States and British North America, including boundary and trade matters, that providing for the surrender of the posts by June 1, 1796, was of most immediate concern to Dorchester and Simcoe. And it was especially important, as the Secretary of State, now the Duke of Portland, pointed out to Simcoe, to obtain the "peaceful acquiescence" of the Indians in this surrender.[55]

Acquiescence was in fact the only course left open to the Indians south of Lake Erie. The terms and tenor of Jay's Treaty dashed any lingering hopes of British military support in their quarrels with the Americans, while their defeat at Fallen Timbers had convinced them of the futility of further resistance without it. For its part, the United States was now ready, which it had not been in earlier years, to salve the Indians' pride and the British conscience by admitting that the Indian lands had not been ceded in 1783, and that it was a matter of negotiating for them with the Indian confederacy. They could, of course, be sure that these negotiations would be successful. In the summer of 1795 the Treaty of Greenville was concluded by which the western Indians abandoned their claims to most of the present state of Ohio and recognized themselves as being under the protection of the United States. The more unwavering among them withdrew to the northwest, into the Michigan region, where they would make another, and again unsuccessful, stand some fifteen years later against the advance of the American frontier.[56]

Whatever hopes Simcoe may have had of a neutral barrier, of making Upper Canada dominant in the interior of North America, even of disrupting the upstart republic, had now of course to be abandoned. It was, however, some consolation to know that the executive branch of the American government had shown vigour and responsibility and goodwill during the recent crisis; perhaps there could now be the prospect of peace and stability along the border, giving the new province an opportunity to grow and prosper. It was as important as ever to retain the friendship of the Indians in the vicinity of Upper Canada, and to look to its defences, but Simcoe wished it to be known that he had no feelings of enmity to the United States.[57] For the rest he kept his views on the new state of affairs to himself.

In any event Simcoe was at the end of his stay in Upper Canada. For some time he had been discouraged and embittered by Lord Dorchester's constant frustration of his plans for developing the province, a mood that was intensified by recurring ill health. He left the province in July 1796, and for a year and more afterward it was thought that he might return. He was assigned to other duties, however, and never saw the province again.

As Simcoe sailed back across the Atlantic he may have reviewed the results of four years' arduous service in the new province of Upper Canada. He undoubtedly felt that he had done everything possible to accomplish his original objectives, but he must have felt that he had received singularly little support and encouragement for many of his most important plans. Both from London and from Quebec he had met with hindrances and with negatives in his attempts to strengthen the security and prosperity of his province against its republican and democratic neighbours. He had aimed, for instance, at planting the British constitution to the fullest extent possible in the interior of North America – to give Upper Canada the very image and transcript of the British Government and Constitution – only to meet with objections and disallowance on the part of the authorities at home. A prime essential, in his mind from the beginning, was to establish the aristo-cratic principle as an integral feature of provincial government. Accord-ingly, he had appointed lieutenants in the counties to be a focus for the ambition of leading residents, in order that a territorial aristocracy might be nursed into vigorous life, and the legislative council made a counterpart of the House of Lords. He had also tried to accelerate the growth of towns as a means of counteracting "those pernicious principles"[58] which emanated from the North American frontier. This was to be done by sprinkling garri-sons around the province, about which urban growth could develop, and by providing for the early incorporation of emerging towns, with councils chosen "in such a manner as to render the Elections as *little popular* as possible, meaning such Corporations to tend to the support of the Aristoc-racy of the Country."[59] But the Secretary of State had frowned on both these projects, stating them to be "very unfit to be encouraged by a Parent State in a dependent Colony." The lieutenant-governor must keep all power consistent with the constitution in his own hands, not let it "fritter down" in a way to allow local interests to become demanding. London was con-cerned to avoid a recurrence of the attitudes behind the American Revolu-tion; Simcoe was certain that these could not emerge in a truly loyal colony blessed with the full benefits of the British Constitution, including and indeed emphasizing its aristocratic elements.[60]

Simcoe's scheme contemplated an early and generous expenditure of money on the new province to ensure its military security, to promote in-ternal improvements, and to provide a striking contrast with the struggling settlements on the American side of the border. A "due support" now would be the surest economy in the long run.[61] But London was in no mood for enlarged expenditures, remembering that the province was already costing upward of £20,000 a year and bringing nothing back in return, while Dorchester at Quebec rigidly exercised his powers as commander-in-chief to denude the province of troops when there was no clear military reason for their continued presence, all the while icily ignoring Simcoe's pleas that the troops were part of his program of provincial development. From Navy Hall came an outraged protest telling of "reasonable Hopes & views" being "blighted and destroyed."[62] In related matters, having to do with the supply-ing of the troops in the province and the supervision of the Indian Depart-ment, the Lieutenant-Governor had also long suffered from the arbitrary and uninformed authority coming up tardily and erratically from Quebec.

Simcoe's plans for laying a sound foundation in the realm of the mind and the spirit had also received less encouragement than he had hoped for. As already indicated, the Secretary of State had shown little sympathy for Simcoe's educational plans, pointing out that "the Country must make the University, and not the University the Country."[63] As Simcoe said more than once, however, Upper Canada was a new province, but its inhabitants were not a new people; if they were to take their rightful place in the Empire, they should at once have adequate facilities for civilized existence. Nevertheless, Whitehall persisted in the view that school-masters in the elementary subjects would satisfy present needs; advanced students could repair to Quebec or Montreal or Nova Scotia.[64] Simcoe knew that they would not go to these places. Once again he had failed to convince his superiors that a bold and imaginative policy would pay rich dividends in the interior of North America.

As was also mentioned at the beginning of the chapter, the full establishment of the Church of England and the immediate appointment of a bishop had been prominent parts of Simcoe's plans for Upper Canada before he had left England. These steps were essential in a new province "situated amongst a variety of republics" if "distinction of rank" was to be upheld and the "democratic influence" lessened.[65] After he had reached the province he was more convinced than ever of the political importance of strengthening the Church of England as a means of combatting the influence of the "Sectaries" and of "forming the Character, Temper, and Manners of the People of this infant Colony to British Habits and to British Principles."[66] Only five years before, in 1787, the first Anglican episcopate in the British colonies in America had been established with the appointment of a bishop of Nova Scotia, and the two Canadian provinces were under his jurisdiction. In 1793, however, this impossibly large see was divided, with Jacob Mountain becoming Bishop of Quebec.[67] Simcoe had to be contented with this arrangement; it would be forty-six years before a separate bishopric was established in Upper Canada. Mountain took an active interest in the interior province, visited it in 1794, and he endorsed and repeated Simcoe's requests for stronger support of the church there.[68] The Duke of Portland, however, scaled down the Bishop's plans, and reminded Simcoe that financial support from England was to be considered as only a temporary assistance until "the Church Lands shall become sufficiently productive" to support the clergy.[69] Simcoe knew that these lands would not serve this purpose for a very long time to come.

These various restrictions on his grand design for the province must have weighed upon the Lieutenant-Governor's mind as he left for home. It is doubtful, however, that he was equally conscious of the ways in which the materials within the province had proved to be intractable. To be sure, Upper Canada had grown, and in a measure had prospered, but it was not turning out exactly as he had intended. Settlers were indeed coming in from the United States; but close observers were convinced that these people were attracted more by cheap and good land than by the superior institutions available under British rule. His plans for administering the vacant lands had not avoided that curse of North America, jobbery and speculation. A gentlemanly class had been encouraged by generous grants, without any sign as yet of a duly ordered aristocratic society, or that those encouraged would always support the lieutenant-governor. Attempts to give the Church of England a position of pre-eminence had not brought the flock to the fold; most of the people continued to be "Dissenters" or the despised "Sectarian fanatics." The legislature had done useful and effective work in laying provincial foundations, but it was apparent that the executive arm had a limited influence in directing its proceedings. In short, Simcoe had helped to nurse a new province into being, but its inhabitants, busy with their own projects and their own local affairs, showed only a tepid interest in the goals he had set for them. The solid core of the population was Loyalist, strongly attached to Britain, but it would be British in a way that was not Simcoe's.[70]

CHAPTER 3

A Frontier Province
1796-1812

The men who headed the government in the following years had little of Simcoe's vigour and imagination. The first incumbent, Peter Russell, the Receiver General, became Administrator[1] when Simcoe left. He was a cautious and timid man, worried of offending his superiors, and easily depressed by minor irritations. Aware that he might be superseded at any moment, he attempted no new departures, but simply carried on Simcoe's plans, as nearly as he understood them. Some improvements in land-granting procedure were effected, and in general a reasonably capable but rather plodding government succeeded the somewhat whirlwind Simcoe era. Lacking the respect of his associates on the executive council and the authority of a lieutenant-governor, this elderly functionary had little opportunity and less desire to make a positive imprint upon the province over which he presided so uneasily and so fretfully. Fortunately for him there was an easier atmosphere along the border in a period when Anglo-American relations were improving, following Jay's Treaty, and when there was increasing hostility between France and the United States.

General Peter Hunter, who assumed the reins of government in August 1799, also made little impression upon Upper Canada during the six years until his sudden death in 1805. He was a professional soldier, and something of a martinet, who seems to have regarded the province as one more regiment to be commanded. Since he had also been appointed to the post of commander of the armed forces in British North America, he was a part-time lieutenant-governor who had to spend a large part of his time at Quebec. During his prolonged absences he left a committee of the executive council in charge of the day-to-day running of the government, armed with batches of signed proclamations and other documents on which the committee was to fill in the blanks when they were issued. At the outset Hunter declared that the government was to be carried on exactly as heretofore. Nevertheless, his occasionally arbitrary conduct left resentments that were vented on his successors.

After another temporary administration, this time of a year's duration and presided over by Alexander Grant, an old and infirm naval officer entirely lacking in political ability, a new lieutenant-governor arrived in August 1806 in the person of Francis Gore. This man, who had been a junior military officer and had then gone into the colonial service, governed the province for five years, whereupon he asked for a leave which took him out of Upper Canada during the period of the War of 1812. In 1815 he returned for a final two years. He seems to have been a person of some capacity, shrewd and active and attentive to his duties; at times he was also impetuous and wilful. But even if he had had the temper of an angel, he would not have been able to avoid the difficulties that were heaped upon him during his first years in the province. He arrived at a time when many irritations were being felt, and when there was an ample supply of trouble-makers to take advantage of them. As these internal gusts blew themselves out, he was faced with the renewed danger of war with the United States following the *Chesapeake* affair in 1807. In short, during Gore's first term, Upper Canada had its first small taste of internal dissensions, accompanied by threats of external danger. Inevitably for a pioneer society, the dissensions centred about settlement, land-granting, internal improvements, and the rivalries and jealousies of a small political community. And to these topics we must now turn.

In the years before 1812, the peopling of Upper Canada went forward steadily. Simcoe's policy of welcoming settlers from the United States was continued after he left the province, although his successors were less convinced than he had been that the migrants from across the lakes were inspired by a sense of British loyalty. Still, the province needed populating, the Americans undoubtedly had the skills needed to develop a pioneer region, and there was no certain evidence that they would constitute a dangerous element. There was little chance of getting a population from Great Britain, as long as the war went on in Europe; meanwhile, leading men in the province wanted to see it opened up, and perhaps they might be able to sell land to some of the newcomers.

The first wave of these people has sometimes been described as "late loyalists," a term of limited accuracy, since most of them did not migrate for political reasons. Yet some of them were relatives of the original Loyalists, drawn into the province by reports from the latter about its advantages.[2] Some were disillusioned by events in the new republic, such as the Whiskey Rebellion in western Pennsylvania in 1794, and by the hold which large land companies had over much of the accessible new land, particularly in New York State. Some, indeed, were attracted to upstate

New York by the advertisements of the land companies, and then decided that they would fare better across the lake. Having reached Oswego or the mouth of the Genesee River they simply coasted along the south shore of Lake Ontario to the Niagara River. There they went north of Lake Erie, into Upper Canada, rather than south toward the Ohio country, where there were still hostile Indians and where swamps made access difficult. Settlement of Ohio was indeed going forward at a great pace but, despite the founding of Cleveland in 1796, it came mainly from the south, from Virginia, and then across the Ohio River. Upper Canada was reached before northern Ohio, and indeed before much of northwestern New York.[3]

A letter published in Philadelphia in 1795 and later reprinted in a little book on the Canadas which appeared in Connecticut in 1799 suggests the view of Upper Canada that was probably in the minds of people interested in moving to the province. The system of government was praised, and it was stressed that the British parliament had "renounced forever the right of taxation"; moreover, taxes within the province were barely felt, since the British government paid for the whole of the civil establishment. The people regulated local matters, through "constables, path-masters and other town officers, in the same manner as formerly in the other colonies, now the United States." The author stated that the soil was ideal for agriculture, and that it was easy to send products to market by way of the lakes, the St Lawrence River and the great port of Montreal.[4] There was nothing in this description to discourage an American on the move from coming into a British colony, especially at a time when national feeling was still embryonic in the new republic. The ensuing peaceful invasion put settlers in all the vacant townships along Lake Ontario west of the Bay of Quinte, and in several of those along Lake Erie. Although roads were still almost non-existent, water communication made possible the dispersal of settlement along a five-hundred-mile front in a period of less than twenty years.

An important phase of this movement deserving special attention is that which brought Quakers, Mennonites, Dunkards, and other "plain folk" into the province, especially from Pennsylvania and New York. The movement was partly political in origin, since these communities, pacifist by creed, were often unpopular with their American neighbours by reason of their neutrality during the late Revolutionary War. Simcoe let it be known that Quakers would be welcome in the province, and that they would be exempted from bearing arms.[5] Militia acts subsequently passed by the provincial legislature included provisions to this effect. The movement was also a search for good and cheap land on the part of a people who were competent farmers and who wanted to see their children grow up about them living according to the old ways. Adherents of these closely knit religious communities made very effective pioneers: they were hard-working, frugal,

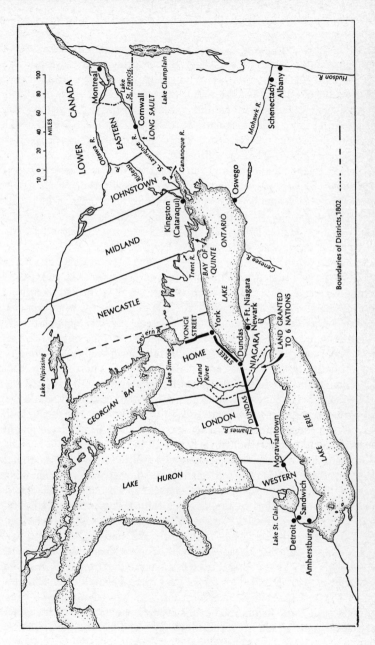

2 : Upper Canada about 1800

ready to come to one another's assistance in attacking difficult tasks, and determined to put down deep and strong roots.

A few English-speaking Quakers and a larger number of German-speaking Mennonites were established in the townships west of the Niagara River before the end of the 1780's, and this movement continued in the next two decades. In 1799 the Acting Surveyor General wrote that "Nineteen covered waggons, with families, came in to settle in the vicinity of the county of Lincoln, about the month of June last; and the facility with which some of these people travel, particularly in crossing the small rivers, deserves to be noticed. The body of their waggons is made of close boards and the most clever have the ingenuity to caulk the seams, and so by shifting off the body from the carriage, it serves to transport the wheels and the family."[6] A scattering of Quakers was also to be found among the Loyalists farther east, particularly in the Bay of Quinte area. At the other end of the province Moravian missionaries brought in a group of Christian Indians from the Ohio country and established Fairfield (Moraviantown) in 1792.[7] At the end of the decade a much more significant enterprise was inaugurated, when two Mennonites from Pennsylvania arrived to spy out the land along the upper reaches of the Grand River. Joseph Brant had recently persuaded the government to agree to the sale of the northern portion of the Indian Reserve to a group of land speculators, and the Mennonites eventually bought 60,000 acres from these people. From 1801 onwards a steady stream of settlers from central Pennsylvania made their way in Conestoga wagons north through New York to Niagara and then northwest to Waterloo County, the first inland settlement in the province.

Quakers and Mennonites were also the first successful settlers in York County, after being narrowly preceded in that region by two disappointing ventures in colonization. Beginning in 1794 William Berczy had brought a few dozen German settlers, recently arrived in New York, into Markham Township, but when his rate of progress failed to satisfy the government, his grant was revoked. The settlement lasted, but grew slowly. The second venture involved the attempt to settle French Royalist émigrés who had fled the Revolution on lands north of York. Count de Puisaye was the leader of this ill-starred colony which was put on the land in 1799, but it was a failure from the beginning. Its members lacked the skills needed for pioneer farming in Upper Canada. Already, however, a more tenacious type of settler was finding his way up Yonge Street, as a few families from New York State took up land in the middle 1790's. They were followed after 1800 by a larger influx of Quakers and of German-speaking migrants, both Mennonites and Lutherans, mainly from Pennsylvania, who stamped their character on several townships north of the capital. These people, and their kind, were not straggling misfits, not the flotsam of the frontier. They brought enough capital to buy good land, which they knew how to recognize, they brought healthy cattle and they brought sturdy furniture, they built grist mills and saw mills, and they made substantial farms. They came to stay.

Other Americans were coming in, too, many of them Methodists, but also of other Protestant denominations and sometimes of no religion at all. They came to find a suitable field for their talents and energies, ready to find that field anywhere on the continent. Now it was Upper Canada, but in twenty years' time some of their kind would be as ready to move into the Mexican province of Texas, always searching for the best opportunities. Some of them made a business of opening up new districts. They acquired land cheaply, cleared it, built a log house, sowed a crop, and then presently pulled up stakes after selling out at a profit. Others, like many of the Scotch-Irish from Pennsylvania,[8] settled down with as much finality as did their Quaker and Mennonite neighbours. Not all the Americans became farmers. With that versatility which flowered on the frontier, they could turn to a variety of occupations. They built mills and roads, they set up as black-smiths and as tavern-keepers, and they taught school.

These newcomers were usually disliked and distrusted by government officials and magistrates and half-pay officers and by many of the old Loyalists, yet they were advancing the civilization of Upper Canada by diversifying its economy and society. Some of them cared little that this was a British province: they took the oath of allegiance easily and it rested lightly upon them. For others, not this much could be said; they were Americans still, although in the King's dominions, and expected to remain so. All of these people, of whatever religious and political outlook, out-numbered the old Loyalists and the few residents who had come directly from Britain by about four to one on the eve of the War of 1812. Although the province's government closely followed British forms, and its leading citizens were consciously and determinedly loyal to the mother country, in many other respects Upper Canada was an American community after being for twenty years in the path of the American westward movement.

This influx elicited many reactions, within and without the province. For instance, it gave Thomas Talbot a strong talking-point when in 1802 he asked for a large grant of land to provide a base for an extensive colonizing scheme. An army officer just past thirty, Talbot was at this time a lively and courtly aristocrat who had abruptly sold his colonel's commission to return to the province he had known as a secretary to Governor Simcoe. western forests, guiding the development of Upper Canada along sound military ambitions, Talbot was now anxious to spend all his energies in the western forests, guiding the development of Upper Canada along sound paths. In applying to the Under Secretary of State for his grant, he stressed that the motley population streaming into Upper Canada was producing a "growing tendency to insubordination and revolt," which could best be checked by encouraging immigration from the British Isles. British migrants were already coming in some numbers to the United States, because they knew nothing of the attractions of the inland province; he promised to try to "turn the attention of these people to Upper Canada," where their "more moral and orderly habits" and "their attachment to their native Country" would prove most beneficial. Accordingly, Talbot was granted 5,000 acres along the shore of Lake Erie, and additional land was also to be reserved for his colonizing plans. Talbot, whose name is writ large on the settlement of the southwestern portion of the province during the following genera-tion, in fact accepted many American settlers, but he always remained true to his purpose of promoting loyalty and orderliness in his growing domain. In 1804 Lord Selkirk, who had been similarly distressed by the prevalence of American land-seekers in Upper Canada, also started a colonization scheme at Baldoon, near Lake St Clair, but it failed.[9]

Within the province, concern over the growing American population was often voiced. It was claimed, for example, that the Americans along Yonge Street had no respect for the government, wanted "to have the Election of all their own officers," and had school-masters in their midst who poisoned "the minds of the Youths, by teaching them in Republican Books."[10] Even in the eastern part of the province, in the County of Prescott, there was difficulty in the militia, caused by people who had "chiefly emi-grated from a Country which breath [sic] the highest respect for a spirit of Democracy."[11] Another correspondent in the eastern part of the province, the Roman Catholic priest (and future bishop) Alexander Macdonell, wrote that Highlanders in the Glengarry settlement should be encouraged as "a strong barrier against the contagion of Republican principles so rapidly diffusing among the people of this Province by the industry of the settlers from the United States." They should be provided with Gaelic-speaking clergymen and school-masters, and should have lands reserved for their future increase, to prevent their children from moving into the American settlements, where their principles received "an unfortunate tinge."[12] Lieutenant-Governor Gore believed that the people from Kingston eastward were dependable, but the region from York westward to Long Point was inhabited chiefly by "Persons, who have emigrated from the States of America and of consequence retain those ideas of equality & insubordina-tion, much to the prejudice of this Government, so prevalent in that country." He felt that it would be a "very serious Evil" if local offices fell into the hands of "new Settlers of . . . doubtful Loyalty." He argued that troops must be clearly in evidence about the province, since "the American impatient of Restraint must see a military force at hand ready to reduce him and confine him to order."[13] In short, the rapid influx of American settlers, who more than doubled the population in the first decade of the nineteenth century, gave worried provincial leaders something of the feeling of sitting on a powder keg.

As this settlement went on, the provincial government continued to wrestle with the ever-present problems of land-granting procedure. Simcoe's successors persevered in the decision to wind up the township grants, since further experience only confirmed the executive council's belief that township grants were being used for speculative purposes by American land-jobbers, and that if they produced any settlement it was of an unreliable kind. New regulations were also put into force in the latter 1790's aimed at denying grants to those who wanted them for speculative purposes. Nevertheless, land was granted readily, even lavishly. Hunter declared, shortly after his arrival, that "more Lands have already been granted than will in all probability be occupied and settled for half a century to come," an exaggeration to be sure, but an indication of the generosity of the Russell period.[14] Hunter sought to tighten procedures by ordering that townships receiving settlers should be filled up before new ones were opened, by examining the character of applicants more carefully, and by speeding up the process of issuing patents. In this last move, however, the government appeared to be more interested in the fees to be realized than in the enforcement of settlement duties, despite certain regulations on this subject. Hunter also caused sharp cries of anguish and indignation by ordering a strict revision of the Loyalist roll (the "U.E. list"), which resulted in the striking off of nearly a thousand names from 1802 to 1804. This step followed an earlier decision to limit the royal bounty to Loyalists who were resident in the province by July 28, 1798, a decision which had already ruffled the feelings of interested people. (In 1806, bowing to the din being raised in the province, Gore agreed to entertain further applications for placement on the U.E. list.)[15]

One reason for Russell's bad reputation in land matters arose from his request to the home government that he and his colleagues on the executive council might receive substantial grants. These were to compensate for the inadequacy of their salaries and the high cost of labour and servants, and to put them on a basis of greater equality with merchants who, with no public responsibilities, were able to purchase lands cheaply by the tens of thousands of acres. The Secretary of State replied that the present councillors might receive grants totalling six thousand acres, as compensation for their expenses when the capital was moved to York, but this was not to be a precedent for the future.[16] Sizable grants continued to be made to military officers, to prospective colonizers such as Talbot and Lord Selkirk, already mentioned, and to various other persons of influence.

Land sold on the open market was almost as cheap, and often better in quality, than "free" land, on which fees had to be paid. Consequently, the most extensive holdings were accumulated by purchase rather than by government grants, which could never be more than five or six thousand acres to any one individual. In particular, there developed an extensive traffic in Loyalist rights, as the children of the Loyalists disposed of lands to which they were entitled, but for which they often had little use. D'Arcy Boulton, the Solicitor General, asserted in 1805 that it was well known "that three-fourths of his Majesty's bounty had been lavishly thrown away."[17] It is also probable that local officials and their friends used their strategic position to make advantageous purchases when government or other land came on the market.

A major feature of land policy continued to be the regulation of the various reserves. Apart from the Crown and Clergy Reserves the largest category consisted of school lands. In 1798, following permission received from the home government, the executive council set aside ten townships, and parts of two others, comprising about half a million acres, for the future support of grammar schools and a university. The Surveyor General was also required, as townships were surveyed, to reserve for the use of the Royal Navy certain lands on which good masts or other suitable timber were found. Lands were also reserved to be sold to finance the building of roads. Various other reserves were made from time to time. In short, the imperial government was more concerned to hold back land until it had increased in value, in order to accomplish a variety of public objectives, than it was to foster immediate settlement. This policy was not confined to Upper Canada, but it was to fail here, as it did everywhere else that it was tried.[18]

It was the Crown and Clergy Reserves, consisting of about two and a half million acres in the organized townships, which occupied the main attention of the executive council. Given the settled policy of the home government that these lands should not be sold until they would fetch a good price, it was clear that they would not be sold for a long time to come. In the meantime, both London and York desired to get some sort of immediate return from them, and consequently turned to schemes for leasing them. The problem here, of course, was that when the price of land, either granted or purchased, was so low, there was little inducement for farmers to rent rather than buy. The answer proposed by the council was a system of long-term (twenty-one year) leases at very low rates, increasing as time went on. A few leases were taken, sometimes by Quakers and Mennonites who wanted to form compact settlements with their neighbours, and sometimes by people who intended to take the timber off the land; in fact, however, those contemporaries who prophesied that leasing the Reserves would bring in little revenue proved to be correct. This was merely the first attempt to deal with a problem that would be with the province for many years to come. As yet the Reserves did not constitute a vital issue, since there was still plenty of land available in the province; dispersed settlement and poor communications could be attributed to many causes, of which the Reserves were only one.

As settlers came in and land was granted and sold, the first outlines of Upper Canada's economic development became visible. Here was a sparse and widely scattered population, spread thinly along the St Lawrence and the Lakes, rarely extending more than a few miles into the interior. No accurate count was taken, but it appears that the number of inhabitants had reached about seventy-five thousand in 1812, after three decades of settlement. It was an almost entirely rural community, with Kingston and York each containing fewer than a thousand souls and the other villages even lower numbers. Hence, the majority of the residents were engaged in the tasks of clearing the land and tilling the soil, using the primitive tools, the back-breaking methods, and the wasteful techniques inseparable from pioneer agriculture in the days before the industrial revolution had touched the business of farming. To a large extent each family was self-sufficient, not through choice but through necessity, putting up its own buildings, perhaps with the help of neighbours, growing most of its own food, making many of its own clothes, sometimes even fashioning its own household and farming implements. They waited eagerly for the itinerant pedlar (often from Albany, New York), and looked forward to the day when they could command a more varied assortment of finished goods, and concentrate their energies on cash-producing activities. Already, they did this as much as possible. It was only in retrospect, when nostalgia had set in, that the primitive life of the pioneer took on a roseate hue. The pioneer himself was determined to get out of that stage as quickly as possible.

In most respects the life of the Upper Canadian farmer differed little from that of farmers on many another North American agricultural frontier, in the wooded temperate zone, both before and after this time. He concentrated on growing wheat, which required the least labour and brought the best return of all crops, and less frequently raised other grains, such as oats and barley. Vigorous efforts by the imperial and provincial governments to promote the growing of hemp, badly needed by Britain during the war years, came to little, because that crop required too much skilled labour and brought too low a price, even when extensively subsidized, to attract the pioneer farmer. As on other frontiers the provincial farmer turned much good grain into rather ordinary whisky, partly to ease the problem of transporting a bulk commodity. He also followed precedent by seeking a return from the timber cleared off his land. Although many trees were simply girdled and left to die, others were sent to the saw mills and in the eastern part of the province some timber was sent to Montreal on its way to the British market. The timber rafts were often used as vehicles for the transport of other commodities. The timber trade of the Ottawa Valley was just getting started in this period. For most farmers trees produced the best cash value in the form of potash, which soon became a leading export. Finally, there was the necessity of building up adequate herds of livestock. In the first stages of settlement cattle, hogs, and sheep were acquired from the neighbouring American states, either purchased or brought in by the settlers, but after 1800 the process was being reversed when Upper Canada began to export cattle to new American settlements, such as those in northern New York. This evolution was a normal phase of frontier development.

In some ways, however, Upper Canada enjoyed advantages over many another frontier community. Paramount among these was the assistance provided by government. At the very beginning, as noticed in the opening chapter, the first settlers, who admittedly were not engaged in a normal migration, were provided with provisions, seed, implements, and other necessities. As the first surpluses of flour, pork, and peas became available there was a ready market for them at the military garrisons in the province; moreover, the government bought up these supplies at higher than the going price as a further encouragement to the infant settlements.[19] The government was also willing to put vacant space on the King's vessels at the disposal of shippers "at little or no expense until after other means of conveyance were sufficiently multiplied."[20] After the British garrisons were withdrawn from the posts in 1796, the American garrisons replacing them continued for some years to buy supplies from Upper Canada, as did the new settlements on the south shore of Lake Ontario and of Lake Erie. Although residents of the province took little direct part in the fur trade, some of the lines of communication passed across their territory, allowing them to make sales to those engaged in the trade. When a market for wheat developed in Lower Canada and the mother country, the Upper Canadian exporters were able to take advantage of it; although lacking adequate roads, they had at their disposal the resources of the Great Lakes~St Lawrence route, superior in some respects to the Ohio~Mississippi route used by the farmers of the American interior. In fact, the pull of the St Lawrence was so strong that it attracted much American trade: exports from some northern states went to market via Montreal and Quebec, while merchants from these cities used the waterway to sell large quantities of British and West Indian products south and west of the lakes. Among other advantages enjoyed by Upper Canada were the absence of threats from the Indians and the fact that the British government paid the salaries of the leading executive officers and put money into the province through the military establishment, the Indian Department, and the payment of pensions.[21]

The listing of these various assets should not, of course, obscure the existence of obstacles to economic progress, notably the lack of roads and of money. Making roads is always a problem in a pioneer country, but it was particularly so in Upper Canada, where settlement was thinly dispersed over hundreds of miles, where the land was heavily wooded and watered by many streams, and where immense quantities of unoccupied land resulted from the Reserves, the Indian lands, and the large holdings of absentee owners. When the government did turn to road-building, its concern was to lay out a system of trunk roads, with an eye to defence requirements, even though such roads were not always of immediate economic value to the settlers. Simcoe's successors continued his plans by arranging for the building of a road eastward from York, by continuing work on Yonge Street, and by bringing Dundas Street eastward to York. In theory, local roads were to be built under the direction of District officials, particularly the Justices of the Peace, relying heavily on statute labour; but the difficulties mentioned above, as well as a strong disinclination to local taxation, made progress disheartening ly slow. Accordingly, members of the Assembly early turned to efforts to get provincial funds for roads in their communities, with the result that road-building and political manœuvring were soon closely intermixed. Everyone complained about the roads and the lack of them, but little was done.[22]

Like all pioneer settlements, Upper Canada suffered from a lack of capital and from an inadequate circulating medium. An important consequence of this situation was that a handful of merchants, first at Kingston, and later at Niagara and York and some other villages, acquired a commanding position in the province's economic life. These merchants were usually agents of large Montreal firms, and received credit from the latter for the purpose of doing business in the western regions. At first the merchants were concerned only with the fur trade, but as agricultural surpluses began to accumulate and as trees were cut, they began to deal in wheat and flour and potash and lumber. Also, they were receiving manufactured items from their Montreal principals, who in turn had imported them from overseas. The local merchants were prepared to buy products, and make payment by delivering goods or by issuing letters of credit. They were in a strategic position, vis-à-vis their Upper Canadian customers, to set prices, both on what they bought and on what they sold. (Of course, they did not have a free hand in these arrangements, since their operations were being closely watched and supervised by their masters in Montreal.) It was not long before farmers found themselves increasingly in debt to the merchants, and obliged to take whatever terms the latter were willing to extend. When certain merchants, in the early 1790's, acquired a monopoly from the Commissary General for supplying the garrisons there was a particularly loud outcry, in which the Assembly and Lieutenant-Governor Simcoe joined.

Simcoe, in fact, frequently pointed to the dangerous power of the merchants, but it was in the nature of things and not easily diminished.[23]

While these outlines of economic life were beginning to appear, some progress was also being made in other phases of provincial life. Concern over the lack of schools was manifested in a joint Address of the Legislature sent to the King in 1797. The consequence, as already mentioned, was a grant of about half a million acres to be set apart for the support of grammar schools and, eventually, for a university.[24] This arrangement seemed to promise a munificent endowment for the future support of education, although it turned out that much of the land in the townships chosen was of very poor quality. Even had it been otherwise, however, there was no possibility of realizing any immediate return from it, given the current price of land. Meanwhile, scattered individuals in the little villages about the province were beginning to take in a few students, notable among these being John Strachan, although he was by no means the first. Of modest origins but with a sound Scottish education, this talented and ambitious young man was just twenty-one when he arrived in Kingston in 1799. Postponing his hopes of starting a college, he began to tutor the children of Richard Cartwright and of other prominent residents. In 1803 he was ordained as a clergyman of the Church of England, and sent to Cornwall where he also opened a school. Over the next few years a number of boys from leading families passed through his hands, and on them Strachan exerted a profound influence. In later years it became apparent that he had educated the governing class of the coming generation. At the same time a recent migrant from Ireland, Dr W. W. Baldwin, also opened a school at York, and other ventures of the same kind were started from time to time. Numerous American school-teachers were to be found in the province and, as already suggested, they were viewed with many misgivings.

These little private academies, valuable though they were, did not, of course, answer the educational problems of the province. In 1804 and 1805 proposals were made in the Assembly to establish public schools in the province, but failed to pass. In 1806 a bill for "the more general dissemination of learning throughout the Province" went through the assembly, but the legislature was prorogued before the legislative council was ready to vote on it. Then in 1807 an Act was passed establishing eight grammar schools, that is, one in each District, and providing that each school-master be paid £100 annually out of provincial funds. This act is a landmark, since it acknowledged the necessity for public support of education, but it nevertheless encountered much opposition. Certain members of the Assembly who had earlier pushed for school legislation voted against it, and within a few years of the establishment of the schools complaints were being sent to the legislature. It was argued that the system benefited only the residents of the towns in which the schools were located, and the well-to-do else-where who could afford to pay boarding and tuition fees. It was stated in a petition from the Midland District in 1812 that the school in Kingston, "instead of aiding the middling and poorer classes . . . casts money into the lap of the rich, who are sufficiently able, without public assistance, to support a school in every respect equal to the one established by law."[25] There was, however, little sentiment in the Assembly for broadening the system of education, and it was not until 1816 that an act supporting common schools was passed. In the years before the war only the barest start was made in fashioning a satisfactory school system.

Provincial leaders continued to express acute concern over "the miserable State of Religion" resulting from the lack of Church of England clergymen. These clergy had to be recruited entirely from the mother country during this period, and although the British government included some £500 in the Upper Canada estimates for this purpose little progress was made. The sum was not large, and in any event clergymen were apparently not very anxious to come out to Upper Canada, or when they did, to stay there. In 1799 Russell reported that there were "only three Clergymen of the established Church to officiate throughout its great Extent."[26] and the situation did not improve markedly in the years down to the outbreak of war. London continued to insist that the province make provision for the support of the church until the Clergy Reserves became productive, only to be answered by pleas of poverty from York.

Concern over the weak state of the Church of England was heightened by the knowledge that other denominations, without any public support, were growing ever stronger. In 1797 the Chief Justice estimated that not more than a fiftieth part of the population belonged to the Church of England.[27] In the eastern part of the province the Calvinist groups and Lutherans stemming from the original Loyalist population were securely rooted, and the Roman Catholic element was reinforced by the arrival in 1804 of a group of Highlanders, including disbanded troops, led by Fr Alexander Macdonell. But by far the most extensive development was the movement of "Dissenters" into the central and western parts of the province, resulting from the American immigration previously described. As well as the Mennonites and Quakers, there were Baptists and Presbyterians, various small sects and, above all, Methodists, the largest religious group in the province. Adherents of these denominations maintained close associations with the parent religious bodies in the United States.[28] Nearly all their clergy came from that country. These men, and especially the itinerant "saddlebag" preachers of the Methodist church, were not regarded as *bona fide* clergymen by the Anglican leaders of the province. They were denounced as untrained, ignorant fanatics, part-time exhorters, who could stir up a meeting, probably mixing politics with religion as they went along, but who were not capable of elevating the minds, manners, and morals of the people of Upper Canada. They were a dangerous element, "highly prejudicial to the peace of Society."[29]

Given these religious trends, it is not surprising that the Marriage Act of 1793 failed to satisfy a majority of the residents. As a partial concession to growing opinion an Act was approved in 1798 extending the right of solemnizing marriages to Lutheran, Calvinist, and Church of Scotland ministers, provided they were certified by the magistrates in quarter sessions as regularly ordained clergymen and had taken the oath of allegiance. It was the deliberate purpose of the government to confine the extension "to such of the Protestant Dissenters, as tho' non-conformists here, are members of an establishment elsewhere, and would for that reason bring with them those sober & regulated modes of thinking both on political & religious subjects which are the usual consequences of habitual conformity to an established ritual, & which form perhaps the best barrier against the encroachments of either infidelity or fanaticism, & the inseparable companion of each, sedition." Needless to say, the excluded denominations, especially the Methodists, were not satisfied with the law, and petitioned for the right to have marriages solemnized by their own clergymen. For three decades bills broadening the law passed the Assembly, only to be rejected by the legislative council. The Act of 1798 continued to set the rules for the solemnizing of marriages until 1831, and was a growing source of grievance for those excluded.[30]

Such were the main features of the economic and social scene, in the fifteen years after Simcoe's departure, which helped to determine the nature of the political controversies of the period. The main centre of political activity was of course the capital at York which by 1797 had definitely been chosen as the permanent seat of government, despite the objections of local officials who were loath to leave Newark. Certainly York had little to recommend it, beyond the anticipated advantages of its location. At first there were no roads leading to it from east or west, and then after 1800 the roads that did exist were often nearly impassable. From 1803 onwards the Lieutenant-Governor felt that the state of the roads made winter meetings of the legislature feasible, but it was still nearly impossible to reach the capital by land on many occasions during the year. The town grew rapidly, but it was a somewhat forced growth which made the price of labour even higher than elsewhere in the province. Officials who came out from England felt trapped after they had settled down in York; they could not live at a reasonable standard on their salaries and sometimes were without the ready money to return home. In 1798, for instance, the Attorney General complained that he had to dig his own potatoes and cut firewood, "however incompatible with my station and education."[31] Russell felt that the town badly needed "a few more families of Education & fortune – & good Clergymen."[32] Some adequate private dwellings were erected by leading residents, but in 1804 Hunter reported that "there is not at present a single Building here, for any one public Office," while the legislature and the courts met in a little structure consisting of two rooms, which was also used for other public purposes and as a church.[33]

It was on this little stage that the political and social leaders of the province played out their roles. They sought relief from the dullness of society by drinking a great deal of madeira and port and rum, and by eating immense quantities of meat, including local game, and bread pudding and plum pudding and mince pie. There was more than one actual or threatened duel. They gossiped interminably before and after the assemblies where they danced and showed off their best clothes. They played cards or they read aloud to one another from *Don Quixote* or *Gulliver's Travels* or *Joseph Andrews* or the Bible. When news of a victory against the French was received, although it was many weeks late, they illuminated the town by building great bonfires and placing candles in their windows. Sometimes they went sailing in the bay or on the lake.[34] It was a tiny place, miles from anywhere, and its chief business was politics. Presently the spirit of politics began to run very high.

In the little controversies that began to appear there was no hint of dissatisfaction with the form of government and no question of uncertain loyalty to the mother country. In 1799, for instance, the Assembly, desirous of showing support for the war against France and finding a small surplus in the accounts, asked that "this mite" be laid "at the feet of His Majesty . . . as a mark of our devoted attachment to His Royal person and Family, and of our grateful sense of the blessings we enjoy under his Government." In the next session the Assembly similarly expressed their happiness "in the enjoyment of Blessings which flow from the possession of a Constitution, approaching as nearly as our local situation will admit, to the British Constitution itself."[35] Yet differences of opinion inevitably began to arise over the manner in which this constitution should operate in the province. Understandably the executive wished to have members in the Assembly who would forward the government's program and give form and leadership to its proceedings. Russell complained that the members were "in general ignorant of Parliamentary Forms and Business, & some of them wild young Men who frequently require some Person of Respectability and experience to keep them in order." But the voters had shown little disposition to vote for government nominees. At a by-election Russell encouraged the Attorney General to present himself, promising to pay part of his campaign expenses but, alas, the "low Ignorance of the Electors" defeated his wish "by preferring an illiterate young Man of their own level & neighbourhood."[36] This anti-official feeling went so far that in 1811 a bill was introduced, although defeated, to make ineligible for a seat in the Assembly anyone holding an office of profit or emolument under the Crown. Strachan thought that this Assembly was "composed of ignorant clowns," but expected improvement when some of his own pupils got into the House.[37]

Little points of friction also began to develop between the assembly and the legislative council over the powers of each branch. Like all representative bodies the former sought steadily to draw more authority to itself, particularly in matters of finance, and to lessen the scope of the appointive branch. On the other hand the council, whose members were conscious of being drawn from a more respectable portion of provincial society (nearly all of them, for instance, were magistrates, and accustomed to the exercise of wide powers in their local communities), had no intention of deferring to a group of men of the most ordinary ability and education. There was also the feeling that members of the executive council, and perhaps even the Lieutenant-Governor, shared in this sense of superiority to the Assembly. In relatively minor matters, such as the appointment of a Clerk of the Assembly or the manner of settling a disputed election, some members of the Assembly began to develop wounded sensibilities over what they took to be slighting treatment on the part of the other branches of government. More serious was the legislative council's frequent practice of amending or rejecting bills, especially money bills, which the Assembly thought to be peculiarly its own concern.[38]

The feeling of irritation in the Assembly reached a first climax during the session of 1806, when the members noticed that the executive had taken a sum, amounting to £617 13s. 7d., out of the provincial treasury without a prior appropriation by the Assembly. General Hunter had, in fact, begun this practice in 1803, but only now was it questioned by the Assembly, while Grant was Administrator. There was no great objection to the use to which this money had been put; the Assembly, however, asserted that these were monies raised by provincial taxation and could be spent only after specific appropriation by the Assembly. In an address, described by Grant as "intemperate," the Assembly asserted "that the first and most constitutional privilege of the Commons" had been violated, asked that the money "so misapplied . . . be replaced in the Provincial Treasury," and that orders be issued prohibiting the practice in the future.[39] Eventually the matter was smoothed over when Gore gave the desired assurances, but the incident had produced political controversy of an intensity hitherto unknown in the province.

It is sometimes said that where there is smoke there must be fire, and it has been been indicated above that in the relations between the Assembly and the other branches there were some incendiary possibilities. It is equally true, of course, that where there is smoke, especially where there is a great deal of it, there are likely to be smoke-makers at work. It was the fate of the province at this time to have a particularly active little group of smoke-makers, busy at their self-appointed task of making the most of existing controversies and of seeking to raise up new ones. These men were all recently arrived from the British Isles, and they all felt that they were deserving of better and more lucrative posts than they had so far received. They were viewed by the leading figures in the province as demagogic and scheming intruders who were deliberately and wilfully disturbing the peace. The newcomers, in turn, regarded those entrenched in government as a "shop-keeper aristocracy" who were managing the province for their own pecuniary benefit. An added edge was given to the exchanges from the fact that some of the complainants were from Ireland, while many of those prominent in the executive were of Scottish origin; in consequence, there were charges against "Scotch pedlars" on the one side, and on the other side fears were expressed that the trouble-makers were connected with the United Irishmen whose rebellion had only recently been put down, in 1798.

The first two of these individuals to arrive in the province, both from Ireland, were Joseph Willcocks and William Weekes. The former reached York in 1800, where for some years he had a rather tempestuous but not politically important existence. He made both friends and enemies easily, receiving sufficient local favour to be appointed to various posts, especially the shrievalty of the Home District. When sworn witnesses testified to his abusive denunciations of both the provincial and British governments he was dismissed from the office of sheriff, in April 1807. Weekes arrived in the province about 1801, by way of New York, where he was reputed to have served for a time in Aaron Burr's law office. After being accepted to practise as an attorney, he entered the Assembly in 1805 by winning a by-election. He took his seat on February 27, and he gave notice on the following day of a motion to consider "the disquietude which prevails in this province by reason of the administration of Public Affairs." When the question was put, on March 1, it was defeated by a vote of ten to four.[40] In the 1806 session he took a leading part in drafting the resolution on the removal of money from the provincial treasury without legislative appropriation, and figured prominently in other actions of the Assembly that were disturbing to the executive. Later in the year, while acting as counsel at the Niagara assizes, he used language which brought him into dispute with a magistrate of that district. Weekes thereupon challenged the magistrate and was himself killed in the ensuing duel.

It was constantly emphasized by lieutenant-governors during this period that important official appointments could not as a rule be given to residents of the province, because of their generally low level of education and training. When vacancies occurred, they usually had to be filled from overseas. In the summer of 1805 the province received a new Surveyor General in the person of C. B. Wyatt, from England, and a new puisne judge of the Court of King's Bench in the person of Robert Thorpe, from Ireland by way of Prince Edward Island, where he had also held a judicial appointment. It was scarcely to be expected that people within the official circle would cause trouble, yet that is what now happened.

Wyatt was not a major figure in the little drama, and at another time might well have gone about his duties without becoming involved in political controversies. But he was dissatisfied, upon his arrival, to find that the Surveyor General's fees had been somewhat reduced just prior to his appointment. Perhaps for this reason he showed sympathy for the Assembly's tentative attempts to harass the government in 1806 by bringing the books of his office before a committee of investigation without receiving permission from the executive council. He repeated the offence in the session of 1807, and when Gore complained, Wyatt replied "that the House of Assembly was omnipotent, and that it was his duty to obey,"[41] hardly the doctrine to endear him to his associates in the government. Apparently an impetuous and inexperienced young man, he also became involved in a quarrel with a subordinate in his office, and attempted to dismiss this individual, although lacking such power. As well, he was accused of having erased a name from the survey in order to substitute his own. The upshot was that Gore suspended him from office early in 1807, and Wyatt returned to England. There he was able to clear himself of the charge concerning the erasure (which had evidently been done in good faith), and later he was awarded damages in a libel suit laid against Gore. He did not regain his office, however, or return to Upper Canada. Perhaps his greatest offence had been his friendship with the malcontents, especially Thorpe.

The provincial leaders were disturbed by the Surveyor General's conduct, but they were alarmed and infuriated when a judge of the Court of King's Bench set himself up as a popular tribune with the apparent purpose of unseating the local government. Thorpe was the leading figure in this little group, and from his talents and official position much the most dangerous. Moreover, he was the prime mover who encouraged Willcocks, Weekes, and Wyatt toward more extreme opposition and criticism. It is hard to avoid the conclusion that he was a born trouble-maker. He had the friendship of important men in Great Britain including Lord Castlereagh, and he had legal attainments sufficient to secure judicial posts in Prince Edward Island, Upper Canada, and Sierre Leone, but he was caught up in quarrels and controversies wherever he went. The root cause of his difficulties was an overweening sense of his own importance combined with an unbounded contempt for all who stood in the way of his advance. He seems to have felt that he was appointed to Upper Canada as an agent of the home government to investigate the shortcomings of the local government and save the province from the evils that undoubtedly existed. He quickly decided that he could best perform this mission if he were promoted to the vacant Chief Justiceship; when the Attorney General (Thomas Scott) received this appointment, Thorpe's indignation knew no bounds. Already well advanced on a demagogic course, he redoubled attacks on the local government, with the result that he was eventually suspended from his duties and, in effect, forced to leave the province.

Soon after his arrival, he was writing to the under secretary in London to inform him of the parlous state of affairs under Grant, who was put down as "quite inefficient."[42] After five months in the province he was ready to give a bill of particulars of how General Hunter and a "few Scotch instruments" had "nearly ruined this province," with the result that nothing had "been done for the Colony, no roads, bad water communication, no Post, no Religion, no Morals, no Education, no Trade, no Agriculture, no Industry attended to." Since the same conditions continued under Grant, Thorpe was finding it "necessary to set about conciliating the people" in order to smooth the way for the new lieutenant-governor. A few days later he informed his correspondent that he was giving direction to the House of Assembly "so as to prevent mischief." Gore later reported that this had involved coming within the Bar of the Assembly to encourage and advise Weekes in his anti-government measures.[43]

Clearly Thorpe had a nose for trouble, and he had no difficulty in turning up subjects about which there was a good deal of grumbling. He made much of the Loyalists' dissatisfaction at their apparent neglect by the government and at what they took to be the preference for fee-paying applicants. He made the sound point, made also by former Chief Justice Allcock and others, that a Court of Chancery was needed to render equity judgements in cases where the common law could not provide justice. There was probably also more than an element of truth in his criticism of the calibre of the men in the executive council, and of their favouritism to friends and connections. Yet the extravagant descriptions of Hunter's régime, of which he knew nothing at first hand, and the designation of the Council as "overbearing reptiles" and "servile instruments" suggests personal pique or deliberate malice rather than any genuine concern with provincial problems. These feelings became more evident and open after he learned that he was not to be Chief Justice. While on circuit in the central and western parts of the province he used the opportunities presented by grand jury addresses to denigrate the government and to offer himself as "the humble instrument of restoring harmony and happiness." This procedure, alarming in itself, was made the more so from the probability that Thorpe was himself inspiring, indeed composing, the addresses in question, and drawing them out of centres of predominantly American population. Gore charged, moreover, that these addresses were presented by six or seven members of the juries, "without the concurrence of the rest, not in Court, but at the Judge's House, several days after the Court had risen."[44]

At his first meeting with the new governor, who had recently arrived in the province, Thorpe "found him imperious, self sufficient & ignorant, impressed with a high notion of the old system, surrounded with the same scotch Pedlars. . . . " Obviously the old system was to be continued and, to save the province, he found it necessary to accept nomination to the Assembly, in place of the ill-fated Weekes, even though "this popularity is oppressive."[45] Ignoring representations about the impropriety of a judge sitting in the Assembly, he accepted the call, was easily elected, and so was available for the session of 1807. During that session he attempted to form and lead an opposition party, but with very indifferent success. On some important questions he stood alone, or almost alone.[46] His conduct at this time, on top of his previous activities on the bench, was final proof to leading residents of the province that the Justice was a dangerous disturber of the peace. Robert Hamilton, for instance, complained vigorously to the Governor's secretary that Thorpe had referred in open court to the Justices of the Peace as "petty Tyrants," and that he was stirring up the "Common People" to defy the forces of law and order.[47] Pressure was put upon the Lieutenant-Governor to stop his course, and Gore, who was filling his dispatches to London with accounts of Thorpe's scandalous conduct, was equally alarmed. As he pointed out some months later, Thorpe's attempts to appeal to the people were most dangerous "in this Province, where Republican Principles prevail so much," and where most residents were "impatient of control."[48] The executive council advised the Lieutenant-Governor that Thorpe's conduct, based on his appeals to the "Lower Classes of Individuals with whom he has held communication," had "had an uniform tendency to degrade, embarrass, and vilify his Majesty's Servants and Government of this Colonoy."[49] When the time approached for the 1807 summer circuit, Gore left Thorpe's name off the commission, and requested action by the home government. Castlereagh's response was to order that the justice be suspended, and he left the province toward the end of 1807. By the following March Gore reported that "the ferment which has been excited in the Public mind, by what is called Mr Thorpe's Party, appears to be gradually Subsiding."[50]

Nevertheless, Gore and the provincial leaders were still not free from attack. In the summer of 1807, after his dismissal as sheriff, Joseph Willcocks had begun publication at Niagara of a newspaper entitled the *Upper Canada Guardian or Freeman's Journal*, the first anti-government paper so far to appear in the province, and he also gained election to the Assembly. There he had little influence for a time; indeed, in 1808 he was imprisoned by his fellow-members for a libel on them published in his newspaper. Yet he was re-elected by his constituents, and undoubtedly had a certain following in the province. His paper presently failed for financial reasons, but he continued in the last couple of sessions before the outbreak of war to oppose the government in concert with few like-minded members. He showed some signs of becoming a useful critic, particularly in the field of education. During the War of 1812 he deserted to the Americans, and was killed fighting in their ranks.

Still another cause of concern to Gore was the publication in England in 1809 of a pamphlet entitled *A View of the Political Situation of Upper Canada*, bearing the name of John Mills Jackson as author. Jackson was an Englishman, of good family and connections, who bought some land in Upper Canada, and came out to have a look at it in August 1806. He soon fell in with Thorpe and Willcocks, spending much of his time with them damning the government over bottles of port. Gore stated that his hostility "arose from his being refused a quantity of land, on account of his improper conduct." Presently Jackson returned to England, and the above-mentioned pamphlet appeared. This publication rehearsed the charges of inefficiency, oppression, favouritism in land-granting, misapplication of money by the executive, and so on, which had been the stock in trade of Mr Justice Thorpe, who was generally believed to be its real author. The appearance of the pamphlet was disturbing to Gore, because Jackson was sufficiently well placed to have his effusion taken seriously in England, where a question on the government of Upper Canada was asked in the House of Commons. Accordingly the Lieutenant-Governor had to spend long hours preparing detailed refutations of Jackson's extravagant and often irrelevant charges.[51] When a copy of the pamphlet reached Upper Canada, the Assembly unanimously denounced it as "a false, scandalous and seditious libel." When, however, the Assembly adopted an address to the Lieutenant-Governor approving his administration and "testifying their abhorrence and detestation" of the pamphlet, four members, including Willcocks, refused to side with the majority.[52] Two pamphlets were also written in answer to Jackson's.[53]

But Gore's troubles during this first period of his tenure of office were nearly at an end. To be sure, he had much to suffer from another oddity sent from England in the person of William Firth, the Attorney General, who seems to have spent most of his term in the province in a constant state of indignation and bad temper; but his complaints, although Willcocks tried to exploit them, had little effect, and he shook the dust of Upper Canada from his boots in 1811. Gore followed later that year when his request for leave of absence was approved, leaving the government in the hands of Major-General Isaac Brock as Administrator.

Some later observers professed to see in the little squabbles of the half-dozen years following 1805 the beginnings of an authentic political reform movement, but it is doubtful that they should be so considered. Certainly there were some stirrings, some incipient divisions between the leading figures in the executive and legislative councils, the merchants and the local magistrates on the one hand, and those who felt left out or ignored on the other. The eighteen-year-old John Beverley Robinson, who was growing up in the former circle, wrote to a like-minded friend in 1809 that the contest over the speakership of the Assembly indicated that the house was "nearly equally divided between Blackguards and Gentlemen."[54] But there were no clear-cut alignments at this stage. It could not be said, in the first place, that there was a strong and overbearing government; the executive councillors were few in number, old and tired, and able to exercise little influence on the Assembly, while the Lieutenant-Governor lacked the power or ability to dominate affairs. Hunter was often away in Quebec, Gore well-meaning but sometimes imprudent and erratic, and Thorpe was probably not far wrong in describing Russell and Grant as "old women." The government sometimes used hole-in-corner methods, was sometimes petty and inefficient, but it was anything but oppressive or tyrannical.

Those who were disposed to criticize the government shared little common ground with one another. Some Loyalists, for instance, were clearly irritated, particularly over land policy, and one of them, David Rogers, a nephew of the famous Major Robert Rogers, was consistently anti-government during several sessions of the Assembly. But he had little sympathy with adventurers from overseas like Thorpe and Willcocks, although he occasionally co-operated with them. In fact, one of Rogers's main complaints, which he probably shared with others of Loyalist origin, was that all the best jobs went to Europeans, and the "natives of America" were neglected.[55] The Loyalists thought of the province as their own; they were jealous of intruders, either from Britain or from the United States. (By contrast, one of Firth's complaints was that those in control of the province discriminated against Englishmen: here was a theme that would come up periodically for another thirty years.)[56] Yet other Loyalists, and these the most important, held posts of prominence, particularly in the magistracy, in all the local districts. They were the established leaders of the province, and regarded as such, whatever went on at York.

Then there were the new American settlers, constituting a majority of the population. These people, who had little active loyalty to anything

British, were greatly feared by many provincial leaders, and one of the main complaints against Thorpe was that he was stirring them up. More will be said about disaffection among this group in the next chapter, but here it should be noted that many of them, such as the Mennonites and Quakers, did not mix in politics at all, and others were too busy improving farms, erecting mills, and generally getting on in the world to have very much interest in agitation. Their interest in better schools, a more sensible land policy, and greater local self-government would later put many of the American settlers behind an emerging reform movement, but many events had still to take place before that movement came into being. In the meantime, as one critic of Jackson's pamphlet pointed out, their very presence was proof that the province was not suffering from oppression or tyranny: Americans, who were so "jealous of their independence," would never have left "a land of reputed liberty, for a Province where the Governor had the power of endangering their safety."[57]

In short, during Gore's régime the province was faced with many heavy tasks: roads to be built, land policy problems to be solved, schools to be erected. There was little revenue, and a rather inefficient government. The population was growing, but it was widely dispersed and heterogeneous in composition. There was little sense of community, and much distrust. Inevitably there were feelings of irritation swirling here and there upon which malcontents could play for a time. But there was no coherent movement for political change, as there could not be in so undeveloped a situation.

Thus unformed and rather out of sorts with itself, the province faced the threat of invasion from the south.

D

CHAPTER 4

Invasion Repulsed
1812-1815

On June 18, 1812, President James Madison signed a declaration of war against Great Britain, thereby facing the people of Upper Canada with the danger of immediate invasion. Despite its internal location and its apparent remoteness from the great centres of international politics the infant province now found that the power struggles of the Atlantic world could reach across the Lakes and River to threaten its very survival. Once again, and not for the last time, Upper Canada and its sister provinces discovered that their safety and security were jeopardized when Anglo-American relations deteriorated.

For the inhabitants of Upper Canada it was of relatively little moment to know precisely why the President and Congress had determined upon war. It was enough to know that the mother country and the neighbouring republic were now enemies and that armies would soon be marching against the province. Yet the origins of the war did much to govern its course and so deserve a brief notice.

For nearly twenty years, since the outbreak of war between France and Britain in 1793, the United States had been grappling with the problems of a neutral nation in the face of a great European War. In the 1790's, when George Washington and John Adams had held the presidency, determined diplomacy had kept Anglo-American differences within bounds, while war with France had been narrowly averted. With the renewal of the Anglo-French war in 1803 and its ever-deepening intensity, the threats to American neutral rights took on a new magnitude. Thomas Jefferson was now President of the United States, a man passionately devoted to peace and unwilling to put his country in a state of military and naval preparedness. At the same time he was determined to enforce respect for American rights, which were being violated by British and French restrictions on trade and by the British practice of impressing seamen from American ships. In this dilemma he sought to bring the great belligerents to book by cutting off all

American trade with them and the outside world through the Embargo Act of 1807. But this drastic measure had relatively little effect upon the belligerents, while it infuriated large sections of the American population, especially in New England. The Embargo Act had to be withdrawn in 1809. Nevertheless, Jefferson's successor, James Madison, continued the main lines of this policy, but without any better result. After every other means had failed of maintaining the national honour and integrity in the face of what were regarded as the humiliating restrictions of the British commercial system, Madison as a last resort asked for a declaration of war against Great Britain. It was a war for which his country was unprepared and which was bitterly opposed by large numbers of its citizens.

Equally, however, it was a war that had been loudly demanded by the so-called "War Hawks," a group of young Congressmen from the South and West. These men were filled with Anglophobia and with an ardent American nationalism; moreover, they represented areas that had been economically hurt in the trade struggle with Britain. These men welcomed war as a chance to retaliate against Britain by attacking her scattered, sparsely populated and apparently almost defenceless North American colonies. Some of them dreamed not only of carrying the American flag into the British colonies, but of keeping it there. They also saw war as an opportunity to end what they regarded as British machinations among the Indians in the northwest, and so strengthen American control of that region.[1]

As American leaders made their plans, it was obvious that their attention would focus particularly upon the interior province of Upper Canada. The Maritime Provinces were out of reach, protected both by British sea power and by the buffer of the New England states, which opposed the war. Much of Lower Canada was guarded by the fortress of Quebec, although Montreal was vulnerable to a well-organized attack. But Upper Canada seemed to be a plum ready for the picking: accessible, defended by only a few regular soldiers, and containing a predominantly American population that would presumably welcome the invaders as liberators. Prominent Americans such as Thomas Jefferson and Henry Clay assured their compatriots that the conquest of the western sections of the Canadas would be a "mere matter of marching," or that it might be accomplished by the Kentucky militia alone. Although the American government had done almost nothing to prepare its country for war, by these calculations little preparation was needed.

For their part, officials in Upper and Lower Canada had watched the recurrent crises in Anglo-American relations in the certain knowledge that war would bring an invasion of these provinces. They also knew that the invasion would have to be resisted by the forces at hand, since the hard-pressed mother country could spare no troops while the conflict with Napoleon was at its height. The prime task would be to hold Quebec; if necessary, all the western country would have to be abandoned until help could eventually come from across the ocean. This drastic decision would only be taken in the event of impending disaster, however, and in the meantime all efforts must be made to defend the provinces.

The greatest scare before the actual outbreak of war came in 1807, as an aftermath of the *Chesapeake* incident, when American feeling was so inflamed that war seemed to be imminent. In the following months a number of actions were taken that made the test easier to meet when it came in 1812. The Provincial Marine (consisting of armed ships on the Great Lakes under army command) was strengthened, giving the British command of Lake Ontario. The one regiment of British regular troops in Upper Canada (the 41st) was reinforced, and some more arms were brought into the province. The Provincial Militia Act was overhauled and improved.[2]

Such were the modest preparations that had been made when Major-General Isaac Brock arrived at York in October 1811 to take command of the forces and to act as administrator in Gore's absence. An experienced soldier, who had seen service in the French wars and had been stationed in British North America for nearly a decade, he had a thorough grasp of the strategic requirements of the approaching conflict. In the next eight months he rapidly pushed forward defensive measures in every possible way. As events would soon show, Brock was in himself an invaluable asset, for he brought to the province a quality that was to be extremely rare in the coming war: military leadership at once vigorous, imaginative, and professional. And he was a man of forceful and magnetic personality, who could inspire and rally the fighting men of the province, both whites and Indians.

In fact, Brock's most critical and most ticklish immediate problem was that of the Indians. The western tribes had never accepted as final their defeat at the hands of General Wayne in 1794, and in the intervening years they had watched with bitter resentment the steady advance of the American frontier into the Michigan Territory. For some time Tecumseh, the most capable Indian leader to appear since Pontiac, and his brother the Prophet had been travelling far and wide, trying to weld all the exposed tribes into a confederacy aimed at resisting the American advance. Inevitably they looked to the British for help. In this situation Sir James Craig, Governor and Commander-in-Chief at Quebec, and Francis Gore at York, had had to walk a very dangerous tightrope. It was vitally necessary to retain the friendship of the Indians, since their help would be essential in the event of war. Yet they must be restrained from making an attack on the Americans, which might lead to counter-attacks against Upper Canada. Hence, the Indian Department became increasingly active after 1807, re-

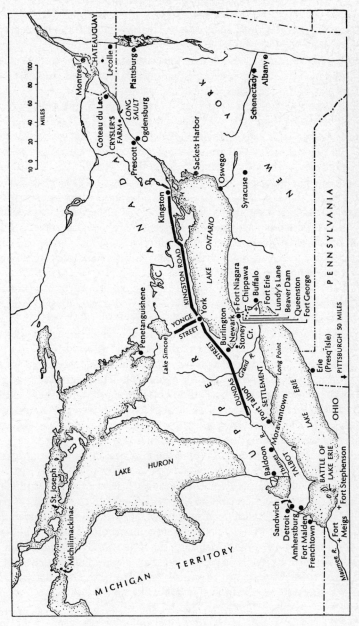

3 : *Upper Canada during the War of 1812*

building the old ties with the Indians and at the same time warning them against any acts of aggression against the United States. If the Indians were needed, they would be ready; if war did not come, no irretrievable actions would have been taken. Americans, then and after, refused to understand that the British purpose in seeking an Indian alliance was defensive, not one of stirring up the tribes to go on the war-path.

Brock soon showed that he grasped the essentials of British policy toward the Indians. On December 3 he reported to Sir George Prevost, who had recently succeeded Craig, that the Indian Department had tried unsuccessfully to prevent the Indians from making the attack which had led to their recent defeat at the Battle of Tippecanoe on the Wabash River. At the same time, however, he also wrote at considerable length of his plans for the defence of the province, giving prominence to the need for capturing the American posts of Detroit and Michilimackinac in the event of war, if the co-operation of the Indians were to be secured. Here was a preview of the opening stages of the campaign of the following summer. Ten weeks later he was urging even stronger measures to combat American efforts to overawe or to divide the Indians.[3]

At the same time that he was attempting to ensure Indian support, Brock was also seeking measures from the provincial legislature to meet the anticipated crisis. Worried by the number of "doubtful characters in the Militia," he asked that militiamen be required to abjure allegiance to any foreign country before being given arms. Also, he asked for power to suspend the writ of *habeas corpus* if war conditions should require it. To his surprise and alarm, however, the Assembly refused to pass either item, and Brock concluded that the "great influence which the vast number of settlers from the United States possess over the decisions of the Lower House is truly alarming." Later, however, a trip through several parts of the province made him more cheerful; he "found everywhere a good disposition . . . a very general determination, to defend the Province, in the event of hostilities with the United States."[4]

This mood of optimism did not last very long. Before the end of June the news of the American declaration of war had reached the Niagara region, where it was greeted with "consternation" on both sides of a border that had been accustomed to "habits of friendly intercourse." Brock could take little comfort from any lack of enthusiasm on the New York side, when he was faced with a provincial population that, despite long anticipation of the dread event, appeared to be stunned and apathetic now that war had finally come. After a month had gone by, he complained:

My situation is most critical, not from any thing the enemy can do, but from the disposition of the people — The population, believe me is essentially bad — A full belief possess them that this Province must inevitably succumb — This prepossession is fatal to every exertion — Legislators, Magistrates, Militia, Officers, all, have imbibed the idea, and are so sluggish and indifferent in all their respective offices that the artful and active scoundrel is allowed to parade the Country without interruption, and commit all imaginable mischief.

If only he had an additional regiment to add to his handful of troops, to stiffen the resolve of the inhabitants! "Most of the people have lost all confidence – I however speak loud and look big."[5]

Like most commanders, Brock was dissatisfied with the number of troops at his disposal. There were only some 1,600 regulars in the province, about two-thirds of them consisting of the 41st Regiment, the only line battalion, then stationed across from Detroit. This was indubitably a tiny force to defend so large a province, yet it contained more trained fighting men than the American commanders could muster for the invasion of Upper Canada at the beginning of the war, or for some time afterward. This small but efficient army, combined with naval command on the lakes, made Upper Canada in some respects better prepared for the impact of war than was its large but unorganized opponent.

There were several thousand regulars in Lower Canada, but apart from the 49th Regiment, sent into the province later in the summer, these could not be spared for service in the interior. Brock would have to get along with what he had, and Prevost advised him to avoid offensive measures, especially since these might heal over the internal divisions so obvious in the republic.

Brock, however, was not content to wait. He believed that quick strokes were vital to revive the spirit of the provincial population. He had already sent orders to the commander of the British fort at St Joseph's (south of the present Sault Ste Marie) giving him permission to attack Fort Michilimackinac, and this mission was readily accomplished. Thus one of Brock's aims, as stated in the previous December, had been fulfilled, and with the result he had hoped for. The Indians now came streaming to his side, and their support would be essential in gaining his other immediate objective, the capture of Detroit.

In the summer of 1812, however, this objective seemed to be quite beyond Brock's grasp. In the previous spring the War Department at Washington had ordered the assembling of a western army, which was to be one of the three prongs of an invasion to hit at Canada through Detroit, Niagara, and the Richelieu route. In June General William Hull, governor of the Michigan Territory and the commander of this western army, had set out from Dayton, Ohio, and he and his force of some two thousand regulars and militia reached Detroit early in July. On the twelfth of that month, some of these troops crossed the Detroit River, and Upper Canada thereupon had its first taste of invasion.

On the next day General Hull addressed a proclamation to the people of Canada, which he obviously hoped would make them either neutral or actively sympathetic toward the American cause. In a careful combination of promises and threats, he tendered them "the invaluable blessings of Civil, Political, & Religious Liberty," promised them protection in their *"persons, property, and rights,"* and informed them that they were to be "emancipated from Tyranny and oppression and restored to the dignified station of freemen." At the same time, however, he warned the provincial population that "No white man found fighting by the side of an Indian will be taken prisoner."[6]

Although the bombastic quality of this proclamation was ridiculed at the time (as it has often been since), and was promptly answered in vigorous tones by Brock, it is obvious that Hull achieved some of the objects at which he was aiming. Two days later an agent of the Indian Department at Amherstburg (where a British garrison continued to hold its ground) reported that the militia in the vicinity were already falling away and returning to their homes, although the Indians under Tecumseh were still faithful. The first reports reaching General Brock indicated that the "insidious proclamation" was having a "considerable effect on the minds of the people – In fact a general sentiment prevails that with the present force resistance is unavailing."[7] Later reports showed that a number of inhabitants in the western district were joining the American standard, and that the safety of the regulars was being endangered by the uncertain conduct of the militia. It was obvious to Brock that his presence was badly needed in the threatened area. For the time being, however, his civil duties prevented an immediate departure, since a special meeting of the legislature was to assemble at York in a week's time.

Brock set great store by this meeting, hoping that the impact of actual invasion would produce more co-operation than he had received from the session earlier that year. After a week's time, however, it was obvious that the Assembly was no readier than before to go as far as he wished in such matters as tightening the militia regulations and sanctioning a partial suspension of *habcas corpus*. At a time when "the Militia was in a perfect state of insubordination," refusing "to march when legally commanded," and manifesting "a treasonable spirit of neutrality," he could see no value in keeping the legislature longer in session. Accordingly, he prorogued the legislature after nine days, intending, if necessary, to proclaim martial law under the terms of his military commission. It must have been with mixed feelings that Brock read the Assembly's concluding address joyously remarking on "the spirit of loyalty" and the "flame of patriotism" that was "burning from one end of the Canadas to the other."[8]

That night (the fifth of August) Brock set out for the west, having previously arranged to collect in the Long Point area a force to relieve Amherstburg. Since the Americans had no military vessels on Lake Erie and had been unable to secure effective control of the country south of Detroit, he faced no obstacle but a buffeting wind during his trip to Amherstburg, which he reached early on the fourteenth, with some 40 regulars and 260 flank-company militiamen.

He arrived to find that the invasion itself had already collapsed. Worried by his failure to secure his communications to the southward, and by rumours of Indians descending on him from the north, Hull had already drawn his men back across the river. Aware of the mood of defeatism that had seized the bewildered American commander, Brock determined to move against him immediately. His first step was to demand the surrender of Detroit, threatening that his Indians might get out of hand if fighting were to take place. Then, collecting a force of some 1,300 regulars, militia, and Indians, he crossed the river early on the fifteenth. Fearful for the women and children behind his lines and distrusting his green troops, the discouraged Hull surrendered without firing a shot. By his bold move General Brock, with his small but well-trained army and his invaluable Indian allies under Tecumseh, had broken one prong of the American invasion; for a year the Territory of Michigan was to be an appendage of Upper Canada. Brock had also revived drooping morale in the province. More than that, the victory led many doubtful residents to commit themselves openly to the British cause, a decision from which they could not easily retreat in the darker days ahead.

Again taking advantage of British command of the lakes, Brock hurried back to Niagara to face the second prong of the American invasion.[9]

Here, along the right bank of the river, from Fort Niagara near its mouth back to the Falls, several thousand American troops had been collecting during the summer. They were still far from being an effective army, but Brock was prevented from knocking them off balance by an armistice which Prevost had concluded with the American commander-in-chief, General Henry Dearborn. Brock had no choice but to wait until the Americans were ready to attack him, which they finally did at Queenston on October 13, by which time they had more than four times as many troops as Brock could muster on the other side of the river.

When the first reports of the landings reached him at Fort George, Brock was uncertain whether they were a feint, with the real attack to come from Fort Niagara. When, however, he learned that the crossings were taking place in strength, he galloped the seven miles to Queenston, leaving his

D*

second-in-command, General Roger Hale Sheaffe, with orders to follow with the main British force as soon as possible. Brock arrived at Queenston in time to find American troops capturing the heights, and to see boats pouring men across from Lewiston. Gathering a few men together, he immediately determined to recapture the heights, but was shot dead as he charged up the escarpment. The hero's fall was soon avenged, however, when the troops under Sheaffe arrived and forced the surrender of nearly a thousand Americans. The invaders had already suffered heavy casualties, and were without hope of reinforcement, since the New York militia suddenly remembered that they were not required to fight outside their state and refused to cross the river.

The third thrust of the American offensive came to nothing, when Dearborn's move against Montreal in the following month petered out at Lacolle. Other minor engagements were equally indecisive, and the year ended with the Canadas still intact. Making full use of his available resources, one man by his dynamic and aggressive leadership had given the provincial inhabitants hope that they might yet survive the onslaughts being prepared against them, and the memory of his example was to be a powerful inspiration to the provinces for the rest of the war and indeed beyond it. Upper Canada had not seen the last of disaffection, treason or neutralism, but the successes at Detroit and Queenston Heights gave the loyal leadership of Upper Canada a command of the situation which it never lost during the remaining war years.

An illustration of the manner in which provincial leaders sought to harness the new spirit was found in the establishment of The Loyal and Patriotic Society, in December 1812. Its purposes were "to afford aid and relief" to militiamen and their families, who suffered from distress resulting from the war, and to bestow medals "for extraordinary instances of personal courage and fidelity in defence of the Province, either by His Majesty's regular or militia forces or seamen." Any person in the Province who subscribed a pound or more annually could be a member. The medal planned for distribution was to show on the reverse side the following scene:

> A streight between two lakes, on the north side a Beaver (emblem of peaceful industry) the ancient armorial bearing of Canada. In the back ground an English Lion slumbering.
>
> On the south side the streight, the American Eagle planeing in the air, as if checked from seizing the Beaver by the presence of the Lion, Legend "UPPER CANADA PRESERVED."[10]

This legend was an accurate statement of the facts, yet already history was being rewritten while it was being made, for the promoters of the Society went on to assert that the "unexpected declaration of war . . . instead of dispiriting its brave inhabitants [had] animated them with the most determined courage." John Strachan, who had recently moved to York to become the Anglican rector, confidently announced, in a sermon asking for subscriptions, that "It will be told by the future Historian, that the Province of Upper Canada, without the assistance of men or arms, except a handful of regular troops, repelled its invaders, slew or took them all prisoners, and captured from its enemies the greater part of the arms by which it was defended." Here was initiated the hardy myth of a predominantly Loyalist population, volunteering their services "with acclamation," and so saving themselves with only incidental assistance from British regulars. This was sound doctrine for the building of enthusiasm, but it was scarcely an accurate statement of what was actually happening.[11]

In point of fact, the short-term militia raised in Upper Canada frequently proved to be little more reliable than their counterpart across the lakes. A large proportion of the population was of recent American origin, and many of these were disaffected or at least preferred to sit on the fence until prospects became clearer. Some of the American settlers quickly moved across the line, although in contrast, others became so angry at the invasion of their new home that they became flaming patriots, eager to kill as many of the intruders as came their way.[12] To complicate matters further, it is clear that some residents of impeccable Loyalist origins either joined the American cause or showed open sympathy for it.

Leaving aside questions of national sympathies, there was the more important fact that a short-term militia raised in a sparsely populated agricultural society could not be a very efficient fighting arm. However willing its members might be to face the enemy, and their zeal was often most intense, they were inevitably part-time soldiers, bound to drift away as harvest time approached, or when word came that their families might be in danger from American raiding parties or from resident Indians, supposedly friendly, but perhaps on the prowl. Reliance had to be placed on regular troops and on local corps raised on terms approaching those governing the regular forces. These corps, which were far from the ordinary short-term militia, combined with the British regulars and the Indians to provide the backbone of defence and the spearhead of counter-attack, and of all these the British regulars were the most essential. This small band of professional soldiers was a force which the Americans could match on only rare occasions.

The effectiveness of the land forces depended, however, on another consideration which was one of prime importance in determining the nature of the War of 1812: naval control of the Great Lakes. We have already noticed that Brock's quick action at Detroit and his return to the Niagara River were to a large extent made possible by initial British control of Lakes Erie and Ontario. In the long run the fate of Upper Canada depended on the ability of its defenders to control or, at least, to use these lakes. When the British were defeated on Lake Erie in 1813, the southwestern peninsula fell into American hands. Lake Ontario was far more important: for the moving of troops and supplies (given the sad state of the roads), and as a first line of defence against American invasion attempts. Hence the growing naval base at Kingston was the key to the defence of the province. And of even greater importance was the control of the St Lawrence down the river from Kingston to Montreal and beyond. The province was at the end of a long lifeline, up which came supplies and, eventually, reinforcements. If the United States could cut this lifeline at any point, the province west of that point would be within their grasp. Obviously, sound strategy dictated an attempt to cut the lifeline as far downstream as possible, preferably at Montreal. In a general way, this necessity was understood by American leaders, but they were never able to concentrate their energies sufficiently or to find the right commanders to lead their troops to victory along the old invasion route to Canada. Moreover, this route was hard to use because of the indifference and hostility of the eastern states. Therefore, they kept pecking away at the periphery, counting apparently on the hoped-for fifth column in Upper Canada to drop the province into their lap. But the poorly prepared invasions, the hit-and-run raids, and the conduct of their undisciplined soldiers greatly increased the will to resist in the province.

The American leaders did set out, however, to wrest control of the lakes from the British. In October 1812 Captain (later Commodore) Isaac Chauncey arrived at Sackets Harbor to assemble and build a fleet which soon gave him naval superiority on Lake Ontario. In the following spring he and his military associates should have used this opportunity to attack the naval base at Kingston, but they were deterred from doing so by unfounded reports of powerful troop concentrations there. Instead, on April 25, soon after the lake could be used and before the St Lawrence was open for sending troops to the interior, Chauncey put some seventeen hundred soldiers (commanded by General Dearborn) on board his ships, with the purpose of destroying provincial strength to the west.

The first objective of the armada was the capital at York, where important naval and military weapons and stores were known to exist. On the morning of April 27 the American troops stormed ashore and quickly dispersed the garrison. General Sheaffe, who had succeeded Brock as the political and military head in Upper Canada, retreated toward Kingston with his small band of regulars, as the main magazine of the fort was blown up, killing and wounding over two hundred of the invading troops. Other public property was also destroyed to prevent its falling into enemy hands. The capital remained under American occupation for a week, during which time the parliament buildings were burned, and some looting took place by

American soldiers, whom Dearborn had difficulty in keeping under control.

The attack on York accomplished its main purposes because between them the British and Americans destroyed or carried away a large amount of badly needed military and naval material, including a large ship being built in the harbour. Much of the British weakness on Lake Erie later that year stemmed from these losses, and American command of Lake Ontario was for the time being strengthened. But the most notorious incident of the occupation of York was the burning of the parliament buildings. Dearborn denied that his men had had anything to do with their destruction, and the true story of their firing has never come to light. The British and the Canadians, however, understandably concluded that Americans had been responsible.

Upper Canada now entered upon the darkest period of the war. At the end of May, Chauncey's ships appeared off the mouth of the Niagara River and landed troops which attacked and took Fort George. The British commander, General John Vincent, was forced to retreat westward, with the intention of making a stand at Burlington, at the head of the lake. The whole of the Niagara peninsula lay open to the Americans. At this same time the British also tried their hand at an amphibious attack, when they sent an expedition against Sackets Harbor, intending to take advantage of Chauncey's absence in the west to destroy that important American naval base. The ships were led by Sir James Yeo, who had just taken command of the Great Lakes naval station, now under the Royal Navy, in place of the Provincial Marine. The troops were accompanied, although not actually commanded, by Sir George Prevost. A landing was successfully made, much destruction resulted, but the attack was not pushed home. Sackets Harbor was not put out of commission, and soon revived.

With this failure at one end of the lake and apparent disaster at the other, the possibility that all of the province west of Kingston might have to be abandoned was very much in people's minds. Disaffection and discouragement, which had been so noticeable in the previous summer, again revived. The militia deserted in some numbers, or at least simply returned to their farms. In many instances settlers refused to provide food and assistance to British and Canadian troops. Some residents, including two members of parliament and a former member, joined the American side. Sir George Prevost, at Kingston preparing for the attack on Sackets Harbor, wrote of "the growing discontent and undissembled dissatisfaction of the mass of the people of Upper Canada" and of his need to bring up his "best and reserved soldiers" if the Niagara and Detroit frontiers were to be held. He felt that the militia could not be relied upon.[13]

Yet the military situation, as it turned out, was far from irretrievable. The Americans threw away some of the fruits of their successes by lack of co-ordinated effort and by failing to keep Vincent on the run. Chauncey returned to Sackets Harbor, more concerned with repairing the damage there than with army co-operation. Then, on the night of June 5, Vincent's outnumbered men, in a surprise bayonet attack devised and led by Lieutenant-Colonel John Harvey, turned on their pursuers at Stoney Creek. In a sharp battle the Americans were dislodged from their positions, had their two generals captured, and retired disorganized and dispirited toward Niagara. In a few hours a small number of daringly led regulars had not only saved the central portions of the province from probable occupation, but their victory would free troops from Kingston to harass from the rear the autumn offensive against Montreal. On the Niagara front the Americans never regained the initiative in 1813. Less than three weeks later they suffered another humiliating defeat when some six hundred of their men were surrounded and captured by a smaller Indian force at Beaver Dam. General Peter B. Porter, a prominent citizen of Buffalo, described the army as lying "panic-struck, shut up and whipped by a few hundred miserable savages."[14]

Abandoning further thought of offensive action on the Niagara front for the time being, the American Secretary of War, John Armstrong, transferred the regulars eastward to reinforce the projected autumn campaign against Montreal. Becoming more and more uneasy, the American militia commander General George McClure finally evacuated Fort George in December and drew back across the river. Before he did so, however, he burned the town of Newark, leaving several hundred inhabitants to shiver in the cold as they watched their houses go up in flames. Despite the greater attention paid by posterity to the (perhaps accidental) burning of the parliament buildings at York, this was the first real atrocity in a war that had generally been fought in a fairly clean manner. It was yet another result of leaving war in the hands of jittery "citizen soldiers."

The British reaction was swift and drastic. A week later six hundred regulars crossed the river, put the garrison of Fort Niagara to the bayonet, and additional troops then proceeded to lay waste the American side of the river, burning Buffalo before the end of the month. The year ended with the Niagara peninsula clear of invaders and with the American side of the river tasting the bitter fruit of war.

Meanwhile, the province had been assaulted at each extremity and with opposite results. The Americans had been succesful in the west, that is, on the periphery, but had failed in the east, where they might have cut the province's lifeline.

After the Detroit disaster the command of the western army of the United States was assigned to William Henry Harrison, the governor of Indiana Territory, a more effective leader than the unfortunate Hull. His opponent was Colonel (later Brigadier-General) Henry Procter, charged with holding the southwestern peninsula and the gains across the Detroit River with a small force of British regulars and the Indians under Tecumseh. He repulsed Harrison's first move against him, at Frenchtown, south of Detroit, but his own attempts to keep Harrison off balance failed when he was unable to take either Fort Meigs or Fort Stephenson, at the southwestern end of Lake Erie. He was thrown back on the defensive, forced to wait for the inevitable American attack, and with Indian morale badly shaken.

The American leaders realized that the key to success in this region lay in wresting naval control of Lake Erie from the British. At Presqu'Ile (the present Erie, Pennsylvania) a shipbuilding program was initiated, which was energetically carried forward by Captain Oliver Hazard Perry in the spring and summer of 1813, and which enjoyed advantages, especially its access to the growing iron industry of Pittsburgh, which the British could not match.[15] By the end of the summer Perry had a stronger squadron than his naval opponent, Captain R. H. Barclay, and then had the supreme luck to float it unarmed over the shallow bar outside Presqu'Ile and into the lake, and then get his guns mounted without being attacked. Barclay and Procter now faced a hopeless dilemma. Without communication by way of Lake Erie they could not receive even the minimum supplies needed to support their forces, including the Indians, along the Detroit, while Barclay was not strong enough to challenge Perry. Yet he had to try, if the British forces were not to die on the vine, and using cannon from Fort Malden to arm his flagship he sailed out from Amherstburg on the ninth of September to challenge the American squadron. On the next day, at Put-In Bay, his entire flotilla was destroyed or captured, and he and the survivors of his crews taken prisoner in a bloody battle.

Procter now had no choice but to fall back toward the head of Lake Ontario. He delayed fatally in doing so, however, and Harrison caught up with him at Moraviantown on the Thames on October 5. There the small force of exhausted British regulars and the Indians under Tecumseh were scattered by Harrison's much larger army. Tecumseh was killed, and Procter forced to flee for his life. Harrison now had an opportunity to attack the British forces in the Burlington-Niagara region from the rear, but he unaccountably returned to Detroit. His victory ended the Indian menace in the Michigan-Indiana region once and for all, and did something to strengthen the hands of American diplomats at the subsequent peace conference, but it proved not to be a mortal blow at the security of the province.

Such a blow could have been struck by the eastern armies of the United States, in their campaign against Montreal, but these armies were led with almost incredible ineptitude by Generals Wilkinson and Hampton. Although at times outnumbered by about ten to one, miscellaneous forces of

British, English-Canadian, and French-Canadian regulars, provincial militia, and Indians plagued the advancing American armies, and then turned them back at the battles of Chateauguay and Crysler's Farm on October 26 and November 11. The most important of the 1813 campaigns projected by Secretary of War Armstrong had collapsed in humiliating defeat.

The Canadas, and especially the upper province, had survived the most dangerous year of the war, a year when they could still expect no substantial assistance from overseas and when American troops were better trained although, as it turned out, not much better led, than in 1812. The lifeline along the St Lawrence had been protected and, of almost equal importance, Yeo had held his own against Chauncey on Lake Ontario. Here no real battle had been fought, which in effect meant a defeat for Chauncey, since he had to stop the shipbuilding program at Kingston if the American offensive were to succeed. With Napoleon's strength ebbing in Europe, Canadians could look forward more confidently to 1814 when help would surely come from the mother country. Under these circumstances American successes on Lake Erie and at Moraviantown were of relatively minor importance.

Secretary of War Armstrong intended that Kingston should be the main objective of the American campaign in 1814, but he failed to make his plans clear to Dearborn's successor, General Jacob Brown.[16] Moreover, Chauncey had no wish to risk his fleet in an assault against the rival port. Accordingly, Brown marched his men away from Sackets Harbor to have another try at an offensive across the Niagara, expecting to receive naval support from Chauncey. Units of the army were well drilled near Buffalo by the young Brigadier-General Winfield Scott, who had already shown the qualities that made him a great commander, and the best American army to take the field during the war crossed the river at the beginning of July, easily taking Fort Erie and intending to push northward toward the lake, and on to Burlington and York.

British troops from Fort George and along the lower river rushed south to stem Brown's advance, and General Phineas Riall led them in a reckless attack against the larger American army at Chippawa on the fifth. But on this occasion American regulars proved to be the equal of British regulars, and Riall's men were forced back. Brown's plans now received a check, since Chauncey failed to appear with the naval support needed for an advance to the north and west. While Brown waited for Chauncey, and tried to decide what to do next, the commander of the forces in Upper Canada, General Gordon Drummond, hurried to the scene from Kingston to take personal direction of a reinforced army.

The two forces came in contact with each other at Lundy's Lane, a mile west of Niagara Falls, on the late afternoon of July 25, and in the next several hours fought the bitterest battle of the entire war. Each side hurled desperate charges against the other in the dusk and darkness, with the honours of war about evenly divided. Casualties were heavy in both armies, as Drummond, Riall, Brown, and Winfield Scott were all severely wounded and Riall taken prisoner. By midnight, however, the Americans were too exhausted to make another attack, and fell back leaving Drummond's men in possession of the field. They, in turn, were too exhausted to pursue. The American offensive thrust was now spent, and although Drummond's assault on Fort Erie in the middle of August was bloodily repulsed, no further advance of any consequence was attempted. In November the new American commander, General George Izard, blew up Fort Erie and went into winter quarters on the New York side.

During the 1814 campaigns there had been further examples of sympathy for and co-operation with the enemy on the part of American-born residents of the province. In May nineteen of those who had been caught were brought to trial at Ancaster; fifteen were convicted, of whom eight were hanged. Indictments were also obtained against seventy former residents who had left the province. As a further move against such people the legislature passed an act in March 1814, providing for legal action to seize the lands of persons who had voluntarily withdrawn into the United States, without licence from the government. All of this made for a rather ugly atmosphere at times, providing opportunities for accusations which originated out of personal spite as well as from concern over treason and disaffection.

It should also be noted that throughout the war, and especially in its later stages, there were frequent examples of friction between military and civilian authorities that had nothing to do with disaffection. The Assembly consistently refused to give the commander-in-chief, who was also always the acting lieutenant-governor, as much power as he wished to suspend *habeas corpus* and declare martial law. When he or his subordinate officers did suspend civil processes, usually for the purpose of ensuring an adequate supply of food to the troops, there was considerable resentment. In February 1814 the Assembly declared General de Rottenburg's proclamation of martial law to be "arbitrary and unconstitutional and contrary to and subversive of the established laws of the land," and in the following month criticized the commander of the forces for not giving sufficient credit to the militia for their services and sufferings.[17] The Assembly was quite convinced in its own mind that it had done its best to safeguard the province, and that the people (that is, the voters) had done so, too. Despite the peril in which the province stood, the Assembly remained suspicious of the power of the military, who were accused of making illegal midnight arrests, of harsh impressment of supplies, and of favouritism in the award of supply contracts. The hard-pressed commanders were understandably exasperated at this stiff-necked attitude. Their difficulties, however, were small compared with those of their American counterparts, who were faced with the fact that a whole section of their country—New England—openly and vigorously opposed the war. A very large part of the provisions consumed by British and Canadian troops came from New England sources.

With Izard's withdrawal across the Niagara, the war ended for Upper Canada. After two and a half years of effort the forces of the United States had failed to hold an inch of land on the Canadian side of the Niagara River, and Fort Niagara was still in British hands. In the southwest, the Americans held Fort Malden, and were able to send raids as far west as the Grand River without encountering real opposition, but in the northwest the British still held Michilimackinac and dominated an extensive region beyond. Finally, although he had two larger ships on the stocks, Chauncey had for the time being lost the shipbuilding contest on Lake Ontario at the end of the year, as Yeo sailed the lake in a ship-of-the-line pierced for 112 guns.

In the latter half of the year the loyal inhabitants of the province had been cheered by the knowledge that Great Britain was now mounting extensive counter-offensives against the United States, although they were chagrined by the outcome of some of these. In August an expedition from Nova Scotia took and held one hundred miles of the Maine coast from the New Brunswick border to the Penobscot River. In that same month occurred the famous British raid on Washington, in retaliation for earlier American raids.[18]

But the most formidable British effort of 1814 was the invasion of northern New York which Prevost led to Plattsburg on Lake Champlain in early September. Heavily reinforced by seasoned Peninsular veterans, Prevost was leading the most powerful army ever to take the field during the war, and leading it against a much smaller force which had been weakened to provide men for Izard's command along the Niagara. Yet this invasion failed miserably, as invasions so often failed during this war. Prevost waited for the outcome of the naval action between the British fleet led by Captain George Downie and the American fleet led by Captain Thomas Macdonough, and when the latter emerged completely victorious Prevost drew his army back into Lower Canada. This little action on Lake Champlain proved to be one of the decisive battles of the war, since it discouraged the British from making further offensive moves and made it easier for the United States to get an acceptable peace treaty. The last major action of the war, Andrew Jackson's repulse of the British invasion at New Orleans, came after the signing of the treaty.

Having entered the war as a means of defending his nation's honour,

Madison was ready to end it as soon as a suitable opportunity arose. Accordingly, an early offer of mediation by the Russian Czar was readily accepted by Washington, and when Castlereagh preferred direct Anglo-American negotiations Madison was equally ready to participate. Five commissioners from the United States met with three representatives of the British government at Ghent in August 1814 to begin the hard bargaining needed to produce a peace settlement. As it turned out, the maritime grievances which had done so much to bring on the war were not dealt with at all; in particular, the British would not budge on the matter of impressment, and the United States had decided to abandon this question in the interests of ending the war. At first the British negotiators took a very strong stand, assuming that they had the Americans at a serious disadvantage, and demanded protection for the Canadas in the form of boundary revisions, unilateral American disarmament on the Great Lakes, and an Indian buffer zone southwest of Lake Erie. American fishing privileges in British-American waters were also to be cancelled. The American diplomats stubbornly resisted these demands, however, and more than once the discussions seemed at the point of being broken off. Eventually, a belief that their military position in North America could not be much improved combined with growing concern over the European situation convinced the British government that the war with the United States must be wound up as quickly as possible. The above-mentioned demands were drastically scaled down or withdrawn, and on Christmas Eve, 1814, a treaty was signed which conformed very closely to an earlier American draft. All conquests were to be restored. Disputed and doubtful aspects of the international boundary between the United States and British North America were to be determined by joint commissions. In short, the war had simply been brought to an end, and the real peace settlement was to follow.

The people of Upper Canada had no part, of course, in the working out of this settlement, and were not directly affected by much of it. They were very real beneficiaries, nevertheless, since recent events had shown (what all the rest of the century would continue to show) that the Canadian provinces could never enjoy real security when hostility existed between the United States and Great Britain. Hence it was to the advantage of the provinces to see Anglo-American relations improved, provided no essential Canadian interest was damaged in the process.

One phase of the settlement that was of direct concern to Upper Canada and its sister province was the limitation of naval armament on the Great Lakes and Lake Champlain, contained in the Rush-Bagot Agreement of April 1817 (formally proclaimed a year later). This proposal had originated with the United States government and was clearly in its interest, since it could confidently expect to win any shipbuilding race started in the future.

Yet the British government could see no alternative except an expensive contest now, which would be very hard to win. The Agreement, of course, did not make for an "undefended border" or for an end of friction along that border. Many hundreds of thousands of pounds came out of the British taxpayer's pocket during the next generation, and even later, for the strengthening of land fortifications and other works, notably the Rideau Canal and the defences of Kingston. The United States also strengthened its own fortifications from time to time within the next half-century. It was, nevertheless, a gain to the Canadians to know that the great internal water highways were to be freely and peacefully used.

Other phases of the settlement which made "the truce" of 1815 into "a real peace"[19] touched the settled regions of Upper Canada in only a few places. The boundary commissions provided for in the Treaty of Ghent were mainly occupied with problems to the east, especially in the region of Maine and New Brunswick, but one of them did determine the ownership of certain islands in the upper St Lawrence and the Niagara Rivers. The last main phase of the settlement, the Convention of 1818, was of the greatest importance for future Canadian-American relations; it dealt with the fisheries in Atlantic waters and placed the boundary west of the Lake of the Woods along the 49th Parallel as far as the Rocky Mountains. Beyond, the Oregon country was to be under joint Anglo-American occupation.

Although remote from the current concerns of the people of Upper Canada, this settlement in the west would in the long run be of immense significance for them. It staked out and defined a new empire in place of an old one now lost forever. The old empire, the Michigan-Wisconsin country, was the especial interest of the Montreal fur-traders. They had fought hard to regain it, and in conjunction with British troops had taken Michilimackinac and much of the region west of Lake Michigan, holding these throughout the war, only to see them relinquished in the Treaty of Ghent. With this decision Upper Canada also lost any chance of having an accessible western frontier under British political control for future expansion. But far away, beyond the northwestern borders of the province, lay another empire, the great prairie country. Within half a century the Upper Canadians would be reaching out to that country, across a thousand miles of broken wilderness, intent on realizing their own form of "manifest destiny." By finally destroying old hopes, but leaving open the possibility of new ones, the peace settlement did much to determine the outlines of the later Canadian nation.

CHAPTER 5

A Briton Banished
and a Union Averted

A British traveller visiting Upper Canada not long after the war noted that the conflict formed an "important era" in its history, so much so that the people dated every occurrence as having happened "before or after the war." A Kingston newspaper editor saw something more significant: "the proofs of loyalty everywhere given . . . and even by the American emigrants" had confirmed and strengthened the population in their British allegiance; "the line of separation" between the province and its republican neighbour "was more distinctly drawn."[1]

Suspicion of American republicanism increased generally throughout the province, but it was at its highest among those in or close to the government, who were more than ever determined that all policy must be aimed at maintaining that line of separation. Men such as John Strachan and his former pupil John Beverley Robinson, who were to provide the conservative leadership of the coming generation, emerged from the conflict convinced that they had narrowly escaped absorption by the United States. Their still-infant province was fated to go on living beside "a powerful and treacherous enemy" who would seize the first opportunity to repeat the attack. The war had shown how essential it was to hold fast to the British tie as the only sure means of protection. Indeed, the great worry of Robinson, Strachan, and others like them was that the British might abandon them or, out of ignorance of North American conditions, take some heedless action that would put the province in jeopardy. For instance, in 1815 and 1816, when there was talk of transferring the capital from York to Kingston, the move was vehemently opposed on the ground that Americans would interpret it as the first stage of withdrawal from the interior.[2] To the Tory mind of Upper Canada the British needed almost as much watching as did the Americans.

The political and psychological consequences of the war proved to be far more significant than its physical effects. Apart from distress in the Niagara area and in some of the western counties the province had suffered little injury that could still be discerned a few months after the return of peace. The war years had in fact been a time of considerable prosperity, when large sums of money had been spent to carry on the conflict. Army bills, issued on the authority of the government of Lower Canada and backed by the British government, had provided Upper Canada with its first adequate circulating medium, paper money that was redeemed at par. Farmers had received high prices for their goods, and merchants had flourished from the business of supplying the armed forces. In some instances roads had been improved in order to facilitate the movement of troops. It was generally accepted by contemporaries that the war although "in some cases injurious to individuals was a benefit to the Country at large."[3]

After this wartime prosperity the province had to a great extent to fall back upon its own resources as plans were made for the future. The first, primitive stages of pioneer settlement had been left behind, and everyone looked forward to a period of more rapid growth, to an expansion of settlement and the beginning of major works of public improvement. The first regular stage-coach lines between Kingston and York began to run in 1817, and in that same year the first steamboat appeared on Lake Ontario. Banking schemes were projected, as will be seen later.

Nevertheless, the years just after the war were a time of economic frustration for the people of Upper Canada, not made easier by the knowledge that their republican neighbours were "going ahead" at a rapid rate. Prices fell after the army ceased to be a customer. Hard money became scarce, and there was no adequate paper money to take the place of the army bills. A post-war depression, which also hit the United States in 1819, lay at the root of many of the irritations and discontents evident in Upper Canada shortly after the war.

In these circumstances many in the province looked hopefully to the mother country for further assistance, with attention being concentrated on the subject of claims arising out of the war. Although losses were not great for the province as a whole, they had been severe in some sections. If prompt and adequate payment were made, a fillip might be given to post-war economic adjustment. The British government, which had just fought a much longer and far more terrible war and was facing post-war problems beside which Upper Canada's were puny, hoped at first that the claims might be met from the proceeds of the sale of the confiscated estates of traitors. Hearings were held, and an original total of some £400,000 was arrived at as representing the claims to be paid. It was soon obvious that the confiscated estate sales would not begin to cover the claims, even when they had been drastically scaled down, and the province renewed its pleas for compensation from the mother country. Complicated and protracted negotiations dragged on for many years to come before partial payments were forthcoming. The failure to make prompt grants of lands promised to certain categories of militia also led to irritation.

Apart from the war claims the leading focus of post-war dispute lay in the decision to discourage further American immigration into the British provinces. This decision was considered by imperial and provincial officials to be essential to the security of the provinces, but in Upper Canada it aroused much general resentment, despite the antagonism toward the United States, born of the war.

Well before the war ended military and political leaders voiced concern over the number of residents of doubtful loyalty who were fast turning Upper Canada into "a compleat American colony." If the influx were resumed with the return of peace, it would inevitably alienate the province "from the Mother Country and betray it . . . to the incroaching power of the United States."[4] Accordingly, General Sir Gordon Drummond, administering the government of Upper Canada, heartily approved a plan broached to him by Lord Bathurst (Secretary of State for War and the Colonies, 1812-27) of assisting Scottish Highlanders to settle in the province. These people were determined to emigrate, and the British government was now ready to offer them inducements to go to the colonies rather than to the United States. Drummond reported that he would be glad to have Scottish immigrants in "a Country already too much inhabited by Aliens from the United States, very many of whom are avowedly disaffected to the British Government, and as many more of doubtful principles." The Scots should be established close to the American border, thus providing "a kind of defence . . . of the very best materials and people loyal and attached to the Government, who would afford at the same time, a counterpoise to that ill disposed and disaffected part of the population, which it is so much regretted has crept from time to time, during a Series of Years into it." Drummond also wanted more Anglican clergymen brought into the province to counteract the influence of the "itinerant fanatics, enthusiastic in political as well as in religious matters," who "were in the habit of coming hither from the United States," and who "succeeded but too well in disseminating their noxious principles."[5] Considerations of defence and security were uppermost as future settlement policies for the province were being fashioned.

As the war drew to an end Bathurst's plans became more concrete. First, it was arranged to demobilize some of the British regular troops, especially those with families, at the end of the war, and to give them lots along the frontier as a barrier against American invasion or peacetime encroachment. Second, a number of "industrious families" would be sent out with the spring fleet of 1815 as a first experiment in government-sponsored colonization. Such settlers would come mainly from Scotland and Ireland (in fact, they all came from Scotland), and would be given "every encouragement and all reasonable assistance" to ensure their establishment in Upper Canada. Finally, Bathurst announced a new policy, which was to have far-reaching consequences, when he ordered that no land was to be granted "to Subjects of the United States," and that every endeavour was to be made to prevent their settling in either of the Canadas.[6]

The details of the new settlement scheme became known to the government of Upper Canada in the spring of 1815. Free passage on the ships being sent out to bring back the troops would be granted to emigrants and their families. Heads of families would be given one hundred acres of land, as would male children when they reached twenty-one years of age. Free rations would be provided for a limited period, while axes and other necessary implements would be furnished at a reduced price. The government promised, under certain circumstances, to pay salaries to clergymen and schoolmasters accompanying emigrants. As a means of discouraging anyone from going on to the United States after receiving a free passage across the Atlantic, deposits were to be required, to be returned after two years to settlers who were still living on the land that had been allotted to them. In this program the British government professed that it was not trying to stimulate new emigration, but simply to divert to the Canadas that "surplus population" which would otherwise proceed to the United States. Drummond was instructed to give careful attention to the settlers, to make certain that they would see the advantages of staying in the provinces.[7]

Although the government of Upper Canada was kept informed of these plans, their actual implementation was assigned to military officers responsible to the governor-in-chief, in Lower Canada, since the whole project was military in purpose. Francis Gore, back in the upper province, thus had to watch a settlement program for which he had to provide land, but over which he had little control and which he felt to be an invasion of the rights of his government. There was soon friction between the two provincial authorities, and little had been done to prepare for the first immigrants when they arrived at the end of the summer. Eventually, however, a range of townships west of the Rideau River was made available, and military and Scottish settlers moved onto this rather rocky and swampy land in the spring of 1816. Many of the soldiers, as might have been expected, soon drifted away, but the Scots around Perth proved to be tenacious, building there a sturdy and enduring community. This first experiment in imperial colonization had a very limited success for the expense it involved, and Parliament became very wary of assisted emigration schemes. It was also viewed with much suspicion by the government and leaders of Upper Canada, who did not like a settlement project which was under the supervision of outside military officers and a cause of considerable expense. The military objective was also somewhat lost sight of, although it was argued that the country along the Rideau should be protected since the Ottawa-Rideau waterway was planned as a military route connecting Montreal and Kingston. The Perth settlement proved to be no more military in character than any other community in the province.

As well as assisting with the military settlements, Gore had to carry out Bathurst's instructions to keep American citizens out of the province. This was an order with which the Lieutenant-Governor was in full sympathy, but at first he was nonplussed as to how it should be obeyed. He found, shortly after his arrival in September 1815, that Americans were once again "pouring into the Province," while he had no legal power to halt the influx except that provided by a provincial sedition act (of which more will be heard later) authorizing "the dismissal from the Province upon very slight grounds, of all such as have not been resident six months, or taken the oath of allegiance." The direct and immediate use of this statute was not contemplated, but on the advice of the executive council he ordered the magistrates throughout the province not "to administer the Oath of Allegiance to any Person not holding Office in the Province, or being the Son of a U.E. Loyalist, without a special authority in such case" from the lieutenant-governor's office. Thus, American citizens would always be open to prosecution under the sedition act; more important, probably, was the fact that, since it was impossible to secure a land title without taking the oath of allegiance, the order would be effective in discouraging further American immigration. The magistrates were also asked to report on the number and character of aliens from the United States or elsewhere coming into the Province "to reside therein, in any Capacity, either as Preachers, School masters, Practitioners in Medicine, Pedlars or Labourers."[8]

But the provincial authorities were convinced that it was not enough merely to stop new immigration. Many residents who had previously taken the oath of allegiance, and many who were natural-born subjects, were returning from wartime sojourns in the United States as if nothing had happened. These too must be kept under supervision. Also, the U.E. List must be kept free of the stigma of disloyalty. An order went out from York stating that the sons and daughters of Loyalists were not to receive their allotments of land until they could prove "that the Parent retained his Loyalty during the late War, and was under no suspicion of aiding or assisting the Enemy – and if a Son, then of Age, that he also was Loyal during the late War, and did his duty in defence of the Province – and if a Daughter of an U.E. Loyalist married, that her Husband was loyal, and did his duty in defence of the Province."[9]

At first, these measures of the imperial and the local executive authorities had the support of the provincial legislature. When the wartime

Assembly met for its last session in February 1816, it showed an eager willingness to be co-operative in all matters. It seconded the efforts of the executive against the disloyal by passing a bill to punish residents who, having taken the oath of allegiance, had left the province during the war and had now returned. This bill was so harsh that the legislative council insisted on softening it in some respects.

Moreover, the members were in a generous mood, of a kind unparalleled in provincial annals. They voted £500 to the retiring Speaker of the Legislative Council, Chief Justice Thomas Scott. They provided Gore with a provincial aide-de-camp and then, unanimously, voted £3,000 to buy him a service of plate in gratitude "for his firm, upright, and liberal administration." (He had been back in the province for six months, after being away throughout the war years.) They provided for the appointment of a provincial agent, to reside in England, and to be named by the lieutenant-governor. (He named his own secretary.) And they capped all this by voting £2,500 to defray the expenses of the civil administration – the first such appropriation in the province's history. In all this, as well as in the other measures of the session, there was little or no hint of party divisions or party spirit. Here, if ever, was a loyal representative body, readily supporting and advancing the measures of the executive branch.

But such happy accord was not an accurate reflection of contemporary opinion. This Assembly, elected back in 1812, was apparently little aware of the feelings of dissatisfaction and frustration which were swirling about the province.

These feelings could not find expression in any organized movement of political protest, which as yet did not exist. Instead, the first indications of opposition to official policies came from men of some prominence, who were acting only for themselves and concerned only with their own personal interest. They were large landholders, speculators, as Gore called them, who objected to the order aimed at excluding American settlers. The best known of these, William Dickson, was actually a member of the legislative council, as well as a commissioner appointed to administer the oath of allegiance. When the decline of immigration from the United States began to affect sales of his land, he flatly refused to obey Gore's order to withhold the oath of allegiance from Americans. Such people were the only possible purchasers of the large tracts of land owned by Dickson and men like him. There was no immediate prospect that many settlers would be received from Britain, and those who might come would be too poor to buy much land from private owners. Americans with money in their pockets, however, might be attracted. Although Dickson and his friends were as anxious as any official that Upper Canada remain a British province, they saw no reason to fear an influx of hard-working American freeholders, who were ready to take the oath of allegiance. They represented, in fact, the only immediate means by which the province could be built up.

As punishment for his defiance of the Lieutenant-Governor, Dickson's name was removed from the commission for administering the oath. But the subject was taken up during the first session of the new Assembly, in the early spring of 1817. The prime mover now was Colonel Robert Nichol, who represented Norfolk County along Lake Erie. Nichol was far from being a radical or a spokesman for frontier democracy. He had an outstanding record of war service, and his considerable property interests in the Niagara area had suffered heavy damage from American raids. In the Assembly he had always sturdily supported the policies of the executive. But by 1817 he was both exasperated at Gore's refusal to back his claims for reward and compensation arising out of the war and in sympathy with his friend Dickson on the subject of American immigration. He now began a career of criticism of the administration which lasted intermittently until his death in 1824.

In the session of 1817 he responded to Gore's request for a larger supply bill than usual by securing the establishment of a committee to investigate the state of the province. The resolutions of this committee, apart from one concerned with land grants for the militia, expressed strong opposition to the whole policy of keeping American settlers out of the province. The first three, which merely pointed to the previous encouragement of American immigration, were approved by the Assembly, in a two-to-one vote, but before the remaining resolutions could be introduced, Gore hurriedly prorogued the legislature. He professed to believe that their real purpose was to transfer "this devoted Province to the United States of America,"[10] a remark that revealed an attitude characteristic of nearly all official reaction to criticism in these years.

The resolutions kept from the Assembly touched on matters that were close to the hearts of many residents of the province: the need for more population and the injury sustained by keeping out Americans, the obstacles to settlement posed by the Crown and Clergy Reserves, and the desirability of putting these up for sale instead of continuing the current leasing policy.[11] There was no quarrel, as yet, with the purposes of the Reserves, simply a desire that their extent be reduced.

But Gore saw the resolutions as expressing the cupidity of land speculators, who were hoodwinking ignorant members of the Assembly into supporting them. He assured Lord Bathurst that if the influx of Americans were not restrained "the next declaration of Hostilities by America, will be received by Acclamation, and the Loyal population of the Colony, will be reduced to defend themselves from the disloyal."[12] Shortly after sending off this dispatch Gore once again left the province, this time never to return, and it was his successors who had to deal with the thorny problems raised by the American-born settlers in the province.

Another indication of the irascible and touchy atmosphere in post-war Upper Canada is found in the events of the following session of the legislature, early in 1818. This time the controversy was purely constitutional in form, and to some extent in substance. It was the old problem, fought over so many times in British constitutional history, of the power of the purse. In the long run there could be only one result in Upper Canada, as elsewhere: the complete victory of the representative house; but here, as elsewhere, the victory was not immediately or easily won. And here, too, the contest was not simply over constitutional forms, but also over political and economic interests which stood to gain or lose by the outcome.

The controversy came into the open when the legislative council undertook to amend a bill sent up to it from the Assembly regulating trade with the United States. The question was argued in purely constitutional terms, with the council maintaining that since it had the power to reject money bills (which this one was, in part), it could amend them as well. The council also asserted, correctly, that its amendments were in line with imperial trade legislation. The Assembly, however, with the aggressiveness of colonial popular bodies, claimed that it had all the powers of the British House of Commons in the matter of money bills, and denied the right of the council to amend them in any respect. Back of the contest lay two conflicting points of view: on the one hand, there was the mercantile wish to provide easy entry of American goods in order that these might be attracted down the St Lawrence; on the other, the agrarian fear, represented in the Assembly, that such entry would pose dangerous competition to the farmers of the province.

Presently, relations between the two Houses were so strained that all normal communication between them ceased, bringing the business of the session to a full stop. The Assembly, as far as can be ascertained from its Journals, was unanimous in its stand, and ready to open up the whole question of provincial finance, much of which was not under its control. It was only two years since the provincial legislature had been asked to contribute to the support of the civil government, and it was now apparent from the accounts that some of the money voted in 1816 and 1817 had been used for purposes (such as pensions to certain retired officials) which did not have the approval of the Assembly. If that body were to vote money, it should be used in ways the Assembly favoured. With no intercourse between the Houses, the Assembly voted a supply message of its own, sent directly to the Administrator, who refused to accept it without the concurrence of the legislative council.

The Assembly's grievances were collected into an address, directed to the

Prince Regent, which used Simcoe's statement of 1792 that the province enjoyed a constitution which was the very image and transcript of that of Great Britain to buttress its claim in the matter of money bills. At the same time the legislative council was criticized as being too closely identified with the executive, since many members of the one council also had seats in the other. This address was the last straw for Samuel Smith, acting as Administrator after Gore's departure. He promptly prorogued the legislature, bringing it abruptly to a close for the second year running, this time without supply voted and with the members of the lower House in a very bad humour.

The question of financial control would inevitably come up again, but when it did party differences would prevent the unanimity in the Assembly displayed in 1818. Meanwhile the province was undergoing an experience which did a good deal to bring such party differences into being. Its grievances, its discontents, its irritations, such as they were, were now in the tender care of a self-appointed physician who had come to pronounce cures.

It was the fate of Upper Canada to attract a number of fiery Scots who did much to enliven its history, although it cannot be said that they did as much to advance the solution of its problems along useful and constructive lines. Without John Strachan and William Lyon Mackenzie the province would have been a duller but possibly a happier and more normal community. And without Robert Gourlay it would have been spared reams of violent, acrimonious and often aimless abuse, producing bad tempers on all sides and leading finally to petty persecution. Gourlay had little that was helpful to offer Upper Canada, and yet his career there threw a flood of light on the harsh and unyielding attitudes of the men who held political power. In the long run, the way in which they hounded him out of the province did much to increase demands for a broader and more flexible political system.

Robert Gourlay was a congenital dissident, an inveterate scribbler, a stiff-necked individualist who sooner or later fell out with nearly everyone he knew, whether friend or foe. From early manhood in Scotland and in England he had been involved in controversies, lawsuits, and quarrels of all sorts. He had many good qualities. He was personally incorruptible, genuinely devoted to the public good, apparently well versed in the science of agriculture, and industrious to a fault. But his enthusiasm and sincerity were so overbalanced by his intense egotism, his exaggerated touchiness, and his unvarying habit of rushing into print at every opportunity, that he could accomplish little in the world of practical affairs.

Gourlay arrived in Upper Canada in the summer of 1817, driven there by the collapse of his fortunes at home. He and his wife owned several hundred acres of land in the province; further, they were related to some prominent people, including the above-mentioned William Dickson. At first, Gourlay's plans were uncertain; but after touring the Perth settlement and the Genesee country in New York State, he felt a call to inaugurate a grand scheme of emigration to Upper Canada. Britain badly needed to get rid of her surplus population, while Upper Canada badly needed more settlers. Although he believed that the Perth settlement had been hopelessly mismanaged (he succeeded in finding mismanagement wherever he turned) it nevertheless showed how much the poor were benefited by emigrating to Canada. But it was equally important, in his view, to attract substantial propertied emigrants from home, the sort of people who were going to the Genesee country and elsewhere in the United States because of their ignorance of Upper Canada.

He discussed his ideas with several leading provincial figures, meeting general encouragement from them and was given permission to publish an address "To the Resident Land-owners of Upper Canada," dated October 1817, in the *Upper Canada Gazette*, the official government newspaper. Here he set forth the benefits that would result from "an enlarged and liberal connexion between Canada and Britain," which would make unnecessary any reliance on American immigration. The first requisite for bringing about this new order was the "drawing out and publishing a well-authenticated statistical account of Upper Canada," and to get this started he annexed a set of thirty-one queries to his address, to which he hoped to get replies from every township in the province. If he received enough answers he promised to publish them in England.[13] To give further currency to the address and the queries he had seven or eight hundred copies of them printed in pamphlet form and distributed throughout the townships.

So far all had gone well. Only one person of importance appears to have opposed Gourlay at this stage. John Strachan, the rector of York and since 1815 a member of the executive council, considered Gourlay to be a presumptuous trouble-maker who ought to be opposed rather than sanctioned by the government. The very idea of stirring up the public to express opinions on the conduct of affairs was enough to disturb Strachan, and especially objectionable was the notorious 31st Query: "What, in your opinion, retards the improvement of your township in particular, or the province in general; and what would most contribute to the same?"

Still, Strachan's was a minority opinion at this stage, and throughout the province there was much enthusiasm for Gourlay's scheme. Many township meetings were held, in which magistrates and other leading residents participated. Presently Gourlay had received more than forty sets of answers to his queries, providing a great deal of information on economic conditions in the province. The replies to the 31st Query advanced many explanations for the province's slow rate of progress, such as bad roads, remoteness from markets, and the difficulties of navigating the St Lawrence, but two stood out. First, there was the extreme dispersal of settlements resulting from the enormous amounts of land held by absentee owners for a rise in price and from the lands tied up in Crown, Clergy, and other reserves. With many millions of acres of uncultivated lots and blocks of land scattered throughout the province, compact and flourishing settlements could not possibly develop. Second, there was the "want of people," especially men of capital and enterprise, caused both by the lack of a "liberal system of emigration" and by the policy of shutting out American settlers.[14]

But Gourlay could not long confine himself to the task of gathering information. After a tour through the western part of the province at the end of 1817, he concluded that the government had been guilty of vicious mismanagement, and in a second address to the land-owners he acquainted them with the "reigning abuse" that he had uncovered. This effusion, dated February 1818, was verbose and unorganized, and filled with vague attacks on Lieutenant-Governor Gore, who had left the province just before Gourlay arrived. He bitterly criticized Gore's efforts to discourage American settlement, although he still urged his readers to rely on Britain. To be sure, their property would rise to twice its value "were Canada united to the States," but a "liberal connection with Britain" and efficient government in place of "a system of paltry patronage and ruinous favouritism" would increase the value of property by ten times. By way of action, Gourlay demanded an immediate legislative inquiry into the state of the province, to be followed by a "commission appointed to proceed to England with the result of such inquiry."[15]

Whether in response to Gourlay's call or not, there was a motion for a "Committee to take into consideration the state of the Province" in the session of the legislature that met immediately after the publication of Gourlay's second address.[16] But shortly thereafter the Assembly became involved in its wrangle with the legislative council over money bills, and the session was abruptly ended, as already noted.

The news of this event – hearing the cannons from York boom across the lake at Niagara – produced in Gourlay a frenzy of outrage. The failure of the legislature to appoint a commission of inquiry convinced him that nothing could be expected of either governors or legislators. The existing system was incurably bad, and must be radically changed or overturned. Its basic fault lay in the governor's power to dispense patronage – "to give away land at pleasure . . . to dispose of all places and pensions – to make and unmake magistrates – to appoint militia officers, custom-house officers, inspectors, school-masters, registers – to grant licences, pardons, and I know not what; – to be worshipped as 'His Excellency,' and to have sufficient means to provide dinners and drink to all and several, suppliants and sycophants." With a governor having such power to threaten and to cajole, Gourlay concluded that no Assembly could be truly independent of him.[17]

Accordingly, he again took to his pen, and within a day had turned out another tirade for the instruction of the eye-weary resident landowners. He informed them that the only hope for improvement lay in appealing directly to the Prince Regent or to the Parliament of Britain. This should be done by petitioning "in collective bodies," which Gourlay asserted was just as legal as individual petitioning. He proposed a scheme of township meetings at which representatives would be chosen, who would later meet in a provincial convention to "dispatch commissioners to England with the petitions, and hold correspondence with them, as well as with the supreme government."[18] That is, Gourlay proposed the assembling of a popular body that would assume at least some of the authority of the provincial legislature.

Township meetings were now organized. Although fewer in number than those of the previous autumn, they again attracted many prominent and substantial men. By this time the provincial government was exceedingly alarmed by Gourlay's activities, but under Smith's ineffectual leadership, there was uncertainty about what to do. This lack of firm leadership was most galling to the Attorney General, John Beverley Robinson. This strikingly handsome, sharply intelligent and rigidly conservative young man, of Loyalist origins and with war service not long behind him, followed his mentor Strachan in believing that Gourlay's activities must be stopped. He could not find that either the township meetings or the convention were unconstitutional, but he did regard them as a most dangerous type of popular movement. While recently completing his legal studies in England, Robinson had been horrified by the popular tumults led by such demagogues as Cobbett and Hunt. Gourlay not only knew these men, but appeared to be imitating their activities in Upper Canada. In England, however, the troops could be called out to restore order; except for a few small garrisons, Upper Canada had been almost entirely denuded of soldiers after 1815. Moreover, the word "convention" had unfortunate overtones of the American and French Revolutions.[19]

But Smith would not act, and the only step open to Robinson was to prosecute Gourlay for libel, in the hope that he might be silenced. In a draft of the proposed address to the Prince Regent, to be sent with the commissioners, Gourlay had referred to scandalous abuses in the land department, to corruption worse than anything to be found elsewhere in the British Empire, and had used many other such extravagant phrases. On the basis of these and other passages, Gourlay was arrested at Kingston in June for criminal libel while on a tour of the eastern section of the province, and let out on bail. Later in this month he was also arrested at Brockville, and similarly released to stand trial later in the summer. In August sympathetic juries acquitted him on both charges. This method of silencing him had failed.

Meanwhile township meetings had selected representatives to attend the dreaded convention at York on July 6, which in fact turned out to be a very mild affair. There were only fourteen delegates, about half of them of Loyalist origin and several of them magistrates. Their deliberations were public and the minutes of their meetings were carefully recorded and published. The tone of their discussions was cautious, with the lead being given by Gourlay himself, who was invited to speak, although he was not a voting delegate. He advised a "change of measures"; instead of sending a commission directly to England, one more attempt should be made to get action from the provincial authorities. With a new governor (Sir Peregrine Maitland) coming out there was hope of a change for the better. Accordingly two addresses were adopted, one intended for the Prince Regent, which the new governor was to be asked to forward, and the second, directed to Maitland himself, criticizing the recent conduct of both the legislative and the executive authorities and asking for an early election, to be followed by an investigation of the state of the province.[20] Although provision was made for two branch conventions to meet later at Ancaster and at Kingston, it was obvious that the convention was not really trying to usurp the role of the legislature.

Nevertheless, the leaders of the provincial government were apparently greatly alarmed as well as bitterly resentful of Gourlay's personal attacks on them, and they poured out their hearts to Sir Peregrine when he arrived in August. This veteran soldier, the son-in-law of the Duke of Richmond, was to be lieutenant-governor of Upper Canada for a longer period than any other holder of the office, and then to hold other important posts in the colonial service in later years. He had been tested in a long series of campaigns culminating in his command of the first brigade of guards at Waterloo. He had all the strengths and weaknesses of his kind: a keen sense of duty, impeccable honesty, and a genuine desire to further the welfare of the province over which he governed; at the same time, his temperament was cold and aloof, and his views were narrowly conservative. Of more immediate import, he had a well-developed habit of command, and was at once ready to take stronger measures against Gourlay than had Smith's "feeble Administration."[21] In particular, when the legislature met in October, Maitland proposed a new law to prohibit the assembling of conventions. This measure was quickly approved, Upper Canada's rather mild equivalent of the Six Acts passed a year later in England. Maitland also refused to receive the petitions brought to him by the committee of the late convention.

Gourlay, of course, was brought to a new pitch of indignation by this course of events, and as always expressed himself violently and volubly in

E

the newspapers after hearing that the law against conventions had passed. John Strachan believed, however, that things were now falling back to a peaceful state, and that Gourlay's influence was ebbing.[22] In this opinion he was doubtless correct, although there was probably much feeling in the province that the law banning conventions was extreme.

In December 1818, however, without the knowledge or approval of the government, Gourlay was arrested and brought before a court of magistrates at Niagara under the terms of the provincial Sedition Act passed in 1804. By this Act anyone who had not lived in the province for six months and who had not taken the oath of allegiance might be arrested and required to prove that his words, actions, and conduct were not intended to promote or encourage disaffection. If he did not give proof to the satisfaction of the judge or other official before whom he was arraigned, he could be ordered out of the province. If he did not leave, he could be jailed, without bail, and tried for the offence of not leaving. If then found guilty, he could be banished. If he still did not leave, or returned without a licence, he could be put to death.[23] This act, which had originally been inspired by fear of the Irish rebels who might enter the province following the uprising of 1798, was applicable to Gourlay under a strict reading of its terms, since he had visited in the United States within the previous six months before his arrest. Also, he had not taken the oath of allegiance in the province, although he had taken it at home.

Gourlay felt the full rigour of this harsh law. He was given ten days to leave the province and when he refused was put in jail, where he remained for eight months. Finally, he was tried at the assizes in August 1819, with the Chief Justice presiding, and ordered to leave the province at once. He crossed into New York on the following day, and returned to Britain before the end of the year.

From a legal point of view the prosecution of Gourlay was within the terms of the Act of 1804. It should also be noted that the action was not instigated by the government, which apparently thought his arrest to be imprudent and inexpedient. Still, the government made no effort to discourage the action, and probably concluded that this was the surest way of getting rid of Gourlay. In their eyes he had raised up a good deal of "sullen discontent" where none needed to exist, and had given Upper Canada such a bad name at home that "the Province is considered in a state of insurrection or near it and rich Emigrants are prevented from coming out." Maitland was so determined to punish those who had co-operated with Gourlay that he refused to grant land to any members of the militia who had been involved in the convention, and in a spirit of vindictiveness dismissed all those holding militia or civil appointments who had shown any open sympathy for Gourlay, unless they abjectly recanted.[24]

Nothing could have been more absurd than to bring a charge of sedition against a man whose great ambition was to tie Upper Canada more closely to the British Empire, and who, as he said of himself, was often imprudent, sometimes foolish, but never for a moment harboured a criminal design. But to call into question the government's use of its powers and to make unfavourable comparisons of conditions in Upper Canada with those across the line was enough to damn a man in the eyes of the leaders of Upper Canada, even without Gourlay's insulting and sometimes scurrilous language. Gourlay thought it "self-evident" that her North American colonies could not "be retained to Britain for many years, on principles less free and independent than those which govern the adjoining country"; they must be given more liberal treatment or they would "fall into the arms of the United States."[25] This was meant as counsel for the prevention of such annexation; to Strachan and Maitland, it was mischievous and seditious talk. Like everyone else who criticized the existing political system, Gourlay was put down as a republican by its defenders.

In the long run, the expulsion of Gourlay proved to be a serious mistake on the part of those who had engineered and condoned it. As an organized opposition movement took form during the following decade, it turned again and again to this episode to find ammunition which could be fired at Maitland and his advisers. For instance, the Assembly consistently passed bills during the 1820's to repeal the Sedition Act of 1804, and the legislative council blindly allowed the issue to be kept alive by rejecting them just as consistently, until 1829 when the measure was finally accepted. The "Banished Briton" came to be regarded as a martyr who had been ruthlessly broken by an arrogant oligarchy; his name cropped up periodically over the next forty years as a standing proof of the evils of the government in these bad old days.

For the time being, however, the excitement died down as quickly as it had arisen. With Maitland's approval, the law banning seditious meetings, passed in 1818, was repealed early in 1820, and the newspaper publisher who had been jailed for printing Gourlay's letters and addresses was pardoned. There was some apprehension in government circles over what effect the recent agitation would have on the elections for the Assembly held in 1820, but it proved to be unwarranted. To be sure, the elections were marked by much violence, whisky and rum flowed freely, heads were broken, efforts were made to keep people from voting, and religious and national prejudices were loudly proclaimed. All this, however, was perfectly normal in an Upper Canada election, then and for years to come, and had little or nothing to do with the Gourlay episode. Although a few men who had supported or sympathized with him were returned, the new House, which had just been considerably enlarged (to forty members), proved to be tractable enough, so much so that Maitland reported himself to be well pleased with it.[26]

As the Gourlay affair subsided the attention of political and business leaders was increasingly centred on the imminent possibility of bankruptcy in the provincial government. Efforts to avoid this catastrophe were in turn partly responsible for involvement in a much larger question, a project for reuniting Upper Canada with its sister province along the St Lawrence. As events were to show, a much greater crisis than that of the early 1820's was needed before sufficient pressure could be built up to end the political division of 1791, but the whole episode was to throw much light on provincial attitudes and problems as well as to foreshadow many of the debates and alignments of the months preceding the enactment of the Union Bill in 1840.

The threat of bankruptcy arose out of the old difficulty – as old as the province of Upper Canada – of how to exist without a seaport; in particular, how to secure a fair share of the customs duties collected at Quebec on goods destined for the inland province. Such duties made up a very large proportion of Upper Canada's revenue, four-fifths, according to a joint committee of the legislature;[27] without them, outstanding obligations, such as pensions promised to disabled militiamen of the War of 1812, could not be paid, and public works could not be planned for a growing and ambitious community. Moreover, the financial situation at this time was made more difficult by the fact that the province had, since 1817, assumed responsibility for civil government charges that had earlier been paid by the British government. In short, the province was at the mercy of Lower Canada for vital revenues, while lacking any certain means to ensure their payment.

It will be remembered that an agreement, lasting only two years, had been made in 1795 providing Upper Canada with one-eighth of the duties. Afterward, the province preferred to keep a record of the goods passing through Côteau du Lac, at the boundary between the two provinces; by comparing this amount with the total imported at Quebec it was possible to arrive approximately at the upper province's share of the revenues collected there. Nevertheless, payments lagged from time to time, and Upper Canada built up considerable claims for arrears. In 1817 a new agreement was made, to last until 1819, promising Upper Canada one-fifth of the proceeds, but shortly afterward a bitter quarrel broke out in Lower Canada between the governor and the Assembly over financial control, with the result that in two successive years (1819 and 1820) the Legislature of Lower Canada made no arrangements to continue the agreement. In the hope that the money would turn up soon the Legislature of Upper Canada empowered the lieutenant-governer to borrow on this expectation. As 1821 wore on, however, and no agreement was reached with the commissioners finally appointed by Lower Canada, the financial outlook became extremely precarious. Since the government of Upper Canada could do nothing itself to break the deadlock, its only recourse was to appeal to the imperial authority. In January 1822 the legislature chose Attorney General John Beverley Robinson to proceed to England to seek the intervention of the British government.

There, Robinson found a much larger scheme afoot than the adjustment of trade relations between the two provinces – nothing less than the union of the two Canadas. This of course was not a new idea. The mercantile leaders of Montreal, who had opposed the partition of 1791, had never given up hope that political unity would be restored to the commercial empire over which they presided. Now that political deadlock had gripped the lower province, they seized the opportunity to convince the mother country that the unwise experiment in division should be quickly ended. With the end of the Montreal fur-trading empire, marked by the absorption of the North West Company into the Hudson's Bay Company in 1821, it became doubly imperative to organize for the effective exploitation of the new staples of wheat and timber. Yet the French Canadians were now both politically conscious and, under their popular leaders, especially Louis Joseph Papineau, politically organized; in the Assembly they could effectively block all plans for the commercial development of the St Lawrence and Great Lakes region. As things were, said old John Richardson of the Montreal firm of Forsyth, Richardson and Company, Canada was not worth holding; only union would "remove many impediments to the common prosperity and improvement, and make this a British instead of a foreign Province."[28]

The pleas of the mercantile leaders of Montreal and Quebec were reinforced by those of the English-speaking residents of the Eastern Townships, who had grown to number forty thousand. These people were denied adequate representation in the Lower Canadian Assembly, and were "subjected to foreign laws in a foreign language." Their growth was stunted by a legislature which openly discouraged any further English-speaking immigration into the province. Only by union could the vacant lands be occupied by an English-speaking population, and Lower Canada made into a truly British province.[29]

It happened that in the early months of 1822 the British government was receptive to these arguments. Union would not only limit the power of the French Canadians, but it would also have the effect of nullifying any tendencies toward American republicanism on the part of the upper province. What could be neater than to tie the two provinces together, in order to weaken the dangerous tendencies of each? Accordingly, a bill was prepared that provided for equal representation of each province in a united legislature (although the upper province's population was less than half that of the lower's) and for the keeping of all records of the legislature in the English language, with all debates to be held in that language after fifteen years. Membership in the legislature would be limited by a high (£500) property qualification, and the hand of the governor would be strengthened by giving him the power to appoint two members of the executive council of each province to sit in the Assembly, where they might debate but not vote. By these and other terms it was anticipated that the tide of French-Canadian nationalism would be stemmed and reversed, democratic tendencies checked, and the influence of the executive strengthened.

But the bill failed when it was introduced in the House of Commons in the summer of 1822. Opposition members objected that so important a change in the Canadian constitution should be made without consulting the people of the Canadas, and the government withdrew the bill rather than go on with it at the tail end of the session. All that the House would readily accept was the Canada Trade Bill, by which Upper Canada was guaranteed one-fifth of the duties collected at Quebec, with the promise that this proportion would be readjusted every three years according to the amount of goods brought into each province—an arrangement that lasted until the union of 1841.[30]

This sequence of events was a matter of profound relief to Attorney General Robinson. He was glad to see the union project dropped, since he had no instructions from York on the matter. In any event he had no wish for a close union with the French Canadians. On the other hand, he had got the trade bill, largely of his own drafting, which was the object of his trip.

Yet Robinson was aware that the British government might well revive the union plan after Canadian opinion had been heard, and assuming the inevitable outcry from Lower Canada there was a good chance that the bill would be amended in that province's favour. He warned his associates at York that Upper Canada might end up as a mere dependency of the lower province, and that the people of Upper Canada should hasten to express their views on union.[31]

In fact, a vigorous debate on the union was developing in each province. In Lower Canada, as expected, opinion generally followed racial lines, with the French Canadians vehemently denouncing the scheme and the English-speaking community strongly supporting it. In Upper Canada there were more uncertainties, and feelings were not so heated, but it presently became apparent that prevailing opinion was hostile to the bill, with the exception of the eastern sections of the province where interest in the improvement of the St Lawrence was strongest. As one moved west opposition to the bill mounted. Petitions revealed that certain details were specially disliked, such as the one requiring a high property qualification for members of the

Assembly (it was argued that in some counties not a single resident would be eligible); the provisions for strengthening the influence of the executive in the representative body were also attacked. The broadest objection, however, had to do with the dissimilarity of the peoples of the two provinces, who were "distinct in their origins, language, manners, customs, and religions," and would inevitably engage in bitter quarrels if required to live within one political unit.[32]

It soon became apparent, also, that, despite its sympathy and community of interest with the merchants of Lower Canada, the governing group in York shared the dislike for the bill that Robinson was expressing in London. They did not wish to pull up stakes in York, just as they were getting well settled in the little capital, or relinquish control of a government which they thought of as their own to direct. Under this government, they felt, Upper Canada had progressed more rapidly than had her sister province, and they had no wish to become involved in the quarrels that were bedevilling the latter. Moreover, an enlarged Assembly, with members from both provinces, would be quite impossible to control. As it was, the government had to use every kind of influence at its disposal to get its measures through the local Assembly; in the one proposed, the executive authority would find "all the French joined by all the radical English arrayed" against it, an accurate prophecy, incidentally, of the situation after 1841. John Strachan was also worried that the interests of the Protestant religion in general, and the Church of England in particular, would have little protection in a body that might well have a Roman Catholic majority. He believed that the union could be made acceptable only by placing the capital in Upper Canada ("on the Ottawa beyond Perth") and by giving Upper Canada a preponderance of members in the Assembly, not just an equal number. This arrangement would involve "no injustice – to make this a British Colony we must have a decided majority."[33]

It was Strachan's considered view, however, that an attempt to yoke the two provinces would fail. He realized, despite the above remark, that any terms acceptable to Upper Canada would be regarded as a great affront by the French Canadians. Schemes for political reorganization must go "much further" if "lasting tranquillity" were to be produced. He had in mind a measure "as would without any positive enactment sink the French name, their language and narrow ideas of Commerce," while sparing their feelings in the process. This magic was to be accomplished by a union of all the British North American provinces. In a general parliament "the French would be only a component part and would merge without any sacrifice of national vanity or pride &c.," by the simple device of requiring that all its written and oral proceedings, as well as those of the law courts, should be in English.[34]

Strachan's former pupil was thinking along the same lines as he continued his discussions with Colonial Office officials in London. In the hope that he could interest them in the broader scheme, Robinson drafted a plan for a general union which he submitted to the Colonial Office and which he supported in a pamphlet published in London. He argued that such a union would show to all the world, and to the United States in particular, that Great Britain was determined to protect all these colonies against aggression or infiltration. He denied that union would lead to a movement for independence, since the colonies were fully aware of the advantages of membership in the empire. There was also no danger of a movement for annexation to the United States. "More free they could not be," since they enjoyed "all the substantial advantages of independent states"; while if they joined the republic, they "would shrink into comparative insignificance as the remote sections of a territory already too far extended, and as unimportant and unfavoured members of a great confederacy in the councils of which they could expect to have little influence."

If, Robinson went on, the colonies became a distinct kingdom, under a viceroy, within the empire, perhaps the first of several that might be formed, many beneficial results would follow. They would develop a greater sense of "community of interest and feeling among themselves," have a more important role on the world scene, get away from "petty factions and local discontents," and widen the distinction between their institutions and those of their republican neighbours.[35] Here, then, in 1823, was some vision of the later Confederation and of the later Commonwealth, from a young tory lawyer from Little York.

But the plan evoked no enthusiasm within the Colonial Office, where it was quite rightly regarded as impractical because of the slow communications between the Atlantic and inland provinces. Union of the two Canadas was still the preferred solution, despite evidences of mounting opposition in the provinces. This opposition prevented any action in 1823, but in 1824 the under secretary, Wilmot Horton, tried to revive the subject. Another bill was drafted in which John Strachan, who was in England on ecclesiastical business, had a hand. When Strachan tried to safeguard what he took to be the interests of Upper Canada by adding several new conditions after the bill was drafted, it was obvious that his suspicions were as strong as ever. And like Robinson before him, he again made a plea for a general union, and again without success. Dual union also came to nothing, largely because of the unbroken front presented by the French Canadians, and the project remained in abeyance until after the Rebellions of 1837.

This outcome was a bitter blow to the majority of the English-speaking community of Lower Canada, which appeared to have lost all chance of being rescued from the French-Canadian sea in which they felt themselves to be adrift. But the people of Upper Canada showed no desire to try to save them at the risk of being engulfed themselves. The conservative governing group fully shared this sentiment, and yet, equally, shared the ambitions of the mercantile community for the commercial growth of the St Lawrence and Great Lakes region. Presently they hit on a device which seemed to avoid all difficulties: Montreal should be annexed to Upper Canada. In 1828 W. H. Merritt advised the Colonial Secretary that, although Union was opposed because of the "fear of French domination," the annexation of Montreal would "satisfy every man in the Upper Province."[36] By one stroke a large section of the English-speaking population of Lower Canada would be liberated, while the Montreal French Canadians thus acquired would be helpless; Upper Canada would have a seaport and no longer be a commercial dependency of the sister province; and the whole length of the St Lawrence needing improvement would be under one government. With a seaport, Upper Canada would be brought out of its inland seclusion, in fact, brought more fully into the British orbit, and thus more effectively detached from American influences. It was a dazzling conception, and the conservative and commercial leaders of Upper Canada could never fully understand why everyone concerned did not endorse it with enthusiasm. The idea was of course anathema to the French Canadians, and the reform movement in Upper Canada also opposed it in later years. Its advocates, however, remained loyal to it until union with all of Lower Canada was finally forced on them in 1840.

Thus the little ruling group at York had survived two threats to their position, neither of them very formidable. They had put down a highly vocal critic who had provided a focus for incipient discontent but who was too eccentric to be a very serious political opponent. They had staved off a union that would have brought to an end their own distinct political identity, but antagonism to that union was so strong in the other province that there was never much possibility of its being carried out. The results of these first trials of strength were reassuring but in no way conclusive, for more dangerous threats to their authority and policies were brewing within the province. All along, they had regarded the large American population in Upper Canada as the fundamental obstacle in the way of achieving their design for the province, and as yet they had found no answer to this problem.

It is time, then, to look more closely at the men in power at York and at the forces preparing to challenge their ascendancy.

E*

CHAPTER 6

The Family Compact
and the Alien Question

During the decade of Sir Peregrine Maitland's administration (1818-1828) Upper Canada began to move away from the simple pioneer society which marked the first generation of its history, and to manifest many signs of growth and progress. A start was made in meeting its greatest need – more population – as first a trickle and then a stream of settlers began to arrive from overseas. Essential works of public improvement, especially canals and roads, were planned and pushed forward. For the first time the province was provided with banking facilities, necessary for more diversified economic activity. Attention was given to schools, a university was projected, and the activities of religious bodies were vigorous and expanding. The leading members of the government were honest, intelligent, and energetic men, desirous of promoting the public welfare.

It should, on this reckoning, have been an optimistic, thriving community, filled with that exuberant enthusiasm so characteristic of North American frontier regions as they began to realize some of their potentialities. It had superb natural resources in its fine wheat-growing lands and in its easily exploited timber. It had a nucleus of skilled, hard-working settlers, and it was not lacking in quick-witted projectors ready to engage in new ventures. It was spared the bitter racial and cultural strife that wracked its sister province of Lower Canada.

Yet, for all this, Upper Canada was becoming an unhappy community, with deep political divisions emerging. As time went on, extravagant and demagogic debate so filled the air that the real needs of the province were often forgotten. In the year that Maitland left the province, the Assembly was captured by an organized political opposition whose members were convinced that only a fundamental alteration of the system of government could cure what they regarded as the rampant misrule of the preceding years. The province was well started down the road that led to an armed uprising which, although pitiful and even ridiculous in itself, at least revealed the abnormal and hysterical state of much of the public mind. Clearly, in so promising a situation, many things had gone badly wrong.

Our point of departure in understanding Upper Canada's descent, first into bitter and destructive political wrangling, and then into rebellion, must be some discussion of the term "Family Compact." This epithet, which came into use about 1828, had only a limited accuracy since, as Lord Durham later pointed out, its members were not all tied together by family connection, nor were they the ingrown, selfish, and reactionary group that the phrase was meant by their opponents to suggest. Nevertheless, although they often differed among themselves on many matters, they did share a common point of view on certain fundamentals which they held to tenaciously, and which they proudly proclaimed. The term has persisted, and continues to be useful to describe the relatively small, tightly knit group of men who dominated the government of Upper Canada in the 1820's and to a somewhat lesser extent in the following decade.

The members of the Compact were simply the leading members of the administration: executive councillors, senior officials, and certain members of the judiciary. They were in control of the day-to-day operation of the machinery of government. They did not have complete freedom of action, since the lieutenant-governor was the head of the administration, and could have thwarted them if determined to do so. Moreover, the lieutenant-governor's actions were always subject to review and to reversal by the authorities in London. Still, he usually came to see things the Compact's way, and London, while a more difficult problem, was far away in the days of the sailing ship. Also, the Compact saw to it that like-minded men received the lesser appointments throughout the province. As a result, little local "family compacts" emerged among sheriffs, magistrates, militia officers, customs-collectors, and others.

In one sense, there was nothing new in this situation. There had always been a small core of executive officers and judicial advisers around the governor or administrator who had largely held the reins of power. Such a group was inevitable in the old colonial system of government and in a society where relatively few men had the training and education needed for the leading government offices. Only a few malcontents, like Thorpe, who would not or could not break into the inner circle, had complained. In Maitland's day, however, the system became at once clearer and narrower, the stakes became greater, and criticism mounted. The aftermath of the war and of the Gourlay agitation, the new tasks facing the province, and the accidents of personality, all combined to form a more sharply defined image of oligarchical rule.

About half the leading members of the Compact were of the second generation of Loyalist families, relatively young men of sound education, high intelligence and proper ambition, brought up in a tradition of unswerving devotion to the King and the Mother Country. Outstanding among them were John Beverley Robinson, Christopher Hagerman, G. H. Markland and, later, John Macaulay, the last three from the Kingston area. It might be noted that these men did not always carry the Loyalist community with them. Many people of Loyalist stock were part of the opposition in the Assembly, and many more of them regularly if not invariably voted for its standard-bearers.

The remaining leaders of the Compact were men, or the sons of men, who had come out from Great Britain, usually before the end of the eighteenth century. Notable among these was the Reverend John Strachan, who was admired and respected by his younger colleagues and associates, many of whom were his former pupils. William Allan, the leading business man of the Compact, and members of the Boulton family were also representatives of this British-born group. It was frequently charged that the Compact kept the door of the club closed against newcomers from Britain, but the charge had little substance. They could not have done so if they wanted to, and they did not want to. When reliable people appeared who saw the needs of the province as the Compact did and were above pandering to the crowd, they were cheerfully accepted.

But the hard core remained Strachan and his young men, all of whom had lived in the province through the war, and had worked and fought in its defence. Those dangerous years had hardened their loyalty, and determined their views on what was sound policy. They quickly acquired positions of power after the war. Strachan was appointed to the executive council in 1815 and to the legislative council in 1820. Robinson became Attorney General in 1818, after acting in that post during the war, and was elected to the Assembly in 1820, where he led the government forces until he was appointed Chief Justice in 1829. Maitland relied heavily upon these two strong and forceful men, conservative in politics, Anglican in religion, whose qualities were soon impressed upon the whole administration. Maitland was never putty in their hands, for he too was a strong and determined man. Moreover, his advisers, as befitted their political outlook, readily accorded him the respect and deference owing to the King's representative. Each strengthened and fortified the other in the task of governing the province.

The design which Strachan and Robinson and their associates sought to impose upon the province was clearly defined, and despite the opposition which it aroused it was not an ignoble one. In its fundamentals the design stood independent of the political power and the economic advantage which its advocates might acquire for themselves by accomplishing it. Yet their power and advantage were so obviously by-products, and the means they used were so often petty, ruthless, and selfish, that their opponents can readily be excused for failing to see the design at all. And if they did, they rejected it.

The cardinal point in the design was that this pioneer North American community was and must remain an integral part of the far-flung British Empire, which they regarded as the grandest, the freest and the noblest political organization that man had ever developed. In the minds of the Compact leaders Upper Canada was not a mere "possession" of Great Britain but part of the British nation overseas, where British subjects had the same rights and obligations as at home. They had a strong sense of nationality but it was one of British nationality, and they had no desire for any other. In the modern connotation of the term, there was little that was "colonial" in their outlook. They did not kowtow slavishly to everything and everyone from the British Isles, and they vigorously defended Canadian interests, as they understood them, before the imperial authority. They could and did denounce unnecessary Downing Street interference in local affairs as vehemently as any of their opponents.

But they willingly and cheerfully conceded that the interest of the whole, in which they passionately believed, had to take precedence over that of any of its parts. From the Empire the province received vital assistance in its economic and social advancement and, even more important, protection from the enemy to the south. Outside the Empire, they would live in a grubby little backwater; within it, they were equal members of the world's proudest and foremost political community. No wonder they sometimes seemed to be more British than the King. By turns they were depressed and infuriated to see how little the British at home knew or cared about the British communities overseas, and particularly their own. Hence, they followed the course of British domestic politics with intense interest, always fearful that the anti-imperial elements at home might come to power, and cut them adrift.

The second basic tenet in their creed was an open contempt for the rising tide of democracy. In the face of it they held fast to the eighteenth-century conception of a balanced constitution, in which the popular or representative element, although essential, was only one part. The royal authority and the appointive branch (out of which something approaching an aristocracy might yet be formed) were equally vital parts of the constitution. The two councils should be in the hands of men of training, of education, and of proven loyalty. Appointed officials should as a general rule hold office for life; and they should not bend to pressures coming from the popular branch. The Compact hoped to have majority support in the Assembly, to be sure, and it sometimes did, on many although never on all questions, but they did not feel that lack of such support lessened in any way the authority which they wielded.

Government did not, in their view, derive its authority from the consent of the governed, but from the King, from history, and from religion. They believed strongly, as a third basic tenet, that there was an established church in Upper Canada, as technically there was not, and that it must be protected and supported. This was not a matter of religious prejudice or intolerance. They had no thought of trying to persecute anyone for the cause of conscience, they accepted the right of everyone to worship God in his own way, and they enjoyed good personal relations with men of other denominations. But they believed that any sound society must have a religious focus, and that meant an established church. In Upper Canada, as in any British colony, that church was the Church of England, of which the Crown was head.

The British tie, a balanced government, and an established church – these phrases go far to suggest the Compact's design for Upper Canada. But there was still another element of almost equal importance with these: economic progress. The leaders of the Compact were not rural reactionaries or tory squirearchs. They felt no antagonism to the bustling world of business. They were interested in trade, in banks, in canals, and in settlement schemes. Frequently, indeed usually, they were more imaginative and more forward-looking than their opponents in such activities, and drew therefrom much of the political support which they enjoyed in the province.

From this preliminary sketch of the outlook of the Compact's leaders, one could easily deduce how deeply they disliked and distrusted the society and government of their American neighbours. These recent enemies were still intensely anti-British, they were the source of unsound ideas and practices regarding government and religion, and they were powerful economic competitors. Upper Canada could never realize its destiny, as conceived by the Compact, unless its population was constantly kept alert to the military and ideological dangers arising out of their close proximity to the United States.

They pointed, for instance, to "the workings of faction" in New York State, "where the minds of the people were eternally kept in agitation" by candidates in their perpetual "scramble for office." They hoped that Canadians would realize the advantages of "the mildest of governments," in which they had "a due share in the formation of laws," with the costs of defence borne by "a generous Parent," the rights of property fully protected, and "a degree of liberty" as complete as that "so much boasted of by their neighbours, without the drawback of incessant party violence and political intrigue." They pointed to the alarming outcome of the New York Constitutional Convention in 1821, where universal suffrage had triumphed, "the elective principle . . . pushed to its extreme," and office-holding restricted to short terms that could only lead to corruption as politicians seized "the passing opportunity" to grasp "at the republican loaves and fishes." More generally, the whole system of republican government was put down as "contrary to the universal order of nature, from the Divinity, downwards, to the communities of the meanest insects"; it was confidently predicted that "many now living" would "see an entire disruption of the North American Federal Government"[1] – as, indeed, many did. In the meantime, it was a source of constant danger, and had to be carefully watched.

This prospect should have convinced the people of Upper Canada of the "distinguished privileges" which they enjoyed as British subjects. Yet the brute fact was that the province displayed many of the blemishes so apparent in the states to the south. The population was still overwhelmingly American in origin. In many communities the tone of the society was as "republican" and as "Yankee" as anything to be found across the lakes. Reports reached the government that the Fourth of July was sometimes celebrated with enthusiasm.[2] Inns and mills were commonly run by Americans who were said to dispense disloyal sentiments along with hospitality and flour. Even many schools and religious groups were tinged with republicanism. Obviously, if Upper Canada was to become a place where genuine British feelings could flourish, the political power of the existing American population had to be curbed, immigration from the Mother Country encouraged, and educational and religious growth directed along correct lines. The Family Compact's design for the province had to be consciously fostered; it would not come about of itself.

They went about the task with confidence and vigour. They had the machinery of government in their hands, and they had the support and encouragement of nearly all the respectable men of any standing in the province. Occasionally there was to be found a curiosity such as Colonel Nichol or Doctor Baldwin who refused to see the light, but such men were not really dangerous, and they were few. There were, of course, the upstart demagogues, as there had always been, a Thorpe, a Willcocks, or a Gourlay. But men of this type had been silenced before, and they should get even less of a hearing in the future as the province matured along sound lines.

"Another reptile of the Gourlay species" did appear, in the person of William Lyon Mackenzie, and at first he must have seemed to be of very little consequence. Of humble but fiercely proud and independent Highland background, Mackenzie had had the usual sound Scottish elementary education, supplemented in his case by voracious if indiscriminate reading and the rigorous upbringing of his Presbyterian mother. Endlessly active, extremely systematic in small matters and incurably impetuous in large ones, his nature was filled with many contradictions and one basic consistency:

he was instinctively suspicious of the great ones of this earth. He was twenty-five when he reached Upper Canada in 1820, and presently he became a partner in a general store in Dundas. A short man with a large head, it was as a "conceited red-haired fellow with an apron" that he first came to the notice of John Beverley Robinson.[3] But there was ink in Mackenzie's veins, and presently he left the store to come before the public as the editor of the *Colonial Advocate*, which first appeared at Queenston on May 18, 1824.

From the beginning Mackenzie took as his mission that of disturber of the peace. There had been too much deference to those in authority, too little plain speaking. Meanwhile, the country had been languishing "in a state of comparative stupor" while its "more enterprizing neighbours" had been thriving and prospering. He intended to stir the province out of its apathy. He charged that it would never advance as long as it was in the hands of an inactive military governor, surrounded by favourites, and represented by an Assembly which was so easily corrupted by "pensions, powers places, titles, honours and emoluments" that its habitual attitude was one of "cringing submission" to the executive. He further charged that Upper Canada's needs were not understood in England, and that the province "should be allowed a little more freedom of action, and be less subject to a distant parental control." The provincial record was in sad contrast to the vigorous administration of De Witt Clinton across the border in New York. Yet Mackenzie was no republican. He preferred "British liberty" to "American liberty" and a limited, constitutional monarchy to the "American Presidency."[4]

The Attorney General dismissed this opening blast, which included a reference to him "as the most subtle advocate of arbitrary power in the Canadas" with disdain. It was annoying to find that the province contained such "malignant and uneasy spirits," but he also knew that "the Government of Sir Peregrine [was] strong and unassailable" and that every District contained "men who would not forget the experience of former demagogues." This latest one was "too contemptible an adventurer to notice."[5]

Yet Mackenzie was both noticed and read. His little weekly sheet was the liveliest newspaper that had yet appeared in the province, and it was soon circulating far beyond the Niagara region. In November he moved across the lake to the capital at York, to report the Assembly's debates and keep the government under closer surveillance. A closer view did not improve his opinion of the manner in which the province was being governed, although he had no clear idea about what should be done to remedy matters. He spoke rather vaguely of the need for introducing the English constitution "into the colonies, in all its purity, and with such alterations as suit our local situation and scattered population." He frequently advocated the union of all the British North American colonies, with full powers over their internal affairs, a proposal, as we have seen, that Strachan and Robinson had already made. And he shared with these men a belief that the British Empire was "the greatest and wisest that ever has been," although he quickly added that *"we colonists* do not enjoy our just privileges as members of that empire." He found much to admire in the United States, but more to abhor. He was highly suspicious of its "quack systems of liberty . . . which after telling us that all men are equal, allow their votaries to buy and sell justice, and mock the ear with the language of freedom in a capital polluted with negro slavery." It would be a calamity if the colonies fell under American control, but unless more prudent men were sent to govern them and unless Great Britain developed more liberal policies for them, the colonists would be more and more attracted by the American siren.[6]

These ideas and proposals were stimulating, but of themselves would not have gained the little editor much notoriety. But a strange demon drove Mackenzie on. He could not be content with criticism of the system of government, and with suggestions for its improvement. Perhaps the demon was not so strange; perhaps it was only the journalist's normal propensity for personalities, heightened in Mackenzie's case into an extreme tendency toward scandal-mongering. At any rate, in the late spring of 1826, his paper suddenly nosedived into the depths of scurrility, indeed skirted the edges of obscenity, as it set out to invent falsehoods about the family backgrounds of leading members of the government. For instance, in commenting on the Virginia origins of the Robinsons, he asserted that they were "descended from mothers who came there to try their luck and were purchased by their sires with tobacco at prices according to the quality and soundness of the article" and that their "blood has been vitiated and syphilized by the accursed slavery of centuries." Strachan was described as a "diminutive, paltry, insignificant Scotch turn coat parish schoolmaster."[7] These vulgarities had nothing to do with political criticism; they were simply the gutter press at work. And to the credit of the reading public of Upper Canada, they did nothing to advance the cause of his newspaper. It was dying of inanition when, on the eighth of June, some young men whose families had been traduced broke into his shop, destroyed his press, and scattered the types.

It was an understandable reaction, and yet of course a foolish one. As a friend of the government leaders realized immediately, it could "be the means of affording the blackguard a sort of triumph at the expense of respectability."[8] And so it turned out. Mackenzie instituted a civil action, made use of the legal processes which he sometimes claimed were rigged against the common people, and was presently awarded damages of £625. A great victory for freedom of the press had been won, or so the tradition has come down, and soon he was back in business. With a better press, paid for by the Family Compact.

Such, then, was the Compact's first brush with the man who had declared personal war on them and who would one day try to overthrow them by armed force. Despite this misadventure, which did credit to the hearts of their sons, although the heads of the fathers might regret it, it was still hard to regard this little man as a dangerous antagonist. He was another scribbler, like Gourlay, but hardly an important political force. The fact that "such vermin," in Robinson's phrase, were loose in the province only added to the urgency government leaders felt for accomplishing their design for the province. And for all the trouble that a Scotch ink-spiller could cause, they were more concerned about another and more formidable obstacle to the development of Upper Canada as a loyal and truly British province: its large American-born population.

This, as we know, was not a new concern. It will be recalled that official policy after the War of 1812 had discouraged the further immigration of Americans into the province, that Gore had sought to do so by refusing to let them take the oath of allegiance, and that this order had been protested by the Assembly. When the dispute was referred to England Lord Bathurst tried to settle it in a dispatch intended to clarify the status of Americans in the province. He stated that Gore had been incorrect in denying Americans the opportunity to take the oath, but on the other hand the Assembly was also incorrect in believing that the mere fact of having taken that oath qualified an American to hold land in the province. A citizen of the United States was not so qualified until he had been naturalized. Bathurst went on to state that the provincial government should take steps to dispossess of their lands those Americans who had come in since the war.[9]

The naturalization procedure to which Bathurst referred had been laid down in a British statute of 1740. By this Act "Foreigners and Strangers" who had been "born out of the Ligeance of his Majesty" might be naturalized in the American Colonies after seven years' residence provided they took the oath of allegiance, an oath abhorring the "damnable doctrine" that princes excommunicated by the Pope might be deposed and murdered, an anti-Jacobite oath and, except for Quakers and Jews, received the Sacrament of the Lord's Supper in some Protestant and Reformed Congregation.

Bathurst's ruling raised so many dangerous questions that the provincial government quietly put it aside for the time being, after the Attorney General pointed out some of the difficulties which it would lead to. To begin, there was surely no legal distinction to be drawn between American citizens who had come into the province since the war and those who had entered between 1783 and 1812. The latter were just as much aliens as the former. Therefore, if the Act of 1740 was to be enforced, it would affect a very large proportion of the whole population. (In fact, it would probably be over half the population in 1818, although Robinson did not make an estimate.) Robinson doubted, however, that this Act applied to Americans who had been born before 1783, within the King's allegiance, or to their children born after 1783, since children acquired the nationality of their parents. Yet this line of argument led to the absurd conclusion that all American citizens, inside or outside the United States, who were born within its confines before 1783, or were descended from such, were still British subjects.[10] It is not surprising that the government of Upper Canada shuddered at the sight of Bathurst's dispatch, for all their dislike of the American settlers.

It was known to everyone that no attempt had ever been made to naturalize American settlers through the law of 1740, whether it applied to them or not. They had been welcomed into the province from the time of Simcoe down to the outbreak of the war; indeed, it was not always easy to distinguish them from the Loyalists, many of whom had also left the United States after 1783. The American-born had in many instances taken the oath of allegiance, since they had served in the militia, been appointed to public offices, been elected to the Assembly, and had been granted or had purchased land in large quantities. According to some estimates, well over half of the privately owned land in the province was in their hands or had been at some time. Yet, if they were to be regarded as aliens, their titles and those of people who had acquired from them would be thrown in jeopardy. Maitland and his advisers had no desire to stir up this hornets' nest.[11] Indeed, at no time during the ensuing controversy was there any intention on the part of the government of deliberately disturbing existing property relations. On the contrary, many assurances were given that these could and should be safeguarded.

Men close to the government did, however, evince a marked hostility to these people when they concerned themselves with politics. Some of them were elected in 1820, as they had been in previous Assemblies, and their presence was much disliked by Robinson and Hagerman. The main antagonist of the government, to be sure, was the unpredictable but troublesome Colonel Nichol, once again in an anti-government mood, sometimes aided by a new member, W. W. Baldwin, a doctor and lawyer from Ireland, who had lived in the province for twenty years. But "foreign importations" helped to make the House difficult to manage. Still, they were there, and had to be suffered.[12] At first, there was no thought that they could be disqualified.

The question was given a new and sharper turn in 1821 when Barnabas Bidwell won a by-election in the strongly Loyalist constituency of Lennox and Addington. Bidwell was born in Massachusetts, was educated at Yale, had served in Congress shortly after the Revolution and later in the legislature of his native state. Still later he was treasurer of the County of Berkshire, Massachusetts; in 1810 he was accused of malversation of public funds, but he disappeared before being brought to trial. In 1812 he turned up in Upper Canada, where he started a school and later took up the practice of law in Kingston. He took the oath of allegiance during the war. Gourlay's *Statistical Account* contained some useful and informative sketches from his pen. It may have been this association with Gourlay which caused John Strachan to take an instant dislike to him as soon as Bidwell's name appeared before the public. Soon after he took his seat he introduced a bill providing for the equal division of intestate estates, sufficient to damn him as "democratical" in Hagerman's eyes.[13] Certainly, he was consistently on the opposite side to Robinson and Hagerman during his weeks in the Assembly.

Shortly after Bidwell's election Robinson presented a petition, signed by 126 freeholders of Lennox and Addington, asking that Bidwell's election be declared null and void. It was urged, first, that as a refugee from American justice he was morally unworthy to sit in the Assembly and, second, that on assuming his various offices in the United States he had taken oaths abjuring allegiance to Great Britain which were not cancelled by his subsequent and, as the petitioners believed, undoubtedly insincere oath of allegiance taken in Upper Canada. In all likelihood this petition was got up on behalf of the defeated candidate, and not at the instance of the government. The government, however, was happy to see the question before the Assembly, but was not very well satisfied with the outcome. Bidwell was expelled by a majority of one vote, solely on the score of moral character, after the charges of legal incapacity were dismissed by a majority of eight votes.[14]

In the voting the Assembly divided largely along east-west lines, with the hard core of opposition to Bidwell found east of York, and his strongest support coming from the members west of the capital, where most of the American-born settlers lived. The western members could also count on much eastern support on the question of the legal capacity of Americans to sit in the Assembly. After the expulsion the Assembly proceeded to pass a bill, which became law, disqualifying from membership in their House all persons who had taken oath of abjuration against His Majesty's Government or who held office in the United States or who had committed serious felonies or other offences. It was clear that the Assembly majority regarded all other American-born residents as free of any legal incapacity.[15]

Nevertheless, when Marshall Spring Bidwell, the son of the expelled member, presented himself at the ensuing Lennox and Addington by-election, the returning officer refused to accept him as a candidate on the grounds that he was an alien. He too had been born in the United States, had come to Upper Canada with his father, and had taken the oath of allegiance there. His legal status was thus the same as his father's, except that he was not disqualified by the Act just mentioned. The Assembly promptly condemned the returning officer's action, and declared that "so far as allegiance is concerned" the younger Bidwell was "eligible to a seat in this House."[16] He was subsequently elected, and in later parliaments twice served as Speaker, in which position he led the reform forces in the Assembly.

The controversies over the two Bidwells brought the alien question fully into the open, where it remained as a first-class political issue for more than five years. The tangled nature of the question itself, intransigence on the part of the government side, a generous serving of demagoguery on the part of the opposition, and a good deal of fumbling contributed by the Colonial Office, all helped to drag out the debate.

For Maitland and his advisers there were two distinct questions, which they wished to keep separated. One concerned the security of land titles, which they were entirely willing to respect and safeguard : indeed any other course meant chaos. On the other hand, they were now completely convinced that the non-Loyalist American-born settlers who had come into the province after 1783 were aliens, without the right to vote or hold office until they conformed to British law or were accorded legislative relief. On the whole, they were on sound legal ground in so arguing, although everyone knew that their motives were essentially political in reaching this position. They considered that many of those people had been openly pro-American or at best half-hearted in the British cause during the war, while others had come in after 1815, perhaps fresh from service in the American army. It was incredible that these people should automatically have the same rights as those who had fought for the King before 1783, their descendants, and those who had emigrated from Britain.

Their opponents, however, and they included a majority of the Assembly, refused to make any such distinction between property and political rights. They asserted that a sinister campaign was under way both to despoil the American-born of their lands and to deprive them of political rights which they had long been exercising. They asserted flatly that all the American-born were British subjects, since they or their parents were born within the King's allegiance in the old colonies before 1783, and had not lost it when the independence of the United States was recognized. They stressed that these people had been welcomed into the province, had always, until the current campaign, been accepted as British subjects, and had loyally defended the province during the war. They also asserted that the Loyalists were almost equally threatened by the alien issue, since many of them had come in after 1783. This charge proved to be very effective, gaining them much support in Loyalist centres, especially in the counties immediately west of Kingston.

The issue could not be settled in Upper Canada. The legislature was dead-locked, since the legislative council accepted the view of the executive on the issues involved. And even if the legislature had been agreed, it did not have the power to settle questions of nationality and naturalization. Accord-ingly, both sides appealed to Britain for a solution. Maitland began with a request that the British government give assurances to the American-born that their property titles were safe, and he also wanted a "decisive enact-ment" excluding aliens from the Assembly. He regarded such a step as essential to the security of the province. He made no suggestions for ending the alien status of the American-born. In contrast, the Assembly asserted that if the American-born had not fully complied with the naturalization law it was only "from ignorance of the law and unavoidable difficulties," and asked the British parliament to take early steps to guarantee to them rights which they already morally possessed.[17]

London's answer to these requests was an opinion of the law officers of the Crown, based upon a recent British judicial decision on the same subject, to the effect that both the Bidwells were aliens and had no right to sit in the Assembly. All inhabitants of the United States who had willingly stayed on in that country after 1783, and accepted American citizenship, had thereby dissolved their ties of allegiance to the British Crown. The question, said the law officers, was now "finally determined."[18] Maitland was, of course, pleased with this opinion, but he saw at once that it would only increase the furore mounting in the province. In the elections of 1824, for the first time in the province's history, a clear-cut majority of anti-government men had been elected to the Assembly, who could be counted on to use every opportunity to make political capital out of the issue. Accordingly, he renewed his request that the imperial parliament "quiet the apprehensions" of the American-born in the matter of their land titles.

This dispatch was received too late in the current session for Parliament to act, but Maitland's plea was so urgent that Lord Bathurst gave permis-sion for the passing of a provincial act conferring the civil rights and privileges of British subjects on aliens living in Upper Canada, although such a measure would normally have to be reserved "for the signification of His Majesty's Pleasure," as the phrase went.[19] From the wording of this dispatch it would appear that Bathurst realized something that Maitland had never willingly faced: that any real "quieting of apprehensions" had to encompass both property and political rights. The two houses at York now had an opportunity to settle the question.

But it was soon apparent that they could not possibly agree, when left to themselves. The Assembly would have nothing but a simple declaratory Act stating that the American-born had been, were, and should always be considered to be natural-born British subjects, thus denying entirely the British ruling that they were aliens. Robinson and a small group of members, mostly from the eastern counties of the province, were overwhelmed in the voting. The legislative council, on the other hand, reflecting the wishes of the local executive, brought in a very limited measure, which stated that these people were aliens, and that they were to be afforded relief only in the matter of their property rights. The Assembly indignantly rejected this line of argument, and once again appealed to the British government to prevent a construction of the law, which was "to the prejudice, terror and disfranchisement of a large portion of the inhabitants of this Province."[20] And to rub salt in the wound, the Assembly followed up this address with another praising the American-born residents, complaining of the policy of discouraging new settlement from the United States, and asking that this policy be reversed.

Maitland was appalled to find such arguments endorsed by a large majority of the Assembly. It was but another proof that a state of feeling existed in the province that had to be counteracted. He formally enquired of his executive council whether "the recent conduct of the Assembly" did not demonstrate the political necessity of establishing a university where the "principal young men might receive an education likely to impress upon them common feelings of attachment to the Crown, and of veneration for the Church of England." Needless to say, the Council agreed.[21]

The province was now in an uproar. The Assembly saw the bitterest debates that had ever taken place in that body, with the leading antagonists being the Canadian-born, Virginia-descended John Beverley Robinson, who denounced the Americans and all their works, and the English-born John Rolph, who represented a predominantly American-born constituency in the western part of the province. Rolph, both a lawyer and a physician, was a mysteriously complex, even devious man, who during a long career on the reform side never fully revealed himself to anyone, but he was also an exceedingly clever debater, the acknowledged leader of the opposition forces at this time, and the first man to appear in the Assembly who could stand up to Robinson on equal terms.[22]

Outside the Assembly petitions were being circulated, addresses composed, and generally, tempers were running high. On New Year's Eve, at the end of 1825, as an illustration, a harmless little episode occurred which was blown up into a *cause célèbre*. A group of sixteen to eighteen members of the Assembly, fresh from acrimonious debates, attended a theatrical performance given in a local tavern by a touring company of American players.

Most of the members had found solace from their labours in the manner appropriate to the season and place. At the end of the performance and after the playing of British airs, one member, a retired army captain named John Matthews, who was a prominent critic of the government and Rolph's colleague from Middlesex County, called for "Hail Columbia," apparently as a compliment to the performers. This gesture irritated another member, who was a staunch supporter of the administration, and he sarcastically called for "Yankee Doodle," meaning that this tune should be even more congenial to the feelings of the majority side. Some loud words were exchanged, a bit of pushing was indulged in, and the members went home to a much-needed rest.

The incident should have been forgotten with the old year. When the commander of the forces and governor-in-chief, Lord Dalhousie, heard about it, however, he had his military secretary inform Captain Matthews that his conduct had been "utterly disloyal and disgraceful," ordered him to Quebec, and suspended his pension. (Matthews returned to England, and finally got his pension back, after much trouble and expense.) This harsh and stupid action, in which Maitland, by the way, was not directly involved, worked up the Assembly majority into a fury of indignation. A committee report spoke darkly of a "political inquisition," and of a campaign to "humble the independence of the legislature." If such things could happen, then indeed "this fine province" had "become a distant appendage of a mighty empire ruled by a few aspiring men with the scourge of power."[23] Perhaps Maitland wondered, when he read these words, whether one university would be enough to prepare a more respectful and respectable Assembly.

Meanwhile, with the failure of the local legislature to act, the question of alien status had once again been referred to England. This time, the Colonial Secretary obtained the passage through Parliament of an act declaring that any persons naturalized by the Legislature of Upper Canada would be entitled to sit in either House and to vote for members of the Assembly. Bathurst then sent a copy of this Act to Maitland, and at the same time detailed in very specific terms what sort of provincial enactment the British government would be prepared to approve. First, persons who had American citizenship when they came into the province were aliens there, and to be regarded as such. Second, the bill must be purely retrospective, "to relieve the actual Inhabitants of the Province"; those entering in the future must be governed by the Act of 1740. Third, persons who had already been domiciled in the province for seven years could immediately acquire the privileges of British subjects, while the others could do so after completing the seven-year term, provided each class took the oath of allegiance and renounced allegiance to any foreign state.[24]

The American-born in the province, of course, bitterly resented these terms. Under them they would have to acknowledge that they were aliens, and had been since coming into the province. For instance, those who had served in the militia during the war were now traitors in American eyes, since they fought against the country of which they were classified as citizens. Even if they had already taken the oath of allegiance, they must nevertheless repeat it now. Their names were to be enrolled in permanent registers for all to see. Despite all this, they would still be British subjects only in Upper Canada, and would once again be aliens if they visited Montreal.

Nevertheless, work on a bill based on Bathurst's terms started in December 1826, and it was eventually passed in the following February. The Assembly went about the task with very poor grace, rejecting the bill on one occasion, but finally passing it by a majority of four votes. Apparently it had to be this bill or nothing, but they clearly felt that a gun had been held to their heads. As the bill went through its final stages a campaign of mounting criticism was being organized, which culminated in the sending of Robert Randall, a Virginia-born member of the Assembly, as a delegate to England to ask for its disallowance there. In sending the bill to Bathurst, Maitland pleaded for its early approval as the only means of ending the ferment, which he said was the work of a few agitators. He argued that the great body of the American-born were satisfied with the bill.[25]

Despite this plea Maitland and his advisers had never really wanted the bill, preferring action by the British parliament or even no action at all. Still, they had faithfully followed instructions and got the bill through a most reluctant Assembly. It was therefore with intense annoyance that the local executive received word that the Colonial Office intended to disallow the very bill it had asked for, and for reasons that could command very little respect at Government House in York. Apparently Bathurst had forgotten that no naturalization bill should contain a clause requiring abjuration of allegiance, since it had always been denied, in negotiations with the United States, that British subjects could make such abjuration. Much worse than this slip, however, was the clear indication that the Colonial Office had been influenced in its decision by Robert Randall and the petition he brought with him. It was a sorry spectacle, it seemed to Compact eyes, to see the home authorities bowing to the importunities of agitators.[26]

The extent of Randall's success in London was revealed in the next set of instructions on the subject from the Colonial Office. They represented an almost complete capitulation to the point of view represented by Randall. The provincial legislature was invited to pass a new bill immediately naturalizing all persons who had at any time received grants of land from the provincial government, or who had held any public office in the province, or who had taken the oath of allegiance, or who had come in before 1820. Any of these who had already taken the oath of allegiance would not be required to do so again. Persons who had settled since 1820, and who were not otherwise covered, could be naturalized upon completing a seven years' residence.[27]

Maitland was indignant at this turn of affairs. He bluntly charged the British government with being "but imperfectly" aware of the situation in Upper Canada. At home, in Britain, naturalized subjects could not sit in Parliament or hold offices under the Crown, yet foreigners, without renouncing their American allegiance, could now enter the legislature of a province which had only recently had so much experience of wartime treason and disaffection. Maitland also felt that his superiors had treated him meanly and discourteously. They had listened to and credited an irregular petition (it should have been submitted to the Lieutenant-Governor for forwarding, according to accepted procedures), and had not given him an opportunity to comment on it, although it severely condemned his own government.[28] Maitland and his advisers felt that they needed better support than this from home if they were to govern Upper Canada effectively.

Still, Maitland had no choice but to put the new terms before the legislature, and to accept a bill based upon them. The bill avoided any description of the American-born residents as aliens; it simply stated that they were to be "admitted and confirmed in all the privileges of British birth." The bill also declared that property could not be disturbed on the ground that it was held or derived from aliens. Although dissatisfied with some features of the bill, the British government confirmed it, rather than see the controversy continue.[29] In effect, the alien question as a leading political issue had been ended, although it cropped up occasionally for several years to come, since many American-born residents still neglected to take the oath of allegiance and were frequently challenged at election time.

Bitter exchanges marked the last stages of the controversy, as both sides realized that Maitland, the executive council, and the conservative group generally, had suffered a sharp and humiliating defeat. It was a defeat with important political consequences. The reformers, as the government's opponents were now coming to be called, had all along realized that votes were the essential stake in the contest, and they never let the American-born residents forget who had secured their rights and their property. On the whole, the latter were suitably grateful, and their votes became the largest single prop of the growing reform movement. It was no coincidence that, in the elections for the Assembly following immediately after this controversy, the Family Compact and their supporters suffered a resounding defeat.

The leaders of the provincial government were most exasperated by the outcome of the alien controversy. Still, there was no cause for despair if

Upper Canada were to receive a sufficient influx of loyal immigrants from the Mother Country who could counteract the influence of the unreliable American population. We must turn now to see what efforts were made in the 1820's to satisfy the province's greatest need, more people; how the government superintended the settlement process; and how these matters, too, became enmeshed in partisan political debate.

CHAPTER 7

Settlement and Land Policy
in the 1820's

In the decade following the end of the Napoleonic Wars the western world's greatest folk movement of modern times was slowly getting under way. At first thousands and then tens of thousands of people left the shores of Europe to find new homes across the seas. Later the annual exodus would be numbered in the hundreds of thousands and in the quarter-century before the First World War it would reach the astonishing figure of well over a million. The exiles sought new countries wherever these might be found, whether in Australasia, South Africa, or South America, but the great majority of them made directly across the Atlantic to North America. The United States received most of these migrants, and so experienced a mighty enhancement of its political, economic, and military power, but the British colonies to its north were also swept onward toward nationhood by their share of this great human tide. Upper Canada, receiving more immigrants than any other British colony, thus shared vitally in one of the great epics of the nineteenth century.

The tide was slow in reaching into Upper Canada, and we shall see only its first stages in this chapter, and indeed in this book. It did not attain its first crest until the early 1830's, and the first full flood came later, in the 1840's and 1850's. But some of the problems attending immigration from overseas were first faced, if not solved, in this early period of trial and error, and some of the groundwork was laid for later progress.

For a time, many continued to hope that the province's need for more population could be met by a renewal of the American inflow. In 1826, for example, the Assembly deplored the fact that "many thousands of families, with wealth and industry" were moving out of the eastern states into "the western territory of the United States" instead of into Upper Canada where they might have come if they had not been discouraged by government policy.[1] But Sir Peregrine Maitland held strongly to the view that "the speedy settlement of the Colony however desirable is a secondary object compared to its settlement in such a manner as shall best secure its attachment to British Laws and Government."[2] In fact, this debate was becoming somewhat academic, since Americans were now bypassing Upper Canada in favour of the western states and territories that had lately been freed of the Indian threat. It was obvious that the further peopling of the province would have to depend largely upon recruits from abroad.

Indeed, many thousands of people had been leaving the British Isles since the end of the Napoleonic Wars. Under desperate postwar conditions unemployment had reached heights never seen before, wages had gone steadily downward, and poor rates had become unbearably heavy. Many influential observers were now convinced that the dire forecast of Thomas Malthus, announced some time earlier, that population would increase faster than the food supply, was already being borne out. The suffering masses began to move out, and the government was now ready to encourage the exodus of what was regarded as a "redundant" population.

An emigration fever gripped Britain. The subject was discussed interminably in Parliament. The leading reviews gave it prominent attention. Books tumbled from the presses, and soon there was an extensive literature on the subject. Notably there were the writings of Morris Birkbeck, an Englishman of some substance who brought a number of his countrymen out to Illinois shortly after the war ended. In 1817 he published his *Notes on a Journey from the Coast of Virginia to the Territory of Illinois* and in the following year his *Letters from Illinois* appeared. These books made the attractions of the western prairies well known to British as well as European readers. Birkbeck was soon followed to America by scores of travellers who, on their return, brought out books discussing the advantages and disadvantages of moving to the New World. As a rule, these writers devoted most of their space to the United States, but they usually gave at least a few pages to the Canadas, if only to provide the inevitable description of Niagara Falls. Some, however, spent the larger part of their North American tour on the British side. Presently there was a vigorous debate over the respective merits of the United States and the British provinces.

Some writers followed Birkbeck in dismissing the latter as of little account in comparison with the flourishing republic. An Upper Canadian newspaper denounced these "exaggerated and even false accounts" that were luring British subjects into a country "the *avowed* enemy" of their native land.[3] In most of the books, however, the provinces received high praise, and their advantages were prominently displayed for intending emigrants. The land was fertile, plentiful, and easily obtained. Taxes were lower than in the United States, since the mother country paid for colonial defence and contributed to the support of the civil government. The winter climate was not nearly as cold, especially in Upper Canada, as was commonly thought at home, while the summer climate was much healthier than that of the western prairies. One could get to Upper Canada by way of the St Lawrence and the Lakes, or up the Hudson and the Erie Canal (after 1825), without the long overland trip needed to reach the American west. Upper Canada had all the advantages of a new country, without the defects to be found in the republican states. In it one could enjoy the familiar British laws and institutions, without the tithes, the game laws, the high taxes, and the stratified class system that bore so hard on the poor and the middling people in Britain. At the same time the provinces were free of the blot of slavery and of the political corruption to be found in the republican portion of North America. For those with patriotic feelings there was the supreme advantage that one could still remain a British subject, and avoid contributing to the strength of a country that was emerging as a dangerous rival of the mother land.

These were only a few of the arguments to be found in the dozens of travel books published in the decade or so after 1815. They did much to make the British public more aware of Upper Canada and to advertise its potentialities to people who were contemplating emigration. Yet the impact of these arguments was slow in being felt. To the consternation of British patriots emigrants who freely decided to leave, and who could finance themselves, continued for several years to go to the United States in far larger numbers than to the colonies. Migration followed established trade routes, and many more ships left British ports for New York and other American ports than for Quebec. The American-bound ships also tended to be more comfortable and better appointed. Opportunities for the man with a small amount of capital were still thought to be better in the republic than in the provinces. Indeed, patriotic considerations appear to have had very little influence on people who made the momentous decision to emigrate. Even those who were in no way disaffected or discontented at home were ready to settle in a foreign country if the material prospects seemed to be best there, while many, especially from Ireland, left in such a bitter mood that they were determined never again to live under the British flag.

Sometimes, to be sure, British immigrants who landed in the United States eventually went on to Upper Canada, after encountering personal disappointments or discovering that they did not like American ways. James Buchanan, for many years the British consul at New York, made a practice of meeting incoming ships with the purpose of steering passengers on to the provinces. In particular, it grieved him to see his fellow Irish Protestants lost to the empire simply because they knew nothing of the opportunities in Upper Canada. After some correspondence with Lieutenant-Governor Gore in 1816 and 1817, he convinced the latter to agree to receive people of this class who could be persuaded to go on. Enough of them did so to form the

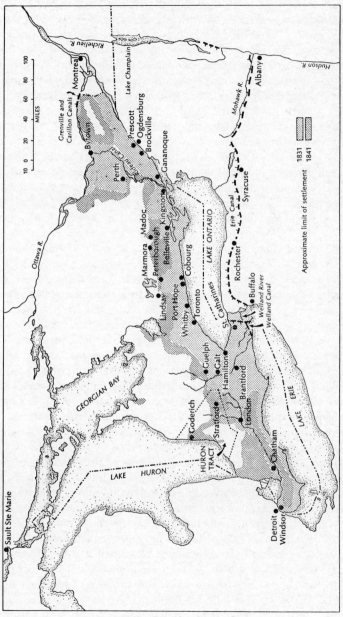

4: *Upper Canada about 1841*

nucleus of settlement in the townships of Cavan and Monaghan. Buchanan continued his missionary work, with less success, for several years.[4] On the whole, however, the British provinces lost more people than they gained in this sort of exchange, since a consistently larger number went on to the United States after first landing at Quebec or Saint John.

With the tide of voluntary emigration moving strongly toward the United States, Upper Canada for several years depended heavily upon various government schemes aimed at assisting or subsidizing particular groups to leave the British Isles and settle in the colonies overseas. Already, as previously mentioned, a number of Scottish peasants had come out under government auspices to form the Perth settlement near the Rideau River. In 1820 they were followed by about two thousand more Scots, this time unemployed weavers and their families from Lanark and nearby counties, who were assisted in various ways by the British government, and who also settled in the Rideau district. But the concept of assisted emigration gained its most persistent supporter when Robert Wilmot became Under Secretary of State for the colonies in 1822.[5] An ardent advocate of emigration as a cure for the evils afflicting Britain, he was equally enthusiastic about the colonies as a destination for the emigrants. He believed that the tie between the mother country and the colonies would grow stronger and be of mutual advantage to both, if the surplus population of the one were transferred to the empty regions of the other. It was a project well worth spending money on; not only would it alleviate present misery but it would strengthen the empire for the future. As it turned out, Parliament was never very enthusiastic about Wilmot Horton's schemes, and eventually turned against them altogether. It was hard to prove that assisted emigration had any real effect upon conditions at home, and it seemed to be very expensive for the number of people moved. Nevertheless, the idea was given a limited trial, with the result that Upper Canada received a few thousand settlers when it badly needed them.

The condition of the poor was worse in Scotland than it was in England, but it was worst of all in Ireland. There it was so shocking that the tumult and open violence already endemic in several counties threatened to blossom into a serious political uprising. It occurred to the British government that if a number of people in the most troubled districts were offered a free passage to Upper Canada and assistance in getting established on the land there, not only would Ireland be quieted but the emigrants would become good subjects when they had a fair opportunity to get on in the world. In 1823 the task of superintending such a scheme was offered to Peter Robinson, who was in London with his brother, the Attorney General, at the time of the union discussions. Robinson accepted the commission, and was soon in southern Ireland taking the names of those who wished to make the trip. At first he encountered some suspicion among people who thought it might be a device for transporting them to the penal colonies. Before long, however, he had more names than he could accept. Nearly six hundred, all but ten of them Roman Catholics, were chosen and sent to Upper Canada, where they were located between the Perth settlement and the Ottawa River.

Two years later Peter Robinson brought out another and larger contingent of Irish settlers, some two thousand, most of whom were placed north of Rice Lake. Here, around the new village of Peterborough, named after him, a flourishing community almost immediately sprang to life where only a few scattered settlers had lived before. Nearly all of the newcomers were young farmers and their families, who with some assistance from the government were soon at home in the backwoods of Upper Canada. When Sir Peregrine Maitland visited them in the following February he found them full of gratitude for their removal from the misery of their former existence. The government had been right in believing that they would prove to be peaceable and useful subjects when they had a chance to make an honest living. They were even said to be living peacefully with their Irish Protestant neighbours – surely the acid test.[6]

From the point of view of the emigrants themselves, and of Upper Canada, the two Irish settlements were highly successful, especially the second one. But the British parliament, after an extensive review of the whole subject by parliamentary committees in 1826 and 1827, concluded that they had cost too much to be repeated. In any event such schemes were not needed to induce the redundant population of Ireland to emigrate, since many thousands were leaving every year without government help. The fact that nearly all of them were going to the United States was of little moment to members of parliament who were more concerned with the state of the budget than with imperial projects.

Although direct parliamentary aid thus ended, other forms of local and indirect assistance were used in the 1820's to bring people out to Upper Canada. In some instances private individuals of some standing who had themselves decided to emigrate gathered together a few score or more of their less fortunate neighbours and shepherded them across the Atlantic. Sometimes landowners who were anxious to clear their estates of useless tenants contributed to pay the expenses of those willing to leave. English parishes eager to escape the burden of poor rates similarly assisted the destitute toward a new life in Upper Canada or elsewhere in America. The government allowed pensioners to commute their pensions for land grants in the colonies, an unfortunate experiment, as it turned out, since most of these men were too worn out or otherwise unfitted for the hard work of pioneer farming. More successful was the plan which allowed army and

F

navy officers to sell their commissions in return for land. It provided Upper Canada with men of capital, education, and ability who quickly exerted an influence in the province out of all proportion to their numbers.

Some of these forms of assistance, particularly the last one mentioned, persisted into the following decade. After about 1825, however, the un-assisted emigration of private individuals emerged as a far more important factor in the settling of Upper Canada. By this time a growing number of farmers, professional people, indeed, people of every walk of life, were plan-ning to move out, not because they were destitute, but because they felt themselves to be steadily slipping, unable to maintain, let alone improve, their current scale of life. Often they were more concerned for their children than for themselves. They decided that it was wiser to sell out everything, buy passage to America, and use the remainder of their savings to make a fresh start there. Whereas most of the assisted emigrants came from Scot-land and Ireland, a large proportion of the unassisted settlers came from England. By the end of the 1820's the movement was well under way, and it reached its high point for this period in 1831 and 1832, when people poured into Upper Canada at an unprecedented rate.

On the whole, the tale of British emigration to Upper Canada does not have the dark hues to be found in some other phases of the population move-ment to North America. For all, of course, it was a dangerous gamble, which many did not win. Some, especially the paupers and destitute on the over-crowded timber ships, died of disease on the long and difficult ocean voyage. Others injured themselves on their first days in the woods with an unfamiliar axe. Still others could not stand the work or the loneliness of farming in the bush, and drifted away to the little towns or across the line, never realizing their dream of becoming independent freeholders. Some who found work on the canals were killed by falling rocks or by gunpowder blasts, or died of fever. Most of them, however, quickly became accustomed to their new surroundings, and set about their new tasks with cheerfulness and determination. It was not very hard to feel at home in a province where many of them already had relatives and friends, and where familiar political, legal, and religious institutions and practices existed. For all the novelty and the strangeness of the new land, they were not uprooted in the sense that central or even western European immigrants were when they came to America. They were welcomed by the residents and by the provincial government, and they were free to take part in its social and political life, as equals, without any of the barriers that faced other immigrants in other times and places. They soon made their impact upon the province, as will be seen in later chapters.

While this population movement was getting under way, it was obvious to every informed person, whether in Upper Canada or in Britain, that basic changes had to be made in land policies if the province was to be efficiently prepared to receive a growing immigrant population. Past regulations and practices had proved to be hopelessly inadequate and unsatisfactory. For over thirty years land policies had sought to accomplish nearly every imaginable purpose except that of encouraging compact and effective settlement. Land had been used as a means of rewarding various classes of persons who had a claim upon the government, such as loyalists, ex-service men, executive councillors, judges, and others. It had been used as a payment for services rendered, as in the case of surveyors, who for many years were paid in land rather than cash. Since many of these people could not possibly use all the lands they had received, they left them in a wild state or sold them, often for a song, to speculators who amassed huge holdings. Yet the speculators in turn could not sell their lands profitably, partly, at least, because of the government's policy of discouraging American immigration. More notoriously, land was used as a means of financing and supporting various public projects, present or future: defraying the cost of government, supporting "a Protestant clergy," providing for schools and colleges, and building roads. Hence, millions of acres were reserved throughout the province, not to be alienated until they would bring a sufficient price to accomplish the intended purpose. That is, the government was the biggest speculator of all, holding back lands until the labours of nearby settlers had increased prices. By 1824 some eight million acres of land had been granted to private individuals, of which a little over three million acres were occupied, and of this only about half a million acres were under cultivation, leaving almost five million acres being held for speculation. The various reserves amounted to more than three million acres.[7]

It will be recalled that since the time of Simcoe the basic land-granting system had been one of making free grants of two hundred acres to ordinary settlers on which fees had to be paid when patents were issued. The applicant was required to reside on his land, and to fulfil certain settlement duties before he was eligible for his patent. In fact, however, little attempt had been made to enforce these duties by officials who were anxious to receive their fees. Thus once again land fell into the hands of people who did not use it.

The result of all this was that by the start of the 1820's a small population of some one hundred thousand was sprinkled over an extensive area stretching for five hundred miles along the St Lawrence and Lake Ontario and Lake Erie. These people lacked adequate means of keeping in touch with one another, religious and educational activity faced almost insuperable obstacles, and it was difficult to get produce to market. It was a primitive society, with few of the amenities of civilization, in which an almost brutalizing amount of work often brought little return. The price of land remained low, and that which had been easily acquired was easily given up. The geography of the province partly explained the dispersion of settlement, since water communication along the Lakes made it relatively easy to take up the front townships at an early period, but land policies had also been heavily responsible.

Discontent with provincial land policy was voiced soon after the end of the war. In 1817 when the Assembly declared its opposition to the policy of discouraging American immigration, it was also ready to pass resolutions declaring the Crown and Clergy Reserves to be "insurmountable obstacles to the forming a well connected Settlement," and asking that these reserves be opened to settlement by putting them up for sale.[8] More comprehensive evidence of widespread resentment against the results of provincial land policies was revealed in the answers to Robert Gourlay's queries later in that same year. When asked what was most retarding their improvement, the township meetings gave prominence, as already noted, first, to the amount of land in the hands of absentee owners and, second, to the land locked up in Crown, Clergy, and other reserves. Gourlay himself was probably never more closely in tune with public opinion than when he wrote that "hitherto, public land has been disposed of in a way which has at once sunk its value and prevented its improvement." He also reflected a commonly held sentiment when he attributed the more rapid growth of the neighbouring states to the superiority of American land policy.[9]

As a matter of fact, those in authority were already well aware that the practices of the past were unsatisfactory. Lord Bathurst indicated as much when in 1815 he ordered that the size of the grant to be made to an ordinary applicant be reduced from two hundred to one hundred acres, on the ground that the smaller amount was all that the average farmer could effectively use. A year later he informed Gore that the British government would support any legal measures taken to resume large grants that remained uncultivated. Gore himself declared in 1817 that the whole system of free grants had failed and should be ended.[10] Men in or close to the provincial government, such as the two Robinsons, were proposing changes.

But Sir Peregrine Maitland was the first lieutenant-governor to make a serious attempt to improve land-granting procedures. He ordered that every recipient of land, even Loyalists and military claimants, must erect a habitable house and fence five acres in every hundred before he could receive a patent. He raised fees, both to increase revenue and to discourage application for more land than could be used. (Indigent settlers could, however, receive fifty acres free of all charges.) And he narrowly interpreted earlier promises of land made to militia veterans of the recent war, since such grants usually went to men who already had land.[11] More important, Maitland exerted pressure to secure a more effective tax on wild lands, intended to force speculators to put up their lands for sale at current prices.[12]

Maitland's efforts showed a genuine desire to grapple with the land problem, yet they had little real effect while they irritated many elements in the province. The wild-land tax could do little to force a speculator to sell his land when there were few buyers, and at a time when the government was busily concluding treaties with the Indians to open more land to settlement and also making arrangements for the sale of a large part of the reserves. There was simply too much land on the market for any effective stand to be taken against the speculators. And when tax-delinquent land was sold, it went for low prices to men who bought it as an investment. In other words, the wild-land tax often played into the hands of the speculators.[13] Among those who were ruffled were the children of Loyalists who muttered at being required to improve their lands, like ordinary grantees, and militia veterans who talked of broken promises. Reformers in the Assembly, although they supported the wild-land tax in principle, objected to the feature of the Act that placed the proceeds in the hands of tory magistrates for local road improvement. Moreover, the critics of the government were gradually broadening their criticism of land-granting procedures, demanding more information about the amount of the fees collected and the way these were used. They would never be satisfied with a system that left control in the hands of the executive.

Nevertheless, both the provincial and imperial governments were already preparing for a more fundamental attack on the land problem, one that would go beyond the improving of procedures, the enforcement of settlement duties, and the taxing of wild lands. There were several motives behind the approach toward a new policy. It was hoped that attempts by the Assembly to determine or to deflect the course of policy might be disarmed or forestalled. It was further hoped that new arrangements might yield a larger revenue from provincial lands, thus lessening or ending the British government's need to make financial outlays and at the same time making the provincial government more independent of the Assembly and more efficient in directing economic progress. Finally, the British government was moving toward a uniform policy for all the colonies, intended to accelerate emigration and development throughout the settlement regions of the empire.

The first impulse toward change came from the government leaders at York, particularly John Strachan and John Beverley Robinson, who were dissatisfied with the administration of the Crown and Clergy Reserves, two-sevenths of all the surveyed lands in the province. The leasing policy, followed since the beginning of the century, had clearly failed. Relatively few leases had been taken, and payments on these were heavily in arrears. With respect to the Clergy Reserves, Strachan was at first inclined to lay the blame to lax administration, and in 1819 at his instigation they were placed under the supervision of the Clergy Reserves Corporation, made up solely of dignitaries of the Church of England. Strachan hoped that the Corporation would be able to protect the Reserves more effectively from outside attack, and also develop them more energetically and more fruitfully than the Land Board of the executive council had done. In both these hopes he was to be disappointed.[14]

Maitland and Robinson concentrated their attention on new arrangements for the Crown Reserves. From the beginning of his administration Sir Peregrine had fastened on "the vast political importance" of these Reserves, as a bulwark of executive authority and as the "best source of future influence and link of attachment between the Province and the Mother Country"; he noted that it "had always been a favourite object with the Democratic party to get rid of the Crown Reserves."[15] Soon he was anxious to make more effective use of these lands as the only way out of a dilemma that loomed ever larger before the provincial government. On the one hand the British government was forever preaching the need of economy and steadily reducing the amount of its financial contribution to the support of the provincial government. On the other hand the Assembly was gradually asserting more sweeping claims to vote and appropriate all revenues raised in the province. In its growing need for more money to further economic and educational advancement the government saw the danger of falling into greater reliance on the Assembly and of having to concede claims which it regarded as both unconstitutional and improper. Everything pointed to the need for more revenue from the Crown Reserves than was brought in by the leasing policy. Some form of sale was apparently the answer.

While officials were coming to this conclusion at York, a series of events with a different point of origin was leading to a similar view in London. Here, the active agent was the old unsolved question of the claims of various residents of Upper Canada for losses and damages suffered during the war. It will be recalled that the failure to pay these was a source of considerable discontent in the years after 1815. At the close of 1820, in an effort to bring this matter more forcibly before the British government, spokesmen for the claimants appointed three prominent men in Great Britain to act for them. Two of these men, for various reasons, took little part in the affair, but the third threw himself heart and soul into it. He was John Galt, a well-known Scottish novelist, who was anxious for the fee which a successful result would bring him. A vigorous, outspoken man, quite unawed by government bureaucrats, he at once put his fluent pen to work demanding action on behalf of his clients.

After much discussion the British government agreed to pay a proportion of the claims, but insisted that any further contributions would have to be matched equally by the provincial government. At the same time it was hinted that the British government might be more generous, if the provincial government would agree to assume a larger share of the cost of its civil expenses.[16] It soon became clear, however, that financial weakness made it impossible for the government of Upper Canada either to raise money for the claimants or to pay more of its own way. At this stage Galt began to wonder whether the natural resources of the province might be made to yield a revenue to be used for one or both of these purposes, and a discussion with Alexander Macdonell, now the Roman Catholic Bishop in the province, convinced him that this approach was worth pursuing. Soon he was again belabouring the Colonial Office officials with criticisms of current land-granting practices and with suggestions for the sale of the Crown and Clergy Reserves.

As it happened, his importunities came at just the right time. The provincial leaders were casting about for a new policy toward the Reserves, while the British government was open to any reasonable suggestion that would lessen its annual appropriation for the support of the civil expenses of the colony. Consequently, when Galt suggested the formation of a land company, which would buy up the Reserves, he found Lord Bathurst and Wilmot Horton very willing to explore the proposal. Land companies had frequently been used to develop new regions in the United States, one had recently been formed to colonize in Australia, and perhaps the time had come to use them in the Canadas. Galt had connections with London capitalists, whom he was given permission to approach to see whether the necessary investment funds might be available for the project. In a short time he had a scheme worked out which formed the basis of an agreement made between Lord Bathurst and the subscribers, late in 1824. A company was to be formed, to be known as the Canada Company, with a subscribed capital of £1,000,000 sterling. The Crown would convey to the company all of the Crown Reserves and one-half of the Clergy Reserves laid out in the surveyed townships before the date of March 1, 1824, excepting certain lots which had been previously granted, leased, or otherwise occupied. In return, the company would make specified annual payments to the Receiver General of the province and give an annual accounting of its operations to the Lieutenant-Governor. Five commissioners were to go to Upper Canada to establish the price to be paid for the lands. Lord Bathurst undertook to secure necessary enabling legislation from Parliament and a royal charter.[17]

Galt must have been disappointed to note that nothing was said about remuneration to those claiming war losses, nor did the Canada Company ever have any direct or indirect connection with this subject which had helped to bring it into being. (Partial compensation was later extended to the claimants by the British and provincial governments.) Galt was now so enthusiastic about the Company, however, that he transferred all his energies into the work of getting it organized. He received an appointment as Secretary and as one of the five Commissioners and early in 1825 proceeded with his colleagues to Upper Canada to make an inventory of the lands to be acquired by the Company and to determine the price to be paid for them.

At this stage Sir Peregrine Maitland and his advisers viewed the arrangements with the Canada Company with more than a touch of suspicion. They were ready, as already suggested, to contemplate new plans for the Reserves, but they were rather out of countenance at the British government's swift proceedings taken without benefit of any advice from York. The members of the Family Compact were always apprehensive of Downing Street brainstorms that were visited upon them unheralded. Maitland had also formed an unfavourable impression of Galt, from the latter's impulsive correspondence with the Colonial Office, and this impression was not improved by personal contact. As on so many other occasions, however, the most formidable figure to be reckoned with proved to be the Venerable John Strachan. When the commissioners submitted their report, calculating that 1,384,013 acres of Crown Reserves and 829,430 acres of Clergy Reserves should be conveyed to the Company, and that an average price of 3s. 6d. (provincial currency) an acre should be paid for these lands, Strachan went immediately into indignant action. In his opinion this price was far too low as the Clergy Reserves contained some of the most valuable lands in the province. The government realized that Strachan's allies, especially the bishops in the House of Lords, were so powerful that there was no choice but to capitulate. It was decided that the Clergy Reserves should be withdrawn from the transaction; instead, the Company would receive a block of one million acres of land (later increased to 1,100,000 acres, to allow for swamps and ponds) in the western part of the province, recently acquired from the Indians. This soon became known as the Huron Tract.

With this adjustment made, other difficulties were soon ironed out, and the charter was issued in August 1826. By the final terms the Company was to pay a total of £344,375 7s. 2d. sterling for the Crown Reserves and the Huron Tract, but it was to be allowed to withhold one-third of the price of the latter and devote this money to public works and improvements in the Tract. The Company was to make annual payments to the provincial government over a period of sixteen years (1827-1843), beginning with £20,000, then ranging from £15,000 to £19,000, and concluding with eight payments of £20,000 each. The following expenses were to be met out of this money, with the balance to be at the disposal of the provincial government: £8,500 for the civil establishment, replacing the annual grant from the British parliament, which would now cease: £1,000 as an annual grant toward the building of a college; £400 as an annual salary to the Roman Catholic bishop and £750 for the support of Roman Catholic priests; £750 for the Presbyterian clergy in connection with the Kirk of Scotland; £400 as a pension to Colonel Talbot as a reward for his exertions in settling the province; and £2,566 3s. 8d. over a period of seven years as compensation for officers of the land-granting department who were no longer to receive fees under new regulations, but who would still have duties to perform.[18]

John Galt, as Secretary and soon Superintendent of the Company, left England in October 1826 to inaugurate its activities, accompanied by an old Scottish literary friend, William "Tiger" Dunlop, who was to hold the post of Warden of the Forests. Galt had in his pocket a letter from John Strachan, which must have done nothing to make the ocean voyage more enjoyable. It was Strachan's advice that the Canada Company should "support the Colonial authorities and never . . . take side against them." Although Galt was warned "never to meddle in Colonial politics," at the same time he was advised to rely entirely upon Robinson, Strachan, and their friends. Their assistance would be vital, but would not be forthcoming unless Galt confided in them and in them only.[19] At least Galt could never plead ignorance of the terms needed for happy relations with the Family Compact.

Nevertheless, Galt approached his tasks with confidence and in high spirits. On his way to the province he stopped at the offices of the Pulteney Estate and the Holland Land Company, in western New York, both of which had been carrying on large settlement enterprises for several decades. From their officers he received a wealth of practical information, out of which, allowing for local variations, he formed "a system of management applicable to the Canada Company."[20] Soon he and Dunlop were tramping through the forests, planning roads and other improvements, founding the town of Guelph and, generally, making plans to attract buyers to the Company's lands.

Galt had a wonderful time; he went at the work with energy and with imagination, but his career in Upper Canada proved to be a brief one. Part of the trouble was that he failed to follow the spirit and the letter of Strachan's advice with sufficient faithfulness, with the result that there was soon a complete break in personal relations between him and Sir Peregrine. That cold, punctilious proconsul apparently regarded the high-spirited novelist as a thoroughly unsound character. Indeed, Maitland and his advisers tended to regard anyone of independent mind, who went his own

F*

way, in this light. More immediately important, however, was the fact that Galt lost the confidence of the Company directors in London, who felt that he was spending too much money for the returns he was realizing. Profits would inevitably be slow in the early stages of such an enterprise, but the directors refused to face this fact. Galt was unceremoniously replaced. Later on the post was given to a man named Thomas Mercer Jones, who became a son-in-law of John Strachan. Henceforth, there was little friction between the Canada Company and the provincial government. For a time the Company continued to face heavy financial weather, but with increased immigration after 1830 its affairs took a turn for the better, and for the rest of its long history, extending down into the 1950's, it proved to be a profitable investment for its shareholders.

How useful it was to Upper Canada is, however, another matter, one on which there is still much difference of opinion. Many people at the time, and later, believed that it brought a salutary vigour to land settlement. It brought into play larger amounts of capital than had been available before, for the building of roads, bridges, and other improvements; it advertised Upper Canada with a new effectiveness; and it attracted large numbers of settlers into the province who might otherwise have gone to the United States. On the other hand, it was argued that its improvement program was often badly planned and directed, that it sold its lands at too high a price, and that, in the Huron Tract, it became a powerful and sometimes tyrannical overlord, holding in its hands the fate of thousands of struggling farmers. Since no careful and intensive study of the Company's operations has yet been made, it is hard to pronounce definitely for one side or the other in this dispute, especially when there are obvious facts to support each. It seems to be clear, however, that many of the accomplishments claimed for the Company would have come to pass without it, in the quickening economic climate of the early 1830's, while the financial buttressing which it provided for the executive branch intensified the political struggle of the years before the Rebellion.

The emerging opposition forces in the province were antagonistic to the Company from the beginning. Mackenzie disliked the idea of a group of English stockholders profiting from the labours of the Canadian farmers, and argued that if American land-granting practices were followed the Reserves could quickly be sold without the assistance of the Company.[21] Complaints of this kind grew in number and in volume over the next dozen years.

In the same period that the Canada Company was being established, the provincial government adopted a new system for granting the remaining Crown Lands. As already indicated, the old system of making free grants upon the payment of fees was disliked by nearly everyone who had any connection with it. It opened the door to charges of favouritism and it provided opportunities for speculation. Settlement duties were either ignored or evaded. At the same time the system brought in little revenue, a matter of particular concern to the economy-minded British government, which was looking for ways of reducing the cost of colonies. There was general agreement that a plan for selling the Crown Lands would be preferable in every way to the system of free grants, which was in any event a misnomer, since the scale of fees had been steadily increased. Accordingly, in 1825 Lord Bathurst proposed the adoption of a sales system which had been used in New South Wales and which he hoped to extend to all the colonies. After making some changes to fit local circumstances the Government of Upper Canada agreed to this plan, and put it into operation in 1826.

In the new system the vacant Crown Lands in each district were evaluated and a scale of minimum prices in each was established. Lands available for sale were then advertised in the newspapers, and by other means, with the minimum (or "upset") price stated, and to be sold to the highest bidders. Purchasers were to pay in instalments. A Commissioner of Crown Lands was appointed, the first being Peter Robinson, who was to make detailed reports to the provincial government, but who was to be directly responsible to the British government. Loyalists and military claimants would continue to receive free grants, as before, and there was a provision for grants to poor settlers on a quit-rent basis. Otherwise, all lands would henceforth be sold, with the proceeds to go into the provincial treasury. As already mentioned, officers who had hitherto received fees were to be compensated out of the payments made by the Canada Company.

This sales system brought Upper Canada closer to American practice, yet unfavourable comparisons continued to be made for many years to come. Payment in instalments was in effect a credit system, opening the way to over-ambitious purchases and burdensome debts, while in the United States sales were on a strictly cash basis. Comparisons of price could never be very exact, but it was generally believed that equivalent lands cost much more in the province. Particularly irksome was the lack of adequate land-office facilities, partly a result of the dispersed nature of the population. Very often a prospective buyer had to journey a great many miles to a land office, and then wait several days for the sale to commence. As a rule, offices across the line were closer to the lots up for sale and used simpler and better understood procedures. In consequence, contemporary observers continued to point to the more efficient land policy of the United States as the reason why Upper Canada was steadily losing settlers to that country.[22] Such criticism was often exaggerated, since Canadian policy was neither as bad nor American as good as such sharp contrasts suggested, and the great drawing power of the United States would still have operated if the former had been much better. Nevertheless, the rapid growth of the American west was convincing proof to many in the province that land-granting procedures were still hopelessly inadequate.

The new system, although an improvement over its predecessor, failed to realize the government's hopes. For one thing, it was too late for any new system to be very effective, since the damage had already been done by the lavish grants of the past, especially those to privileged claimants, which were still to continue. Furthermore, just as the new system went into effect, the Canada Company acquired over two million acres of the best lands in the province, and presently some of the excellent Clergy Reserves lots would be available. The Crown Lands Commissioner was faced with too much competition from these sources and from private sellers to be able to sell his lands to much advantage. And, of course, the new system did nothing to still the rising tide of criticism coming from the Assembly, which would never be satisfied with a system over which it had no control.

These changes led in turn to a new policy for the Clergy Reserves. After Strachan and his colleagues had rescued the Reserves from the clutches of the Canada Company, they were still faced with the twin puzzles of how to make them yield a better revenue and of how to still the rising clamour against them – a clamour which Strachan himself unnecessarily stimulated, as will be noted later. The Anglican leaders decided that they must also press for a sales policy, to meet competition from the Canada Company and the Crown Lands, although they wished to continue leasing as well. To meet their wishes, an imperial Act was passed in 1827 allowing for the sale of one-quarter of the Reserves, with a maximum of one hundred thousand acres to be sold in any one year. In instructions accompanying the Act the Colonial Secretary stated that lots hindering the progress of settlement should be first offered for sale.[23] Within a short time the Clergy Reserves were selling briskly and at good prices. Henceforth, they could not be seriously criticized on the score that they were obstacles to settlement. By the end of the 1820's, however, the Clergy Reserves were a political and religious, not mainly an economic, issue.

These various changes did much to rectify the mistakes of the past, and to make land more readily available to new settlers. But they were not sufficiently sweeping to satisfy a new school of colonizers coming into prominence in Britain. This school derived its inspiration from Edward Gibbon Wakefield, a zealous theorist who had to work behind the scenes because of his somewhat unsavoury personal reputation. (In 1826 he had tricked the daughter of a wealthy manufacturer into marrying him, carried her off to France, and had subsequently been put in jail. There he had taken to reading about emigration, on the reasonable assumption that it might be wise for him to leave England when he got out.) Wakefield was vehemently opposed to the policy of "shovelling out paupers" to colonies, and then allowing them to become freeholders on easy terms. This system resulted in a population of poverty-stricken small farmers without capital to develop their own holdings, and it also deprived new countries of a needed labour force. Instead, he urged that land be sold at a price high enough to ensure that it could be bought only by men with sufficient capital to develop and improve it. Poor settlers should be prevented from acquiring land, but should work as labourers, either on the land or on public works. Only after they had accumulated enough savings should they be able to hold land on their own.

Wakefield preached his theory to all who would listen and soon attracted the support of several influential men, including high officials in the Colonial Office. The result was a dispatch dated November 21, 1831, from the Colonial Secretary, Lord Goderich, announcing a new policy to the Government of Upper Canada, which in part although not wholly embodied Wakefield's theories. Land was to be sold at higher upset prices than before, and sold at auction to the highest bidders. No settlement duties were to be exacted, since the private interests of a man who had paid a good price for his land would be sufficient incentive to ensure its development. Under no circumstances were poor settlers to be given land.[24] As it turned out, however, the Government of Upper Canada had great difficulty in adhering to this policy. However satisfactory it might be for Australia, it was another matter to apply it in Upper Canada, where poor settlers would simply move across the line into the nearby states if they could not get land. The result was constant wrangling between imperial and colonial authorities, with Wakefield, who felt that his theory was not receiving a fair trial from either, watching the scene with growing irritation. He was to have an opportunity to pay his respects to both when he came out to Canada with Lord Durham in 1838.

As a general comment, it may be well to suggest that undue importance should not be attached to government regulations. We have seen that the excessive grants at an early period and the reservation of millions of acres placed great obstacles in the way of compact settlement. Yet, as on many another North American frontier, land seekers had a remarkable capacity for ignoring the property rights of absentee owners and the edicts of a distant government. The land was there, and they often used it without asking anyone's leave. To a very considerable extent, Upper Canada was settled by squatters, and it was never practicable to evict very many of them; the speculators and the government simply had to make terms with them. In this somewhat irregular but characteristic fashion, some of the worst features of a defective land system were nullified.

Finally, we should note that not all large landholders simply stood by, waiting for land prices to rise. Two may be mentioned who worked vigorously and successfully, one on a limited and the other on a very extensive scale, to place settlers on their lands, and so brought into being flourishing communities.

The first of these was William Dickson, a Scot who had entered the province as far back as 1792, and had soon become a successful merchant in the Niagara district. With his profits he had begun to buy land, especially a large tract, northwest of Hamilton, encompassing the township of Dumfries, which the Six Nations Indians had previously alienated. After he failed to shake the government's policy of discouraging American settlement, he determined to secure settlers from his native Scotland. He sent an agent home, advertised widely there, and carried on an extensive correspondence with leading Scotsmen. Soon he was attracting a steady stream of immigrants, who were at once placed on the land and given various kinds of assistance in the early stages of their new life. He appointed an energetic and competent young Pennsylvanian named Absolom Shade to superintend the settlement of the township. Together the two men founded the village of Shade's Mills (renamed Galt in 1827 after Dickson's old friend the Superintendent of the Canada Company), while Shade vigorously forwarded the erection of mills, roads, and schools.[25]

But the most remarkable settlement promoter in the province's history was Colonel Thomas Talbot. It will be recalled that this 31-year-old army officer, descended from one of the most famous families of the Anglo-Irish aristocracy, had in 1803 received the usual field officer's grant of five thousand acres, and that in addition part of an adjoining township had been reserved along the shores of Lake Erie for his colonizing activities. In May of that year he and five assistants set out by boat from above Niagara Falls and landed at the mouth of a creek almost directly south of the present city of London, Ontario. At that time the nearest white settlement was forty miles away to the east, and the uninhabited wilderness stretched even farther to the west. From this base, which he named Port Talbot, he and his men began to clear land, and in the next year, he built saw and grist mills.[26]

In its inception Talbot's plan was little different from that of many another township "developer" in the early years of the province. By his arrangement with the government he was to be entitled to reserve for himself 200 acres of land for each settler whom he placed on 50 acres of his own land. Assuming that he filled up his 5,000 acres by such grants, he would thus accumulate an estate of 20,000 acres adjoining the original grant that would compare favourably with the holdings of his forbears in Ireland. In fact, he departed from the terms of his grant by locating settlers on 50-acre lots and then reserving a surrounding 150 acres, with the intention of continuing this plan, perhaps indefinitely, in the nearby townships. He clearly intended to derive a large personal profit from his colonizing activities.

In the beginning his settlement grew slowly enough; after five years he had placed only twenty families on his lands.[27] He soon realized, however, that his plans could never be fulfilled until adequate roads were built linking his townships with the settled communities, and he secured an appointment from the government at York as a road commissioner, which enabled him to locate settlers along a route eastward from Port Talbot. In effect he was acting as an unpaid agent of the provincial government, doing its work in order to advance his own interests. As time went on he greatly exceeded the authority vested in him by the provincial government, which then tried to clip his wings. When this threat appeared, Talbot appealed to London, where his great influence prevailed despite the outraged cries emanating from York.

In this way Talbot steadily enlarged the area of his activities in southwestern Upper Canada. He pushed ahead with road-building until he had satisfactory communications eastward toward the head of Lake Ontario and westward to the Detroit River. By the end of the 1820's he had built a road nearly three hundred miles long, the best road of its length in the province. Or, rather, his settlers had built the road. He succeeded in getting all reserved lots moved back from the road, leaving it free for continuous settlement. He then required every settler to clear half the road in front of his lot, as well as one hundred feet adjoining it, and he also required him to clear ten acres elsewhere on the grant and to build a habitable dwelling. These were normal settlement requirements, but Talbot enforced them more rigidly and more consistently than was done in any equivalent portion of the province. The settler had to stay on his land for five years before he was eligible for a certificate, which could then be exchanged for a patent. If a man failed to obey Talbot's regulations, he was summarily dispossessed and his land given to someone else. Talbot's methods were high-handed, insulting, and even tyrannical, but they achieved results. His "principality," as he called it, grew steadily, and soon he was embarrassed by more applications than he had land to satisfy. In order to meet these requests and, also, in order to extend his personal sway, he managed in one way or another to extend his superintendency over an area that went far beyond the limits not only of his original grant but of the lands for which the provincial government made him an agent. In the process he did build up a large estate for himself, which he left vacant in the worst speculating tradition. At the same time, however, he spent so much of his own money developing the settlement that, except for his vacant land, he derived little pecuniary benefit from his activities. Willingly or not, he was more engrossed in the superintending of a flourishing settlement than in the accumulation of a personal fortune.[28]

In his log house on a cliff above Lake Erie, the old Colonel pursued his hermit-like existence, the most notable "character" in the province. He rarely visited the outside world, although he sometimes entertained guests of prominence. His heart was in his principality; for the rest, he was content to watch at his sitting-room window until the rays of the setting sun informed him that it was time to begin the day's serious drinking.[29]

Talbot's rigidly tory outlook, combined with his eccentric personality, made him many enemies within his own settlement. Eventually, moreover, the settlement became too large to be managed by an aging man who kept no records that anyone could understand but himself. Toward the end of 1837 both the British and the provincial governments acted together to require Talbot to wind up his agency and turn it over to the latter. By this time, in the words of his most recent biographer, the Colonel had settled

> twenty-seven townships extending more than 130 miles from Long Point to the Detroit River, and north to the boundary of the Huron Tract. Under his supervision half a million acres of land were reclaimed from forest and swamp and brought under cultivation; and thousands of persons were settled without the evils of non-residence and speculation that plagued the regions under the control of the government.[30]

It was a unique record of achievement, and Talbot well deserved the pension that had earlier been granted to him. His most effective work was done before the onset of the great migration of the 1830's, during which more efficient procedures were used by the government. In the years from 1815 to 1830, however, working in a remote section of the province, where he could ignore the government when it might hamper him, yet make use of its authority, he had avoided most of the evils which restricted settlement in other parts of the province.

CHAPTER 8

Economic Growth
in the 1820's and 1830's

In 1824 a young English aristocrat, who would one day serve as Colonial Secretary and later as Prime Minister, made a North American tour with three friends. In the privacy of a journal not published for over a century E. G. Stanley remarked upon the slow rate of Canadian economic growth as compared with that of the United States, noting "the universal energy and activity which pervades the latter, and the general supineness and listlessness in which the former appears to be sunk." In particular, he emphasized the long and narrow shape of the Canadas, with only one outlet to the sea, and that one frozen over for half the year.[1] This type of remark, which was frequently made by other contemporary observers, embodied a fundamental truth. Given the technology available in the nineteenth century, the nature of their geography, and their scanty population, the British North American provinces were in fact limited to a modest rate of economic progress in these years, and for long afterward. Not until the opening up of the west and the north, and the exploitation of resources which were unknown or could not be used in the earlier period, would rapid expansion be possible. Meanwhile, the Canadian task in the nineteenth century, to a great extent, was that of a holding action.

Nevertheless, one had indeed to be a "cursory traveller" (as Stanley admitted he was) to see only "supineness and listlessness" in the Upper Canada of the 1820's. After the post-war depression lifted in the early 1820's there was solid progress in agriculture and lumbering, and small processing establishments of various kinds became more numerous throughout the province. Strenuous efforts were made to improve communications both within the province and with the outside world. The need of more elaborate business organization was recognized in the attention that was given to banking. The beginnings of overseas immigration, already described, were a source of optimism and encouragement. On the whole, despite some exceptions that will be evident, it cannot be said that political unrest in this decade had any very firm economic underpinning, a statement that would not be so true for the 1830's.

Wheat-farming continued to be the basis of the provincial economy in most of the settled parts of the province. Each fall new fields of winter wheat were sown where trees had been chopped or burned during the previous year, and summer saw a larger surplus available for sale. The tightening of the British Corn Laws in 1815 limited exports in certain years, but following 1822 these were amended to give the British provinces a sizable preference over foreign importers. Moreover, there was a good local market in the immigrants, the gangs of canal workers, the employees of the Canada Company, and the men engaged in lumbering. This market also took much of the surplus of other crops, such as timothy hay, oats, potatoes, corn, and barley, while much grain went to the small but numerous distilleries. In the southwestern part of the province tobacco-growing became firmly established in these years.

Clearing land for arable farming provided important secondary occupations in this pioneer period. Not only did many men find employment by specializing in this task, but it produced important cash crops. The burning of trees produced ashes in such quantities that for a time in the early 1820's they were the province's leading export in the form of "pot and pearl ashes." "Asheries" were dotted about the province to which ashes were sent to be leached and dried for the British textile industry. Also, farmers spent their winters as part-time lumbermen cutting trees and getting logs ready to be floated down on the spring floods to the nearest sawmill. At first, the mills were on the lake front, but with the advance of the settlement they moved farther into the back townships. Sawn lumber not only made it possible for farmers to get out of log huts and into frame houses, but it also provided a valuable export, much of it going to nearby American centres.

The sawmill, usually started by one of the more affluent or enterprising settlers, was the nucleus from which many a village and town grew. Presently a gristmill would be added, often as part of the same establishment, where farmers could get their wheat milled into flour. The miller frequently took his payment in a proportion of the flour made and he then sold this locally or to a merchant engaged in the export trade. Soon there would be a demand for other services. Tanneries, woollen mills, wood-working establishments, paper-making plants, blacksmith and wheelwright shops and, most numerous and ubiquitous of all, distilleries were set up to meet local demands. Stone quarrying and the making of bricks and pottery were other activities. At Marmora and Madoc, north of the Bay of Quinte, iron ore was mined and smelted, although with limited success, and there was similar activity in the Long Point region. All in all, definite signs of economic specialization were evident in the province.[2]

In most parts of the province lumbering was or soon became subsidiary to agriculture, but in the Ottawa Valley the reverse was true. As early as 1800 Philemon Wright, from Massachusetts, had established himself near the site of the later city of Hull, where he soon decided that lumbering was more profitable than farming. Before the War of 1812 square timber was being floated down the Ottawa on its way to Quebec, and after 1815 the trade moved rapidly up the river, as the construction of dams and timber slides made it possible to overcome the obstacles posed by falls and rapids. This industry, which depended entirely upon the colonial preference in the British market, produced a distinctive economy and society marked off from any other section of the province. Life in the shanties and on the rafts was rough and violent, made more so by the frequent fights between the French Canadians and the Irish immigrants who provided most of the work force. The lumberman's life alternated between periods of intense activity and equally intense efforts to spend the season's wages as quickly as possible in the nearest tavern. The social effects of the timber trade were often deplored; in contrast to the New Brunswick scene, however, they were confined to only one section of Upper Canada and hardly came to the notice of the rest of the province. The economic effects were highly beneficial to farmers in the vicinity, for the trade provided the best local market, and at the highest prices, to be found anywhere in Upper Canada. In fact, some farmers moved upriver with the trade, producing solely for the market it provided.[3]

Such were some of the main economic activities of the period, and they exhibit a considerably more diversified scene than that of the first generation of settlement. Further advance depended heavily upon improved communications and stronger business organization.

In the matter of roads there was little progress to report in these years, or for some time afterward. Despite increasing population, dispersed settlement still made it difficult to provide a good system of main and, particularly, of local roads. Much effort was expended in the Talbot settlement, in the military settlements, and along the Rideau Canal, by the Canada Company, as well as by provincial and local authorities, yet the general condition of roads remained poor. Although hard-surfaced roads were becoming common in Britain and in the older parts of the United States, the roads of Upper Canada were for the most part hard only when frozen over in the winter. In the spring they were a sea of mud, and in low-lying stretches they did not dry out even in the summer, although a bone-shaking corduroy of rough-hewn logs might get vehicles across. District officials lacked, or claimed they lacked, the financial resources to get on with the task, with the result that there was mounting pressure on the provincial legislature to assist in the building of purely local roads. Numerous appropriations were made, but few contemporaries were satisfied with the results.

The main roads were somewhat better, although a good rain might make even these impassable upon occasion. Dundas Street running west from the capital was improved after the war, but the Danforth Road to the east fell into disuse. Instead, another road nearer the lake, known as Kingston Road, became the main highway. Along this road a weekly stage-coach line began winter service in 1817, taking from two to four days to make the trip between York and Kingston. By the early 1830's there was daily, and somewhat faster, service (except Saturdays and Sundays) all the year round. From 1828 there was also stage-coach service up Yonge Street and to the western parts of the province.[4] In the 1830's these provided, by contemporary standards, a fairly comfortable trip in winter and in dry midsummer weather, although most travellers found it wise to take full advantage of the regular and frequent stops at taverns along the way.

An essential feature of any community's communication system is its postal service. Throughout its history as a separate province most residents of Upper Canada were convinced that they were cursed with one that was utterly inadequate. Inevitably it was slow and otherwise deficient, especially in the newer districts given the dispersed nature of the settlement and the poor roads, but many residents believed that the real cause lay in the organization of the Post Office itself, over which the province had no control whatever. Real power was in the hands of the Postmaster General in Britain, while his subordinate, the Deputy-Postmaster General at Quebec, administered the service, with relatively little discretionary authority, for the British North American provinces. Residents of Upper Canada believed that distant officials could never keep abreast of the ever-changing needs of a rapidly growing province. Indeed, as early as Simcoe's time, requests had been made for a separate establishment in Upper Canada, but to no avail.

The quality and quantity of postal service did improve steadily, especially after the advent of steamboats on the lakes after 1815, but the stream of complaints did not abate. British authorities took the view that the Post Office shall pay for itself, that service could not be extended to new settlements until there was some assurance of enough traffic to support the extension. At the same time the revenues derived from the postal service were withdrawn from Upper Canada. To be sure, they were used for the general improvement of the service to and from the province, but nothing definite was known about where the money went or how it was used. In 1821 the Assembly asserted that the organization of the Post Office violated the British pledge of 1778 never again to tax a colony, and in 1825 it was asserted that the Post Office should be under the supervision of the provincial legislature, a demand that was periodically renewed over the next several years. Unfavourable comparisons with the superiority of the American post office were a stock-in-trade of the critics. It was increasingly insisted that the system was illegal, since it was a form of taxation, although John Beverley Robinson quoted Benjamin Franklin to the effect that postage was not taxation. Finally, the Law Officers of the Crown did declare the system illegal, and a new arrangement was proposed which, however, was rejected by the Assembly.[5] The organization of the Post Office remained a subject of dispute down to the time of the Union.

Better roads and a better postal service were obviously matters of major interest, but for the inland province improved water communications were of greater importance. As Upper Canada began to produce a surplus of grain and flour and some other foodstuffs and as the lumbering trade expanded, there was a growing desire to get products to the British market in the cheapest and most expeditious manner. This desire was felt most particularly by the little groups of merchants and mill-owners and store-keepers in the villages and small towns along the lakes. After the unusual prosperity of the war years, from which they had profited more than any other element in the province, they subsequently fell upon very difficult days. Under the best of conditions they operated on a very narrow margin of profit in forwarding grain, flour, ashes, and other goods down the lake and river to Montreal, but after the drastic fall of prices occurring about 1818 they found themselves being swept into insolvency. They could not collect from farmers to whom they had extended credit. They could not meet their obligations to the Montreal houses from which they had in turn borrowed heavily, while the latter were also pressed hard from London. It was an old story, repeated time and again in the economic history of North America.

There was no entirely satisfactory answer to this problem. Given slow communications, primitive credit arrangements and fluctuating prices the best calculations of business men would frequently go awry, even if they were not tinged by the lively optimism that so often caused such men to over-extend themselves. Nevertheless, there was one phase of the problem that cried out for an answer and, if solved, could ease all the others. Transportation costs were inordinately high, and were placing an almost unbearable burden upon the conduct of trade.

Thus attention came back to the lakes and the river, to the St Lawrence route. Such an observer as E. G. Stanley might disparage this "one outlet" as frozen over for nearly half the year, but Canadians viewed it very differently. Surely it was an incomparable system, reaching far into the heart of the continent, a water highway not only for the British provinces but one which tapped the trade of the growing American west. On the continent only the Mississippi could compare with it, but the St Lawrence had the great advantage of bringing out goods to the high seas at a point much closer to Britain and Europe. The fact that it was blocked with ice in the winter months was not an insuperable disadvantage; in any event, it was one shared by the competing Erie-Canal~Hudson River route. But it did have one glaring and exasperating defect: although nearly all of it was perfectly navigable, even for the large vessels of the time, its course was broken by the rapids above Montreal and by the falls and the rapids in the Niagara River. Until these obstacles were circumvented the St Lawrence route operated with only partial efficiency.

Plans for improving the St Lawrence route had been forming for a long time, and some first steps had already been taken. Back in the early 1780's the Royal Engineers had built tiny canals, thirty inches deep, but sufficient for bateau navigation, around the rapids just above Montreal, and these had been enlarged after 1800 to allow for the passage of Durham boats. At Niagara the historic portage road was on the American side, but a new one, eleven and a half miles long, was built on the Canadian side, between Queenston and Chippawa, in the early 1790's. These arrangements, imperfect though they were, did allow the route to be used, and as long as it had no serious competitor they were sufficient to attract trade down from the west. Nevertheless, it was slow, expensive, and goods frequently arrived in a damaged condition.

Demands for more effective improvements acquired a new note of urgency after 1817, when the State of New York began construction of the Erie Canal. This canal, to stretch more than 350 miles from the Hudson River to Lake Erie, represented a deliberate plan to outflank the St Lawrence route, to attract the trade of the west down to New York Ciy, and to take it away from Montreal. As the future would show, the plan succeeded brilliantly, and the canal was an important although by no means the sole factor in the rise of New York to economic primacy in North America. But the merchants and political leaders of Upper and Lower Canada refused to concede the victory to New York without a struggle. They continued to have faith that, properly improved, the St Lawrence route was vastly superior to "Clinton's Ditch," constantly suffering from a shortage of water. Their faith would be justified, although not fully so until the middle of the twentieth century.

In the meantime, however, the prospect was gloomy, indeed, that the plans of the New Yorkers could be frustrated. Effective improvement of the St Lawrence would tax Canadian energies and resources to the full, yet those energies and resources could never be effectively organized as a result of the partition of 1791. In the lower province, where the greater financial power lay, the Assembly was preoccupied with its running battle with the executive and felt little sense of urgency for schemes of internal improvement. The Montreal merchants were desperately anxious for action, yet they were unable to make any considerable contribution of their own to the work. The British government favoured improvement, and possessed the authority and resources to support it. But its primary concern was with defence, and as will be seen that concern ran counter to the aims of the Canadian commercial community.

In Upper Canada it was felt that the mother country would provide assistance, but only if the provinces did something to help themselves. Yet it was hard to see what could be done at a time when the upper province faced bankruptcy owing to the failure to receive its share of the duties collected at Quebec. Indeed, some Upper Canadians, either because they resented their subordination to Montreal or because they wished to alarm that provincial metropolis into action, sometimes pointed out that they did not have to rely solely on the St Lawrence route; if necessary, their goods could reach tidewater through the United States. Some wheat from Upper Canada was already finding its way across the lake to be milled at Rochester, and in later years much lumber would be sold in the American market. Yet for all the advantage of having this alternative market and route, the leading figures of Upper Canada never seriously doubted that they must make every effort to develop the St Lawrence route. In 1821 a committee of the Assembly chaired by Colonel Robert Nichol placed every possible emphasis on such development, and recommended the appointment of commissioners to explore the whole subject of canal-building along the route.[6]

Commissioners were duly appointed and after a survey of the problem they submitted reports in 1823. In an apparent attempt to represent the subject in its larger imperial aspects, much stress was laid on the advantages of canal-building in the matter of defence, and routes were suggested which stressed that feature. For instance, it was recommended that the connection between Lakes Ontario and Erie should be made by a canal, sixty-two miles long, extending from Burlington Bay to the Grand River. This route would be long and expensive but it would have the advantage of being well away from the American frontier. Similarly, support was given to the project of making navigable the Rideau waterway between the Ottawa River and Kingston. If this were done, and the necessary canals built on the Ottawa and just above Montreal, troops and supplies could be moved into Lake Ontario without passing under American guns along the St Lawrence. Finally, the need for canals around the rapids in the St Lawrence below Prescott was also urged. Such a program was far beyond the means of the province. All Sir Peregrine Maitland could do was lay it before the British government, and hope for assistance. Lord Bathurst's reply was more exasperating than helpful. The British government would lend the province £70,000, but only if the local legislature would engage itself to certain firm guarantees, quite beyond its present financial capability.[7]

Lord Bathurst also urged that of the three basic projects under discussion priority should be given to the improvement of the Rideau waterway, the one that had the most immediate interest for the British government. It was in fact an interest of a decade's standing when Bathurst wrote in October 1824. Back in the war years British military authorities had often realized how precarious their situation would be if the Americans made a full-scale effort to cut the lifeline between Kingston and Montreal. Fortunately, such an attempt had never been successful, but there was little ease of mind for the future in the knowledge that American military leaders had been planning just such a campaign for the summer of 1815.[8] The significance of the Ottawa-Rideau route immediately began to bulk large in the minds of British commanders in the Canadas, and it was more closely examined in 1816. In the following year, as already noted, military settlements were starting in the Rideau country, as a means of protecting the route and the region back of the St Lawrence. In 1819 the Duke of Wellington urged that early attention be given to the route. About the same time work was begun on the Lachine Canal above Montreal, and on three small canals to make the Ottawa River navigable. It was while examining the Rideau route that the Duke of Richmond, Maitland's father-in-law and the Governor-in-Chief of the Canadas, died in 1819 after being scratched by a tame fox that had become rabid.

For a time there was no effective action and, as we have seen, Lord Bathurst tried to interest the province in the project in 1824. It soon became clear, however, that Upper Canada was much more interested in improvement of the St Lawrence than in the roundabout Rideau route. A British commission sent out in 1825 reported this sentiment, and recommended that the project be assumed by the British government as a purely military undertaking. This commission also uncritically accepted the highly optimistic estimates of the provincial survey on the cost of canalizing the Rideau route. Thus, with no clear idea of its cost, and with no discussion in Parliament, the British government decided to undertake the project.

In May 1826 Lieutenant-Colonel John By of the Royal Engineers arrived in Canada with orders to complete a water communication from a point on the Ottawa River just below the Chaudière Falls to Kingston on Lake Ontario, about 130 miles distant, to be of a uniform depth of five feet. The route was to follow a tangled network of rivers and lakes, through virgin forests and unhealthy swamps, without usable roads and with only the few thousand inhabitants of the struggling military settlements along the way. Like other canal-builders of the day Colonel By's work force would have to rely on the pick and shovel, on wheelbarrows, on oxen, and on simple hand cranes for lifting large stones. Holes for gunpowder would have to be drilled in rock by hand. Both labourers and supplies would have to be assembled and transported from a considerable distance. Altogether, Colonel By faced a truly herculean task, and he had been ordered to complete it in the shortest possible time.[9]

Nevertheless, contracts were quickly let, and the work was soon underway, southward from the little community of Bytown on the Ottawa, and northward from Kingston Mills near Lake Ontario. Difficult engineering problems were met and solved. Men died of malaria or were blown to bits by gunpowder, but the job went forward. Solid masonry locks made their appearance, eventually forty-seven in all. By May 24, 1832, the canal was open for service, and when the Ottawa canals were finished two years later the first St Lawrence seaway had come into being, although it did not use much of the St Lawrence. The British government had completed the costliest military work which it had ever undertaken in North America.[10] It was so costly – about £1,000,000, including the Ottawa canals – that Colonel By, despite his great achievement, ended his career under a cloud of undeserved but indignant Treasury criticisms.

The Rideau Canal was maintained as an integral feature of the Canadian defence system for many years. Sturdy blockhouses were built near its main locks. It stood ready to provide an effective link between the two provinces in the event of another war with the United States. The war never came, and it was the canal's eventual destiny to see in modern times the peaceful invasion each summer of many scores of American pleasure craft.

The Canadian people were, of course, grateful for this expensive contribution to their defence, and they were also grateful for the stimulus which such a large expenditure gave to the country between the Ottawa River and Lake Ontario. For the farmers around Perth it was a godsend, providing them with a good local market for their surplus at a time when no other was available. The farmers were also able to pick up additional income by hiring themselves out as teamsters to the canal contractors.[11] Many roads were built, without expense to the local residents, to aid in the construction of the canal.

Yet it remained true that the Rideau Canal was a British defence work, following a roundabout route, and of relatively little use to the merchants of the two provinces who wanted the improvement of the direct St Lawrence route. In fact, its construction probably delayed work on the river between Montreal and Kingston, where canals were not finally built until the later 1840's. In any event, these canals could not be started until the legislature of Lower Canada showed a willingness to co-operate, of which there was little sign.

The connection between Lake Erie and Lake Ontario was another matter Here something might be done without waiting for the lower province to act. Such, at least, was the view of William Hamilton Merritt, a young merchant and storekeeper who made his home in St Catharines, and operated mills and a distillery at the mouth of the Twelve Mile Creek on the lake-shore west of the Niagara River. Merritt had been born in western New York in 1793, the son of a Loyalist who moved into the province three years later. He served in the War of 1812 as a young cavalry officer, and was captured at the battle of Lundy's Lane. After the war he married the daughter of a New York State senator, a connection which probably increased his interest in the progress of that state. A sanguine, enterprising man, full of plans and projects, he was to spend much of his life holding up the example of New York to the people of his own province as one to emulate and if possible surpass.

Merritt's attention was first drawn to the idea of a canal through the problem he faced in getting enough water for his mills at the mouth of the Twelve Mile Creek. A survey convinced him that it would be possible to tap the Welland (or Chippawa) River, which flowed into the Niagara River above the escarpment, and in turn he was led to think of a canal from the mouth of the Creek to the Welland River. In 1818 he joined with other residents of the Niagara District in a petition to the provincial legislature, urging action on such a canal as a means of frustrating the plans of the Erie Canal builders to capture the western trade.[12] Subsequently, as already noted, commissioners appointed by the legislature reported in favour of a canal extending from Burlington Bay to the Grand River.

This route, which was probably impractical in any event, had no appeal for Merritt, who wanted a canal that would go alongside his properties at St Catharines and the Twelve Mile Creek. Apart from his personal interest, he believed this to be the most direct and useful route for the traders of the province. Accordingly, he abandoned any further thought of a canal to be built by the provincial government. After having a survey made by an American engineer, he and several associates in the Niagara District applied to the legislature to be incorporated as a chartered company, with a capital of £25,000, and with permission and powers to build a four-foot canal from Lake Ontario (starting at the Twelve Mile Creek, of course) to the Welland River, from which craft could enter the Niagara River above the Falls and so reach Lake Erie. In addition, it was proposed to build a branch of the canal from the Welland to the Grand River, thus providing a second entrance to Lake Erie. It was assumed that subscriptions to the capital would be readily forthcoming, after incorporation, and that the whole project would be both inexpensive and easy to execute. Apparently the legislature thought so too and, cheered by the thought that a much-needed public work was going to be provided by a private company, it passed the incorporation bill in January 1824, without much debate. Prominent figures, including Sir Peregrine Maitland, John Beverley Robinson, and J. H. Dunn, the Receiver General, had extended their favour to the plan.

No support had been promised by the provincial government, however, and it also soon became clear that little money could be raised in Upper Canada, or in Montreal, for that matter. Merritt therefore turned to New York, where he was soon in touch with J. B. Yates, a former member of the House of Representatives, with interests in the Syracuse-Albany region. Yates was in the business of managing lotteries, and had idle funds available for what appeared to be a profitable investment. He and certain of his associates were also strong believers in the projected canal, for they saw that it would make possible a cheap and expeditious shipping route from American Lake Erie ports to Oswego, where ships could enter the side-cut of the Erie Canal, then planned (and completed in 1828), and so bring goods to Syracuse and nearby points without a 200-mile barge haul on the Erie Canal. For this purpose the Welland Canal had to be deep enough for sloops and schooners, and not the four-foot ditch originally planned. To get the invaluable support of Yates and other men to whom he was introduced, Merritt agreed to such an enlargement of the canal. In any event he was probably more than willing to contemplate the larger project, which would be more useful to the inhabitants of the province, and which could be regarded as a defence work, since it would allow naval ships to move from one lake to the other.[13] Altogether, New York subscriptions amounted to about one-half of the capitalization at this stage. In addition, Merritt made contact with American contractors and engineers who, with their skilled teams of labourers, would soon be free for further tasks upon the completion of the Erie Canal. Such skills and experience were not available in Upper Canada.

By the end of November 1824 Merritt was ready to turn the first sod, with a full sense that he was also marking a turning point in the province's history. He informed his hearers that they were now about to leave "this dull, supine state" of past years and "mingle in the bustle and active scenes of business." The advantages of the country were at last to be realized, men of capital would now be attracted and, in starting a project as important to the province as the Erie Canal was to New York, they would "witness the same spirit of enterprise here that our neighbours, the Americans, possess in so eminent a degree."

He also informed his audience that there was "nothing novel, new or intricate in the undertaking." It was only necessary to "follow the plan adopted by that celebrated and enlightened statesman, De Witt Clinton," and the canal could be built "without taxing the country one farthing."[14] These were brave but innocent words, as Merritt would later discover. Although the Welland Canal was to be only about one-seventh the length of the Erie, it proved to be much more than one-seventh as difficult to build. Within a distance of about thirty miles there was a drop of over three hundred feet, necessitating many more locks than on any equivalent section of the Erie, and locks with twice the depth of those on "Clinton's Ditch." Most difficult of all was the problem of water supply caused by a ridge of land, about sixty feet high and two miles across, between the Welland River and the brow of the escarpment. Since this ridge was well above the level of the Welland River, it would either have to be tunnelled through or cut through, if water were to be brought northward out of that river.

It was not long before difficulties began to crowd in upon Merritt and his associates. The original plan of putting a tunnel through the ridge proved to be impossible because of flooding, and was abandoned in favour of a deep cut through the ridge. It was also clear that the enthusiasm of the provincial authorities had markedly diminished since so much of the capital had been raised in New York, and was not likely to be revived unless there was definite assurance that the canal would not be controlled by Americans. Yet it was equally obvious that more money would be needed than was contemplated in the existing charter. To solve these and other problems the charter was amended early in 1825, increasing the capitalization to £200,000 and confining the directorate to residents of Upper Canada who owned ten shares or more. Thus the American investors were excluded from any part in the formal management of the company, while men in or close to the provincial government, with only a nominal financial stake in the company, assumed most of the positions on the directorate. The company received a land grant from the government in 1825 which, although of little financial value, was an indication of renewed favour. In 1826 the provincial government made its first loan, of £25,000, to the company, and later that same year the British government promised to assume one-ninth of the cost, provided government ships were passed through the canal toll-free.[15] In 1827 a further £50,000 was loaned by the legislature of Upper Canada and £25,000 came from Lower Canada. Still the financial condition of the company remained desperate as costs continued to run far ahead of estimates, and Merritt now made a determined effort to secure financial help in England. The remaining stock was sold there, and Merritt also came back with a British loan of £50,000, extended in lieu of the earlier one-ninth offer. As the closest student of the company has stated, it "was already degenerating into a privately-controlled institution for the disbursement of public funds."[16]

The company might have been able to stop its borrowings at this stage if construction problems had not intervened. On November 9, 1828, when the canal was apparently within a few weeks of being completed, a series of disastrous slides started in the "Deep Cut," bringing the whole work to a complete halt. The excavators had come to a bed of loose sand that made it impossible to dig the bottom of the canal to a level below that of the Welland River. Extensive surveys were needed in order to work out an alternative mode of proceeding. It was then decided that water would have to be brought from the Grand River by means of a feeder canal. That is, the Grand River would be dammed near its mouth, thus raising its water level about seven feet above Lake Erie, with water to be carried by a twenty-seven mile feeder canal, and an aqueduct above the Welland River, into the ship canal. This was a cumbersome arrangement, and it meant that the mouth of the Welland River was now the only means by which ships could get into Lake Erie, since the feeder canal could be used only by small boats. Nevertheless, it did bring water into the canal, without having to cut so deeply through the ridge, where the bottom of the canal remained above the level of Lake Erie. (It was only in 1881, after several decades of further excavation started in the 1840's, that it became possible to bring water directly into the line of the canal from Lake Erie.)

The new plan, of course, led to much unexpected expense, and the company continued to be desperately short of money. It was only by grasping at every expedient that Merritt was able to pull the company through the year 1829, while the work was being pushed forward. All concerned felt a pardonable sense of accomplishment when two schooners, one from Upper Canada and one from New York, passed through the canal from Lake Ontario to the Welland River at the end of November 1829, but no one seriously believed that the canal was finished. The wooden locks had been built so cheaply (in utter contrast to those on the Rideau Canal) that they were in constant need of repair. Moreover, the currents in the Niagara River above the mouth of the Welland River were too strong for good sailing navigation, while the water supply in the feeder canal failed periodically. In 1830 it was decided to build a new section south from the Welland River, to provide a direct entrance upon Lake Erie. This section was completed in 1833, thus finishing a direct canal of twenty-eight miles from Port Dalhousie on Lake Ontario to Port Colborne on Lake Erie, but one that was still dependent on the precarious water supply from the Grand River feeder canal.

By now the company "found themselves deeply in debt, their funds exhausted, and their credit gone,"[17] despite another £75,000 borrowed from the provincial government and despite constant calls on J. B. Yates, who continued to believe in the canal, notwithstanding all that had happened. And still the canal was a rickety, ramshackle affair. In 1833 Benjamin Wright, formerly senior engineer on the Erie Canal, was asked to make a thorough survey of the canal. Wright recommended extensive alterations and improvements to put the canal in effective running order. These were quite beyond the resources of the company, despite further provincial assistance. In 1837 after the province had provided more than £200,000 in the form of loans and stock subscriptions, the government subscribed for a further £245,000, which was nevertheless insufficient to pay for the improvements called for by a new survey. By this time the canal was no longer regarded as a purely economic project; there was no expectation that revenues, most of which at this time came from tolls on goods to and from American ports on the two lakes, would be adequate to attack the mountain of debt for many years to come, if ever. Yet the canal was regarded as essential both to the progress and defence of the province.[18] In 1841 the company was dissolved. The canal came under the administration of the provincial Board of Works, and a complete reconstruction began, which extended over several decades. The financial history and eventual fate of the Welland Canal Company foreshadowed that of several other Canadian corporations of the future, especially railway companies.

Like the Rideau, the Welland Canal had a marked effect on the region through which it passed, apart altogether from its place in an extensive transportation system. The little communities along the Niagara River, especially Queenston, which had profited from the portage route, now fell behind, while villages along the canal prospered. Water power made available by the canal attracted flour mills, sawmills, and woollen mills. Within a few years the industry of the Niagara peninsula was concentrated to a marked extent along the line of the canal or on rivers directly accessible to the canal.[19]

The Rideau and Welland Canals were the biggest works carried out in Upper Canada before the Union of 1841, but they were far from satisfying the appetite of the inhabitants for internal improvements. As Merritt's son and biographer put it, "a mania for canalling seemed to possess the people," and he noted that his father "was daily in receipt of letters from different parts of the country about canal schemes."[20] It was obvious that others besides Merritt felt "the spirit of enterprise" that was sweeping across eastern North America in these years.

For instance, as early as 1820 a French immigrant named Pierre Desjardins petitioned the legislature for permission to build a four-mile canal from the head of Burlington Bay to the village of Dundas, with the hope of tapping the trade of the country at the western end of Lake Ontario. A company was incorporated in 1826, and the canal was opened in 1837, although the dreams of its projectors were never realized. A smaller but more important work was started in 1823, when the provincial government began to cut through the narrow sand strip of Burlington Beach to allow ship navigation into the Bay. The channel was completed in 1832, thus laying the basis for the future growth of the village of Hamilton, which in a few years far outdistanced its rivals, Dundas and Ancaster.

A far more ambitious scheme was bruited as early as 1827. This was nothing less than a plan to complete a system of navigation back from the mouth of the Trent River to Rice Lake, thence through a series of rivers and lakes to Lake Simcoe and so to Lake Huron. The route had been known since the time of Champlain, and in the late eighteenth and early nineteenth centuries it had been examined several times with a view to assessing its feasibility as an entrance to the upper Great Lakes. In 1833 and 1835, N. H. Baird, a civil engineer appointed by the government, submitted two thorough reports on the route, estimating that a combined canal and road system could be constructed for about £200,000 or a continuous canal for some half a million pounds. Baird strongly urged the merits of the route, stating that from Georgian Bay it was 261 miles shorter than by way of the lower lakes. It was a certain means of outflanking the Americans in the contest for the western trade, while it would quickly open up the interior of the province. In a country lacking good roads, it was the surest way of bringing agricultural produce, lumber, and the ore from the Marmora iron works to market.

In 1836 and 1837 the legislature appropriated limited sums for the proposed improvement, but because of the political and financial dislocation of the years immediately following little had been accomplished at the time of Union. It was not until the early twentieth century that the waterway was partly constructed, long after it had been outdated by the railway. Like the Rideau, it was an expensive government work, eventually used almost entirely by Canadian and American pleasure craft, but in its origins it testified to the enthusiasm of the 1820's and 1830's for "internal improvement."[21]

The "mania for canalling" and other improvements was general throughout the province. All sections and all interests shared in the desire for cheaper and more efficient transportation facilities. The leading figures in the provincial government – the Family Compact – actively supported the various projects of the 1820's and 1830's. There was nearly always a majority in the Assembly, regardless of party, ready to vote money for the projects put before it, with the result that the province found itself with an unbearable burden of debt in the later 1830's. Nevertheless, this subject, like all others before the public, became enmeshed in bitter debate before many years had passed, as critics of the Compact became ever more suspicious of any scheme it sponsored.

The most vocal of these critics, William Lyon Mackenzie, was at first most enthusiastic about the plans for canals. He welcomed the start of the Welland Canal as a means of avoiding dependence on the Erie Canal, although he was skeptical of the original low estimates of its cost, and felt that such a work should be "a provincial undertaking."[22] Less than three years later, however, he was voicing apprehensions about the large subscriptions and loans for a company that had such close ties with the inner circles of the executive government. It could be a way of adding "a little more to the already overgrown influence of the crown," while other undertakings were neglected. At the same time he was made suspicious by the fact that almost all the engineers and contractors on the Welland Canal were American citizens, who could not have the same interest in the welfare of the province that British subjects would have. A year later he made his views clearer by stressing that the Welland should be supported only on a pay-as-you-go basis, and not by borrowing, and that assistance should go not solely to the Welland, but to other projects as well.[23]

As the demands of the Welland Canal Company became more frequent and more urgent in the 1830's, causing a steady rise in the public debt, the enterprise encountered increasing opposition in the Assembly. To a considerable extent this opposition was purely sectional in nature, and cut across party lines, with members from western constituencies supporting the canal and eastern members wanting assistance for other projects closer to home. Nevertheless, a growing proportion of the reformers except for those nearest the Canal, voted against it. Many of them believed, probably correctly, that the Canal would be more useful to American than to Canadian farmers, since it would allow Ohio growers, for instance, to ship their produce to the New York market (where Canadians were largely excluded by tariff), or even directly into the province.[24] It was argued that improvement of the St Lawrence River below Prescott would do much more to benefit the Upper Canadian farmer than would the Welland. But the major contention of the reformers was that roads and bridges were being neglected in the excessive concern for the Welland Canal. Better roads would bring the quickest and most tangible benefits to farmers and, of course, from a political point of view they had the great advantage of being visible local reminders of a member's zeal at the provincial capital. Although the bulk of the reformers never shared Mackenzie's bitter hostility to the Welland Canal Company, most of them did feel that too much of the provincial revenue was being sunk in it, and that there was too close a tie between the governing group and the Company.

The "mania" for internal improvements was not the only indication in the 1820's and 1830's of a growing demand for economic expansion and diversity. In these years the first banks were established, as the province moved away from the simple barter economy of an earlier day. And, like the Welland Canal Company, the Bank of Upper Canada, with its close ties to the Family Compact, became a storm centre of local politics.

The business life of the two Canadian provinces was carried on without the benefit of banking institutions until after the War of 1812, despite early attempts in each province to set up banks. Merchants at Montreal, Kingston, and other smaller centres provided a rough substitute by issuing and accepting various kinds of bills and notes as credit instruments. But such commercial paper was not an adequate means of exchange, nor did the bewildering variety of American and European coins circulating in the provinces provide a suitable metallic currency. The Army Bills issued under British authority during the war years were a welcome innovation, which accustomed people to the use of paper money, but they were withdrawn from circulation soon after the war. At the same time the province was also being denuded of specie to pay for the many purchases made after the return of peace. It was against this background that a group of merchants from the province's leading commercial centre, Kingston, petitioned the legislature for an incorporation act, authorizing them to establish a bank. They noted the large number of English and American banks started in the previous generation; in particular, they argued that the rapid progress of the western territories of the United States owed much to the existence of banks in that country. A bank bill was duly passed, the first passed by a Canadian legislature, and was reserved for the consideration of the home authorities, as all such legislation had to be. In transmitting the bill Lieutenant-Governor Gore noted that the province was being inundated by paper money from across the line, and hence in need of a circulating medium of its own, which a bank could provide.[25]

While action on this legislation was awaited, the first Canadian bank had already opened its doors. In 1817 the Bank of Montreal began to do business as a private assocation, some five years before the legislation incorporating it was formally proclaimed. This bank, like other Canadian banks to follow it, was closely modelled on the Bank of the United States established at Alexander Hamilton's urging in 1791, and which in 1816 had just been revived as the Second Bank of the United States. Hamilton in turn had derived his banking principles from English and Scottish models. Here, then, was an instance of Canada receiving a British institution after it had been adjusted and modified to North American conditions in the United States.

Meanwhile, the Kingston merchants, still waiting for the confirmation of their charter, also began operation as a private association at the beginning of 1819; this move was doubtless stimulated by the fact that the Bank of Montreal was extending its operations into Upper Canada. Soon afterward word came that the Bank Act of 1817 had been approved, but by this time the legislation had expired because of a two-year time limit. It was apparently simply a matter of re-enacting it, in the sure knowledge that it was acceptable to the British government. A bit of sleight-of-hand now occurred, however, by which a bank was established at York, not at Kingston.

In fact, an attempt had already been made to start a bank at York when a petition headed with the name of the Reverend John Strachan had been submitted to the Assembly in 1817 some days after the Kingston petition.

G

The Assembly, which probably doubted that the petitioners represented any very considerable accumulation of financial power, failed to act on the petition. In 1819, however, Maitland, who was undoubtedly influenced by Strachan and his associates, informed London that the Kingston group were an untrustworthy lot with dangerous American connections. The only safe bank would be one with close government ties, and with headquarters at York.[26] Accordingly, the charter was taken away from the Kingston group, and a bill passed establishing the Bank of Upper Canada. To be sure, a bill was also passed chartering the Kingston group, but on terms which they could not meet. In consequence, they continued as a private association into the early 1820's, when a combination of bad luck and bad management forced them to default. It was the first Canadian bank failure.

The Bank of Upper Canada, whose charter was not finally confirmed until 1821, had very close connections with the provincial government, on the model of the First and Second Banks of the United States. One-quarter of the stock was to be subscribed by the government, which was also to appoint four of the fifteen directors. Branch offices on the Hamiltonian model were also expressly allowed. The government immediately subscribed its share, but it proved to be impossible to raise the remainder of the required minimum among private subscribers. The charter was then amended to reduce the minimum subscription needed. In effect government funds, taken from monies in the hands of the Receiver General and from the Military Chest supported the Bank. Nine of the directors were either members of the executive or legislative council, or held important offices under the government, and most of the remaining six also became office-holders within a few years. John Strachan's name led the list of directors.[27] It is no exaggeration to say that the Bank of Upper Canada was a creature of the emerging Family Compact. Moreover, it was a creature which the Compact could carefully protect and foster, since its control of the legislative council allowed it to reject bills passed by the Assembly to establish competing banks. For ten years the Bank of Upper Canada enjoyed a monopoly in the province, except for one or two branches of the Bank of Montreal, which it tried unsuccessfully to freeze out.

The Bank of Upper Canada was an object of criticism from the beginning. It was, in fact, attacked from two quite different sides, by those who wanted more banks, and by those who either wanted no banks at all or at least no banks of the accepted North American type.

The first line of attack came from merchants and business men in various small towns in the province, such as Kingston, where there was still resentment at the treatment received in 1820, Hamilton, and Niagara; and still others in the middle 1830's. These men wanted to avoid dependence on the bank at the capital, and believed that banks in their own communities would stimulate local development. Official spokesmen, representing both the government and the Bank of Upper Canada, resisted these claims, arguing that the Bank was efficiently and competently run and that it would be sounder policy to increase its capital in order that more branches could be established throughout the province. It was better to have one strong bank than to follow the American practice of a multiplicity of weak, inexperienced local banks likely to collapse at the first gusts of adverse economic winds.

This argument had much obvious merit, and it was to be justified by the events following the Panic of 1837. Yet it failed to convince opponents who were put off by the secretive and rather haughty attitudes of the directors of the Bank and who could not see that the Bank was doing anything very effective to promote economic growth. No less a person than John Strachan privately asserted that criticism was justified by the "greed" of the directors in voting themselves "high Dividends and bonuses – instead of keeping large reserves of Profits as a refuge in case of loss."[28] Eventually the Compact bowed to the clamour and allowed two additional banks to be chartered. As will be seen later, the pressure continued to mount, producing a veritable rash of bank bills in 1836-37.

On the other side, the most tenacious opponent of the Bank proved to be William Lyon Mackenzie, who fought it bitterly down to the day he led his followers in rebellion against the government. In 1826 he had already concluded that "this great monied engine, the only one in the colony, is entirely under the thumb of parson Strachan and his pupils to wield at their discretion." His chief complaint was, however, a more basic one. It was not so much the monopoly position of the Bank, and the suspicion that its directors accommodated friends of the government and turned their backs on opponents, as the fact that it was run on the principle of limited liability that infuriated Mackenzie. He found it incredible that stockholders were to be liable only to the extent of their investment, and not to the full extent of their private fortunes in the event that the Bank could not meet its obligations.[29] This viewpoint made Mackenzie an enemy not only of the Bank of Upper Canada, but of all banks. By the end of the 1820's he had become a close disciple of the "hard money" school in the United States that denounced the "paper system" and believed in a purely metallic currency.

As long as he was simply attacking the Bank of Upper Canada Mackenzie carried much of the reform party with him. In 1829, for instance, the Finance Committee of the Assembly recommended that the government stock in the Bank should be sold at auction, and the proceeds used to build roads and bridges. In 1830 a Select Committee on the State of the Currency, of which Mackenzie was chairman, recommended stricter rules for the regulation of banks, and made the ringing declaration that "the prosperity of the farmer does not depend upon the amount of money or bank notes in his possession. . . . It is industry that supports banks; it is not banks that support industry."[30] Such rhetoric was, however, no longer acceptable to a growing number of Mackenzie's fellow-reformers when the larger question of establishing new banks came under discussion. Mackenzie remained true to a traditional agrarian conservatism on this subject, a position in which he was more and more alone. Other reformers increasingly accepted the prevailing spirit of capitalist enterprise that was sweeping the continent in the 1830's, wishing only to break the hold of the Bank of Upper Canada in the interests of a wider diffusion of activity. Just as Mackenzie exemplified the anti-Bank and anti-capitalist attitude of the Locofoco wing of the Democratic party in the United States, so the majority of reformers shared the views of those Jacksonians who wanted to destroy the Second Bank of the United States because it was a restraint on local banks.[31] In consequence, although controversies over banks and banking legislation loomed large in the 1830's, they usually cut across party lines.

In the 1820's, then, Upper Canada began to acquire some of the lineaments of a more complex economy as it grappled with the problem of building canals and roads and of establishing banks. Some sharp disagreements arose over priorities, and since these new projects depended heavily upon the support and encouragement of the provincial government, they heightened the determination of the opposition party to seek changes in the political structure. Nevertheless, the Family Compact carried most of the province with it in its plans for economic progress. The growing resistance to Family Compact rule came less from antagonism to its economic program than from increasingly bitter complaints against its religious and educational policies. To those we must now turn.

CHAPTER 9

Religion and Education
in the 1820's and 1830's

The efforts of the Family Compact to encourage the settlement and the economic advance of Upper Canada along lines that would make it a truly British and loyal province were paralleled by an even more vigorous determination to guide religious and educational growth to the same end. Despite considerable opposition the first set of policies was generally supported in the province and could usually count on the backing of the British government. With religion and to a lesser extent with education it was, however, very different. The Compact's attempt to ensure to the Church of England the position and privileges of church establishment and to give that church a leading role in education, especially in the proposed provincial university, were overwhelmingly opposed in the province. The result was a series of bitter and unrelenting controversies, marked with the kind of passion that only religious divisions can produce. All parties appealed constantly to the British government for support, often to be met by an evasive and indecisive response, which heightened rather than diminished the controversies.

I

The leaders of the provincial government in the Maitland era were no more satisfied with the state of religion in Upper Canada than their predecessors had been before the War of 1812. In their eyes the Church of England was still too weak in relation to the other Protestant denominations, especially the Methodists.

The expansion of Methodism into Upper Canada had been viewed with alarm from earliest times. In 1794, for instance, the Anglican Bishop of Quebec reported to the Secretary of State that "The greatest bulk of the people have and can have no instruction but such as they receive occasionally from itinerant and mendicant Methodists, a set of ignorant enthusiasts, whose preaching is calculated only to perplex the understanding, & corrupt the morals & relax the nerves of industry, & disolve [sic] the bonds of society."[1] In 1814 General Drummond called them "itinerant fanatics, enthusiastic in political as well as religious matters," who came in from the United States to disseminate "their noxious principles."[2] Yet its critics had little understanding of the careful training that lay behind the itinerant system, for it was only after serving a severe apprenticeship in less responsible positions that a preacher was allowed to go forth as an itinerant messenger of the faith. By this time he was a picked and proven man, as determined a missionary as any seventeenth-century Jesuit. Usually, to be sure, he was lacking in any extensive formal education, but he was not lacking in native intelligence, a wide knowledge of human nature, and a considerable fund of general information. Behind him stood the annual conference, with full powers to decide where he would go, to support him, or to discipline him. And he was armed with a doctrine that made a direct and personal appeal to a pioneer farming people. Out in all kinds of weather, with his few possessions in the saddlebags tied on his horse's back, he carried his message of salvation for all who would truly repent and come to Jesus. Despite the hard epithets cast upon him by his critics, for many years it was he alone who brought the consolations of religion into the remote corners of the province.

The Methodist itinerant used all the techniques of the experienced revivalist. His approach was often highly emotional. He threatened his listeners with the tortures of everlasting hell fire if they remained stony-hearted. He painted glorious pictures of the salvation awaiting those who gave themselves to God. He did not believe that the devil should have all the good tunes: enthusiastic hymn-singing was a prominent part of any Methodist service. Like all revivalists he believed in the value of lengthy and continuous contact if the message was to be put over effectively. Out of this belief came the camp meeting, which spread from the United States into Upper Canada in the decade before the war. Although a favourite butt of criticism on the part of European visitors and of clergymen of more conservative denominations, the camp meeting was simply a response to the needs of a dispersed population. The violent emotionalism of its early days gradually gave way to more formalized and more carefully organized arrangements, and eventually it passed out of use, to be succeeded by the indoor protracted weekend meeting. In its heyday, however, the camp meeting was a most effective means of bringing the gospel to a pioneer community, as well as a stimulating social occasion to lonely men and women from the backwoods and an excellent opportunity for courtship for young people. It hardly deserves the bad reputation bestowed on it by disapproving commentators, either contemporary or later.

Although the first Methodist impulse came from the United States, it was not long before the denomination took deep root in the province, and began to send up Canadian shoots. Many of the American preachers became permanent residents and naturalized British subjects, frequently "locating" in a settled community as they grew older. Native-born ministers began to have an increasingly prominent role. Clearly, there was nothing in the American connection to prevent the healthy local growth of Upper Canadian Methodism.

Such was the state of Methodism when British Wesleyans, who had already been active in Lower Canada for some time, came into the upper province shortly after the end of the war. Within a year or two they had placed preachers in towns along the St Lawrence and Lake Ontario as far west as Niagara. This invasion of their own preserve was much resented by the Methodist leaders of Upper Canada who saw it as an attempt to deprive them of the fruits of a quarter-century of diligent effort. For a few years there was much competition between the two groups, but in 1821 they agreed to a division of labour. The Wesleyans consented to withdraw from the upper province except for Kingston, where they had established close ties with the garrison, while the American Methodists would withdraw from Lower Canada, where they had long been active in the Eastern Townships, but would continue to serve the country along the left bank of the Ottawa. In announcing this arrangement to the Under Secretary of State a committee of the Wesleyan Missionary Society stated that they had "heard of no instance" of the Americans "interfering in political questions," and that the American Conference had positively instructed their missionaries to be loyal and obedient to British authority.[3]

Nevertheless, the Methodists in Upper Canada continued to be vulnerable because of their American connections despite the fact that the preaching body was becoming more Canadian with each passing year. To the usual criticisms coming from official and anti-American quarters was added a schismatic movement led by a preacher named Henry Ryan, who demanded a complete separation from the American Conference. Partly as a response to these pressures and partly as a consequence of their continued growth, the Upper Canadian Methodists in 1824 separated from the Genesee Conference to become a distinct Conference affiliated with the Methodist Episcopal Church of the United States. In effect, it had complete autonomy. Even so, the last remaining tie was broken four years later when the Canadian Conference separated amicably from the American parent body. The whole episode was an interesting example of a Canadian body passing through a dependent phase to achieve independence within one generation.

The growth of other denominations must be noticed more briefly.

To a limited extent the history of Presbyterianism paralleled that of

Methodism in the province. From an early period preachers of the Dutch Reformed and American Presbyterian Church moved across the border and established a few congregations. But these churches lacked the highly centralized organization of the Methodists, and never mounted an itinerancy system of comparable efficiency. In the eastern part of the province there were a few Scottish Presbyterians from the earliest days of settlement, and their numbers were increased with the postwar immigration from Scotland. The first preachers who came directly from Scotland belonged to the Secession Church and to other groups that had separated from the Church of Scotland. It was not until the later 1820's that clergymen of the Kirk appeared in the province in any numbers. For several years relations between them and the seceders were marked by much bitterness. Presbyterians of all kinds were probably the second largest denomination, after the Methodists, but they never worked harmoniously together in these years.

The Baptists were another group that first came in from the United States. Missionaries of that denomination were volunteering to enter the Canadian field from the early years of the century, coming in as itinerants and using the revivalist techniques of the other Protestant groups. The congregations that were built up cut their ties with the American church soon after the war, although the American Baptist Home Missionary Society provided considerable financial support for several years to come. Apart from Quakers, Mennonites, Irvingites, Campbellites, Mormons, and some others that were represented in the province by the end of the 1830's, a brief mention may be made of David Willson and the "Children of Peace." Willson was born in Dutchess County, New York, of Irish Presbyterian extraction, and came into the province in 1801. After a few years with the Society of Friends, he left them in 1812 to found the "Davidites" or "Children of Peace." At Sharon, some thirty miles north of York, he built a carefully designed temple which was the focus of the sect's activities until Willson's death in 1866. The Children of Peace were distinguished not only by their love of music and their intricate service, but also by their strong appeal to the poorer classes of society, in which some saw overtones of political reformism. As visitors in New York State were anxious to see the Shakers, so visitors to Upper Canada often made a point of visiting David Willson and his sect.[4] Upper Canada was, after all, not very far from the "Burned-Over District" of northern New York, which produced so many examples of religious enthusiasm in these years.

The Roman Catholic Church came into Upper Canada with the Highland Scots among the Loyalists, and was further reinforced by the emigration of disbanded Highland troops in 1804. The chaplain of the latter, Father Alexander Macdonell, accompanied them, and he soon emerged as the leading figure of his church in the province. In 1819 he was appointed Vicar

Apostolic and in 1826 Bishop of Regiopolis (Kingston), with a diocese comprising the whole province. He was appointed to the legislative council in 1831. Throughout the thirty-five years of his ministry in Upper Canada Bishop Macdonell constantly stressed the unswerving loyalty of his flock, and consistently threw his support to the side of the executive government and the Family Compact. With the Irish immigration of the 1820's the number of Roman Catholics in the province increased considerably, but many of the newcomers, brought up in the O'Connell school, refused to follow Macdonell's conservative lead.[5]

It was on this diverse religious scene that the Church of England waged its contest for men's minds and souls. It enjoyed important advantages and at the same time suffered from serious difficulties. It was not formally the established church of the colony (although its leading clergymen as well as the government leaders consistently regarded it as such), but it had a privileged position and it received far more financial assistance than any of its rivals. On the other hand, a relatively small proportion of the total population, whether of the Loyalists and the later American settlers or of the Scottish and Irish immigrants from the British Isles, had an Anglican background. It was not until the English immigration beginning in the later 1820's that any kind of mass base for the Church of England was provided. Another serious obstacle was that nearly all its clergymen had to come from Britain, and it was not easy to secure them in sufficient numbers. Until adequate educational facilities were developed in the Canadas, the Church of England would remain in a rather precarious position.

Moreover, the Church was not well organized to minister to a widely scattered rural population. The clergy who could be prevailed upon to emigrate often found life in the little towns and villages sufficiently primitive without climbing into the saddle to venture off into the backwoods. There were some Anglican clergymen who were as indefatigable as any Methodist itinerant, but it was not until the 1830's that the missionary efforts of the Church of England were very extensive. It has been commonly believed, also, that the formal Anglican service had little attraction for backwoodsmen who liked a man to preach as if he were fighting bees.

This view, however, would never have been accepted by John Strachan or, indeed, by other leading Anglicans, clerical or lay. They believed that if the Church could be brought to the people, they would immediately respond. The Methodists and others were having some success only because they were working in a spiritual vacuum. Once the Church of England put forward a real effort, the various sects would soon decline. From 1815 onward, therefore, Strachan engaged in an unsleeping campaign to protect and improve the position of the Church of England, a campaign that he carried on from the inner citadels of power. In 1815 he was named an

G*

honorary member of the executive council in acknowledgement of his contributions to the province during the war, and in 1817 he became a regular member. In 1820 he was appointed to the legislative council, where he intended to offset what he regarded as the excessive weight of Presbyterians in that body.[6] As for the Assembly, he counted on a growing influence there through the election of former students of his to that body.

John Strachan, as we have already seen, touched the life of the province at many points. He was blessed with an iron constitution and unshakable nerves. He faced his adversaries and his times of trial, whether they were General Dearborn's troops in 1813 or the cholera epidemic of 1832, with dauntless courage and with unflagging energy. He brought a powerful mind and a talent for incisive expression to the many duties that fell to him or that he assumed. On this little provincial stage he displayed the qualities of a great political churchman, of a Richelieu or a Laud. Like many churchmen of the type, he was a man of humble origins who became a rigid and uncompromising defender of tory positions and a determined opponent of liberal tendencies. He carried the advocacy of his church's claims to such extremes and embroiled it in so many political controversies that a growing number of his own communicants longed for a less ardent leader.

Yet no formula that tries to put Strachan down as a reactionary who failed to understand North American pioneer conditions will explain the man. He was entirely aware that the Church needed clergymen who were both physically and mentally prepared for the tasks of a provincial missionary. He readily accepted the hardships of frontier life, when it was his duty to bear them, and he had little sympathy with those who complained. In church organization he was to prove himself ready for a degree of lay representation, based upon the practices of the Protestant Episcopal Church in the United States, that was revolutionary for its day in British communities. In fact, he was always ready to learn from the American sister church, which he greatly admired. Moreover, he was no believer in narrow privilege. If he favoured an aristocracy, it was one of ability and merit, not of birth. As we shall see later, he pushed for expanded educational facilities and advocated a system of scholarships for bright boys from poor families. Although no democrat, he had no quarrel with the equalitarian structure of North American society. He was thoroughly at home in it, in a career lasting more than sixty years.

What he did quarrel with was the prevailing American doctrine, which he saw seeping into Upper Canada, that the state was purely secular and without direct religious affiliation. There must be an established church, and the state must support it adequately and wholeheartedly. As he was to put it on a later occasion, "There should be in every Christian country an established religion, otherwise it is not a Christian but an Infidel country."[7]

The English parish system must be extended to Upper Canada. The established church must have prime authority in supervising the educational system. It was in believing that a centuries-old system, even then under some attack in England, could be transferred in its entirety to a North American province marked by great religious diversity, that Strachan proved himself to be out of tune with the society in which he lived.

Central to all of Strachan's plans for the church was that great endowment, the Clergy Reserves. As we have already seen, in 1819 he secured the establishment of the Clergy Reserves Corporation in order to bring this land directly under Anglican administration and to make it clear to everyone that the proceeds were to go to the Church of England. In this same year, however, Maitland informed Lord Bathurst that a petition for financial support from Presbyterians in the Niagara District had caused some people to argue that the proceeds of the Reserves should not be confined to the Church of England. His advisers were quite convinced that the latter must be the sole beneficiary, but since there was "a lively feeling throughout the province" he appealed for a definite decision from the British government on the question.[8] The fateful issue was emerging.

Maitland's query was referred to the Law Officers of the Crown, and on the basis of their opinion Lord Bathurst wrote his reply on May 6, 1820. He stated that the provisions of the Constitutional Act of 1791 for the support and maintenance of a Protestant clergy were "not confined solely to the clergy of the Church of England, but may be extended also to the clergy of the Church of Scotland." "Dissenting ministers," who were not "recognized and established by law" were excluded. The two churches were not to share equally. Only the Church of England could be endowed with land for the purpose of setting up parsonages or rectories, and in general it would be most expedient to look first to the support of that church. Where members of the Church of Scotland greatly predominated, however, it would be "both advisable and proper" that lands be reserved for the support of its ministers.[9] This dispatch had a very cold reception from Maitland and his executive council. It was filed away, given no publicity, and every effort was made to forget that it had ever been written. Yet its contents became known to the clergy and laymen of the Scottish church, and reinforced their conviction that they were entitled to a share of the Reserves.

They were soon voicing this conviction in demanding tones, advancing certain basic arguments that were to be endlessly repeated in the next two decades. The Church of Scotland was an established church, so recognized at the time of union in 1707. Since Canada had been acquired after the union, the Church of Scotland was as much established there as the Church of England. The term "a Protestant Clergy" was deliberately used in the Constitutional Act as a formula to cover both churches. Petitions rehearsing these arguments were circulated in the two provinces, and then carried to London. The Assembly of Upper Canada adopted an address, asserting that the two churches were on an equal footing.[10] The leaders of the church in Scotland began to take an interest in the matter, and to add their voice to the growing insistence.

While the campaign was being mounted the forces of the Church of England counter-attacked with equal vigour. A petition from the Upper Canada Clergy Reserves Corporation, signed by Strachan, listed many proofs to show that the term "Protestant Clergy" referred only to their church, argued that religious dissension would result from two establishments, and asserted that the Church of Scotland was the smallest Protestant denomination in the province. In a dispatch backing these arguments to the hilt Maitland urged that the Church of Scotland be given only occasional aid, at the discretion of the government. Charles Stewart, the mild-mannered travelling missionary who was soon to be named Bishop of Quebec, and John Strachan both went to England in 1824. There these two Scots of such contrasting temperaments defended the Church of England against the claims of the Kirk. The Colonial Office was not anxious to become involved in this controversy, however, and postponed a definite decision. When the Reserves became productive it would be time enough to pass on the Kirk's application.[11] Of course, this evasion left each side the more determined to keep up the agitation.

Yet both churches were losing touch with public opinion in Upper Canada, which was little inclined to support the exclusive claims of either one. Although the Assembly had earlier favoured equal treatment for the Church and the Kirk, in January 1826 it asserted that all denominations of Protestants were equally entitled to share in the Reserves. Moreover, if it should be found impossible to divide the proceeds among so many groups, the majority of the Assembly favoured applying them "to the purposes of education, and the general improvement of this Province."[12] To Maitland it was obvious that the Assembly had first taken up the Church of Scotland's case "only to open the door" to this new liberal position; the Assembly's address should be final proof to the British government that giving way to the Church of Scotland would encourage the clamours and attacks of every Protestant sect. The Kirk was equally indignant. Its leading lay spokesman in the province, William Morris, complained that neither the government nor the Assembly was ready to put it on any more respectable a footing "than the most obscure sect" or to give its clergy any more preference than that accorded "the most ignorant itinerants."[13]

New bitterness was injected into denominational rivalries by John Strachan's assertions of the claims of the Church of England. In July 1825, when delivering a funeral sermon marking the death of Bishop Mountain, he not only praised the progress of the church during Mountain's thirty-two years as bishop, but went out of his way to make uncomplimentary comments about the other Protestant denominations, especially the Methodists. In the following spring he went to England, where he remained for more than a year engaged in many tasks, including the negotiations with the Canada Company, the bill for selling the Clergy Reserves, and the chartering of a provincial university. While in England he returned to the theme of his funeral sermon by forwarding to the Colonial Office an Ecclesiastical Chart purporting to show the strengths of the various denominations in the province. The Chart showed some thirty Anglican clergymen serving fifty-eight places either regularly or occasionally, apart from missionary journeys. He was able to find six independent Presbyterians and but two ministers of the Kirk. The other denominations were dismissed contemptuously. Since the Methodists had "no settled clergymen" he had found it "difficult to ascertain the numbers of Itinerants employed" – perhaps there were twenty to thirty. "The other denominations have very few teachers, and those seemingly very ignorant." In an accompanying letter, he further paid his respects to the "teachers of the different denominations" by stating that, with few exceptions, they came from the United States "where they gather their knowledge and form their sentiments." The "Methodist teachers" were particularly open to suspicion, since they were "subject to the orders of the Conference of the United States of America." Only by increasing "the number of the established clergy" could the government prevent the Methodists "from gradually rendering a large portion of the population, by their influence and instruction, hostile to our institutions, both civil and religious. . . ." At the same time Strachan made it clear that he was disgusted by the readiness of the British government to listen to the enemies of the church. It was "sickening to the heart to read the language" of British cabinet officers and members of parliament. The "progress of liberalism" was "bringing everything into disorder."[14]

In these pronouncements Strachan overreached himself, and did his cause incalculable harm. When the Archdeacon, as he now was, returned from England in the summer of 1827, it was to find a seething indignation that had been growing rapidly during his absence.

The opening gun in the counter-offensive had been fired a year before in the form of a long letter, criticizing Strachan's funeral sermon, written by Egerton Ryerson and published in Mackenzie's Colonial Advocate. It was a champion of equal mettle and durability who now entered the lists, for Ryerson during a long and often stormy career was to have an influence at least as great as Strachan's on the religious, educational, and political life of the province. The man who would one day be called "the Pope of Methodism" had just turned twenty-three years of age when his letter appeared.

The son of an Anglican Loyalist who had served in the Revolutionary War and again in the War of 1812, Egerton, like three older brothers and one younger, was converted to the Methodist faith by the itinerants who came westward out of Niagara to the Long Point country where the family lived. After a good elementary education, interlaced with farm work and buttressed by his own reading, he felt the call to preach in connection with the Methodists. In 1825 the Conference received him on trial, and assigned him to the York and Yonge Street Circuit. It was not long afterward that his fellow Methodists asked him to prepare a rebuttal against Strachan's attacks.[15] In such wise, one of the most accomplished controversialists in Canadian history received his first opportunity to try his powers. Always true to his loyalist and conservative origins and always wishing to live within the confines of his religious calling, nevertheless he was seldom long out of the public eye. His powerful and active mind, his vigorous and dominant personality, and his compelling if sometimes erratic passion for civil rights, social justice, and religious equality drove him again and again to take a leading role both in the affairs of his denomination and in the wider world of government and politics.

In his long letter Ryerson took issue with Strachan at every important point. Although expressing his admiration for the Church of England, he denied it any special claims based upon apostolic succession. He disputed Strachan's assertion that no nation was truly Christian unless it had an established church. Above all, he defended the Methodist itinerant preachers, asserting that they were carefully selected, well trained, and well supervised. He denied that they were a subversive influence, pointing out that all but eight of them were British-born and of these eight only two were not naturalized British subjects. The letter was a remarkable performance, and it greatly heartened his fellow Methodists. One of them regarded it as "the commencement of the war for religious liberty."[16] It was in fact the most outspoken and the most effective challenge so far flung at the leaders of the Church of England and their government supporters.

It was also the commencement of a period of intense sectarian debate, made the more bitter when Strachan's Ecclesiastical Chart and his letter to the Colonial Office became known in the province in September 1827. A wide-ranging newspaper controversy sprang up, in which each side made extreme, indeed extravagant, charges against the other. Strachan himself remained silent until March 6, 1828, when he made a lengthy defence of his position in a speech before the Legislative Council. He admitted to some errors in the Chart, but argued that these did not affect its general soundness. Once again he asserted that the Church of England was established in Upper Canada, and was entitled to the full proceeds of the Clergy Reserves.

In turn, Strachan was once again answered at even greater length by Ryerson.[17]

Meanwhile, the Assembly had received a petition bearing nearly six thousand signatures asking for an inquiry into Strachan's "cruel charges" against Methodists, and into the proposed University Charter, and calling for steps to preserve the petitioners and their children "from ecclesiastical domination." The petition, along with some others of the same tenor, was referred to a Select Committee of five, chaired by Marshall Spring Bidwell, who was emerging as the leader of the reformers in the Assembly. The Committee heard numerous witnesses representing both houses of the legislature and the executive government, various clergymen, and private individuals. It asked the witnesses whether the non-Anglican clergymen in the province were for the most part from the United States, whether the Methodist ministers were rendering the population "hostile to our institutions, both civil and religious," whether the people would be more attached to these institutions if the number of Anglican clergymen was increased, whether the population wished an established church, and many other questions in the same vein. With only two or three exceptions, among whom John Beverley Robinson stood out, the witnesses, including members of the Church of England, flatly contradicted the assertions in Strachan's letter and chart, and declared the latter to be full of inaccuracies.

On the basis of this testimony the Committee submitted a lengthy report to the Assembly, the essentials of which were incorporated in an address to the King, adopted by the Assembly on March 20, 1828. The address declared that only a small proportion of the population belonged to the Church of England, and that there was no tendency for the number to increase. The Methodist preachers were vigorously defended. The address went on to say that the people did not want an established church, and recommended, once again, that the Clergy Reserves should be used to advance education and internal improvements. The address also strongly attacked Strachan's University Charter.[18]

Meanwhile a group of reformers determined to repeat their strategy in the alien controversy by making an appeal to England. As the "York Central Committee," they secured eight thousand signatures to a petition, protesting against the exclusive claims of the Church of England, and forwarded it to George Ryerson, one of Egerton's older brothers, who was in England on private business. George Ryerson had it placed before the House of Commons by Joseph Hume, a radical member of parliament who was interesting himself in the complaints of colonial reformers. Ryerson also found that several other MP's were sympathetic to the cause which he represented.[19] The liberal winds blowing in Britain were henceforth to have a powerful effect on the course of political controversy in the Canadas.

In this same period, early in 1828, the forces of the Church of England and the Kirk were equally active in Upper Canada in the circulating of petitions, and these too were forwarded to the mother country. Canadian affairs were beginning to press for attention in British government circles, even more strongly in fact from the lower province than from the upper. In the former the conflict between the Assembly and the executive over financial control had brought parliamentary government to a full stop. Papineau's party collected 87,000 names on a petition and carried it to England, while the English-speaking residents of the Eastern Townships made their complaints known in another petition bearing 10,000 names.

Inundated by this flood of paper the Colonial Secretary, William Huskisson, moved in the House of Commons on May 2, 1828, for a Select Committee to enquire into the government of the Canadas. He stressed the government's intention to make every effort for the improvement of the provinces and its belief that they would one day emerge as "free countries like ourselves." He spoke harshly of the survival of French laws and customs in the lower province, asserting that it was both the duty and the interest of the mother country to "imbue" Canada "with English feeling, and benefit it with English laws and institutions." Noting Huskisson's preoccupation with the problems of Lower Canada, Hume criticized the Secretary for failing to discuss Upper Canada's grievances, particularly those relating to the University Charter and Strachan's Ecclesiastical Chart.[20]

Inevitably, the Select Committee devoted the major share of its attention to Lower Canada, but it did hear several witnesses from the upper province who happened to be in London, including George Ryerson and William Hamilton Merritt. The evidence given by some British officials, notably James Stephen of the Colonial Office, and the general tone of the Committee's Report angered the tories of Upper Canada more profoundly than any other action hitherto taken by British liberals. In the matter of the denominational rivalries the Report, being a mere expression of the Committee's opinion, settled nothing. Still, it gave some comfort to the Church of England's opponents by arguing that although only that church could be endowed with parsonages, the proceeds of the Reserves might be applied to the clergy of any of the Protestant denominations, depending on their respective strengths. The Committee noted that Anglicans made up only a small part of Upper Canada's population, and it deplored Anglican predominance in the proposed university.[21] All told, it was hardly surprising that members of the Family Compact continued to fume over the Select Committee's Report for the next decade and more.

In Upper Canada after the furore over Strachan's Chart had somewhat subsided, there was a brief respite from denominational bitterness. The new lieutenant-governor, Sir John Colborne, who arrived toward the end of

1828, was a Waterloo veteran like his predecessor and much more at home in military than in civil tasks, but by nature he was a more sympathetic man than the cold and aloof Maitland and readier to conciliate public opinion. In particular, he was anxious to avoid the impression that he would rely entirely upon the small group of advisers who had been so close to Maitland and of whom Strachan was the dominating figure. Not only did he seldom consult the Archdeacon, to the latter's intense indignation, but he informed both Bishop Stewart and the Colonial Office that Strachan's activities had been very harmful to the cause of the Church.[22] In fact, he was a zealous friend of the Church of England and as narrowly suspicious of the Methodists as any of his predecessors.[23] But for a time these rigid attitudes were disguised behind a pleasant and agreeable manner, leading the province to wish him well and to hope for a muting of religious disputes. When the strongly reform Assembly, elected in 1828, showed a disposition to quarrel with Colborne, it was rebuked in the ensuing elections of 1830, which saw the return of a conservative majority. There was no real difference between the majority of the conservatives and the reformers on the subject of the Clergy Reserves; both were opposed to the claims of the Church of England, and in favour of using the proceeds of the Clergy Reserves for education. The voters appeared to hope, however, that a conservative Assembly might accomplish more than its predecessor, which had passed bills on the subject, only to have them rejected by the legislative council. In this the voters were to be disappointed.

For their part, the leaders of Methodism in Upper Canada were preparing to play a larger role in the province's life. The Annual Conference, now independent, it will be recalled, of any American affiliation, resolved to sponsor a weekly newspaper, the *Christian Guardian*, which began publication in 1829 with Egerton Ryerson as its editor. At first, the paper largely confined itself to religious and moral questions, especially Indian missions and the temperance movement, but before many months its editorial columns displayed distinct political overtones. Given the nature of church and state relations in the province and the combative personality of its editor, it was inevitable that such overtones should appear. Within a year Ryerson was demanding a complete separation between church and state, arguing that clergymen should be supported voluntarily by their adherents, and that the revenues of government should be used to support "education, the arts and sciences, &c." The general tenor of the *Guardian* was enthusiastically approved by William Lyon Mackenzie. In its early years it was in fact widely regarded as a recruit to the ranks of reform journalism. Time would show that this impression was false, since Ryerson was following his own course, one that now ran parallel to that of the reformers, but would not always do so. He was striking at the "abominable incubus" of "Ecclesiastical Establishment" in order to enlarge the scope of Methodist action, not out of any broad program of political reform. For the time being, however, he was appealing to a large audience, not only of Methodists, and the *Guardian* became the most widely read newspaper in the province.[24]

And it was not long before sectarian feeling was again at a white heat, with a renewed round of petitions and counter-petitions pouring in upon the Colonial Office. One incident in the controversy brought Colborne's true views clearly into the limelight. When the Methodist Conference asked him to forward an address to the King, the Lieutenant-Governor, in an impetuous and petulant gesture, took it upon himself to scold the Conference for its opposition to "Church Establishment," to indulge in innuendo regarding its American connections, to inform its leaders that they were incompetent to express opinions on education, to accuse them of conducting a political journal, to deplore their "officious interference" with the Indians (a reference to Methodist missions), and to warn the Conference that the "small number of our church" would increase as more British immigrants came in. It was an astonishing as well as a highly vulnerable performance, an easy mark for Egerton Ryerson to knock over in five thousand words. Colborne was also soundly rebuked by the Colonial Secretary, when the incident came to the latter's attention.[25]

Meanwhile, the same Colonial Secretary, Lord Goderich, had been wrestling with the problem of the public support of religion in Upper Canada so insistently raised by the flood of petitions and memorials that was reaching his desk. This problem was before him at the same time that he was reviewing the whole question of colonial land policy, making it possible for him to combine his plans for the Clergy Reserves with his Wakefieldian scheme for selling all Crown Lands at good prices and to the highest bidders.

Assuming that the basic objection to the Clergy Reserves was that they were an obstacle to settlement, Goderich proposed to restore peace by stopping all further reservation of land for the support of a Protestant Clergy and by reinvesting in the Crown all existing Clergy Reserves land, to be sold henceforth on the same basis as all other Crown lands. But this plan missed the whole point, since the Clergy Reserves, already being sold and leased at a fairly rapid rate, were no longer a real obstacle to settlement. The basic objection was that one-seventh of the land of the province was set aside as an endowment for the Church of England, with perhaps a little going to the Kirk. And here Goderich offered nothing, for he clearly intended that the Church of England would continue to be supported out of the proceeds of land sales.[26]

A further insight into Goderich's intentions is afforded by his specific instruction that the clauses in the Constitutional Act looking to the erection and endowment of parsonages or rectories for clergymen of the Church of

England were not to be affected in any way by the proposed changes. In a later confidential dispatch he informed Colborne that while he hoped for religious peace in Upper Canada, and favoured some government support for other denominations, he nevertheless hoped for "the widest extension of the Church of England," provided there was no "exclusion or repression of other churches." Most fatefully, he counselled Colborne to use some of the funds available to prepare lands for the endowing of Church of England rectories.[27]

Despite the insistent tone of his dispatches, however, Goderich's plan for re-investing the Clergy Reserves in the Crown was ignored in both provinces. The Lower Canadian Assembly was in no mood to pass any bill sent from the Colonial Office. In Upper Canada the legislature was on the point of adjourning when the dispatches arrived, and although the bill was introduced in the Assembly it did not come to a vote. Colborne and the official group had no enthusiasm for a plan that would deprive the Church of England of exclusive control over the Reserves, while the majority in the Assembly wanted a far more drastic break with the past than Goderich offered. Only a few weeks before, this conservative Assembly had addressed the King, declaring that the great majority of the people was opposed to the establishment of any exclusive or dominant church, and wanted the proceeds from the sale of the Reserves placed at the disposal of the provincial legislature, to be used exclusively for the support of education. And this address had been followed by one to Colborne, announcing that the Assembly would henceforth dispense with the services of a chaplain in order to avoid any appearance of recognizing an established church.[28]

These were the considered views of a conservative Assembly, one which, as we shall see later, expelled William Lyon Mackenzie from its ranks on several occasions. In reform circles criticism of the Church of England was much less restained. The Cobourg *Reformer*, for instance, likened it to "a smitten trunk, surrounded with noisome weeds, and encircled with the windings and twistings of Clerical abuse and abomination – loaded with pomp and cursed with Simony – which stands blighted and blasted by the vengeance of an honest and indignant nation."[29] As the main recipient of government aid and with its leaders making exclusivist claims, the Church of England was obviously in a highly vulnerable and exposed position. Yet its clergy, believing deeply in their mission, saw no choice but to hold firmly to their position, especially when a decision of the British government, effective July 1, 1832, caused a drastic reduction in the stipends paid to Anglican clergymen in the province. In the long run this financial crisis helped the church to become more deeply rooted in Upper Canada than ever before,[30] but one immediate effect was to increase its insistence on receiving all the proceeds from the Clergy Reserves.

At the same time, the Methodist Church in Upper Canada was under-going an even more severe upheaval, with correspondingly greater effects on provincial life. This upheaval arose out of the union of the Canadian Methodists with the British Wesleyans, a marriage forced upon the Canadians.

Neither the provincial nor the British government had been happy at the withdrawal of the Wesleyan missionaries from Upper Canada in 1820, and this feeling was much stronger a decade later. By this time the Canadian Methodists were regarded as a dangerous political force, who ran an anti-government newspaper and who openly supported the forces in opposition to the government. We have already noted Colborne's resentment. How much better everything would be if the Wesleyans came back! They did not dabble in politics, while the inclinations of their leaders were strongly pro-tory, their British loyalty was of course unquestioned, and their atti-tude toward the Established Church was properly deferential. Not surpris-ingly, the Wesleyans began to receive suggestions that they return to Upper Canada.

When George Ryerson heard hints of this possibility in 1831, he wrote from England to his brother Egerton in very hostile terms of the "arbitrary" and tory outlook of the Wesleyans, and prayed that "the Lord continue to save us from the government of an European Priesthood." He rejoiced that "our country lies beyond the Atlantic and is surrounded by the atmosphere of freedom," and recommended looking to the United States for a General Superintendent. "Better to bear the temporary censure of enemies in Canada, than the permanent evil & annoyance of having a Church & State Tory Superintendent from this country."[31]

It was nevertheless inevitable that the British Wesleyans should return to the province, as they did in 1832. They were urged to do so by govern-ment leaders. Their help was needed in the Indian missions, which lacked funds. It could be argued that the withdrawal agreement of 1820 was no longer binding, since that had been made with the American Conference, from which the Canadians had now withdrawn. And with British immigra-tion to Upper Canada rapidly increasing, they felt a new and insistent call to duty in the colony.

The Methodist leaders of Upper Canada reacted quickly and decisively. Hiding feelings of resentment and anxious to avoid a bitter and harmful struggle, they greeted the Wesleyan missionaries with an offer of union, a readiness to accept a British president, and a willingness to surrender their Indian missions to a superintendent appointed by the London Wesleyan Missionary Committee.[32] Two of the Ryerson brothers—John and Egerton—urged these arrangements on the Canadian Conference, and although some of its members were reluctant, the Conference accepted them. In 1833 Egerton Ryerson went to England as the Canadian delegate to settle the terms of union, which were essentially the ones originally proposed by the Canadian Methodists. The union, however, involved one highly disturbing consequence. The British government had recently proposed that £900 be allotted to the Wesleyans out of the provincial funds available to assist religious bodies in Upper Canada. Union would thus implicate the Canadian Methodists in the receipt of government monies, despite their long-standing voluntarist scruples. Ryerson and his associates sought to sugar-coat the pill by announcing that this money would be used solely for the Indian missions, and since the Indians were wards of the government there was no real departure from their principles. In the latter part of 1833 the union went into effect.

The union powerfully affected the religious and political life of Upper Canada. It disrupted Upper Canadian Methodism, for many Methodists in the province refused to accept it, and organized themselves into the separatist Methodist Episcopal Church. Moreover, within the main body considerable friction between British and Canadian elements arose and persisted until the union was dissolved in 1840. Ryerson and his associates, however, tried hard to make the union work, and to reap the advantages of a more respectable and more secure position. They sought to give Canadian Methodism a new political direction or rather, as they would have put it, to take it out of politics. As we shall see, Ryerson broke with Mackenzie and the extreme wing of the reform party. The *Guardian's* tone became less political and more purely religious. The paper continued to speak, though in more muted tones, against church establishment, which seemed incongruous if not hypocritical coming from the organ of a body that now also received government aid.

All this was to have an important influence on the political trends of the pre-Rebellion years, but on the central issue of church and state relations there was little change. The bitter controversies of the 1820's had left too deep a mark. The great majority of the population remained firmly opposed to anything smacking of church establishment, and equally opposed to a division of the Clergy Reserves among religious denominations. This opposition was the one unvarying constant in Upper Canadian politics.

II

In their determination to give the young province of Upper Canada a strong British impress its leaders were as much concerned to foster the right kind of education as they were to encourage sound religious development. Indeed, the two concerns were hardly separate, since in common with most of their contemporaries in other lands, in the United States as well as in western Europe, they believed that children and young people should be educated in a religious setting. Unfortunately for the success of their plans, however, they conceived of this setting in such narrow terms that strong and eventually overwhelming opposition was raised against them. As a result they have seldom received credit for their genuine and arduous efforts to provide the province with an effective educational system.

The prime mover in improving Upper Canada's early schools was the Reverend John Strachan. A product of Scotland's famous schools and a successful teacher in both Cornwall and York, he viewed the scene on the aftermath of war in 1815 with evident dissatisfaction. The only government-supported schools were the grammar schools set up in 1807 – one for each district – good in their way, but too expensive and too remote for more than a fraction of the population. The government did nothing to support elementary education. Here and there throughout the province parents banded together to hire a teacher for their young children, and there were also several private academies of varying quality. If a child was lucky he might indeed get the rudiments of a sound education, as Egerton Ryerson had done. But there was no central direction and no responsible supervision of this hodge-podge of schools, and there were too few of them. They were often in the hands of unqualified teachers, men who had failed in every other calling. Equally harmful, in Strachan's view, was the fact that teachers were often Americans, who used American books. Children were taught anti-British sentiments, a special brand of American geography and even American arithmetic. Finally, there was no institution of higher learning. A few parents were able to send their children to England, but most young people who sought advanced training found it in the United States where, in Strachan's view, they learned "nothing but anarchy in Politics & infidelity in religion."[33] During the remainder of a long lifetime Strachan was to devote a major portion of his energies to an effort to correct this situation in all its aspects. The educational system as finally evolved would be very different from the kind he wanted, yet in a real sense he was its first architect.

The most obvious need was for more elementary schools. Under Strachan's inspiration – this was at a time when his relations with the lower House were good – the legislature in 1816 appropriated £6,000 for the annual support of common schools, the money to be used for defraying the salaries of teachers. Local trustees were to select the teachers, who must be British subjects, and were to make reports to District Boards of Education, also set up by the Act. It was a modest start, but it compared not unfavourably with what was being done elsewhere. Strachan also secured some changes in the grammar schools in 1819, providing for annual reports, for the admission of poor children by scholarships (a provision that apparently came to little) and for public examinations. In 1823 a General Board of Education was established, with Strachan as president, which had a supervisory authority over the province's schools, and had some power to manage the school lands. The beginnings of a planned school system were clearly coming into view.

Meanwhile, however, Strachan and the executive government were taking steps and making plans that would soon envelop all phases of education policy in bitter controversy.

In 1820 the legislature reduced the annual appropriation for the common schools from £6,000 to £2,500, largely because of the financial crisis of that time. At this juncture Sir Peregrine Maitland closed down the common school at York (arguing that other localities needed the small available stipend more than the capital did), and used the building to inaugurate a monitorial school based on the Bell system of National Schools. These schools, organized under Church of England auspices, were having a considerable vogue in England. They were held to be the perfect way to teach large numbers of children at a relatively low cost, since the older pupils gave lessons by rote to the younger. Here, then, in Sir Peregrine's view was a system by which he might combat "the baneful influence" of American teachers and "their republican apparatus."[34] He hoped to see the system spread, and he sought and obtained revenues from the school lands for the support of the National Schools.

This system did not flourish in Upper Canada, and of the few schools established none survived for very long. The Assembly, which had not been consulted in their establishment, later fastened on Maitland's arbitrary action in closing the York School as one of the great grievances of the decade. The incident was kept alive for years, with the dismissed teacher, Thomas Appleton, periodically placed before the province as a victim of executive tyranny. This attempt to put education in Anglican hands produced little but alarm and suspicion in the province. It was obvious that Strachan's "silent policy," as he called it, of concentrating "the command and direction" of education "in our clergy" was going to run into trouble.[35]

At the same time, Strachan was seeking to realize his goal, and that of Simcoe before him, of a provincial university. Efforts to secure help from the legislature failed in 1816 and 1817, but with the arrival of Maitland in 1818, he secured a willing ally who would support his efforts over the next decade until success seemed to be achieved. Maitland's early attempts to interest the Colonial Office in the project were unsuccessful, because at this time the British government appeared to favour the establishment of a university in Montreal to serve both provinces. Nevertheless, in December 1825 Maitland renewed his request for a university at York, and he sent Strachan to England to support the project. Over a period of several months,

Strachan put his case both to the British government and the British public, and he argued it persuasively if not always with complete consistency. By contemporary standards it was clear that Strachan wanted a liberal institution, one that would be open to everyone, without religious tests, except for divinity students and for professors who sat on the university's governing council. He had some difficulty in getting British authorities to agree to such latitude; in fact, they required a slightly tighter Anglican control than Strachan would have preferred. On the other hand, in seeking financial support from Church of England bodies, Strachan stated that the university would be a "Missionary College . . . for a century to come," and that its main function would be to train Anglican clergymen.[36]

After several months of negotiations, Strachan was successful in his quest. On March 31, 1827, Lord Bathurst announced that a Royal Charter had been issued to King's College, that it was to receive £1,000 a year out of the Canada Company payments, and that the British government had agreed to endow the College with 225,944 acres of valuable Crown Reserves in exchange for an equivalent amount of poorer lands from the original School Reserves.[37] Within a short time the terms of the charter became known in the province. The Anglican bishop of the diocese was to be the official visitor, the lieutenant-governor the chancellor, and the archdeacon of York to be the president. It was to be governed by a council consisting of the chancellor, the president and seven of the professors, the latter to be members of the Church of England. There was to be a Divinity School for training Anglican clergymen. Apart from members of this School, no students were to be required to take religious tests.

By contemporary English standards it was the most liberal charter ever issued for the establishment of a university, but its terms were immediately attacked by the Assembly, which was at the same time exercised over Strachan's Ecclesiastical Chart. The "sectarian tendency" of the proposed institution was vigorously criticized, and the King was asked to cancel the Charter and to issue a new one that would not be subservient to the Church of England.[38] A short time afterward the Canada Committee of the British House of Commons added its voice to the rising clamour by advocating that no religious tests should be required of the members of the College Council and that there should be a Church of Scotland as well as a Church of England theological professor.[39]

Despite the outcry a College Council was established according to the terms of the Charter, and it began to sell the university lands and to purchase property in York on which buildings could be erected. Once it was aware of provincial dissatisfaction, however, the Colonial Office drew back, and invited the provincial legislature to submit suggestions for changes which, it was promised, would receive prompt attention. This was a rather fruitless proposal, since there was no chance that the Assembly and the legislative council would ever agree on desirable changes. Seeing the impossibility of such agreement, the new lieutenant-governor, Sir John Colborne, exercised his authority as *ex officio* chancellor to halt all further progress in establishing the university. In any event Colborne felt that a university was less needed than a good preparatory school, and he took early steps to set one up at York, soon to be known as Upper Canada College. This institution, which was endowed with a portion of the school lands, and which received loans from the university endowment, was intended to have the features of the best English grammar schools.

Colborne's action, although it initiated one of the most famous of Canadian schools, did nothing to quiet the rising tempest. Strachan and his associates were outraged at the halt given to the university. Downing Street was ruffled because Colborne had acted without its approval although, characteristically, it gave in. And the reformers in the Assembly saw Colborne's school as an academy for the children of the provincial aristocracy, poaching on school lands and on an endowment meant for the province as a whole. The Assembly continued its drumbeat of resolutions and bills, looking to the cancelling of the Charter and the establishment of the university on a more liberal basis, a drumbeat that remained just as loud after a conservative Assembly was elected in 1830. Out of this controversy a consensus emerged in the Assembly in favour of a state-supported secular university, a fairly novel conception for that time in the western world. With equal determination, however, the legislative council rejected all the Assembly's proposals.

Once again the Colonial Secretary tried his hand, when Lord Goderich, on November 2, 1831, earnestly asked the College Council to relinquish the Charter in order that one more suited to the wishes of the province might be substituted.[40] Strachan and his colleagues, although willing to make a few compromises, flatly refused to give up the Charter. It had been issued by the King, and they meant to keep it. They believed that it was this kind of shilly-shallying on the part of London that kept agitation alive in the colony. They maintained this adamant position until the eve of the rebellion, and then receded from it only slightly. And later, when King's College was transformed into the "godless" University of Toronto, Strachan answered by founding the University of Trinity College.

One early response to the university Charter came from the Methodists. For a few years many of their young people had been attending Cazenovia College in central New York, but in 1830 the recently formed Canadian Conference resolved to establish an institution to be known as Upper Canada Academy, where no system of theology was to be taught and no religious tests required. It was to be financed by small contributions collected on the circuits. Ryerson openly contrasted these arrangements with those contained in Strachan's charter.[41] Lack of funds delayed the opening of the Academy at Cobourg until 1836. Later it was renamed Victoria College, and later still, it was federated with the University of Toronto.

In the Assembly the whole educational system was soon under attack. Taking the view that colleges and schools which were supported by public lands or public revenues should be "equally accessible to persons of all religious persuasions, and of all classes of society,"[42] the Assembly majority found much to complain of in the arrangements governing the common and grammar schools. They objected to the General Board of Education because it was not subject to legislative supervision and because it was presided over by John Strachan. After repeated attacks, they finally secured the abolition of the Board in 1833 and the right to appropriate the proceeds from the unalienated school lands. Above all, they concentrated their fire on the grammar schools, where they also found Church of England influence to be excessive. Although a fair number of teachers were non-Anglicans (usually Presbyterians) it was generally believed that an Anglican clergyman was seldom passed over for appointment when one was available. It was also believed that far too many school trustees were Anglicans, and to change this situation it was recommended that the trustees should be elected. The Assembly also felt that free grammar schools were more important to the province than a university, and repeatedly resolved that the university endowment be turned over to the grammar schools.[43] In these same years, of course, the Assembly was also resolving that the proceeds from the Clergy Reserves should be used for education as well as for internal improvements. The Assembly expressed solicitude for the common schools as well, asking on more than one occasion that one million acres of waste land be transferred to the care of the provincial legislature as a permanent fund for the support of these schools.[44] In much of this there was a genuine interest in education; in even more, perhaps, there was an ambition on the part of the Assembly to enlarge its powers at the expense of the Executive.

Despite the growing rancour of political debate the legislature was gradually working its way to an improved school system during the 1830's. There was little actual accomplishment, beyond an increase of the appropriation for common schools, but out of the welter of bills and proposals came a consensus that helped make possible the constructive accomplishment of the following decade.

One persistent focus of discussion was the question whether the trustees or commissioners who supervised the schools should be locally (and annually) elected or should be appointed by provincial authority. A satisfactory system required both local participation and a firm central direction, but in the political climate of the 1830's it was impossible to consider the subject on its merits. The reformers in the Assembly were strongly opposed to an appointive arrangement which merely extended the control of the Family Compact to all the school districts of the province, while the legislative council resolutely opposed the election of school trustees as a republican device, both cumbersome and expensive, that would not put the best qualified men in positions of authority. There was some merit in each position, but reconciliation had to await a quieter time.

Another phase of the discussion centred on the manner of financing the schools. Reformers, who were anxious to please their constituents as well as to berate the executive authority, argued that adequate funds could be derived from the school lands, from the Clergy Reserves, from the public lands generally, or from all of these. If only these lands were in the hands of the legislature, to appropriate as it saw fit, a magnificent school system could be provided at little or no cost to the taxpayer. Conservative spokesmen, such as Mahlon Burwell, maintained, on the other hand, that the local school districts must learn to tax themselves, and that the provincial government should do no more than match these local contributions. Reversing the usual tendency, it was Burwell and his associates who drew strongly on the American example, citing in particular the system of state and local participation that had been worked out in New York. To be sure, the reformers talked loudly of the superiority of American school systems, but they were always rather vague on the question of taxation. When they did borrow ideas from across the line, as Charles Duncombe did in 1836, following a lengthy trip through the United States, they refused to face the question of how it was all to be paid for. To the legislative council fell the thankless task of standing out for a plan that was within the province's means. All of these problems were in better perspective by the end of the decade; in the meantime, however, they had done much to intensify the bitterness of public debate in the pre-Rebellion years.

CHAPTER 10

The Rise of the Reform Movement

As Sir Peregrine Maitland's term as lieutenant-governor drew to a close in the autumn of 1828 he was an angry and a somewhat bewildered man. He had been responsible for the province's government for ten years. During that period its population had approximately doubled. Settlements had been formed in dozens of new townships, and obvious progress had been made in providing them with roads, sawmills, and grist mills, while in the older districts churches and courthouses as well as private buildings were taking on a more substantial form. Vigorous canal-building projects were under way, and a provincial bank had been established. Elementary and secondary schools were dotted about the province, and a university with a magnificent endowment had recently been chartered. Sir Peregrine felt that the growing economic prosperity and the more civilized aspect of Upper Canada owed much to the honest and conscientious government over which he had presided.

Yet it was a bitter fact that for some two years there had been a rising agitation, which showed no signs of abating. Grievance-mongers had been busily getting up petitions, filled with harsh and extravagant attacks upon his conduct of affairs and, what was far worse, receiving aid and comfort from members of the imperial parliament. And only lately, during the past summer, a provincial election had returned a majority of malcontents and oppositionists to the Assembly. While he believed that the majority of the population consisted of loyal subjects, he was filled with foreboding for the fate of the province as he went off to his new post in Nova Scotia. Like conservative government leaders in other times and places, he could see only a few wicked and seditious men where there was in fact a growing popular movement.

Although there was a touch of exaggeration in Maitland's statement that "for more than eight years [he had] administered this Government with satisfaction," he was on the whole correct in dating the beginning of agitation to the controversies surrounding the alien question. In his mind, almost the whole blame for that agitation lay with British MP's and with the Colonial Office for entertaining mischievous petitions and for failing to support his administration. He accused British MP's and British newspapers and reviews of constantly hinting that Upper Canada "must be humoured" because it was "delicately situated" near "a great and enlightened republic," "and that if we do violence to their feelings or inclinations they will naturally and certainly throw themselves into the Arms of their Neighbours, whose form of Government is supposed to have so many attractions." This Maitland flatly denied: the well-disposed majority in the province valued "themselves upon having a much better form of Government, and one quite as free and much more favorable to human happiness." Nothing was to be gained "by breaking down all barriers between us and the United States." Only a few "political disturbers" and "some hundreds of people" whom they had corrupted and deluded wanted to sever "this Colony from the Parent State." A policy of making concessions to such a "miserable minority" could never succeed, as all past imperial history showed; its only effect would be to encourage them to make ever more extravagant demands.[1]

Undoubtedly, the opponents of the provincial government's naturalization policy had received encouragement from Britain; what Maitland failed to see or to admit was that that policy had alarmed a very large segment of the provincial population and that failure to allay that alarm would have increased, not diminished, the prevailing agitation. He also would not see that in the last years of his administration the efforts of John Strachan, his most trusted adviser, to monopolize the Clergy Reserves for the Church of England and to ensure that the proposed provincial university should be controlled by that church had given grave offence to even more inhabitants than had the alien question.

These two issues provided popular support for the reform movement toward the end of Maitland's régime. There had, however, been many causes of irritation, accumulating over the years, that provided recruits for the movement. Some of these were inevitable in the prevailing form of government and stage of social development; others were rather trifling incidents, reflecting both a narrow and petty attitude on the part of the provincial government and a tendency toward extravagant exaggeration on the part of its opponents.

In any political context the question of who gets the jobs is never far below the surface, if it is below the surface at all. To a great extent, the basic complaint against the Family Compact was that it distributed patronage in a narrow and selfish way. In the long run, the demand for a less exclusive system of government – for "Responsible Government," as the cry became – derived its main impetus from a determination to break the stranglehold of the local oligarchy on appointments bringing prestige and profit. In a pioneer society, where business and professional opportunities were limited, interest in holding a government place, even one carrying a modest stipend, was much livelier than in modern times, when that interest even yet has far from disappeared.

Heartburning over the distribution of patronage had existed from the earliest days of the province, but it became more noticeable as government activities expanded. In one respect the government had always faced a genuine problem in filling posts demanding education and specialized training. There had never been enough qualified men for these posts among the native-born inhabitants, with the result that there was a recurrent tendency to look to Britain for appointees. This was an inevitable and also a sound policy, for it brought into the province men who raised its cultural level, yet it was equally inevitable that it should be viewed with jealousy by those who were passed over. On the other hand, among the British immigrants there were those who felt themselves to be ignored by the provincial government; they, too, raised their voices in complaint. Moreover, and also inevitably, many appointments went to men who lived in, or were willing to move to, the provincial capital. Residents in distant towns often felt that a few men in York were keeping all the good things for themselves, their relatives and friends.

But the Family Compact were not simply looking for men of education and training. They wanted reliable men, men who were devoted to the British connection, men who would assume positions of leadership in their communities, men who felt deeply about the welfare and security of the province. Newcomers from Britain who came out because they were unsuccessful at home and knew nothing about the province were not necessarily reliable. One reason that Strachan wanted a university was to train the most intelligent young men of families who had a stake in Upper Canada for the positions of leadership that should naturally be theirs. Only in Upper Canada, and under the right auspices, could that training be effective. All this was understandable in men who felt that Upper Canada would remain British only if the most careful policy was followed, but in their application of these principles they were intolerant, short-sighted, and selfish. They passed over Methodists and members of some other religious denominations, presumably because of their American connections. They ignored men, and the relatives of men, who had even mildly criticized the government, in or out of the Assembly. They black-listed men who had had any connection with Gourlay's meetings, even long years after that episode. They raised the cry of loyalty at every turn, but they did it so narrowly and so unfairly that many throughout the province came to regard their conduct of government with indignation and antipathy. "A faction of corruptionists . .

soldered together by the principle of avarice," the Family Compact was regarded by its opponents as requiring but one qualification for office – "obsequiousness."[2]

Another persistent cause of antagonism to the provincial government, which had its roots deep in the past, had to do with the control of the revenue. It will be remembered that one important purpose of the Constitutional Act of 1791 had been to provide the provincial executive authority with greater financial independence than the governors of the old pre-1776 colonies had enjoyed. Certain funds were entirely at the disposal of the executive authority and beyond the reach of the legislature: the casual and territorial revenues of the Crown, including receipts from land sales and leases (and the payments from the Canada Company after 1826), and the receipts from the Quebec Revenue Act of 1774. Other funds were raised by laws passed by the provincial legislature, but in a pinch the executive could carry on the government without these funds. Any representative assembly, whatever its political complexion, would eventually fret in these circumstances and grasp for the control of all the revenue raised in the province; and the Assembly of Upper Canada ran true to form.

In the beginning its campaign was mild enough, without the vehement character of the Lower Canadian Assembly's assault, yet it was clear that its demands would always grow and never be satisfied. In the earlier 1820's the Assembly contented itself with calling into question the accounting practices of the government, complaining that monies expended were not clearly detailed. A little later, the Assembly took to skimping on the annual supply bill, thus embarrassing the government without in any way bringing its operations to a halt. Maitland implored the British government to stand firm against any enlargement of the Assembly's control over the revenue.[3]

It was also perfectly clear, well before the rise of an organized opposition party, that the normal workings of the provincial constitution produced collision and discord. Disputes and minor clashes between the assembly and the legislative council occurred frequently. The assembly was already restive under the council's rejecting or pigeonholing many of its favourite bills, while the latter staunchly asserted its right to act as an equal and co-ordinate branch of the legislature. The assembly also complained that the presence of the Chief Justice on the executive council militated against the "pure" administration of justice.[4] On the other hand the Lieutenant-Governor asserted that he was entirely lacking in means to influence the assembly, and could not even be certain that the policies of his administration would be adequately or accurately stated in that body.[5] Friction was endemic under these constitutional arrangements.

Finally, during Maitland's régime there occurred a number of rather petty instances of the exercise of executive authority which were blown up by his critics until they appeared as cruel and heartless "outrages." We have already mentioned the dismissal of the school-teacher, Thomas Appleton, and the action against Captain Matthews. On another occasion the government dismissed the king's printer, Charles Fothergill, after he had voted the wrong way in the Assembly and, later, it cut off payments to William Lyon Mackenzie and Francis Collins, acting as official reporters of the Assembly debates, because of anti-government attacks in their newspapers. A more notorious incident occurred when an innkeeper named Forsyth fenced off a portion of the government reserve beside Niagara Falls. Forsyth was entirely in the wrong, but instead of proceeding against him by a civil action, Maitland sent a small detail of soldiers to tear down the fence. In highly coloured and exaggerated language, which sometimes played fast and loose with the truth, committees of the Assembly sought to prove from these incidents that civil rights and free speech were being endangered by a military despotism. In fact, these actions of the government were relatively mild compared with the summary imprisonment which the Assembly on more than one occasion meted out to its own critics. Representative assemblies have always judged their own actions by a separate standard.

But the "outrage" on which the most ink was spilled revolved about the person of John Walpole Willis, a puisne judge of the Court of King's Bench who arrived in Upper Canada in September 1827. He was the first judge to be sent out from England since Robert Thorpe, and he came from much the same mould. A man of considerable legal attainments and of consuming ambition, he was soon at loggerheads with the government circles in York. Willis may have felt that the provincial leaders should treat him and his high-born wife (the daughter of the Earl of Strathmore) with greater deference than they evidently showed, while the provincial leaders had no instinctive affection for a man whose job might just as well have been filled by one of their own. At any rate, he was soon consorting with known opponents of the government, and apparently seeking recognition as a popular leader. More serious was his action in June 1828 of declaring in open court, and without previous warning to the government, that the Court of King's Bench was incompetent to function without the presence of the Chief Justice, who was in England on sick leave. Thereupon Willis left the bench, and refused to return to it. Administration of justice by the province's highest court was brought to a full stop. After securing opinions from the provincial law officers and from the executive council, Maitland suspended him, and he was removed by the British government when the full story became known. Upper Canada was well rid of Mr Justice Willis.

The episode, however, took place during a provincial election campaign, and reform orators used it as final proof that the province was suffering under an unfeeling military and clerical despotism. This appeal was obviously effective, for the new Assembly was dominated by reform opponents of the government. In the opinion of the Sheriff of York, "there never has been such a feeling of Radicalism existing (openly) in the Country as at the present time."[6]

John Rolph and Marshall Spring Bidwell, who had led the opposition forces in the previous Assembly, were now reinforced by two men who would acquire a prominent place in the Canadian reform tradition: Dr W. W. Baldwin, who was elected in Norfolk County, and his son Robert, who won the town of York for the reformers at a by-election in 1829 occasioned by the appointment of John Beverley Robinson as Chief Justice. The elder Baldwin, who had emigrated from Ireland more than a quarter of a century earlier, was a well-established resident of the provincial capital. Like Rolph, he was qualified to practise both as a doctor and a lawyer, and indeed for a time he had also been a school-teacher. Belonging to a prominent and well-connected family, possessed of considerable property, and an adherent of the Church of England, he might have been expected to gravitate to the ranks of the Compact or at least to be a firm supporter of the government. Yet for some years he had been an outspoken opponent of the ruling clique, and during the 1828 campaign he had toured the countryside building up enthusiasm for the opposition cause.[7] His twenty-four year old son, although always more moderate and more cautious, shared his political outlook. In the weeks after the election Rolph, Bidwell, and the Baldwins consulted frequently over programs and strategy. There was more than a hint that a unified political party was being formed, led by a caucus of reform leaders, or "cabinet," as Rolph called it.[8]

Not a member of the reform leadership, yet a notable figure in the party now forming was one of the newly elected members for York County, William Lyon Mackenzie. He had been busy as early as January, when he had proposed twenty-nine assorted anti-government resolutions to a meeting in Markham.[9] He followed up this sort of activity by publishing a "Black Book," in which he rated members of the Assembly according to their votes in past sessions.[10] To the surprise of most observers, and to the disgust of friends of the government, the fiery little editor was easily elected. The elderly Barnabas Bidwell counselled him to "avoid excess," and to "sacrifice . . . minor points of individual opinion to the general objects of the party."[11] But Mackenzie was never to be a very good party man.

At this stage the young reform party placed strong hopes on an appeal to the mother country. Following the success of the petition on the alien question they were encouraged to believe that liberal-minded men in the British parliament, both in and out of the government, would aid their cause. Accordingly, meetings were held at York in July and August 1828,

H

with the two Baldwins and other members of their family connection as the prime movers, which resulted in a lengthy petition that was sent to E. G. Stanley and to Lord Goderich, with the request that it be presented by them in the two houses of Parliament. The petition set forth a long list of grievances, gave much prominence to the Willis case, complained of the "total inaptitude of military men for civil rule in this Province," criticized the composition of the legislative council, and spoke of the "practical irresponsibility" of executive councillors.[12] When it was learned that the Duke of Wellington had become Prime Minister, W. W. Baldwin sent him a letter expanding on this last point. He asserted that the only hope of the colonists for "*peace*, good *government* and *prosperity*" lay in the adoption of British constitutional practice. There should be "a provincial Ministry (if I may be allowed to use the term) responsible to the Provincial Parliament, and removable from office by His Majesty's representative at his pleasure and especially when they lose the confidence of the people as expressed by the voice of their representatives in the Assembly."[13] Although the reformers were expending their shot on a great variety of targets, it was clear that some of them had glimpsed the surest way of gaining effective control of the provincial government.

This petition was an outrageous document in the opinion of Sir Peregrine Maitland, and he implored the British government to pay no attention to it. In bitter terms he commented on the character and social standing of the members of the committee which had organized the petition. Although the only one of the group having the "character of a gentleman," W. W. Baldwin was noted for assisting "the promoters of discontent." As for the others, they consisted of "American Quack Doctors, a tanner, Shoemakers, Butcher and Penny postman." Except for the Baldwins, none of them was "either known or received in the society of gentlemen here, whatever their politics." He concluded with a clause-by-clause refutation of the petition.[14]

Nevertheless, the petition was given a courteous although non-committal reception in Britain, and was made the occasion of a brief debate in each House. The former Colonial Secretary, William Huskisson, said military men were appointed because qualified civilians would not go to the colonies; he argued against unnecessary interference in the "internal arrangements" of Upper Canada, "especially as its vicinage to the United States placed it in a peculiar situation." The present Colonial Secretary, Sir George Murray, denied that British constitutional practices could be duplicated in the colonies, because the latter lacked an essential ingredient of the political system at home, namely, an aristocracy. The Duke of Wellington saw a military reason for rejecting Baldwin's plea, asserting that the principle of a responsible provincial ministry "could not be safely applied" in a colony "situated on a frontier," as Upper Canada was.[15] There was little encouragement in any of this, but probably the reformers expected little after the Duke of Wellington became Prime Minister.

Before this debate, the reformers had been encouraged by the Report of the Select Committee of the British House of Commons, which became known in Canada in the autumn of 1828. That Report criticized the composition of the legislative council, denied the exclusive claims of the Church of England to the Clergy Reserves, and recommended a broadened university charter. It was interpreted as a great blow to the oligarchy in each province, and as an "extraordinary document" that promised much hope for the future.[16] Of course, the friends of the government had little respect for this "precious report," which was just such a one as "old Bidwell, Son, Rolph, etc." might have drawn up; it was enough to "disgust the *sterling* loyalty of the country."[17] Strachan feared its tendency would be "to prostrate everything British – to nourish discontent – to depress the Friends of Good Govt and to strengthen Levellers and Democrats."[18] Sir John Colborne stated that the Report had "done much harm in both Provinces, by furnishing the disaffected with arguments that suit their views. . . ."[19]

Rejoicing at the discomfiture of the provincial government and its supporters, the reformers increased their efforts to strengthen and broaden their political organization. In Marshall Spring Bidwell's view, it would be folly to rely on a British government led by the Duke of Wellington for the maintenance of their constitutional rights. Only firmness, spirit, and unity on the part of the Canadian people would gain the day.[20] One obvious approach was to establish closer relations with the opponents of the administration in Lower Canada, and with the approval of Rolph, Bidwell, and Dr Baldwin, Mackenzie wrote an exploratory letter to John Neilson, the proprietor of the *Quebec Gazette* and an associate of Papineau. Mackenzie said that Upper Canadian reformers would be glad to receive papers and documents from their opposite numbers, as well as suggestions for joint action. In particular, he wondered whether the Lower Canadians would join in an attempt to assert the principle that the governor's advisers should be changed when they lost the confidence of the legislature.[21] John Rolph, also, rejoiced in Papineau's success and hoped that "the L. C. Patriots would join in asserting the principle and the practice" referred to by Mackenzie,[22] while Bidwell informed Neilson that his associates wished "to cultivate a cordial & confidential friendship with the patriotic members of your House of Assembly, and to act in concert with them."[23] These were the first real overtures of friendship between English-speaking Upper Canada and French-speaking Lower Canada, made through a Scottish-born intermediary, in the person of John Neilson.

Yet the reformers could do little with their victory during the brief parliament of 1829-1830, which was dissolved upon the death of George IV.

In some respects they played the same roles as does a majority in the United States Congress when the presidency is controlled by the other party. They were able to harass and complain, but unable to produce a positive result against a powerful executive. As in the House of Representatives, they elected one of their leading partisans, Marshall Spring Bidwell, to the Speaker's chair, and he directed the majority from that vantage point. They were industrious in setting up legislative committees to investigate real and fancied shortcomings of the administration and, like an American legislative body, they were unable to enforce any real party discipline upon their members.

Nevertheless, the analogy is not very exact. They could never hope to control more than one of the legislative bodies. The legislative council was quite beyond their reach, and it was simply the executive authority in another guise. Their best efforts were rejected or simply ignored by the upper chamber. Perhaps even more important, they lacked any real power of the purse. With sufficient financial resources to carry on the government, Sir John Colborne did not even call upon the Assembly to vote supply, a situation which left the latter as a rather ineffectual debating society.

In these circumstances it was difficult to make much impression upon the electorate, particularly when the new Governor seemed to promise a change from the old ways. In his first months Sir John Colborne sought consciously to avoid some of the men who had been closest to Maitland. Although John Rolph was soon convinced that "Sir John [was] falling into the hands of those who ruled Sir Peregrine and scourged the country,"[24] the general impression in the province was that the new man should be supported, not harried.

This sentiment probably helped to bring the reformers down to defeat in 1830, and it may also be that there was some reaction against the Methodists, who benefited from the upsurge against Strachan in 1828, but who figured rather too prominently in the "saddlebag" Assembly elected in that year. Yet it is not easy to give a rational explanation of election results in a province where the population was widely dispersed and often poorly informed, and where party organization was still primitive. Much depended upon the appeal of the individual candidate, which often stemmed more from his national origin and religious affiliation than from his political program. It has been argued, for instance, that the reformers were defeated because they did not further the economic progress of the province, yet they were active enough in voting money for roads and canals. Nevertheless, they had as yet failed to secure a dependable majority among the voters of the province. In fact, the voters swung in pendulum fashion, between conservatives and reformers, from election to election in these years.

Despite their reduced numbers, the reformers in the Assembly seemed to grow in effectiveness after the election of 1830. Although a minority, they were far better led and disciplined than their opponents. In Bidwell, who now directed them from the floor instead of from the Speaker's chair, they had a resourceful and skilled parliamentarian, while his colleague from Lennox and Addington, the less polished Peter Perry, was a punishing and rough-and-tumble "Parliamentary Bull Dog."[25] On the other hand, the Conservative members appeared to be lost without John Beverley Robinson. The new Attorney General, H. J. Boulton, was an erratic person who never commanded the same respect and support. Perhaps the real leader of the government forces was the Solicitor General, Christopher Hagerman, a man with many of Robinson's qualities, but harsher and more explosive in his toryism. (The two sons of Loyalist stock, Perry and Hagerman, were the most unrelenting of political opponents.) Yet a great many of the conservative members refused to follow Hagerman; on the Clergy Reserves, the university, and a number of other questions, they were much closer to the reformers than to the administration and its spokesmen in the Assembly. John Strachan was revolted by the spectacle: Colborne provided little leadership, Boulton and Hagerman disagreed openly on the floor, "and by trimming the Bidwell party do almost what they please."[26] A conservative newspaper noted that the opposition had "a common and uniform system of action," while the majority had none, "no acknowledged leader – no mutual understanding."[27]

The morale of the reformers remained high despite their recent electoral defeat, because they believed that they were in the van of history, that they were fighting for a cause that was going from strength to strength in other lands and must inevitably conquer in their own province. In 1830 the Bourbons had been toppled in France, the Belgians had gained their independence from Holland, and the Poles had risen against the might of Russia. Much more important, however, was the encouragement they gained from events in Great Britain and in the United States.

Each stage of the bitter fight over the Reform Bill, when England seemed to teeter on the edge of violent revolution, was followed with the most intense and absorbed interest in Upper Canada. The defeat in parliament of the Duke of Wellington and the coming into office of a Whig government, the introduction of the Bill, the election of 1831, the defeat of the Bill in the House of Lords, the threat to appoint peers, and the final victory provided Upper Canadians with the greatest political drama of their lives. Nearly all of them felt that the province's fate was involved in the outcome.

Egerton Ryerson believed that the ministry of Lord Grey marked the end of the "iron age of high-toryism in Great Britain," to be succeeded by a "brighter era" whose "genial influence" would extend to the Canadas.[28] To Mackenzie it was "GLORIOUS NEWS !," promising that "the base mercenary hirelings" in Upper Canada would soon "follow their arbitrary master into oblivion." The people of Upper Canada need but stand up for their rights, and make their wishes known in the mother country, "now that both king and government are on their side."[29] A member of the government group reported that at word of the rejection of the Bill by the Lords, "all the old staunch Goverment men rejoiced, while the opposite party which are many would hang all the Lords up, beginning with Eldon, etc., etc., etc."[30] For his part, Colonel Talbot was "quite in the dismals" as he learned of the further progress of the Bill during the following summer.[31]

The reformers in Upper Canada were so much encouraged that they began to imitate the tactics of their fellow subjects in the mother country. Early in 1832 a "Public Meeting of Freeholders and Inhabitants of the Home and adjoining Districts" was held which recommended "to the several townships, counties and districts of this province, the formation of political societies on the plan of the political societies of England, Scotland and Ireland . . . for the preservation of civil and religious liberty."[32] Here was an obvious reference to the Political Union which Thomas Attwood organized in Birmingham at the beginning of 1830, and which was soon widely copied throughout the British Isles. When the news of the final passage of the Bill reached Upper Canada it gave a further impetus to the formation of political unions, the "mighty fulchrum" that had "moved the *whole British Empire*" and that would "inevitably move all Canada ! !"[33] In this political climate reformers gloried in the British connection; they were soldiers in the same army that was marching to victory in the mother land. In the early summer of 1832, for instance, the prospectus of a newspaper, soon to begin publication in the heart of Colonel Talbot's principality, stated that its "leading design" would be "to defend the political tenets of the reformers on British principles and no other."[34] Although Colonel Talbot brought out his "royal guards" to break up what he regarded as a republican conspiracy, the organizers of political unions were convinced that they were following British precedent.[35]

Nevertheless, Colonel Talbot was not very far wrong in his estimate. For all their genuine protestations that they were acting in the spirit of British reform, the reformers of Upper Canada were heavily influenced by their proximity to the neighbouring republican states.

To be sure, much of the so-called American influence stemmed from the circumstances of the province itself, and was not a slavish borrowing or importation from the United States. A pioneer society of small farmers, with an equalitarian social structure and a fairly even distribution of property, Upper Canada faced most of the same problems and developed many of the same attitudes as did New York or Ohio or Illinois. A tendency toward emotional and sectarian religion, a certain materialism and anti-intellectualism, a resentment of people with education and social standing, a rather sullen attitude towards strangers – all these characteristics of the American frontier flourished richly in Upper Canada along with the more celebrated virtues of individual initiative, hard work, and belief in democracy. Fortunately for Upper Canada, the province was spared some of the worst features of the frontier, such as its lawlessness, its inhuman treatment of the Indian, and its tendency to reject inherited European culture, but there were enough of these features to cause British travellers to feel almost as uncomfortable there as in the western States. John Mactaggart, a Scottish engineer working on the Rideau Canal, echoed the opinion of scores of other observers when he complained that "in Upper Canada the feeling is totally Yankee."[36]

Much of this "Yankee" feeling came directly from the character of the population. Both the old Loyalist stock and the later American settlers – the two groups were now considerably amalgamated through intermarriage – had strongly impressed their manners and customs upon the province by the end of the 1820's The prevalence of such manners and customs was at the same time quite consistent with a marked antipathy to the United States, often arising out of memories of the War of 1812, and in itself denoted no inclination for a closer political association with that country.

Nevertheless, it was the opinion of contemporary observers that the rise of political unrest and the spread of the reform movement were directly affected by events across the border, that the province would have been much quieter if it had not been exposed to pervasive American pressure. For instance, Thomas Carr, a Justice of the Peace in Otonabee, near Peterborough, asserted that "the republican mania has crossed the lines – our ears are incessantly dinned with the institutions, progress, prosperity, and the superlative system of land-granting of these States . . . we must run a race with them, and keep pace also in the career of prosperity; otherwise we are lost to Great Britain."[37] Another competent observer, R. B. Sullivan, the Commissioner of Crown Lands, in a report to the Lieutenant-Governor on the state of the province just after the Rebellion, began his lengthy analysis by noting that "There are no mountains or seas, or differences of language to separate this Province from the United States, and this Province must be materially affected by the state of Politics and of the popular mind in the neighbouring republic."[38] Comments in this vein were repeated almost endlessly in the years before and after the Rebellion of 1837.

Such influence has always been felt in Canada, throughout its history, but it had a special impact in the decade before the Rebellion. These years saw a rapid growth of democratic ferment in the nearby states, giving rise to a great variety of social movements and to Jacksonian Democracy as its most noted political manifestation. Universal white manhood suffrage became general in nearly all the states at the same time that they enjoyed a headlong rate of economic progress. The American example was beginning to have noticeable repercussions throughout the western world; it was inevitable that Upper Canada should feel those repercussions with the greatest force. It was also inevitable that critics of the provincial administration should find not only inspiration but also ammunition from across the border that could be used in their own political battles.

It was against this background of quickening political change in Britain and of expanding democracy in the neighbouring states that the reformers of Upper Canada assailed the power and authority of the Family Compact and fought for a broadened political system. The new winds from the mother country convinced them that it was entirely legitimate and appropriate to maintain the struggle, while the neighbouring states provided a multitude of examples which they felt to be worth emulating.

In the spread of reform sentiment throughout the province no other agency was so effective as the newspaper. For a time in the middle 1820's, Mackenzie's *Colonial Advocate* had stood almost alone as an anti-government paper, but by the early 1830's there were several weeklies "conducted on liberal principles."[39] The *Brockville Recorder*, the Kingston *Spectator*, the Cobourg *Reformer*, the Hamilton *Free Press*, the *British Colonial Argus* (St Catharines), and the St Thomas *Liberal* were notable examples, and in its early years the *Christian Guardian* was usually critical of the government. These papers ranged themselves against such tory and conservative journals as the Kingston *Chronicle*, the Cobourg *Star*, the *Courier* and the *Patriot* (both published in the provincial capital), the Hamilton *Western Mercury*, and the Sandwich *Canadian Emigrant*. It is hard to say which group of papers had the larger audience. It was claimed in 1833 that the *Christian Guardian*, the *Colonial Advocate*, and the Cobourg *Reformer* distributed "as many copies of their journals as any twelve of the Tory papers put together,"[40] although in the following year Mackenzie believed that the tory papers had pulled ahead.[41] All these papers, on both sides, were crammed with politics and most of them were relentlessly partisan in tone. Apparently they suited their public, for they were read with care by their subscribers and then passed around to friends and neighbours. Like Americans, the Upper Canadians were a newspaper-reading, much more than a book-reading, people. Mrs Jameson found the newspapers to be "the principal medium of knowledge and communication," and stated that a commercial newsroom in the provincial capital was "absolutely the only place of assembly or amusement, except the taverns and low drinking-houses."[42] With some exceptions, the papers were often vulgar and even scurrilous in tone, but they provided much more coverage of domestic and foreign news than can be found in small-town papers today.

With these considerations in mind, let us now examine some of the main features of the reform outlook as revealed in the legislative and newspaper controversies of the early 1830's.

The basic complaint of the reformers was that public opinion was ignored in Upper Canada. The government was in the hands of a small, exclusive oligarchy that reserved nearly all jobs for its own members and its hangers-on, that directed economic development for its own profit, that tried to monopolize much of the public land for the advantage of one religious denomination. On a whole range of issues the oligarchy flouted the known wishes of "the People."[43] To be sure, the voice of the people might be heard through their representatives in the Assembly, elected on a broad franchise. It was notorious, however, that the Assembly was nearly powerless as against the executive authority and the legislative council. And the popular branch of the legislature was not always a pure vessel since, it was alleged, the executive had various means of influencing the election of members or of corrupting them after they were elected. Hence the reformers fought for a political system in which public opinion would flow unimpeded and in which those who represented that opinion would hold power.

In making their case against the provincial government the majority of the reformers usually stopped short of making a frontal attack upon the lieutenant-governor. He was the representative of the monarch, the visible link with the mother country, and they were very willing to accord respect to his office. Their main complaint was that the lieutenant-governor surrendered his powers into the hands of an arbitrary and exclusive clique, who were the real rulers of the province. The reformers saw him as a military man, well-meaning perhaps, but untrained and unskilled in civilian affairs, and with little desire or incentive to discover the needs of the province. Sir Peregrine Maitland was accused of spending much of his time in indolence at his summer place near Niagara Falls, and the same kind of charge was made against Colborne.[44] Mackenzie was fond of making contrasts between the supine inactivity of Maitland and Colborne and the vigour of American state governors, and as we shall see later came to favour an elective governor for Upper Canada. But most reformers did not follow in this daring proposal; they confined themselves to hopes that the next man would prove to be more independent of "the faction."

It goes almost without saying that the reformers' complaints against the Lieutenant-Governor and their view of his relations with the executive council were based more on party feeling than on fact. Maitland and Colborne were very conservative men, quite out of sympathy with many of the aspirations of the people of Upper Canada, and lacking in the political ability needed to cope effectively with an aggressive and ambitious representative assembly. But they were neither indolent nor "supine." They were diligent men who worked hard to advance the welfare of the province. They

H*

drew their advice from too limited a circle of advisers, but they were never the prisoners of those advisers. Indeed, John Strachan, who knew the workings of the government from the inside, had a very different complaint against the lieutenant-governors. He, too, felt that military men, who were "in general arrogant self sufficient and supercilious," were unsuited to civil government. They adopted "measure after measure without information and to the great detriment of the Country without the knowledge of the Executive Council or any reference whatever to them—but the Country supposing that they are consulted blame them and not the Governor." Some of this was sheer spite, occasioned by Colborne's attitude toward the university, but the fact remains that the very personification of the Family Compact believed that the lieutenant-governor should be required to "consult on all occasions with the Executive Council," who should in turn "be like the King's Ministers responsible for their advice."[45] There was never any real difference between the conservatives and the reformers of Upper Canada on the need for local control of the internal affairs of the province, although they did differ over the relationship between the executive council and the assembly.

The reformers, as we have already seen, also centred their attention on the role of the executive council. In the view of Dr W. W. Baldwin and of his son Robert, all other desirable changes could be accomplished if the executive council were to be made responsible to the Assembly and if the practice were to be established that the executive council should resign or be altered when it lost the confidence of the majority of the Assembly. Indeed, Robert Baldwin believed that this was the only reform needed. In the long run events would show that the Baldwins were essentially right in urging that a responsible council was the one sure way to end collisions in the conduct of the provincial government and to ensure effective local self-government.

Nearly all the reformers agreed with the Baldwins in this matter and, as we shall see, the demand for responsible government always had a place of high prominence in reform manifestoes and insistence on it was to help to precipitate the crisis of 1836-37 as well as to bring solutions in the years afterward. Yet none of the other reformers was to prove as consistently single-minded on this point as was Robert Baldwin, and for this fact there were understandable reasons. The executive council was a rather shadowy body, mentioned only indirectly in the Constitutional Act of 1791. No one knew, except its oath-bound members, exactly how it functioned, or what its powers were or could be in relation to the lieutenant-governor. Both Strachan and the Baldwins thought that its powers should be greater—a local ministry—although the former, like a good conservative, was not prepared to elaborate a theory on the matter. He simply believed that the governor should act on the advice of the loyal and reliable men in the council. The Baldwins constantly asserted that they wanted the British constitution as it was practised at home: that the Crown (in this case, the Crown's representative) should act on the advice of a ministry that had the confidence of a majority of the representatives of the people, in the Assembly, and that the ministry should resign when it lost that confidence.

But, leaving aside the basic fact that the governor was a servant of the British government and not a monarch, it was by no means a fact that the British Constitution in 1830 worked as the Baldwins described it, although it was beginning to do so. In Britain by the end of the 1820's there was indeed a ministry that was responsible for the King's actions and against which the King, in the final analysis or an open contest, was very nearly powerless. The ministry governed the country. But until 1830 the ministry was not dependent upon public opinion for its power and authority, and to a somewhat diminishing extent this remained so for many years afterward. Public opinion in the modern sense scarcely existed before 1830 and made itself felt only in times of great crisis. The ministers were men of great personal authority, usually members of the powerful aristocracy, or related to it; they manipulated the constituencies, and so won every general election between 1742 and 1830.[46] They did not feel bound to resign simply because they lost votes in the House of Commons, even on important bills. They were not always composed of the members of a single party. They were aristocrats, carrying on the government in the king's name; in the last analysis their authority did depend upon the approval of the House of Commons, but it was no simple servant-and-master relationship.

Certainly it was a far more complex relationship than that contemplated by the Baldwins. In Upper Canada there was no aristocracy, no class of men possessing independent standing and authority. Although rudimentary by modern standards, public opinion was a far more effective force than in Britain, and made itself felt at the polls. The party complexion of the Assembly changed at every election, often drastically. In short, the doctrine of ministerial responsibility as propounded by the Baldwins, would operate far more democratically in the Canadas than it did at the time in Britain. Some conservatives saw this, and exclaimed against a doctrine that would put a Bidwell or a Mackenzie or a Papineau in a ministry or even at the head of one, and that would in any event mean an entirely new council every four years, something that was not true in Britain at this time. But many reformers, looking at the actual operation of government at home, considered it to be in the hands of the aristocracy. They did not believe that a closer approximation to British practices would be of much help to them.

For many of them the legislative council was a much more tangible and immediate target. For years this body had been frustrating the will of the

Assembly by rejecting or side-tracking its bills, and its activity in this respect always increased when the reformers were in a majority in the representative body. It seemed rather pointless to try to win elections if the results were to be nullified by the upper House of the legislature.

Some of the criticism of the legislative council was exaggerated and unwarranted. The members of this body included men of education and legal ability who carefully scrutinized the bills coming to them. They could show that many of these were rejected because they were badly drafted or beyond the powers of the legislature. If the council had not negatived them, either the lieutenant-governor or the British government would have done so. It was easy but unfair to put all the blame on the legislative council, when much of it rested on the legislative ineptitude and unconstitutional ambition of the assembly. Moreover, the council could also show that in measures to develop the province, particularly in the field of internal improvements, it had co-operated fully with the assembly, and that many of its own measures had also been ignored by the other body. Its members asserted, and quite correctly, that the council had powers equal to those of the assembly and was fully entitled to exercise them as it saw fit.

Nevertheless, the legislative council was a highly vulnerable body, and nearly everyone, except its own members, agreed that it was in need of reform. Of the fifteen members who attended at the end of the 1820's, six were members of the executive council and four others held office under the government. Under these circumstances the council appeared not as an independent legislative body, but as the administration in another guise. Sir John Colborne saw at once that the membership should be enlarged, but he had difficulty in finding qualified appointees in a province not overly blessed with men of standing and education.[47] Some who were qualified but who lived in distant parts of the province refused to come to the capital to assume the onerous and unpaid duties of a councillor. Eventually Colborne did enlarge the council considerably, but since most of the new men were of conservative outlook the change did little or nothing to improve the reputation of the council among reformers.

The spotlight was increasingly on the legislative council after 1830 because of the changed emphasis of British colonial policy. It was now made clear that the British government was anxious to interfere as little as possible in the internal affairs of Upper Canada. On matters such as education and the Clergy Reserves, Downing Street was, within some limits, willing to accept any plan approved by the provincial legislature.[48] But this concession availed little as long as one branch of the legislature defied the public opinion of the province. If the council could be altered to reflect public opinion, if the legislature could speak with one voice, then an almost irresistible pressure could be exerted on the executive.

In the minds of most reformers there was only one way to make the legislative council responsive to public opinion, and that was to make it elective. They noted that as far back as 1790 Charles James Fox had favoured such an arrangement, and they were also aware that there were many contemporary British proposals for changing the composition of the House of Lords. At a time when the whole structure of the British Constitution was being vigorously reassessed there was no reason to think that an elective upper chamber violated any fundamental feature of that Constitution.

The reformers needed little stimulus from the outside, either British or American, to hit upon so obvious a device for dealing with a concrete problem. By the end of the 1820's men such as Mackenzie and Bidwell were calling for an "elective senate." A public meeting held at York on January 19, 1832, petitioned the King for a "Legislative Council elective by the People." From that time forward the idea was given a growing prominence in the reform program, although never to the same extent as in Lower Canada. There is some evidence that reformers were influenced by the structure of the United States Senate, although they did not want the indirect mode of election then used for the Senate.[49]

To members of the Family Compact it made little difference whether the idea came from British radicals or American republicans or was original with the reformers. They opposed it unreservedly, as an attempt to make the council "a mere passive instrument for giving effect to an unbridled democratic will."[50] Perhaps the most curious feature of the whole debate was that neither side saw that any form of election would strengthen the legislative council in its contest with the assembly. Strong second chambers have proved to be highly effective brakes on an "unbridled democratic will."

The third branch of government, the judiciary, also came under the scrutiny of the reformers. Particularly after the Willis incident, they argued strongly that judges should be independent of the Crown, as they were in Britain, with tenure during good behaviour and not during pleasure. As matters stood, the judges were thought to be merely an arm of the executive. If any of them displayed independence, they were struck down as Willis had been, and Thorpe before him. The reformers also complained of the presence of the Chief Justice in the executive council, and of his role as Speaker of the legislative council, and of the presence of other judges in the latter body. Sir Peregrine Maitland vigorously combatted reform accusations, but by 1831 Lord Goderich was prepared to concede the point. He offered to place all judges of the Court of King's Bench on tenure during good behaviour, provided the legislature would make an adequate and permanent provision for their salaries, and announced that for the future no judge (except the Chief Justice) was to sit in either council. On the latter subject the Colonial Office kept its promise, but on the former the Assembly refused to make the required provision regarding salaries. The terms of the judges' commissions therefore remained unchanged, and complaints about the independence of the judiciary remained a prominent feature of the reform program. In a subsidiary line of argument, there was frequent objection to the high cost of litigation, a result, it was said, of the oligarchy's arrangements to provide for its "many relatives and friends."[51] References to simpler and cheaper judicial processes in the American states were often made in this connection.

For many reformers faults in the administration of justice were most vivid at the inferior stages. Here, in the Districts, the Justice of the Peace was the dominant figure. Appointed by the provincial administration, he inevitably reflected its bias, and often appeared to be one of its agents. The fact that very few men of reform sympathies ever received such appointments was taken as proof of this point. Acting both individually and as a member of the Court of Quarter Sessions, the J.P. performed many extra-judicial functions, such as supervising statute labour on the roads and levying local taxes. He was regarded by reformers as still another official who was unresponsive to public opinion. They often demanded that some of his duties be taken over by elected persons or that the J.P. himself be made elective, as was the practice in several American states. The sheriff, another government appointee, also received his share of criticism, an inevitable result of the many unpleasant duties he had to perform, including the sale of land for unpaid taxes. A particular complaint arose out of the sheriff's power to select juries who, the reformers claimed, were usually "violent party men," representing the government's point of view.[52] Reformers, led by Peter Perry, favoured a more popular method of selecting juries, and here again they found comfort in contemporary American practice, where a lottery system was often used.[53]

In making their demands for a provincial government that would be subject to public opinion, the reformers often indicated that they had American state governments in mind as suitable models to follow. At a time when the states were relatively more important and the federal government less important than would be true in later years, it was understandable that reformers should be attracted by their example. Like Upper Canada the states were part of a larger political system, yet they appeared to enjoy almost complete control over their own local affairs, suffering but little interference from Washington. There were no built-in antagonisms between branches of the legislature, while the governor was the servant of the people instead of a distant Colonial Office, performing his duties at a fraction of the salary paid to Sir Peregrine Maitland or Sir John Colborne. These contrasts were "standing provocations to discontent now, and will become

bribes to revolt very soon, in our North American colonies; if their grievances are not redressed, and the feeling of the people consulted in the system
of government." "Only think of our attempting to establish a hot-bed of
aristocratic fungi in the near vicinity of the United States of America!"[54]
Fuller publicity for public accounts, lower salaries for government officials
and cheaper justice, less empty formality in the conduct of government, and
a stricter subjection of the military to the civilian power were among the
beneficial attractions which reformers saw in the states across the line. And
all of them were growing more rapidly than was Upper Canada.

In seeking an unsullied expression of public opinion reformers were enthusiastic advocates of the ballot. A petition favouring the idea had been
put before the Assembly as early as 1812,[55] but it was not until the 1830's
that the subject became the centre of vigorous debate. Complaining of the
frequent riot and bloodshed in provincial elections, supporters of the
measure noted not only that it had the backing of prominent British public
figures but that its use was proved by long American experience. A conservative majority defeated the Ballot Bill in 1833, but the reformers easily
passed it in 1835, only to see it rejected by the legislative council. Reformers argued that it mattered not whether vote by ballot "originated, or
is practised, at Algiers, the Cape of Good Hope, or in the State of New
York," while its opponents saw it as "an endeavour of the friends of United
States government to put our institutions on the same footing as theirs, to
destroy our principles of government, for I say the ballot system is hostile
to the principles of the British Constitution."[56] As it turned out, this controversy would persist in Canadian politics for many years to come.

Society in Upper Canada was too young and too simple to produce many
of the movements for social and humanitarian reform that were currently
gripping Great Britain and, to a lesser extent, the United States. Yet there
were a few instances of the same point of view in the province.

In 1826, for instance, Mackenzie was pleased to note that "We are quite
as advanced in legislation as the United States," as shown by John Rolph's
bill to abolish imprisonment for debt, brought in just before a bill on the
same subject was introduced in the United States Senate.[57] Here was a matter that was very much before the British public at this time and that had
been legislated upon in many American states. Many moderate conservatives joined the reformers in pushing the measure, but despite Rolph's efforts
over many years and despite passage in the Assembly in 1835 by a vote of
41 to 5, the measure did not become law in these years.[58]

Efforts to abolish the law of primogeniture received much more attention.
From 1825 onward Marshall Spring Bidwell, the leading advocate of this
measure, regularly introduced bills, providing for the equal division of
intestate estates. Egerton Ryerson stated that Bidwell's speech on the

measure in 1831 was "probably the most able Parliamentary effort that was ever made within the walls of the U.C. Parliament."[59] The bill passed regularly, often almost unanimously and by majorities of varying political complexions, but was consistently rejected by the legislative council. Bidwell argued that primogeniture might be suitable in an old and populous country like England but was out of place in a new and thinly settled community. He drew attention to the fact that it had been abolished in other British colonies as well as in the United States. "He was sure the country would be more free, more moral, more happy, if there was a pretty equal diffusion of property, than if it were principally accumulated in the hands of a few. He wished there might be none very wealthy, and none very poor."[60] Refusing to support such a "levelling system," however, Christopher Hagerman said the bill would "be a death blow to anything like an aristocracy" which he "considered essential to the happiness and good government of any people."[61] Like other tory opponents of the measure, he regarded it as a republican innovation, inconsistent with British principles.

As a final instance of interest in contemporary Anglo-American uplift we may cite the temperance movement. The campaign against the evils of liquor, which had recently been organized in the neighbouring states, was started in the Canadas in the late 1820's. Undoubtedly the campaign received considerable stimulus from the American example, and from American literature on the subject, although little or no direct American influence was present in the founding of the local societies in various parts of the province. It was apparent, nevertheless, that the chief carriers of the movement were clergymen of the evangelical Protestant sects, such as Methodists, Baptists, and certain groups of Presbyterians, which had the closest association with American denominations. It was this fact that gave certain political overtones to the temperance movement in Upper Canada, as well as the fact that some leading reformers, notably M. S. Bidwell and Jesse Ketchum, were prominent members of temperance societies. Anglicans and Roman Catholics, who perhaps had less tradition of attempting to regulate the moral conduct of their neighbours than did the sects with an American background, generally stayed clear of the movement, while men of conservative political inclination usually regarded it with suspicion. It was the view of Colonel Talbot that the "rebels" in his settlement had "commenced their work of darkness under the cover of organizing Damned Cold Water Drinking Societies, where they met at night to communicate their poisonous and seditious schemes. . . ."[62] Few tories would have supported such an outlandish statement, but most of them had little sympathy with a movement that seemed to be yet another American importation.

Such, then, were the views of the men who regarded themselves as the spokesmen of the plain people of Upper Canada. Very few of them were well-educated or even well-read men, and none of them worked out a well-articulated political philosophy. Most of them were considerably to the right of William Lyon Mackenzie, who will appear more prominently in the following chapter, and to the left of Robert Baldwin, who would later, somewhat by default, become their leader. They picked up political ideas and suggestions wherever they could find them, and put them to use in a pragmatic and often piecemeal fashion. They argued in simple and general terms "that all power belongs primarily to the people . . . and that all publick officers are their servants, and derive all their authority from the people."[63] It escaped few of them that in such a political system men who were skilled in appealing to the people – politicians with the democratic touch – would scale new heights of power and status.

CHAPTER 11

Mackenzie and the Grievances of Upper Canada

The history of the province in the six or seven years before December 1837 involves a great deal more than the activities of one little red-headed Scottish newspaper editor and assemblyman. Indeed, he might seem to be a rather insignificant individual when compared with Sir John Colborne, John Strachan, Egerton Ryerson, or William Hamilton Merritt, to name only a few, who exercised power and were constructively engaged in furthering the growth of Upper Canada on many fronts. Not only was Mackenzie not the leader of the reform party, but his disruptive course brought much harm to that party. Nor was his final resort to violence inevitable or in any way beneficial; the rule of the Family Compact could and would have been ended without recourse to rebellion. Notwithstanding, Mackenzie exerted a powerful and at times decisive influence on the course of events. Since he more than anyone else contributed toward making the times abnormal and contradictory, as well as exciting, he deserves some pride of place when they are recounted.

As we have seen, Mackenzie first appeared before the provincial public as an intemperate and often a scurrilous critic of the local oligarchy. Whether it was because people of standing snubbed and despised him as an impudent upstart or because, as he once suggested, of his "rebel" Highland blood,[1] he was anti-government from the start of his public career. As his later life, twenty years of it beyond the scope of his book, showed, he would be so all his life. He was a perverse, angular, cantankerous man. He was entirely unsuited to the life of politics, unable to work with colleagues toward an agreed objective, and quite without perspective. But he was also more than this. He was an omnivorous, if indiscriminate reader and an intense and unflagging student of public affairs. With complete disregard for personal gain or advancement, he put himself unreservedly at the disposal of the plain people of Upper Canada. Much of his effort was misguided or positively harmful, yet he gained a faithful following and he shook the provincial government to its foundations.

As to his goal, Mackenzie was remarkably consistent. He wanted a free government, without "favouritism and prodigality," that would "enlighten the minds of the people, and by every lawful means promote their happiness and comfort."[2] Of course, no government this side of heaven would ever have satisfied him in these respects, but one did not have to be an extremist to find the Family Compact somewhat wanting in the scale.

For many years he had no doubt that British ways were best or that Upper Canada would find its salvation within the orbit of the mother country, especially if it became part of a British North American union. He disliked the tone of American politics, and wanted no part of a country sanctioning slavery. But after an extensive trip in the United States during the first year of Andrew Jackson's administration, his outlook perceptibly changed. Here was democracy at work, and he liked it. In particular, he was enthusiastic about the Jacksonian practice of rotation in office (a polite term for the spoils system). What a wonderful way to get rid of the impudent "puppies and underlings of office" who so abounded in Upper Canada![3] Presently he was serializing the biography of his new hero, Andrew Jackson, in the pages of the *Colonial Advocate*. None of this meant that he wanted a political connection with the United States and its "southern and northern quarrels," but he was more convinced than ever of the feasibility of a "federative union" of the British North American colonies that would do away with "slavish dependence" on England, and he now regarded it as proved that "the representative system of government" worked, and worked well.[4] Opposing the growing English tendency to speak of the "Omnipotence of Parliament," he was sympathetic to the idea of a written constitution, to which all laws passed by the legislature must conform.[5]

But it was the contrast between provincial extravagance and republican frugality that Mackenzie found most glaring. Across the line the public debt of the federal government was being steadily reduced, while in Upper Canada the debt was growing to support the Welland Canal and other improvements. Mackenzie, along with other reformers, denied any opposition to these improvements, but he did argue that the province should not be saddled with increased obligations until it had a government that was responsible to public opinion. In Upper Canada, he asserted, "mismanagement of the public revenue prevails, of so gross and disgraceful a nature that the mere detail looks more like a romance than a reality."[6]

Early in 1831 the British government made what was meant to be an important concession to the two Canadian legislatures when it relinquished control over the revenue raised from customs duties under the Quebec Revenue Act of 1774. Henceforth the legislatures were to be free to appropriate these revenues. In return the legislatures were asked to pass civil list bills making permanent provision for the salaries of certain provincial government officials, who had previously been paid from these revenues. The Lower Canadian Assembly flatly refused to co-operate, but the recently elected conservative Assembly in the upper province was willing to pass such a bill, although it provided less than the executive asked for. It seemed to be a reasonable measure, especially since the revenues conceded were somewhat larger than the sum voted in the civil list bill, and it meant an expansion of the legislature's financial competence. But Mackenzie and some of his reform colleagues bitterly opposed this "Everlasting Salary Bill," claiming that there should be no permanent grants until "a constitutional responsibility" had been conceded. There could be no real check on the government as long as its principal officers were free of annual dependence upon the Assembly for their salaries.[7] Mackenzie and his friends lost this battle, but they never ceased to denounce the idea of a permanent civil list. They were fully aware of how effectively the assemblies in the old American colonies had harassed a financially vulnerable executive authority.

After the passing of this detested measure Mackenzie redoubled his efforts to bring home to the people the iniquities of the government and of the conservative majority in the Assembly. During the summer and fall of 1831 he travelled extensively over the province, and especially in his own constituency in York County, distributing tracts and pamphlets and getting signatures on grievance petitions. This activity, joined with the ceaseless stream of criticism carried in the Colonial Advocate, proved to be highly effective in strengthening and enlarging Mackenzie's political following among the farmers east and west of Yonge Street between the capital and Lake Simcoe. He convinced them that he had their best interests at heart; they in turn looked to him for information and guidance. Among these people were a great many of the old American population that had come into the province some thirty years before, and who were still ruffled by the recent alien controversy. A majority of them, including families of German and Irish origin, became unswerving supporters of Mackenzie.[8]

Supporters of the government watched these efforts of the little agitator with growing irritation. Already, earlier in the year, his endless round of motions and demands for investigation had led to an unsuccessful effort to expel him from the Assembly. By the time that body met again at the end of the year Mackenzie had provided his opponents with better ammunition to use against him, for in the November 24 issue of his paper he had referred to the Assembly as "a sycophantic office for registering the decrees of as mean and mercenary an Executive as ever was given as punishment for the sins of any part of North America in the nineteenth century." Accusing him of a libel against the House the tory leaders pressed a motion for expulsion, which was carried on December 13. It is probable that many of

Mackenzie's reform colleagues had little sympathy with his extreme language, either as used in his paper or in his speech defending himself in the House, but they stood loyally by him. Bidwell saw the issue essentially as one of freedom of the press; in a province where the executive had so much power – over revenues, lands, and banking, and even over the Assembly, through "placemen" – freedom would be destroyed if the opposition press were trampled down.[9] This argument had only a limited relevance, since no action was being taken against Mackenzie's paper.

Less than three weeks later, on January 2, 1832, a by-election was held, at which Mackenzie was triumphantly re-elected, with only one vote being cast for his opponent. He took his seat the next day. Two days later the *Colonial Advocate* was out with a slashing attack on Sir John Colborne, and the following day Christopher Hagerman was on his feet with another demand for expulsion, which was again carried. And this time Mackenzie was declared ineligible to sit again in that Assembly. Nevertheless he was easily re-elected.

When the Colonial Secretary received word of these events, he was greatly alarmed. No good British Whig could ever forget the famous case of John Wilkes back in the 1760's, and be unaware of the folly of a legislature attempting to contend against a resolute constituency. In a confidential dispatch, dated April 2, 1832, Lord Goderich advised Colborne that the Assembly had no power to keep Mackenzie out permanently and instructed him to use his influence with the Assembly to end its vendetta against this "unprincipled demagogue."[10]

Meanwhile, Mackenzie, unable to take his seat, was again touring the country, haranguing meetings, and finding an enthusiastic response to his fulminations against the government and the Assembly majority. Sympathy for Mackenzie had much to do with the organizing of political unions, getting under way at this time. After several weeks of this kind of activity Mackenzie set out for England with a sheaf of petitions under his arm, determined on an appeal from Upper Canadian Toryism to British Reform.

Then followed an extraordinary episode in the history of Upper Canada. Mackenzie regarded himself, and to a considerable extent was accepted by the Colonial Office, as a spokesman for all the dissatisfied elements in the province. He was accorded interviews by high Colonial Office officials, and his endlessly repetitious screeds were attentively read in Downing Street. It need scarcely be said that Mackenzie left no subject untouched. It was a long, hard summer for Lord Goderich and his colleagues, but they felt that they must be polite to a man whom they regarded as the leader of the opposition in Upper Canada. At the same time Mackenzie was making a considerable impact upon opinion in the British capital through a series of articles appearing in the *Morning Chronicle*. No other emissary from Upper Canada was ever taken so seriously in London. Eventually, on November 8, Goderich sent a most curious dispatch to Colborne. In one breath it vigorously discounted many of Mackenzie's complaints, but in the very next it assumed that some things might be wrong after all, which Colborne should seek to correct.[11]

Encouraged by his reception Mackenzie stayed on in London, continuing to press his charges against those in power in Upper Canada. For a man who believed so strongly in local self-government he was most persistent in seeking imperial intervention in provincial affairs. One of his main demands was that the British government should disallow recent bank legislation in Upper Canada. Mackenzie was convinced, and with some reason, that it was his fierce opposition to these bills that had really led to his expulsion, and he was determined to carry on the fight in England. On this matter he met with a good deal of sympathy, for British officials were always rather sceptical of the soundness of colonial banking bills.

This subject was slow in coming to a head, however. In the meantime, in March 1833, Mackenzie was elated to learn from the Colonial Office that a dispatch had gone out to Sir John Colborne ordering the dismissal of both Attorney General Boulton and Solicitor General Hagerman, as punishment for their part in expelling him from the Assembly. Here was success, indeed, with the possibility of more to come if the banking bills were disallowed. Mackenzie could well imagine the discomfiture of his enemies in Upper Canada.

Discomfiture is in fact too mild a word to describe the feelings of tories and conservatives as they learned of the Colonial Office's response to Mackenzie's mission. They were outraged by the tone of Lord Goderich's long dispatch of November 8, which took seriously so many of Mackenzie's complaints. After stating that a dispatch based on allegations from so contemptuous a source did not call for their serious attention, the legislative council returned it to the Lieutenant-Governor. In the Assembly Perry and Bidwell moved to thank the Secretary, but the conservatives by a vote of eighteen to ten carried an amendment regretting that Goderich did not rely on better testimony than that from a man who had twice been expelled from their House.[12] Conservative newspapers were still more outspoken, declaring that the Whig government at home never meddled in colonial concerns without doing "mischief."[13]

But outrage and disdain were succeeded by an almost uncontrolled fury when it became known that Boulton and Hagerman had been removed. The leading pro-government newspaper wondered what "this political imbecile . . . this foolish Colonial Minister" would do next. Everything was reduced to "a state of uncertainty" in which:

The minds of all the well affected people of the country (and they, to the certain ultimate discomfiture of the United factions of Mackenzie, Goderich and the Yankee Methodists *are a vast majority*) begin to be unhinged. Instead of dwelling with delight and confidence upon their connection with the glorious Empire of their sires, with a determination to support that connection, as many of them have already supported it, with their fortunes or their blood, their affections are already more than half alienated from the Government of that country, and in the apprehension that the same insulting and degrading course of policy towards them is likely to be continued, they already begin to "cast about" in "their minds eye," for some new state of political existence, which shall effectually put the Colony beyond the reach of injury and insult from any and every ignoramus whom the political lottery of the day may chance to elevate to the Colonial Office.[14]

Try as they might, Mackenzie and his friends were never able to surpass this tory denunciation of Downing Street rule.

Now, of course, it was the turn of the reformers to roll their eyes heavenward as they deplored this "shameless libel" upon a loyal people. The St Thomas *Liberal* called it "treasonable language" and the Hamilton *Free Press* asked all honest men to support the King's ministers in their reforms, and put down the tory threat of "Revolution and separation from the British government."[15] Public meetings were soon busy passing resolutions to the same effect. The outlook seemed to be very bright. A Whig Government might grant the essential reform demands – a responsible executive, control of the provincial revenue, and permanent tenure to judges and magistrates – and then Upper Canada would soon "become one of the finest countries in the world."[16]

But the reformers soon learned that their battles were not to be won in London. The "lottery" of British politics could work against them just as surely as against the tories. Soon it became known that a new Colonial Secretary had reappointed Hagerman to his old post and promoted Boulton to the office of Chief Justice of Newfoundland. Mackenzie, of course, already had this information, and he returned to the province in the early summer of 1833, disillusioned and bitter after his year in the old country. He was convinced that the reform impulse there was already spent, and that the people of Canada would henceforth have to rely on their own efforts. Canada did have staunch friends in the British Parliament but they were to be found among the radical members of the opposition, especially Hume and Roebuck, not in the government.

Another prominent Upper Canadian made his own journey to England at this time, but he came to a very different conclusion. While on his mission to arrange the details of the union with the British Wesleyans, Egerton Ryerson closely observed some of the leading personalities in British politics. Upon his return to the province he set forth his "English Impressions" in the *Christian Guardian*, which were sharply critical of the radicals in general, and of Joseph Hume in particular. These men were painted as infidels in religion, republicans in politics, and insincere and inconsistent in their concern for human welfare. Such men had no real standing or influence in the mother country, and Ryerson advised the people of the province to cease looking to them for advice and help.[17]

These comments may have been intended to work on Mackenzie's low boiling-point; certainly they succeeded in doing so. Within a few hours the *Colonial Advocate* was on the streets of York in a special edition, describing Ryerson as "Another Deserter," who had gone "over to the enemy, press, types, & all, & hoisted the colours of a cruel, vindictive tory priesthood." To Mackenzie it was plain that Ryerson's new course was the first fruit of the union with the conservative British Wesleyans: "a jesuit in the garb of a methodist preacher" had betrayed the liberties of the people of Upper Canada.[18] For his part Ryerson summoned up his resources of Christian charity to offer a gentle reply, saying that he had often admired Mackenzie's energy but thought him injudicious at times. A week later Ryerson sharpened his pen somewhat, when he accused his fellow editor of an "open and unqualified avowal of republican principles."[19]

Most reformers and most Methodists were extremely unhappy about this quarrel, and tended to blame Ryerson more than Mackenzie for a split that could only benefit the church-and-state tories. To be sure, Egerton's brother John strongly backed him up, with the argument that it was necessary "to obtain the confidence of the government & entirely disconnect ourselves with that tribe of villans [*sic*] with whom we have been too intimate. . . ."[20] But what was undoubtedly a more general reaction came from a group of five Methodist preachers, including Egerton's younger brother Edwy, who said that they were meeting a "torrent of opposition" on the circuits, with subscribers cancelling the *Guardian* left and right. They stated that they and their "brethren in the ministry" had not changed their political views, that they still felt themselves to be connected with the reformers, and implored Egerton to abandon the quarrel.[21]

The majority of the Methodists did retain their reform sympathies for some time, and many of them remained loyal to the cause throughout the decade. If Mackenzie had stopped at this point, Ryerson might have been nearly isolated within his own community. But with his usual abandon Mackenzie pushed his quarrel with Ryerson and the Methodist leadership to such extremes that he lost the reformers a significant portion of their Methodist support.

The leaders of the reform party were becoming increasingly embarrassed by their involuntary association with Mackenzie. From time to time they protested that the little editor did not speak for the party, yet they had no choice but to support him in his continuing contest with the majority in the Assembly. The latter, probably sensing this embarrassment, kept up the farce of expulsion, thus giving Mackenzie a prominence which the reform leaders did not covet for him. While he was in England Mackenzie had again been expelled, re-elected and yet again declared ineligible for membership, despite the known objection of the Colonial Office to this course. After his return he was once more elected, and then twice forcibly ejected from the House amid mob scenes of tumult and disorder. Bidwell complained that the House was making a martyr of Mackenzie and a spectacle of itself, but the majority was determined to have its way.[22] Mackenzie nevertheless had a revenge of sorts, for when the town of York was incorporated as the city of Toronto early in 1834, he was chosen as its first mayor by the aldermen victorious in the municipal election. Whatever misgivings reformers throughout the province might have had about him, Mackenzie's local support was still as firm as ever.

With the new mayor about to take up his municipal duties the House prepared to face one of the consequences of his trip to England – the proposed disallowance of recent banking legislation. In his paper Mackenzie had continued his barrage of attacks on limited liability and note-issuing banks, frequently praising President Andrew Jackson for his veto in the summer of 1832 of the bill rechartering the Second Bank of the United States and calling on King William to emulate this example.[23] A tory paper, The Patriot, twitted him for his sudden tenderness toward the home government, noting that he had "always been a stickler for self Government, but to effect a purpose he can change his opinion as the Camelion its color; sure proof of utter destitution of principle." This paper was indignantly opposed to any "puerile meddling of the Lords of Trade with our tills and money-chests."[24]

The Patriot on this occasion spoke for the business community in the capital and, as it turned out, for nearly everyone in the province as well. Intimations of imperial interference led to a remarkable demonstration in the Assembly, as representatives of all shades of opinion joined in the protest. In this conservative House Bidwell, seconded by Perry, moved an amendment to an address to the King, containing the following words:

> . . . if Your Majesty's Ministers, at a distance of more than 4000 miles, not at all controlable [sic] by or accountable to Your Majesty's Subjects here, and possessing necessarily a slight and imperfect knowledge of the circumstances of this country, the wants and habits and feelings

of the inhabitants, and the mode of transacting business among us, can dictate a different course in relation to measures affecting only ourselves from that which the people by their Representatives, and with the concurrence of the other branches of the Provincial Legislature, have chosen, we are reduced to a state of mere dependence upon the will and pleasure of a Ministry that are irresponsible to us, and beyond the reach and operation of the public opinion of the Province. . . .[25]

Only one member, Mackenzie's friend Jesse Ketchum, voted against this amendment. There could hardly be more convincing proof that men of every political outlook were determined to have local self-government, however much they might disagree over the means. Mackenzie contented himself with stating that "a more plain and distinct declaration of independence has not emanated from any British American Colony since the 4th day of July, 1776."[26] He could hardly be unaware that the rebuke extended to him no less than to the British government.

Following its policy of interfering as little as possible in colonial affairs, the Whig ministry did in fact draw back, and decided not to disallow the banking legislation.

It would, of course, be incorrect to leave the impression that Mackenzie was less devoted to the goal of self-government than any of his colleagues. Banking was one of the questions on which he felt most strongly, and some aberration was perhaps inevitable when he saw the chance of striking down these engines of the money power. Moreover, he probably thought that many of the supporters of the amendment were hypocritical, since they consistently winked at violations of the free flow of public opinion in other areas.

Since his return from England he had in fact lost nearly all of his readiness to turn to the British government for help against the local oligarchy. In replying to a reform address complimenting him on his work in England, he stated that he no longer wished to see the British Constitution "in practical operation in this country," because "a cheap elective, representative government, including both an elected Legislative Council and an elected governor, would be much preferable."[27] In dropping the adjective *Colonial* from the name of his newspaper at the end of 1833, he announced that he was doubtful that he "could any longer conscientiously advocate the continuation of the colonial system as now established, without great modifications." He had become "more democratic" as he observed the contrast between the United States, "where taxes and public monies return among the people to enrich them," and Upper Canada, where "the vast sums drawn from us for Canada Company's lands, Crown and Clergy Reserves, and large portions of the taxes, drain the country of a safe circulating medium."[28] In counselling reformers on how to plan for the forthcoming provincial elections he strongly urged them to adopt the American practice, which he carefully outlined, of regular nominating conventions as the only certain way of getting candidates who would remain "sincere reformers."[29]

He was cutting his ties with moderate men. He had broken with Ryerson, and had criticized the Baldwins for having "left the reformers in the lurch."[30] He attacked Neilson for breaking with Papineau.[31] He was ready to strike out on his own.

At the end of February 1834 he joined with a group of the more radical reformers in and around the provincial capital to assemble a general convention of delegates to nominate candidates. Neither John Rolph nor Dr Baldwin would participate, and Bidwell refused a nomination proffered by the convention. But the group went ahead, nominated candidates for the four ridings of York County, and pledged them in advance to fight for "the full control of the whole public revenue," the ballot, an elective legislative council, a responsible executive council, and several other changes. Each candidate was asked to promise that he would resign if he changed his mind on any of these questions.[32] At about the same time in many other parts of the province similar meetings were held which owed much to the example of Mackenzie and his friends in York County, who provided the party with a detailed program and inspired it to fashion effective local organizations. Men like Bidwell and Perry and Rolph could not oppose such activity, but they viewed with misgivings a movement in which Mackenzie was so prominent. Perry intimated as much when he said at a political meeting in his own county that "no two persons disapproved more at times of Mr. Mackenzie's occasional violence than Mr. Bidwell and himself, but they both supported him on principle, seeing that the people had been insulted in his person"[33] – a reference to Mackenzie's expulsion from the Assembly. These men were well aware of Mackenzie's active and successful efforts to give the reform party a fighting edge, but they also knew that his capacity to embarrass the party remained undiminished. This capacity was soon given vivid demonstration when Mackenzie imprudently published a letter from his close friend, Joseph Hume. Like many of the British radicals, Hume hoped to see the colonies cut adrift, because he saw them as a burden on the British treasury and a means of providing outdoor relief to the aristocracy. When he heard of Mackenzie's latest altercation with the Assembly, in December 1833, he wrote that this incident "must hasten that crisis which is fast approaching in the affairs of the Canadas, and which will terminate in independence and freedom from the baneful domination of the Mother Country and the tyrannical conduct of a small and despicable faction in the Colony." He advised Canadians never to forget "the proceedings between 1772 and 1782 in America."[34]

This letter might be read in two ways. It might simply be a call for the ending of colonial misrule and for a new and less subordinate relation to the mother country. The reformers, who fervently wished that Mackenzie had put it in his letter case instead of in *The Advocate*, tried hard to put this interpretation upon it. But from Hume's known views on the Empire it was more likely to be a call for separation from the mother country, and one in which Mackenzie must be implicated, since he had published the letter with approval. It provided tories and conservatives with a heaven- (or rather Hume-) sent opportunity to denounce reformers as "wretched conspirators" who were now "gibetted together, TRAITORS IN THE FIRST DEGREE."[35] Reformers had some very hard thoughts about Mackenzie as they squirmed through that summer.

If the provincial elections had been held in June, the reformers might have been caught badly off balance, but they were not held until October. By that time the sensation over Hume's letter had died down, and the quarrel with Ryerson, although it left a residue of bad feeling, had not alienated many Methodists from the reform cause. The work of building a strong political organization went on, while Mackenzie sought both to reassure and to invigorate his supporters. Saying no more about his earlier view that the British Constitution could not and should not be established in Upper Canada and that he doubted the value of the connection with Britain, he returned to a course acceptable to a majority of reformers. Once again he emphasized the protection and the assistance which a powerful and liberal mother country could provide to a young and struggling colony. He assured the voters that their demands for control of the public lands and the whole revenue, for a responsible executive council and an elective legislative council would be readily conceded, if they would but "elect an intelligent and patriotic House of Assembly" that could "act in concert" with the "present enlightened government" at home.

In this address, "To the Reformers of Upper Canada," Mackenzie placed special emphasis upon the distress of the farmers. All along, one of the main charges against tories and conservatives had been that they were too tender to the interests of merchants and millers and bankers and too insensitive to the crying needs of farmers. Now Mackenzie returned to the complaint that American agricultural produce was allowed to enter the province duty free and could reach the British market under the preference, as well as compete in the Canadian market, while an American tariff kept Canadian produce out of the United States. Mackenzie accused the conservative legislature of the last four years of having worsened this situation by tax policies harmful to the farmer. At a time when the agricultural prosperity of the later 1820's was ebbing, this was an effective political argument.[36]

An appeal along these lines, united with the strong local organizations built up in the last couple of years, brought victory to the reformers in the elections of 1834. It was apparent to all observers, both inside and outside the party, that the victors were still split into moderate and radical wings, but they put up a brave show of unity. Once again they put Bidwell forward as their candidate for Speaker, and despite Hagerman's determined attempt to put a disloyal, pro-American label on him, the vote for him was overwhelming. As British freemen, seeking only constitutional reform, the members were not to be frightened, in Peter Perry's words, "by imputations of treason, or the whining snivelling cry of loyalty, made by persons who were loyal only to their salaries."[37] They then carried an address to the Lieutenant-Governor, asserting that reformers deeply cherished the British connection, and complaining of tory insinuations to the contrary.[38] As a further gesture aimed at closing ranks the majority passed a resolution expunging from the Assembly's journals "all declarations, orders, and resolutions" related to Mackenzie's several expulsions.[39]

On many subjects it was indeed easy for reformers of all shades to agree. They wanted protection for the farmers against American agricultural imports. They denounced the patronage policies of the executive, which were so discriminatory against reformers. They sought (without much success) for information "respecting the powers, duties and responsibilities of the Executive Council."[40] They repeated their demand for control of the whole revenue, and coupled it with criticism of the Canada Company. They passed bills embodying their views on jury selection, the Clergy Reserves, intestate estates, the University Charter, and many other subjects, which met their usual fate at the hands of the Legislative Council. Despite a resultant sense of frustration they remained hopeful that "obstacles to the peace, welfare and good government of the Province" would be removed; in particular, they wanted a system of "local responsibility," especially needed in view of the "rapid succession" of Colonial ministers who are "strangers to the Province."[41] In all these matters the reform majority was substantially united – and ineffectual.

Once more in the Assembly, and with heightened influence, Mackenzie willingly joined his reform colleagues in passing these resolutions, addresses, and bills. But he never believed that such activity would be sufficient, or very useful. Moreover, he was always suspicious of Assemblies, no matter how reformist they were at the beginning, it was all too easy, as he thought, for the executive to detach and corrupt the more timid and weak-kneed by appointments to office (postmasterships and so on) and by other enticements, such as invitations to the Governor's dinner table. Continuing pressure must be exerted on the government from outside the Assembly, and that body must be watched. Within the Assembly more was needed than futile talk. Mackenzie girded himself for action.

His first step was to free himself for "other and more important duties" by giving up *The Advocate* after more than a decade of arduous, not to say furious, journalism. This was a safe step to take, because Toronto now had another radical paper, *The Correspondent*, edited by William J. O'Grady, an apostate Roman Catholic priest, who was as implacably opposed to the government as Mackenzie himself. Accordingly, *The Advocate* was merged with *The Correspondent* a few weeks after the election.[42]

It was not long before Mackenzie revealed what his "more important duties" would be. On December 9, 1834, a general meeting in Toronto established the Canadian Alliance, and he was appointed its corresponding secretary. This organization intended to encourage the formation of branch societies throughout the province and to "enter into close alliance with any similar association that may be formed in Lower Canada or the other Colonies, having for its object 'the greatest happiness of the greatest number.'" Apparently the spirit of the recently departed Jeremy Bentham was to preside over the Alliance. It intended to "watch the proceedings of the Legislature," to spread "sound political information by tracts and pamphlets," and to "support honest, faithful and capable Candidates" for office. All members must agree in writing to support its political program.

That program included the usual reform demands for a "responsible representative system of Government," sale of the Clergy and Crown Reserves "under the control of the representatives of the people," support for education and internal improvements, the vote by ballot, not only for "representatives" and aldermen but for "justices of the Peace, &c.," and "control of the whole Public Revenue." Amended jury laws, an end of primogeniture, a "responsible Post Office," the "extinction of all monopolizing Land Companies," and the "total disunion of Church and State" were inevitably included among the planks. In addition, however, the Alliance called for the abolition of the legislative council, not content to have it elective,[43] and for a "Written Constitution for Upper Canada, embodying and declaring the original principles of the government." Nothing was said about the British connection except that they opposed "all undue interference by the home government" in the "domestic affairs of the Colonists."[44] In the opinion of the *Christian Guardian*, the Alliance Reformers had abandoned "Colonial connexion and monarchy" for "Republican independence and democracy."[45]

Mackenzie was soon busy at his corresponding duties, believing that "unless we get societies up hav'g one common object to be pursued by the same means," the new parliament would "disappoint our hopes – but if we enlist the people in our cause we are safe."[46] During the next several months branch societies were organized in many parts of the province.

Within the Assembly, Mackenzie saw one role that was worth playing above all others. Like members of the American Congress from time to time, he decided that the best way to get at an independent executive was to investigate it. Satisfied to let his reform colleagues go on with their bills and resolutions, he prevailed upon them to set up a Committee on Grievances, appoint him as its chairman, and fill it with radicals of his own kind. The Reform leaders agreed, probably hoping that Mackenzie would go off with his committee and leave them alone.

Here was a marvellous opportunity to hold a grand inquisition. After years of being scorned and despised by the great men of the province he was now armed with the authority of the Assembly to summon them before him and to put searching and embarrassing questions to them. He was also in a position to ask for papers and documents bearing on past and present government operations, and he accumulated these by the basketful. Now at last both the province and the mother country would see the true extent of colonial misrule.

Mackenzie set about his work with a will, as he and his committee heard testimony from a parade of witnesses over a period of several weeks. From government officials he sought information on financial matters, on the amounts and origins of their salaries, and on the way the province was actually run. In most instances he was greeted with silence, or with haughty and unresponsive answers; some of these men were either uninformed or unprepared to give vital facts on government operations. In either event, the chairman's worst suspicions were verified. On the other hand, he called a number of radical reformers, both assemblymen and private citizens, who gladly answered his loaded questions on the executive and legislative councils, on land granting and the Clergy Reserves, on misappropriation of the revenue, on schools, on banks, on judges, and so on and on. On the one hand, a supercilious and secretive oligarchy; on the other, an outraged and oppressed public.

From time to time Mackenzie sent off preliminary reports to the Assembly, asking for more documents or giving the committee's findings on particular subjects such as the Post Office. But finally it was all gathered together in typically helter-skelter Mackenzie fashion – the voluminous testimony, the assorted documents, and the committee's findings – in a Seventh Report, to make a thick book of grievances. Despite its miscellaneous character, however, the Report did fasten on one explanation of multitudinous evils afflicting the province. The "chief sources of Colonial discontent" stemmed from "the almost unlimited extent of the patronage of the Crown, or rather of the Colonial Minister for the time being and his advisers here, together with the abuse of that patronage." By its control of extensive revenues, beyond the reach of the Assembly, the executive authority could reward or punish the clergy (including the Methodists), all civil officers, the judiciary, teachers and school trustees, and the whole military and naval establishment, to mention only the most obvious. The Crown's influence was further enlarged by its "management of millions of acres of public Lands," its control of "the expenditure of a large annual amount of local taxation," and its influence over such semi-public corporations as the Canada Company, the Bank of Upper Canada and the Welland Canal Company. The whole system had "so long continued virtually in the same hands, that it is little better than a family compact." The province was honeycombed with abuses which "are concealed, or palliated, excused and sustained by those who are interested to uphold them as the means of retaining office, for their private, and not for the public, good."[47] It was the most detailed attack on Family Compact rule ever assembled in Upper Canada.

The report was completed near the end of the session, and presented late at night to a half-empty chamber, whose members had had little opportunity to examine a volume of over five hundred pages. Yet a motion was passed ordering two thousand copies of it to be printed at public expense. Thus it went out to the world with the apparent but not the real approval of the Assembly. With some reluctance the reform majority later endorsed the Report, but some influential reform leaders, including Peter Perry, voted against it, because of its factual inaccuracies, its extreme and unfair remarks about the Methodists, and its blanket indictment of everyone who held an office in the province.[48] Once again Mackenzie had embarrassed his colleagues.

Nevertheless, he had given the government of Upper Canada a mighty shaking. While he was off to Niagara during the summer to investigate the Welland Canal, his Report was on its way to England. There it was received with both apprehension and consternation by the Colonial Secretary, now Lord Glenelg. The Secretary, already beset by dangerous events in Lower Canada, was entirely at a loss to understand what had happened in the loyal province of Upper Canada to produce so violent a document which he assumed, reasonably enough, had the considered approval of an Assembly only recently elected. For some time he had in fact, as had his predecessors, been demanding fuller information from Sir John Colborne on the political situation in the province. Now he became still more insistent, yet Colborne contented himself with saying that the reform Assembly did not represent popular feeling, and that the Report was inaccurate. Such a reply was quite useless to Glenelg, and in justifiable exasperation he informed the Lieutenant-Governor that he might expect to be "speedily relieved" of his post.[49]

Mackenzie, however, was in no mood to go back to the old game of appeals to England and reliance on the Whig government there. And he was finished with taking advice from Joseph Hume, who had optimistically told him that each Colonial Minister would do things the last had failed to do, and who even now was counselling him to welcome Colborne's successor.

They were all the same and they were all bad. Upper Canada would never flourish until Downing Street rule was ended, and until it had a written constitution and an elected governor who would wield the veto as Andrew Jackson did to strike down monopolies and guard against the corruption inherent in legislative bodies. No longer would he "put his trust in princes."[50] And he informed John Neilson that he was "less loyal" than he had been; now he directed his attention only "to the people."[51] Clearly the removal of Sir John Colborne would do nothing to soften Mackenzie's campaign against the system of government in Upper Canada.

But that campaign faced greater obstacles than Mackenzie realized, and would not turn out at all as he hoped or expected.

CHAPTER 12

Conservatives and Rebels
1836-37

I

At the end of 1835 the British government concluded that a powerful movement of political discontent had arisen in Upper Canada and that it represented majority opinion in the province. As embodied in the reform party, that movement had captured the Assembly in 1834 and in the Seventh Grievance Report had called for sweeping changes in the provincial Constitution, notably an elective legislative council, an executive council responsible to the Assembly, and severe limitations on the lieutenant-governor's control over patronage. In consequence, the Colonial Office believed that redoubled efforts must be made to conciliate provincial opinion. Although demands for fundamental constitutional changes could not be met, every effort must be made to remedy practical grievances if the province was to retain its British allegiance. It was in this spirit that instructions were written to Sir Francis Bond Head, Colborne's successor, in December 1835.

On the other hand, it was the view of the Family Compact that the British government wholly misjudged the political state of Upper Canada. The leaders of the Compact believed that conservative forces in the province were far stronger than the forces of innovation, and that they would prevail if given firm leadership and provided with unwavering support from London. Although the political scene was in fact chaotic, and subject to wild fluctuations, the Compact leaders were correct in placing a high estimate on the strength of the conservative forces.

To be sure, there had been a time in the early 1830's when the Compact leaders were seized with the darkest pessimism. The reform spirit in Britain raised the danger, in their minds, that the mother country might cut loose from its moorings and sail out into the uncharted seas of innovation and even anarchy. They believed that the Whig government's policy of conciliating the colonies encouraged agitators to redouble their efforts. In Lower Canada the campaign led by Papineau not only slowed economic progress in the two provinces but threatened the very existence of British rule. In

Upper Canada much of the population was unreliable and growing more republican in outlook. In his first years in the province, the Lieutenant-Governor, Sir John Colborne, seemed to the Compact to show little grasp or firmness. In a fit of extreme exasperation John Strachan cried out that the British Ministry should be told that "if they continue to attend to such persons as Ryerson & McKenzie & break down the Constitution the Conservative party will turn round upon them & first trample on the necks of these miscreants and then govern ourselves."[1]

Nevertheless, the conservatives were never people to confine themselves to handwringing and futile denunciation. While they continued to fight vigorously against their political opponents, they had good reason to think that reinforcements were on the way. The Solicitor General wrote hopefully of "the influx of British Emigrants" that would save them from the " 'Canadian Native' or the neighbouring republic." He noted that the province was "filling with people of wealth and intelligence" who would not be gulled by "such fellows as Ryerson and McKenzie." When "thinking people" of this type began to exert an influence on their neighbours, the "overthrow of these miserable factionists" would be certain. The future security of the province, then, lay with emigrants whose "predilections will be English" and who would "strenuously adhere to the Unity of the Empire." Efforts must be made "to conciliate the Emigrants by every act of kindness in our power" and to warn them constantly of "the mischievous designs of such fellows as Bidwell, Ryerson and McKenzie."[2] Such was the conservative strategy of counter-attack against the reformers. As events were to show, it proved to be remarkably successful.

Sir John Colborne consciously adopted this strategy from the beginning of his term as the only way to make Upper Canada "a really British Colony," and to combat the influence of "Settlers from the United States," who were "generally active, intelligent and enterprising."[3] Consequently, he undertook to do everything in his power to assist the emigrants who were now pouring out of Britain in unprecedented numbers, a great many of them indigent and destitute. He posted agents along their route from Montreal westward to give emigrants information and advice. He placed superintendents in the townships open for settlement, who were to provide temporary shelters and to assign indigent settlers fifty-acre lots on which no payment was to be made for three years. The government undertook to build access roads to new settlements which, incidentally, provided much needed employment to the able-bodied among the newcomers. In addition, Colborne encouraged the formation of emigrant societies throughout the province to draw local authorities and individuals into the work of relieving and assisting those who came. This work took on enormous and fearful proportions in the summer of 1832 when a cholera epidemic raged among the emigrants and was carried to many in the province. But all fell to with a will, and although hundreds died, the crisis was surmounted. Altogether, it was a magnificent effort, an epic in the province's history.

Within three years, from 1830 to 1833, population increased by nearly fifty per cent. After that the influx fell off somewhat but continued at a substantial rate until 1837. All of the settled parts received a share of the increase, but townships around Lake Simcoe, north of Rice Lake, in the southwest between Colonel Talbot's domain and the Huron Tract, and up the Ottawa River received a major part of the new settlement. Colborne tried to steer some of the most reliable emigrants to the western parts of the province, where American settlers were numerous. A Presbyterian minister learned from a recent visitor to York that "it is the intention of the government to raise up such a body of persons attached to the Constitution of Great Britain as may counteract the influence of Yankeeism so prevalent about St Thomas and along the lake shore," while John Langton had to resist Colborne's urging that he go to the western townships.[4]

The great contribution of the tens of thousands of new settlers lay in their work in further opening up the province. No one could be sure what impact they would have on its political life, and whatever it might be it would take time to be felt. They were necessarily almost entirely uninformed about provincial affairs, and since most of them had been too low in the social scale at home to be politically active there, they would be slow in learning an unaccustomed role. Some of them belonged to religious communions that discouraged any concern with politics. Moreover, they were ineligible to vote until they received patents for their freeholds. Most important, they were too busy getting established to be able to look much beyond their own clearings for some time. Their letters home reflected this concern with immediate things: ". . . we have plenty of good food and grog . . . we dine with our masters. . . . We have no poor rates nor taxes of any consequence. . . . We shall never want timber nor water. . . . Bricklayer is a good trade here . . . a poor man can do a great deal better here than he can at home. . . . I do not like Canada so well as England; but in England there is too many men, and here, there is not enough; there is more work than we can do, here . . . our dogs . . . live better than most of the farmers in England."[5] And there were heartaches and disappointments that were not written about.

Nevertheless, interested observers in the province often speculated on what political part they would play. Reformers hoped that men from the middle and lower classes, who had felt the mighty reform surge in Britain, would turn naturally to their ranks. Yet they were disturbed by the influence which the governing group was able to exert in teaching "Emigrants from the old Countries . . . to regard the Reformers of Upper Canada" with a "spirit of enmity." "From the moment an Irishman or an Englishman sets foot upon our soil, his ears are stunned by the cry of Treason and Rebellion which is constantly kept up . . . to deceive the ignorant and unwary." They were taught to view the old American settlers with suspicion, and to call them "Yankees, Republicans, &c., by way of reproach. . . . Hence the supercilious deportment of Europeans towards Canadians when they first come amongst them."[6] In a lengthy letter addressed to his newly arrived countrymen a writer of Protestant Irish origins and reform sympathies, who had long resided in the province, sought to show that the same aristocratic "high church and tory system" from which they had fled was growing up in the province. He pleaded with them not to be deceived by demagogues who tried to convince them that they should take up their shillelaghs to defend "a British colony from Yankees, mosquitoes, bullfrogs, or something or other they knew not what."[7]

But conservatives were confident that they would win over the new settlers. One of their leading newspapers observed that the political conflicts in Upper Canada differed essentially from those in Britain. In the latter, Whigs and Tories disagreed over the powers of the Lower House of Parliament, but both were "alike ardently attached to a Government of Kings, Lords and Commons." In the province, however, the contest was between "monarchical government" and "Democratic Republicanism"; in consequence, "every acceptable individual of the Whig, and even the Radical party in England, with scarcely a solitary exception, becomes what the disaffected party term a 'Tory,' the moment he comes to Canada."[8] Looking more deeply, Christopher Hagerman, as well as many other observers, counted on the change that the possession of property and a new economic security would effect: "however turbulent or discontented individuals may have been prior to their arrival in the province, comfort and plenty soon work wonders on those who are of industrious habits, and loyalty and good-humour speedily follow."[9] And in discussing the elections of 1834, Colborne noted that it was too early to expect them to "be generally affected by the recent Emigration," but that better results could be expected in the future.[10] This proved to be an accurate prophecy.

One important consequence of the immigration was a great strengthening of the Orange Order in Upper Canada. For several decades this fervently Protestant organization had been fighting vigorously against the Catholics in Ireland, so vigorously that by the 1830's the British government, as a contribution to the peace of that strife-ridden island, was striving to disband the Order. But Orangemen were always more British than the King, and they paid little attention to official discountenance. When Protestant Irish came to Canada they brought the Order with them.

The first lodges were formed in the early 1820's. In 1824 the Assembly deplored their existence and advised the public to treat them "with silent disregard." Sir Peregrine Maitland publicly expressed his opposition to them.[11] For several years they were few in number and confined largely to the eastern counties. With the large influx of Protestant Irish in the late 1820's and following, however, their numbers grew rapidly, especially after the arrival in 1829 of Ogle Robert Gowan, who became the leading figure in the movement. He was untiringly zealous in the cause, an effective organizer, and at once at home in the rough and tumble of provincial journalism.

In Ireland, Orange devotion to the British Empire required constant vigilance against the subversive schemes of Roman Catholics, but in Upper Canada for a time it took a different form. In Upper Canada, to be sure, there were the usual riots and broken heads on the Glorious Twelfth as their Papist brethren tried to break up their parades. And good Orangemen could not but be alarmed at the thought of so many French Canadian Catholics just down the river. But for the time being, in the 1830's, the task of keeping Canada British required a different tack. The French Canadians were outside the province, and the Catholics within posed little immediate threat. In later years Orangemen returned to their traditional campaign of keeping the country alive to the dangers of Catholic power, but for the present there was a more threatening enemy: the reformers, with their supposed separatist and republican tendencies.

An order that so loudly proclaimed its loyalty to the Empire was naturally welcome to conservatives and to people who felt that the British connection was in peril. Many residents, including descendants of United Empire Loyalists, who knew nothing of the controversies back in Ireland, gladly joined this militant organization. To be sure, others joined it simply because, like good North Americans everywhere, they had a natural affinity for fraternal orders. Such members often retained previous reform sympathies for a time, but if they remained they usually became convinced that it was disloyal to go on voting for a party labelled as pro-American and anti-British. As we shall see later, the Orange Order played an important role in deciding the crucial election of 1836. By providing, as it often did, the shock troops of Upper Canadian toryism, it proved to be one of the most important consequences of the recent British immigration. An element had been introduced into Canadian life that was to have remarkable durability over the next century and more.

But apart from the ordinary people in the new immigration, who could be expected to remain loyal to their British heritage, Colborne and his government placed especial reliance on the much smaller but still sizable number of men of quality who were arriving at the same time. These men had been far from destitute at home, but had concluded that they could no longer maintain or improve their existing status, or provide adequately for their often numerous families. Among them were professional men, substantial farmers, and of particular importance, military and naval officers who were languishing in the long peace following Waterloo. Many of them brought considerable amounts of money with them. Very often they carried letters of introduction from prominent men in Britain addressed to the lieutenant-governor. The latter received them cordially, and advised them fully on the opportunities available in the various sections of the province. It was hardly an accident that they often received the choice lots in new townships and other advantages. Within a very short time they were likely to receive appointments as Justices of the Peace, militia commissions, and other local posts.

Neither political group in the province ever had any doubt of what the influence of these men would be. A conservative paper, for instance, predicted that when the country had "received over its wide expanse even a slight sprinkling, so to speak, of such incomers, . . . we may rest pretty well assured that the vocation and the importance of the demagogue will soon be both at a very small discount." On the other hand, one reformer, referring to the half-pay officers, complained that the "curse of Canada is an *unprincipled* aristocracy, whose pretensions to superiority above other settlers would disgust a dog . . . getting possession of a few hundred acres of wild land [they think] themselves Lords of Canada."[12]

Some of they may have looked like lords to the average settler, because they had enough capital to hire labourers to clear land and to employ house servants, while they engaged in gentlemanly sports and attended balls and dinners in the provincial capital. But most of them were not so circumstanced, and these did their share of hard work. And it was work done at the edge of settlement, without the amenities by then enjoyed in the older townships at the front. Somewhat self-consciously, perhaps, Mrs Traill, the wife of a half-pay officer, spoke of her kind as "the pioneers of civilization in the wilderness, and their families, often of delicate nurture and honourable descent, are at once plunged into the hardship attendant on the rough life of a bush-settler." Yet into the bush the half-pay officer went, "bringing into these rough districts gentle and well-educated females, who soften and improve all around them by *mental* refinements." In Canada, where property was so easily acquired, it was only "education and manners that must distinguish the gentleman."[13]

And so it happened that the most polite and cultivated society to be found anywhere in Upper Canada flourished in some of the most primitive settlements of the backwoods. There the newcomers of this type preferred to be, where servants were "as respectful, or nearly so, as those at home" and the "lower or working class of settlers" were "quite free from the annoying Yankee manners that distinguish many of the earlier-settled townships."[14] There in the bush one might "meet with as good society, as numerous and genteel, as in most of the country parts of Ireland," consisting not only of "ex-officers of the army and navy" but also of "young surgeons, Church of England clergymen, private gentlemen, sons of respectable persons at home, graduates of the colleges, &c."[15] But not all of these people succeeded; certainly their hopes of becoming gentleman farmers were nearly always disappointed. Some of them returned home, either disappointed or satisfied to have had a brief experience of a novel but essentially dull existence. Others escaped to provincial towns to take up more rewarding and less back-breaking activities. But enough of them remained to strengthen greatly the British cast of the Upper Canadian back country.

In summary, then, while the reformers were improving their political organization in the early 1830's, the conservative side was also being greatly reinforced by immigration from the British Isles. It need hardly be said that the immigrants were not necessarily supporters of the Family Compact, about which in fact they knew relatively little. Probably the great majority of them were quite hospitable to the idea of moderate reform. When, however, the issue appeared to be reduced to a vote for or against the British connection, there was no question where they would stand. They were forerunners of those young men from Britain who filled up the first Canadian contingent in 1914.

II

Despite previous efforts of conservative leaders to emphasize the overriding importance of the loyalty issue, it had never yet been possible to focus all attention on it in a provincial election. This fact was first accomplished by the new Lieutenant-Governor, Sir Francis Bond Head, who arrived in the province at the beginning of 1836.

Historians, with their eyes on the sequel, have usually regarded Head's appointment as one of the strangest ever made by the Colonial Office. He had had no previous experience in colonial government and, indeed, none in politics, as he was the first to admit and proclaim. After a career as a military engineer, which took him to several parts of Europe, he retired from the army as a half-pay major. Later he had an adventurous but not very successful experience as the manager of British silver mines in South America. From this and other journeys he acquired some reputation as the author of sprightly travel books; already he had revealed a facile pen. He was an assistant poor-law commissioner in Kent when the sudden call to Upper Canada reached him; perhaps his vigorous administration of the new Act had brought him to the attention of the Whig government. Following their irritation with Colborne they wanted a new man who would make a fresh start, yet they could not aspire much higher than to a person of Head's attainments. Upper Canada was not an attractive post to qualified civilians, and it had been decided not to appoint another high-ranking military officer.

In an attempt to demonstrate the British government's sincere intention of conciliating provincial opinion, Lord Glenelg provided Head with a long dispatch instructing him on the course to follow.[16] Most of the dispatch took the form of comments on the Seventh Report on Grievances. Although he disputed the Report's extreme charges on the matter of the Crown's control of patronage, he ordered Head to review the whole subject, to limit and reduce its amount where possible, and to make appointments on the basis of qualification, not politics. Regarding other complaints Head was to do everything possible to meet the wishes of the Assembly, and Glenelg re-iterated the British government's determination not to interfere in the internal affairs of the province. The reformers' demand for an executive council responsible to the Assembly could not be conceded, however. True responsibility lay in the Lieutenant-Governor's accountability to the British government which always stood ready to receive and to investigate complaints coming from the province. In short, without promising any basic change in the system of government, Glenelg was ready to support the re-form of all concrete and specific grievances and to defer to provincial opinion in every practicable way. No one could have been more well meaning. But Glenelg apparently assumed that after vigorous debate the provincial legislature would reach agreement on outstanding issues, something that was quite impossible, given the composition of the two houses. Moreover, in Sir Francis Bond Head, he had chosen a strange instrument to accomplish his laudable purposes.

How strange was not long in becoming apparent. Soon after his arrival in Toronto Sir Francis divulged his instructions to the legislature, not just their substance, as Glenelg had ordered, but the full text, which contained material certain to embarrass Lord Gosford, who had come out to Lower Canada a few months before as the head of a conciliating royal commission. Apparently Sir Francis felt very little sense of obedience to his superiors in London. At about the same time he was forming his impressions of provincial politics, which he did with amazing quickness. Taking an immediate dislike to Mackenzie and Bidwell, and being much impressed by Chief Justice John Beverley Robinson, he soon decided that "strong Republican Principles [had] leaked into the country from the United States," and were predominant in the Assembly, whose majority did not represent "the general Feeling and Interests of the Inhabitants." The "Republican Party," as he henceforth described the Reformers, were "implacable" and would never be satisfied by concessions.[17] It was an unpromising beginning for Glenelg's policy of conciliation.

I*

Nevertheless, Head did take one important step that was within the spirit of his instructions. Finding it essential to make additions to the membership of the executive council, he asked informed observers for the names of qualified men who would serve to make the council a more balanced body and one more representative of political opinion. As a result of these inquiries he offered appointments to Robert Baldwin, John Rolph, and J. H. Dunn, the Receiver General. The last named was a member of the administrative group, and had long been active in Welland Canal affairs, but was not directly identified with the Family Compact. The first two were well known as reformers but had been politically inactive in recent years. At first, Baldwin refused the offer, saying that he could not accept office unless his well-known views on a responsible executive council were acceded to. Head, however, argued that he should come in, and then speak for his views from within the council. With much foreboding, Baldwin agreed.

It was not long before he felt his apprehensions to be fully justified, since he was soon quite dissatisfied with the extent to which the Lieutenant-Governor consulted the council. Thereupon, he convinced his colleagues, the old tory members as well as Rolph and Dunn, to unite in a formal complaint which, by coincidence, was very much in the spirit of Strachan's letter to James Stephen of five years earlier. The Council asked to be consulted on all general matters relating to the conduct of government; if this were not to be done, they thought that the public should know how little they had to do with affairs.[18] Head flatly rejected this proposal. With both precedent and Glenelg's instructions to back him up, he argued that the responsibility for carrying on the government was his alone, and could not be shared with the council, although he would consult it whenever he saw fit to do so. All six councillors then resigned, the old members being forced out as well as the new, although they were now ready to draw back.

These resignations fell like a thunderclap upon the reform majority in the Assembly, already disgruntled and irritated by other events. After calling on Head for more information, in which step they were joined by all but two conservative members, they then set up a select committee, chaired by Peter Perry, to investigate and report on the incident. After Head had appointed a new council, made up of men of conservative views, the Assembly, in a straight party vote, passed a motion of want of confidence.[19] As well, reformers throughout the province quickly wheeled their formidable political organizations into line of battle. Meetings were organized. Petitions and addresses were adopted and forwarded to the provincial capital.

The conflict reached a new intensity after Perry's committee made its report in the middle of April. During its deliberations the committee, and the province, had learned a new fact, not directly related to the current controversy, that drove reformers into a fury, and for a time brought all elements of the party together in outraged opposition to the government. The new fact was that Sir John Colborne, in his last important act before leaving the province, had set up fifty-seven rectories as endowments for Anglican clergymen. (Actually, he had had time to sign only forty-four patents, and these were all that were established.) In Colborne's view, this was a perfectly defensible step. Glebe lands for this purpose had been set aside, partly from the Clergy Reserves and partly from Crown Lands, from time to time over the previous forty-five years. Altogether, they amounted to some twenty thousand acres. On more than one previous occasion Colborne and his predecessors had received explicit approval from the Colonial Secretary to take the step, but the rising tide of provincial opposition to the exclusive claims of the Church of England had hitherto delayed action. Now it had been taken, in flat defiance of this opposition, and in a secretive, midnight fashion.

Indignation at this action did much to heighten the language of the committee's report, which was a bitter attack upon Sir Francis Bond Head. His appointment of Baldwin, Rolph, and Dunn was termed "a deceitful manœuvre to gain credit with the country for liberal feelings and intentions where none really existed," while he continued to act "under the influence of secret and unsworn advisers." The committee could not understand why "a Lieutenant-Governor, at a distance of more than four thousand miles from his superiors, is so much more immaculate and infallible than his royal master," who always acted on the advice of his councillors. With a government resorting to "arbitrary principles" and with conditions in sad contrast to the prosperity, activity, and improvement "in the adjacent country," it was clear that the state of public affairs was growing steadily worse. The last straw was the knowledge that "57 government parsons" had been established, "in contempt of all our humble remonstrances"; final proof, if it were needed, of "the necessity of having a responsible Government." All other measures having failed, the committee advised the Assembly to stop the supplies.[20]

Events now moved rapidly to a climax. On April 15 the Assembly approved the committee's report and voted to stop the supplies. Tension was further increased when four days later Mr Speaker Bidwell laid before the House a letter sent to him by Papineau, which denounced the British ministers and asserted that "the state of society all over continental America requires that the forms of its Government should approximate nearer to that selected . . . by the wise statesmen of the neighbouring Union, than to that into which chance and past ages have moulded European societies." On the next day Sir Francis prorogued the legislature, letting it be known that in retaliation for the stoppage of supplies, he would refuse his assent to money bills already passed, a measure that was far more crippling to provincial prosperity than was the Assembly's rather empty gesture. He also took the opportunity to make an appeal to the "backwoodsman" and to "every noble-minded Englishman, Irishman, Scotchman, and U.E. Loyalist"; clearly, he knew where to look for support. In the same breath he assured the province that the best hope for genuine reform lay in cleaving to him, not to a selfish faction.[21]

A month later, he dissolved the legislature and the province was soon in the midst of a bitterly fought election campaign, with Sir Francis boldly assuming the leadership of the conservative forces. He had already concluded that he "was sentenced to contend on the soil of America with Democracy, and that if I did not overpower it, it would overpower me."[22] In vigorous, colloquial, or as he put it, "homely" language, he never missed an opportunity to pin the republican label on his opponents or to assert that all who stood for the British Constitution and the British connection should throw their weight against Bidwell and his party. The reformers also tried to take this ground, arguing that all they wanted was the Constitution as applied in Britain, but they were never able to seize the initiative from the Lieutenant-Governor. When the smoke had cleared early in July, it was at once obvious that the reformers had been routed. Although the vote was close in several constituencies, they would be outnumbered more than two to one in the next house. Bidwell, Perry, and Mackenzie were only the most notable of the party to suffer defeat; only Rolph among leading reformers had survived the landslide.

Many factors combined to produce so striking a political reversal. For many voters, economic considerations bulked large. With the boom in the neighbouring states reaching its peak, just before the crash of the next year, Upper Canada seemed to be losing in the race for prosperity and development. While people were leaving the province for the western states, reformers argued over abstract principles of government, complained about the Welland Canal and the banks, and seemed not to welcome an inflow of British capital. To be sure, in the last Assembly they had voted money for roads, bridges, and other local improvements, but much of it went to their own constituencies in the older settled districts rather than to the struggling townships in the back country. Moreover, in an attempt to provide themselves with some patronage and to keep the money voted out of the hands of the executive, the reformers had set up commissionerships to supervise its expenditure and had distributed these among themselves. This device could easily be made to appear as a political job. It was also well known that the reformers regarded themselves as the protectors of the interests of the farmers, the "honest yeoman." In the last Assembly they had passed a bill, killed in the legislative council, to impose higher duties and other restric-

tions on agricultural imports from the United States. This measure undoubtedly pleased many established farmers, but in newer areas, which still
needed to import food, and in the lumbering centres of the Ottawa Valley,
it was disliked. It was especially disliked by all who were engaged in mercantile pursuits, and who lived by forwarding goods down the St Lawrence.
If to these is added the reformers' often expressed opposition to the Canada
Company and the lukewarm attitude of many of them to British immigration, it is apparent that they had offended important economic interests in
the province.

The reformers were also more vigorously opposed than in any previous
election. Conservative forces were alerted as never before, although now
they called themselves Constitutionalists. They believed that the British
connection – to which the province "principally owe[d] its rapid advancement" – was in danger, and they believed that the provincial Constitution
was threatened with innovation. They were seeking to prevent revolution,
not to impede honest reform. Indeed, reform would be accelerated by a "Constitutional House": the land granting system would be improved, the Clergy
Reserves would be returned to the Crown, immigration would be encouraged, "capital and wealth" would flow in from the mother country "like a
fertilizing stream," and "Sir Francis Head would be enabled to carry into
effect those Reforms and improvements for which he has been expressly sent
here by our good KING."[23] Appeals such as this combined with increasing
political activity roused intense feeling against the "Bidwellian Party."

The victory also owed something to the Lieutenant-Governor's skill as a
campaigner. He never wavered from one simple theme: that the contest
was between a loyal people and a disloyal faction. He sought, with much
success, to sweep away all previous distinctions between tories and radicals,
conservatives and reformers. He announced frequently that he himself was
a reformer, and that the best way to achieve true reform was to support him.
Conservative leaders were delighted by his firm opposition to the radicals
and by the support which he brought to their cause. He knew how to strike
responsive chords in the breasts of many residents. For instance, on one
occasion he denounced the letter from Papineau recently placed on the
Assembly's journal, suggested that there were "one or two Individuals" in
Lower Canada who welcomed the prospect of foreign interference in the
provinces, and then concluded with the rousing challenge, "In the Name of
every Regiment of Militia in Upper Canada I publicly promulgate – Let
them come if they dare!"[24] To the reformers this was ludicrous bombast,
and they did their best to pour ridicule upon it. But to all, and there were
many, who disliked the course of the French Canadian extremists, and who
had memories of the War of 1812, the challenge had a reassuring sound.

As already suggested, Sir Francis made a special appeal to the recent

British immigrants, and it was one which most of them enthusiastically answered. With the election approaching, some of them made hurried efforts to secure their land patents, and hence the franchise, in which efforts the government was very co-operative. John Langton wrote of how he and his friends brought voters in a steamer down the Otonabee River to the polling-place, remarking, "There was astonishingly little fighting considering the number of wild Irishmen we brought down, but they were altogether too strong for the Yankees. . . ."[25] Another resident, recently from Britain, stated that the men in his settlement, "to the number of nearly a hundred, marched in procession to the polling booths," in order to make a demonstration "on the side of religion, order and true liberty."[26]

A remarkable feature of the campaign was the ready co-operation of Orangemen and Roman Catholics to defeat the reformers. The Orange Lodge in Toronto and Bishop Macdonell publicly complimented each other's loyalty. Orangemen voted for Roman Catholic conservative candidates, and Roman Catholics similarly supported Orange candidates. It has been calculated that from one-third to one-half of the reform defeats were caused by this uniting of the Orange and the Green. The Orangemen even abstained from their annual parades on the Glorious Twelfth, just after the election, to show their appreciation of Catholic loyalty. Mackenzie, who had probably been defeated by this joint effort, denounced the "Orange Papists," but the two groups continued to co-operate until after the Rebellion.[27]

The Methodist leaders were also in the field against the reformers in this election. The gulf between the Mackenzie wing of the party and the Methodists had widened after the publication of the Seventh Report, while the denomination had grown more conservative under British Wesleyan influence. When the issue was narrowed to one of loyalty, there was no question where its leaders would stand. The *Guardian* staunchly supported the Lieutenant-Governor and the Constitutional party, with Egerton Ryerson publishing several letters in criticism of the reformers in general and Peter Perry in particular. Some months after the election John Ryerson informed his brother that "Not one Radical was returned from the bounds of the Bay of Quinty Districts. The preachers & I laboured to the utmost extent of our ability to keep every scamp of them out & we succeeded. And had the preachers of done their duty in every place, not a *ninny* of them would have been returned to this parliament."[28]

Undoubtedly, then, the Methodists made their contribution to the defeat of the reformers but, as Professor Sissons has noted, it was probably not as decisive as has sometimes been claimed. Many of the rank and file again voted the reform ticket, as they had always done.[29] Reformers at the time complained more about Orangemen than about Methodists, and put particular emphasis on the role of the new voters. Although the St Thomas *Liberal*, for instance, referred generally to the "unholy exertions of the State-paid Priests," in which group it probably included the Methodists, it also spoke of the "exhibition of ruffianism, club-law and intimidation" put on in every constituency. The editor continued:

> Above all . . . heaps of new Deeds, *the ink scarcely dry on them*, were sent in all directions, not only the week preceding, but absolutely the very week of the Elections. . . . The honest and legitimate constituency of the Province – the old – the peaceable – the respectable settlers were thus overwhelmed, in almost every County, by pensioners and paupers, who never before exercised the elective franchise, who did not know any more about the Constitution of Canada or about the subjects in dispute, between the late House of Assembly and Sir Francis Head, than the man in the moon.[30]

Acting on this last complaint, Charles Duncombe, a leading reformer from the western part of the province, took a petition to England which stated that the Lieutenant-Governor had favoured tory candidates in various ways, and in particular had overwhelmed "legally registered voters" by illegally issued patents.[31] This petition was referred back to a select committee of the newly elected Assembly which, not surprisingly, found no truth in it. The committee was able to show convincingly that patents issued just before the elections could not have influenced the results.[32]

The charge of fraud, as drawn by Duncombe, was clearly exaggerated, but he and his reform colleagues had good reasons for complaining that it had not been a fair election. In 1836, as in previous elections, they suffered from the fact that the election machinery was in the hands of their opponents. Above all, it was intolerable that they should have a recently arrived lieutenant-governor openly in the field against them, accusing them of treason. Undoubtedly there was a real shift of opinion in the provincial electorate in 1836, intensified by the activity of new voters. Many voters genuinely felt that the reformers sought dangerous changes in the Constitution, and that a victory for them would imperil the British connection. Yet, not without some cause, a great many reformers drew the conclusion that a free expression of public opinion was impossible under existing circumstances. Their feeling that the scales were tipped against them was heightened when the newly elected conservative Assembly passed a bill providing that it should not be automatically dissolved at the King's death, which was expected soon. Reformers were quite convinced that this measure would never have been accepted by the Legislative Council, the Lieutenant-Governor, and the Colonial Office, or any of them, if they had been in a majority.

Disheartened by the nature and results of the election campaign, many reform leaders of moderate outlook turned their backs on political life. Bidwell, smarting from defeat after twelve years of representing his county, wrote to Robert Baldwin in bitter tones of the practice of "denouncing every man as disloyal, a revolutionist, a secret traitor, etc., who happens to differ from the Provincial government, on questions of expediency or constitutional principles."[33] He returned to his law practice. Baldwin himself had gone to England before the elections to warn the Colonial Secretary that the province's connection with Britain was being endangered by Sir Francis Bond Head's actions. Although refused a personal interview, Baldwin stated his views in a lengthy memorandum, which fully set out his conception of responsible government as the one means of bringing harmony and stability to Upper Canada. If this "English principle" were denied, the people of the province might be driven to turn "to another Quarter" and "call for the power of electing their own Governor, and their own Executive," but they would never "abandon the object of obtaining more influence than they now possess, through their Representatives, in the administration of the Executive Government of the Colony."[34] Baldwin, too, stayed in private life upon his return.

For the time being, however, the province enjoyed harmonious government, with an Assembly that had confidence in Sir Francis Bond Head and his executive council. In the first session of the new legislature, a large number of bills easily passed through both houses providing for overdue changes in the judiciary, amendments to the University Charter and, especially, internal improvements. In the latter category there was not only more money for the Welland Canal and for roads and harbours but the first railroads for the province were projected. Sir Francis gladly approved all of these bills, although his instructions required him to reserve several banking bills that were also passed.[35] The constitution of 1791 could work fairly effectively when there was a conservative Assembly.

For some months after the election, then, the province was relatively quiet in contrast to the furious political debate of the previous months. Attempts were made by some reformers to rebuild their shattered organizations, but with limited results. Mackenzie, who had returned to journalism with a newspaper entitled *The Constitution* which began publication, somewhat symbolically perhaps, on July 4, 1836, attacked the government and all its works as bitterly as ever, but he seemed to be shouting into the wind. The province as a whole seemed to be more concerned to participate in the prevailing boom that was sweeping North America than to revive the sterile debates of earlier years. Conservatives congratulated themselves on having brought the people to their senses by the firm stand taken against radicalism.

Yet these appearances were deceiving. Farmers had little opportunity to benefit from the commercial boom; instead they were suffering from low prices and lack of good markets. Opponents of the government were suffering from a kind of emotional exhaustion, but they nursed the old complaints as much as ever. Shortly after she arrived from England, at the end of 1836, Anna Jameson, the wife of the Attorney General recently appointed from England, found "among all parties a general tone of complaint and discontent – a mutual distrust – a languor and supineness. . . . Even those who are enthusiastically British in heart and feeling . . . are as discontented as the rest: they bitterly denounce the ignorance of the colonial officials at home. . . ."[36] Sir Francis Bond Head's glorious victory had not really cleared the air very much.

Sir Francis was in fact throwing away the fruits of victory as rapidly as possible. Having defeated the forces of democracy and republicanism, he was then determined to disperse and destroy them. He proceeded to dismiss from office certain men accused of showing sympathy for the reform side in the recent election, including a judge who flatly denied the charge. He urged upon the Colonial Office an end of the policy of conciliation, and its replacement by stern and decisive measures. Not only did he begin to lose some of the support of moderate men in the province, but his action and views met with diminishing acceptance in Downing Street. From the end of 1836 onward he was engaged in an increasingly acrimonious correspondence with Lord Glenelg that led eventually to his resignation. Despite the Lieutenant-Governor's coup the Colonial Office could no longer entrust Upper Canada to this erratic and insubordinate "damned odd fellow," as Lord Melbourne dubbed him on his return to England. Sir Francis had no answer to the problems facing the province.

But these problems, real though they were, did not drive Upper Canada to rebellion. If the province could have been insulated from outside pressures it would have had every prospect of a peaceful political evolution. The British government had no desire to interfere in its internal affairs; instead, it was fully prepared to approve of and assist in the transition to a broadened political structure. And with the gradual rise of effective political parties within the province that transition was inevitably and inexorably coming. A rebellion was not needed to solve Upper Canada's political problems; the rebellion that did come complicated rather than eased the transition.

Upper Canada, however, was not insulated or immunized from outside pressures. Instead, it was caught up in a severe financial crisis that reached in from the larger Anglo-American world of which it was a part and that greatly disturbed its economic life. In addition, and at the same time, it was directly affected by the bitter struggle coming to a head in Lower Canada. And now more than ever, political differences were exacerbated by proximity to the neighbouring republican states. Alternately goaded and inspired by these outside pressures, Mackenzie and a small group of followers determined on their ill-starred plan to overthrow by force a nearly unprotected government.

Of these outside pressures the most clearly disruptive was the financial crisis. After several years of unprecedented business expansion in both Britain and America, the bottom suddenly fell out of the boom at the end of 1836, and conditions became steadily worse during the following year. The causes of the downturn in the business cycle were essentially the same on both sides of the Atlantic – excessive speculation and optimistic expansion by business men, and indeed the public at large, who were eager to seize the opportunities made available by a rapidly growing economy – but the effects were felt with particular sharpness in the young debtor communities of the New World. The latter were heavily dependent upon the British money market for capital. When they could no longer borrow there, when indeed British investors began to liquidate their holdings in America, the western communities found themselves in an intolerable position. That position, moreover, had already been made highly precarious by the policies adopted by the Jackson administration in the United States. By destroying the Bank of the United States the administration had removed the one agent that might have restrained the headlong speculation of the 1830's. Then, in his own attempt to halt the speculation, Jackson issued, in July 1836, a Specie Circular, ordering that henceforth only hard money would be received in payment for the public lands. This measure drained specie away from the banking centres of the eastern seaboard, which were soon also suffering from insistent British demands. By the spring of 1837 business failures and unemployment were followed by the decision of banks throughout the United States to suspend specie payments.

The province of Upper Canada, inevitably affected by business conditions across the line, as well as in Britain, was in a very poor condition to weather the resulting storm. Following the prevailing pattern, the provincial legislature had also borrowed heavily, in an attempt to speed up economic progress, and was in no position to meet its commitments. Bankers in the province were suffering from the same drain of specie as across the line, but because of the Lieutenant-Governor's belief that suspension would be dishonourable, they were unable to protect themselves, unless they met very difficult requirements. This quixotic attitude of Sir Francis soon lost him much of the popularity among conservatives that he had earlier enjoyed. It was W. H. Merritt's view, expressed after the event, that Head's policy of placing obstacles in the way of specie suspension, which was persisted in "against the expressed opinion of the Inhabitants and their Representatives," had done more "to create a feeling in favour of *Responsible Govern-ment* than all the essays written or speeches made on the subject."[37]

Few voices had been raised in opposition to the orgy of bank bills and borrowing that reached its climax in the session of 1836-37. Most reformers were just as enthusiastic for this course as were conservatives. Indeed, it was only at the extremes of the political spectrum that doubts and antagonism were expressed. At one end were some tories who wanted strict regulation of the note-issuing powers of banks, perhaps following a recent New York law on the subject.[38] At the other end was William Lyon Mackenzie who opposed the craze for banks root and branch.

As we have seen, Mackenzie had always opposed the banks. He had followed with the closest sympathy the efforts of Jackson and the hard-money men to break the power of the banks in the United States, and he was determined to follow their example in Upper Canada. Needless to say, he was not deterred by the fact that most reform leaders did not agree with him, any more than Jackson had been deterred by the fact that many in his party had campaigned against the Bank of the United States in order to open the way for an expansion of local banking. When the provincial banks found themselves in difficulties in the spring of 1837, because of the heavy drain on specie reserves, Mackenzie made every effort to mount a campaign against them. He warned the "Farmers of Upper Canada" that they would be "richer and happier" if these "vile Banking Associations" were swept away. He advised them to *"Get Gold and Silver for your Bank Paper, while it is yet within your power."* In particular, he denounced the Bank of Upper Canada for having "controlled our elections, corrupted our representatives, depreciated our currency, obliged even Governors and Colonial Ministers to bow to its mandates, insulted the legislature, expelled representatives, fat-tened a host of greedy and needy lawyers, tempted the farmer to leave his money with it instead of lending it to his worthy neighbour, shoved govern-ment through its hands, sent many thousands of hard cash to foreign lands as bank dividends, taxed the farmers and traders at £18,000 a year for the use of its paper, and supported every judicial villainy and oppression with which our country has been afflicted." In Mackenzie's mind, Upper Canada suffered just as much from the money power as did the United States, but with a vital difference. In that country Jackson, and now Van Buren, were "purging the nation of vile rotten cheating bank folks," while these were still all powerful in the province.[39] Considering the difficulties that bankers had with Sir Francis in the summer of 1837, they must have been astonished to learn how much power they had.

With the bank power ruling Upper Canada and ruining its farmers, Mackenzie was more than ever impressed with the contrast between this sad picture and the glorious scene across the lakes. His paper was once again filled with glowing accounts of the virtuous simplicity of American state governments. Michigan, newly arriving at statehood, had a "government by farmers" while Upper Canada had "a government by strangers from beyond the great sea, who do not intend to become permanent settlers," and were paid salaries five to ten times as high as those of their opposite numbers across the Detroit River.[40] With blithe inconsistency Mackenzie also pointed repeatedly to the rapid progress of the western states, ignoring the fact that this progress was inseparably connected with the banking expansion and business speculation which he so vehemently opposed. Instead, he was secure in his simple faith that Upper Canada, too, could achieve such utopian bliss if it could only achieve a pure agrarian polity, which in fact nowhere existed across the line except in Mackenzie's imagination.

A final factor was needed to turn Mackenzie's thoughts in the direction of armed uprising, and that was the abrupt reversal of British policy toward Lower Canada. Following the failure of Lord Gosford's mission of conciliation, Lord John Russell announced a return to firmness in his Ten Resolutions of March 2, 1837. These Resolutions rejected the demands of the Papineau party and allowed the governor to take funds from the provincial treasury that the Assembly had refused to vote. When the Lower Canadian radicals learned that these Resolutions had been approved by Parliament they immediately intensified a campaign of agitation and organization that led to rebellion within six months.

The passage of the Ten Resolutions brought Mackenzie to new heights of furious indignation. He denounced "the mercenary immoral wretches" who had supported resolutions "more suitable for the Meridian of Russia in its dealing with Poland." He was soon in correspondence with Wolfred Nelson, perhaps the most militant radical leader in the lower province, and he was soon preaching the doctrine of non-importation. "Buy, wear, and use as little as you possibly can of British manufactured goods or British West India merchandize or liquors."[41] Mackenzie now agreed with his Lower Canadian friends that a bold attack must be made against British authority, not simply against the local oligarchy.

By the beginning of July 1837 he was seeking to convince his readers that the Lower Canadians had both the will and the means to make good their independence; moreover, he asserted, "There are thousands, aye tens of thousands of Englishmen, Scotchmen, and above all, of Irishmen, now in the United States, who only wait till the standard be planted in Lower Canada, to throw their strength and numbers to the side of democracy."[42] Two weeks later he began to reprint Tom Paine's *Common Sense*, which had sparked the movement for independence in 1776.[43] At the same time he set forth in great detail a scheme for local reform organizations, some features of which had distinct military overtones. One of his subscribers reported finding a note from Mackenzie folded in his paper, asking him to accompany the editor to Lower Canada "to assist the french" and then return and conquer the upper province.[44] At the end of July he met with a group of radicals in Doel's brewery in Toronto to adopt a Declaration closely modelled on the famous document proclaimed at Philadelphia on July 4, 1776. It ended by asking the reformers of Upper Canada to make common cause with Papineau and his colleagues, to organize political associations and public meetings, and to select a convention of delegates to meet at Toronto "as a Congress, to seek an effectual remedy for the grievances of the colonists."[45] A Committee of Vigilance was named, with Mackenzie as agent and corresponding secretary.

Mackenzie then set out on a tour of the country north of the capital to organize public meetings and to superintend the adoption of the Toronto Declaration and other inflammatory resolutions. More than a score of such meetings were held, and there was similar though less intense activity in other parts of the province.[46] Orangemen and other opponents of the radicals attempted to break up the meetings by force; in turn, the radicals armed themselves with clubs and other weapons. Soon they were drilling and shooting at targets, although with no clear idea in their minds why they were doing these things. Mackenzie sought to convince them, however, that everything was within their grasp if they should move against the government. ". . . Britain has no power here if opinion be concentrated against the measures of her agents. We are far from the Sea – for five months our shores are ice bound – the great republic is on one side of us, the Lower Canadians on another; Michigan and the wilderness, and lakes are to the west and north of us. The whole physical power of the government, the mud garrison, redcoats and all, is not equal to that of the young men of one of our largest townships."[47] This line of argument became all the more persuasive in October when Sir Francis, who was prepared to rest the fate of his government entirely upon the loyalty of the people of Upper Canada, denuded the province of regular troops in order to strengthen the garrisons in Lower Canada.

Meanwhile, Mackenzie and his lieutenants sought to convince their followers that a display of physical force was both justified and necessary. A rising tone of nationalism marked their appeals. Reformers were asked to be "more Canadian" in their "habits and feelings," to throw away their "lip-loyal feelings and sayings of other countries," and to "substitute the word patriotic for the word loyalty."[48] "Foreign" colonial ministers and "foreign" governors were vigorously denounced, while at the same time the advantages of membership in the American Union were set forth in attractive terms. As a state in the Union, the people of Upper Canada would enjoy complete local self-government, universal suffrage, and vote by ballot.[49] Mackenzie's nationalism was now a North American nationalism. With the same grievances that the old thirteen colonies had suffered from, the Canadian people had the same right to rebel;[50] their logical haven after successful rebellion was in the Union that had emerged from the earlier Revolution.

From this rising campaign of agitation, which looked to co-operation with the Lower Canadian radicals and to separation from the mother country, the main body of reformers in Upper Canada kept themselves increasingly aloof. None of the party's prominent leaders, Perry, Bidwell, or of course the Baldwins, had any part in it, although John Rolph's private attitude was somewhat equivocal. In effect, these men abdicated their responsibility to give a lead to public opinion, leaving the field to Mackenzie and his radical associates. And the moderate rank and file of the party also withdrew from political activity rather than follow Mackenzie's leadership. They still believed firmly in the reform objectives but also believed, as one correspondent informed Mackenzie, that they must "be attained in peace." This man asserted that Mackenzie's extremism had nearly wrecked the cause by driving Methodists, Catholics, and Presbyterians into the ranks of Toryism and by making it almost impossible for the British government to continue its policy of conciliation.[51]

These were accurate observations, but Mackenzie was past heeding them. Let the old-line politicians stay on the sidelines and frown; he did not need them or want them. Instead, he was now working closely with a number of men who were ready for action. In the main, these men were drawn from among the old American settlers north of Toronto, who had lived in the province for a generation. They were well-established farmers and artisans, but they had never become reconciled to a government which, they were convinced, discriminated against them at every opportunity, and went out of its way to favour British immigrants at their expense. Notable among them were Samuel Lount, born in Pennsylvania in 1791, Silas Fletcher, born in New Hampshire in 1780, and Jesse Lloyd, born in Pennsylvania in 1786.[52] Working with these men, and in conjunction with the American-born Charles Duncombe in the London district, Mackenzie convinced several hundred supporters that a demonstration of physical force would easily, indeed peacefully, sweep away the oligarchy, the banks, the land-grabbers, and the state-paid priests, and inaugurate a democratic government controlled by the plain people, under which all would prosper.

The blueprint for the new order was published in Mackenzie's paper on November 15, 1837, in the form of a draft constitution for the State of Upper Canada. In presenting it to the public Mackenzie invoked the names of Henry Grattan, John Locke, Algernon Sydney, Benjamin Franklin, John Hampden, William Pitt, Charles James Fox, Oliver Goldsmith, Henry

Brougham, J. A. Roebuck, Joseph Hume, and George Washington in support of the course he was taking. The document itself closely followed the outlines of the Constitution of the United States, although many of its individual clauses were related directly to Mackenzie's long-standing complaints against the provincial government. In particular, he would require that money bills and bills of incorporation be passed only after a three-fourths vote of each House, while the agrarian purity of the new commonwealth was to be protected by a total prohibition against bank charters.

A month before publishing this constitution Mackenzie had sought to convince his associates in Toronto that Head's removal of the troops gave them the perfect opportunity to seize the arms and ammunition in the City Hall and capture the government in one bloodless and decisive move. These more cautious men had backed away from the fatal step at that time, but in subsequent weeks Mackenzie had convinced them that he had the men needed to bring off a successful *coup*. The more respectable members of the conspiracy, particularly John Rolph and Dr T. D. Morrison, now agreed to join the movement at the appropriate time. In every way they tried to cover their tracks in the event of failure. By the middle of November, however, Mackenzie was determined to force the hands of his timid colleagues. On a trip north of the city he set a date for the uprising, December 7, and put plans in motion that could not easily be reversed. The news, toward the end of November, that the Lower Canadian *Patriotes* had risen, was the final proof for Mackenzie that the time to act had come.

On a last trip north of the ridges at the end of November Mackenzie distributed a handbill calling on the "Brave Canadians" to strike for "Independence," and made final arrangements with his trusted friends. But with plans in their last stages everything began to go wrong. First, there was a worried call from John Rolph that the authorities in Toronto were alerted to the uprising – in fact, they refused almost to the last moment to take seriously the possibility of rebellion – and that the date must be advanced in order to retain the element of surprise. This eleventh-hour change threw out of line arrangements for assembling, arming, and victualling the men. Then the disheartening news arrived that the *Patriote* uprising in the lower province had been put down. Rolph now tried to convince Mackenzie that the project was hopeless, but the latter had crossed his Rubicon. In any event the men were already marching.

During the evening and night of December 4-5 some seven to eight hundred of them gathered at Montgomery's Tavern, about two miles north of Toronto. Rebel guards were posted down Yonge Street to prevent any movement into the city, and a well-known tory, Colonel Robert Moodie of Richmond Hill, was mortally wounded as he tried to ride past them. Coming up from the city to reconnoitre, an alderman, John Powell, was captured, but escaped after shooting dead the rebels' most capable military leader, Anthony Anderson. Powell got back to the city with conclusive proof that long-rumoured rebellion was a fact. Now all chance of surprise was gone.

Even so, the rebels were a larger force than any that was ready to meet them as they set off down Yonge Street about noon on December 5. After moving a little more than a mile they stopped to reform their ranks at the brow of Gallow's Hill. There they were presently met by a truce party, sent out by Sir Francis, consisting of Robert Baldwin and John Rolph, men whom the rebels would know and presumably trust. (Rolph was still not identified with the conspiracy.) The rebels were offered a full amnesty if they would go home. Mackenzie asked for the promise in writing, and marched on another mile. Then the government withdrew its offer when it learned that militiamen were on the way. Rolph, however, secretly sent word that the city was still poorly defended, and that an attack would succeed.

And so the last act of the little tragicomedy was enacted. In the gathering darkness of the late December afternoon the rebel army trudged on down Yonge Street, with a few dozen riflemen at its front. The rest were armed only with pikes, pitchforks, and cudgels. As they neared the northern outskirts of the city they were observed by a small picket of some two dozen men, commanded by the sheriff. When the front ranks of the oncoming band were within musket range the sheriff gave his men the order to fire. Fire they did, but having done so, they promptly dropped their weapons and took to their heels, to avoid being crushed by the much larger force opposing them. Samuel Lount, commanding the rebel riflemen, ordered the fire returned. The front ranks then fell to their knees to allow their companions behind to continue the fusillade. But the smell of gunpowder in the fearful darkness brought as much confusion to the rebels as it had to the loyal picket. When the men behind saw the tall hats of the front riflemen disappear from the skyline, they at once concluded that these men had been shot down. Not knowing what hordes of well-armed tories were about to charge them they, too, turned and ran, carrying most of the army with them. Lount and his few riflemen had no choice but to follow them. One rebel had been killed, and two died later of wounds.

With the retreat of the rebel army up Yonge Street to Montgomery's Tavern went the last flickering chance of scattering the government. On that same evening reinforcements led by Colonel Allan MacNab reached the capital by steamer from Hamilton, and by the next morning confusion and near-hysteria had given way to confident determination. A day later, with bands playing and with a couple of pieces of artillery, a force of more than a thousand men marched north to attack Mackenzie's men. Contact was made south of the Tavern, and within half an hour the outnumbered, poorly armed, and almost leaderless rebels were put to demoralized flight. Through a combination of good luck and the help of many sympathizers Mackenzie managed to work his way round the lake to safety on the American side. A slight western phase of the rebellion came to nothing. Dr Charles Duncombe raised the standard of revolt in the country between London and Brantford, but his little band quickly fell away before militia advancing from several sides.

There is no certain way of knowing how much potential support there may have been for the uprising. An initial success might well have enlarged the movement somewhat. Some men who were marching to support Mackenzie quickly changed sides to become rebel-chasers when they saw how events were going. Mackenzie was often identified while escaping, as were other leaders, and yet they were not stopped despite a price on their heads. Nevertheless, the uprising had no broad following. Mackenzie and his associates managed to dupe only a few hundred farm lads and other rather simple people, many of whom paid a bitter price for their adventure, into believing that an armed uprising would cure the province's ills. The vigour with which people from one end of Upper Canada to the other rose to support the government showed that in no sense was Mackenzie the leader of a popular movement. His later admission that resort to force had been a mistake was cold comfort to the men and their families whose lives he had helped to ruin and to the reform cause which he had greatly injured.

Mackenzie's attempt to use force against the government, coinciding with the much more formidable rebellion in Lower Canada, was bound to disturb the political and social life of the province. Nevertheless, it had been a very small affair, engaging the support of only a fraction of the population. Within a few days all was quiet, with no possible chance of renewed disorder of any consequence originating within the province. If Upper Canada had been left free to absorb the consequences of the December rising a normal atmosphere might well have been restored in a relatively short time. But it was not left alone. Intervention from across the American border, lasting over several years, was to bring far more alarm, expense, and bloodshed than the rebellion itself produced, and was to complicate seriously the process of political and social transition.

The reasons behind this intervention were many, varied, and changing, and here they can be alluded to only briefly. To many Americans the fact that the Canadas still maintained a political tie with Great Britain was in itself proof that they must be suffering from tyranny and oppression; now they had imitated the patriots of '76 by rising to strike off their shackles. Assuming that the rebellions represented a widespread popular movement that had been put down by British regulars, and that the provinces still yearned to be free, Americans instinctively extended their sympathy and many of them saw a duty to give their active support to the downtrodden Canadians. And these sentiments were reinforced by other considerations. A mood of Manifest Destiny was seizing the United States, and one of its aspects was the belief that Americans had a moral obligation to extend the "area of freedom" throughout the North American continent. Yet such feelings were general and vague; more was needed to bring action. In particular, there was an unstable border population, made restless by the panic of 1837, and ready for adventure especially if it was coupled with the promise of free land in Upper Canada. More substantial elements in the American population were ready to see the rank and file so occupied, and also ready to take advantage of anything they might accomplish. The recent history of Texas, and its emerging importance in American politics, could never be far from people's minds at this time.

Thus it was that Mackenzie received an enthusiastic welcome when he arrived in Buffalo on December 11. After he had spoken of the bitter oppression under which the people of Upper Canada were labouring, many volunteers offered to join his cause, and a campaign to collect weapons and supplies was soon under way. Within two or three days a motley little band had established themselves on Navy Island, on the Canadian side of the Niagara River, where Mackenzie proclaimed a provisional government for Upper Canada and offered land in the province to all who would join him.

At first, the government and the people of Upper Canada watched these events with some calmness, assuming that American authorities would soon stop these hostile actions against a neighbouring province. But federal power was distant and ineffectual, and local and state officials showed little desire to act. When Colonel Allan MacNab of the militia saw that the American-owned steamer *Caroline* was openly and without hindrance engaged in ferrying men and supplies from the American side to Navy Island, to build up power for a raid on Upper Canada, he instructed Commander Andrew Drew, R.N., to destroy the ship. Not finding her at Navy Island, Drew's naval party continued across the river, where they set fire to the *Caroline*. She was sent down the river, and broke up before reaching the Falls. In the boarding operation an American citizen was killed and others were injured.

This incident greatly heightened tension along the border. The Assembly of Upper Canada applauded the action, while many Americans were outraged at this violation of their territory. To the existing motives for filibustering against Upper Canada that of retaliation was now added. Moreover, the *Caroline* affair darkened Anglo-American relations for several years to come.

By the spring of 1838 "Patriot" preparations were in full swing all along the border of the two provinces. Mackenzie and other refugee Canadians had little part in these activities, which were led and supported almost entirely by American citizens. The favourite form of organization was the secret society, of which the Hunters Lodges came to be the largest and best known. It was only gradually that official American action against these offensive preparations became effective. For many contemporary Upper Canadians the outstanding consequence of the Rebellion of 1837 was the threat, which on several occasions became a reality, of further invasion from the United States, in a time of Anglo-American peace and of quiet within the province.

CHAPTER 13

An End and a Beginning
1838-1841

I

The conservative leaders of Upper Canada believed that the Rebellion provided final proof of the utter bankruptcy of British colonial policy under the
Whigs and a final opportunity to break with the mistakes of the past. The
attempt to conciliate agitators and the failure to give full support to men
of proved loyalty had brought the Canadian provinces to the edge of disaster. Reckless statements in parliament and in British periodicals on the
future of colonies had encouraged Americans to hope that the mother
country might not defend the provinces. It should now be abundantly clear
to the British government that those who sought innovations in the provincial constitution were disloyal at heart, ready to appeal to the sword,
ready to combine with the anti-British rebels of Lower Canada, and ready
to call in foreign invaders.

Yet despite nearly a decade of rebuffs the loyal people of Upper Canada
had sprung in overwhelming numbers to the defence of the provincial
government. The most notorious among the "restless and unprincipled
agitators" had either fled the province or were in prison on charges of high
treason. Upper Canada was now alerted to the deep-seated antipathy of
French Canadians to British rule and to the malevolent hostility of the
American border population. Surely the eyes of the British government
would at last be opened to the need of supporting the loyal majority in
Upper Canada, of firmly establishing British rule in Lower Canada, and of
strengthening provincial defences against the "lawless vagabonds" across
the border. If these conclusions were drawn in Downing Street, and the old
illusions put aside, then perhaps the Rebellion might prove to be a blessing
in disguise. Upper Canada might yet look forward to the enjoyment of
"rational liberty more secure in the future than we have felt it to be in the
past."[1]

On their side, the reformers of Upper Canada found their ranks shattered and in disarray. Some of their most trusted leaders, such as Bidwell, had left the province; others were under surveillance, or in custody. A number of their most effective newspapers ceased publication at the time of the Rebellion.[2] The suspension of the Habeas Corpus Act just after the Rebellion was an open threat to reformers. Under these circumstances they had to content themselves with protesting that the great majority of the party had remained firmly loyal during the crisis, that they had stood ready, "almost to a man . . . to oppose rebellion and act against any external or internal enemies of the country."[3] They argued that true reformers had never wanted separation from the mother country or the adoption of a republican constitution. Any who had wanted these things had merely to cross the lines and live in the United States. By staying in the province the reformers demonstrated their loyalty and proved that their only wish was for the redress of genuine grievances. They had nothing whatever to gain from a "rash insurrection" which could only silence "for many years to come the voice of Reform, even the most rational and temperate."[4] Reformers insisted that "the people of this province" had not put down the uprising in order to continue the Family Compact in power, but there was a dispirited tone in their protestations.[5]

With the tories apparently more firmly in the saddle than ever, many reformers concluded that the prospects were utterly hopeless. In sizable numbers they began to sell their farms, often for a fraction of their value, and to move off to the American west. Several well-known reformers, including Peter Perry and a newcomer named Francis Hincks (about whom we shall hear more later), formed the Mississippi Emigration Society for the purpose of organizing this movement. Some of its directors made a journey to Washington to seek a large tract of land in the new-formed Territory of Iowa, then opening up to settlement. Although this overture proved to be unsuccessful, since the request violated American land regulations, the emigration of individuals went on. Many left for political reasons, while others were driven out by the continuing economic depression.[6] John Ryerson, who had attacked reformers with such vigour only two years before, now lamented that the loss of "so many useful & respectable citizens" would "be the means of smashing to peaces [sic] everything like reform or liberal interests in church or state."[7]

Thus it was a sorely troubled province that the new Lieutenant-Governor entered toward the end of March 1838. The Family Compact, the legislative council and the conservative Assembly were all filled with bitterness at the weakness of past British policy, and determined to use their present opportunity to make the province secure for loyal men. The jails were filled with captured rebels, and two of them, Samuel Lount and Peter Mathews, were on trial for their lives. Reformers throughout the province were struggling against a general suspicion of treason or at least disaffection, and were filled with irritation by many instances of petty persecution. At the borders lay the constant threat of invasion by the so-called Patriot movement being organized in New York and other neighbouring states. Public works were at a standstill, and the province lay under an over-whelming debt. Hundreds, perhaps thousands, were leaving for the western states.

No drastic changes were to be expected from the Lieutenant-Governor, however. He was Sir George Arthur, a veteran of the colonial service, who had been superintendent of British Honduras, and for a dozen years Lieutenant-Governor of the convict settlement of Van Diemen's Land. He had been appointed to Upper Canada just before the Rebellion broke out, and had sailed just after the news of it reached England. His primary task was to restore and maintain order, and to achieve this objective he was instructed to place full confidence in the loyal elements that had saved the province. Quite understandably, Arthur interpreted this group to be the conservatives, and more particularly the Family Compact. Although the Compact leaders were rather reluctant to see Sir Francis Bond Head leave them, they were soon very well pleased with his strong, determined, and much more experienced successor.

The Compact leaders thus had every reason to expect that their views would continue to prevail in the conduct of the government of Upper Canada, but the omens were very mixed for a stronger British policy. On the one hand it was encouraging to learn that by Act of Parliament, passed in January 1838, the Assembly of Lower Canada had been suspended and that temporary legislative power had been vested in a Council to be appointed by the governor. Less reassuring was the news that the governor selected to administer this autocratic system was to be the Earl of Durham, a man noted for his connections with British Radicals and as a principal leader in the fight for the Reform Bill of 1832. Somewhat nervously, John Macaulay noted that although "called a Radical peer," Durham was "clever, and therefore I do not think he will do any harm, for he will not fail to see what policy the true interests of Canada and the Empire will dictate."[8]

Behind the appointment of Durham there was, however, little either to justify or to dispel the fears of Toronto tories. Faced with a formidable rebellion in Lower Canada and a less serious uprising in the upper province, the British government had decided that the time had come for a thorough inquest into the affairs of the Canadas. To carry out this inquest Lord Durham was given broader powers than any of his predecessors. Not only was he appointed Governor-in-Chief of the Canadas, Nova Scotia, New Brunswick, and Prince Edward Island, but he also received the new title of Governor General, which was to encompass Newfoundland as well as the provinces already named. In addition, he was named High Commissioner "for the adjustment of certain important questions depending in . . . Lower and Upper Canada respecting the form and future government" of these two provinces.[9]

Nevertheless the Prime Minister, Lord Melbourne, was not clearly determined upon a new departure in Canadian policy when he pressed this most difficult appointment upon Durham. Like most British politicians of his day Melbourne knew little and cared little about the North American colonies. He shared the common belief that their connection with Great Britain would be severed at no distant date in the future. Yet he had to act to deflect criticism from his government, and he had to appoint a man of commanding stature. Durham was such a man. He was also an unruly colleague who might be less dangerous to the government outside the country than in it. Motives of political expediency rather than any vision of a new imperial policy governed Durham's appointment.

While the Canadian people awaited the arrival of Lord Durham (he reached Quebec at the end of May 1838), Sir George Arthur was tackling his more limited task of restoring order and normal conditions in Upper Canada. A week after he reached Toronto, Lount and Mathews were sentenced to death. Despite petitions bearing thousands of signatures and tearful pleas from the families of the condemned men, Arthur refused to intervene. The two men were hanged on April 12. The execution of these two men, one a former member of the Assembly, and both well liked by their neighbours, created a great sensation in the province, which was not used to such stern proceedings. Yet they had both taken arms against the government and their guilt was abundantly clear.

Arthur had no doubt that an example had to be made of Lount and Mathews, but he was puzzled as to what further action should be taken against the hundreds of prisoners in provincial jails. He was soon made aware of the bitter party feeling pervading the province. From the executive council and from many other sources he received urgent pleas for severe punishment as the only means of rooting out disaffection and of discouraging invasions by the American Patriots. Yet he was also aware that passions would never be allayed by a vindictive policy. Accordingly, he concluded that there was no need for further capital punishment, but that some of the worst offenders should be transported to the penal colonies for lengthy terms. He would set the rest free at once in the hope of bringing about an improved temper in the province.[10] Although some tories would have liked a harsher policy, the most responsible among them, including Chief Justice Robinson, accepted the Lieutenant-Governor's view. Robinson argued that an even milder policy would be possible, were it not for the aid and encouragement which the disaffected were receiving from across the border.[11]

Indeed, it was this factor – the threat or the fact of border raids – which largely governed the treatment of prisoners at this time and for two years or more in the future. Without these raids the passions raised by the Rebellion would have been much less intense. In June 1838, after many weeks of rumours, there were two invasions of the province, one across the Niagara River into the Short Hills and the other across the Detroit River. Although they were easily repulsed, they were further proof to conservatives of the need for firm measures.

In this atmosphere it was difficult for opponents of government policy to speak out without encountering the charge of disaffection or even of treason. Yet signs of reviving political debate were soon evident. Many in the province were encouraged when one man of unimpeachable credentials raised his voice, or rather his pen. In May a letter signed by "A United Empire Loyalist" appeared in the *Upper Canada Herald* of Kingston, which strongly criticized Sir Francis Bond Head for his treatment of Marshall Spring Bidwell and vigorously defended Bidwell and the vast body of reformers in the province from any connection with the late insurrection.[12] It soon became known that the author was Egerton Ryerson. The letter was widely reprinted in provincial newspapers and also published as a pamphlet. Shortly afterward Ryerson resumed the editorship of the *Guardian*. The incident promised a revival of loyal opposition unencumbered by radicalism. The Canadian Methodists, increasingly restive in the union with their more conservative British colleagues, were girding themselves to renew the struggle against what John Ryerson had earlier called "the dominion of a military & high church oligarchy."[13]

But the leading focus of reviving reform sentiment was a newspaper founded under the auspices of moderate men, which appeared in Toronto at the beginning of July. This was *The Examiner*. Its editor was Francis Hincks, a young man who had come out from Ireland a half-dozen years earlier and who had at once become a close friend of the Baldwin family. Brought up in an atmosphere of nonconformist liberalism, Hincks instinctively opposed the Family Compact, yet his business training and his intense personal ambition made him much more interested in practical accomplishment than in dogmatic radicalism. He was to be completely at home in the opportunistic party politics of the coming era. For the time being, however, his task was to press the argument that "any attempt to re-compose society" without taking account of the large body of moderate reformers could never succeed. These men should "speak out boldly and fearlessly" in the confident hope that Lord Durham would assist them to achieve "a system of government which would give satisfaction to all."[14] They should put their reliance on the "British Constitutional principle of Responsible Government." Echoing Robert Baldwin, Hincks emphasized that this principle involved "no change in the constitution," but "simply a resolution of the home government" that it should henceforth be observed. The prospect of a responsible executive council would soon win over those who had been tempted by the republican device of the direct election of a multitude of local officials.[15]

The moderate reformers were able to put their views before Lord Durham when he made a brief visit to Upper Canada in the first part of July 1838. After a visit to Niagara Falls, which included an attempt to woo American opinion along the border region, Durham made a short formal visit to Toronto. Among those to whom he granted interviews were Dr Baldwin and his son Robert, and although he could talk to them for only a few minutes, he showed a willingness to receive their views in writing. It was the younger man's letter that proved to be of far-reaching importance.

Robert Baldwin congratulated Durham on being the first British statesman "to avow a belief in the possibility of a permanent connection between the colonies & the Mother Country." He asserted, however, that this prophecy would come to pass only if the people of the colonies acquired control over their own "domestic concerns." "It is the genius of the English race in both hemispheres to be concerned in the Government of themselves," and those in North America would no more "be satisfied with less" than the people at home. Once this control was conceded, all talk of grievances would end; without it, the colonies would surely be lost. He enclosed a copy of his letter of July 13, 1836, to Lord Glenelg, fully setting forth his view that executive responsibility could be applied in the colonies, and observed that the outbreak of the Rebellions had lent weight to the argument in this letter.[16] As the sequel was to show, this correspondence, buttressed by copies of The Examiner also sent to him, had a powerful influence on the recommendations that Durham later made.

Durham's view of political affairs in Upper Canada was also much influenced by Charles Buller, his closest adviser, who quickly concluded that politics in the province were "a mere question between a petty, corrupt, insolent Tory clique . . . and the mass of the people. You can hardly conceive how popular you are with the latter, and how furiously the others are said to rage against you."[17] The reformers were gaining a powerful ally.

II

But Lord Durham's full impact on provincial politics lay several months in the future. In the meantime, in the summer and autumn of 1838, Sir George Arthur strove to maintain quiet within Upper Canada and to prepare for the expected Patriot invasions from across the border. A stream of exaggerated reports came into the Lieutenant-Governor's office, mainly from magistrates, militia officers and clergymen, telling of widespread disaffection

K

and subversive activity,[18] while informants from across the line kept him aware of preparations on the American side.[19] Arthur was on the alert for trouble when rebellion again broke out in Lower Canada at the beginning of November.

In the calculations of the Patriot leaders on the American side this uprising was to be the signal for renewed insurrection in the upper province, which would then be aided by invasion. In fact, however, the Lower Canadian rebellion was quickly put down, and all remained quiet in Upper Canada. Nevertheless, on November 11, a considerable body of some four hundred Patriots crossed the river at Prescott. They were immediately engaged by local militia and a few regulars. Many of the invaders escaped back across the river, but about half of them took refuge in a large stone windmill, where they were soon forced to surrender. Altogether about thirty of them were killed and one hundred and sixty made prisoners. Losses among the militia were relatively heavy, considering the numbers engaged. At a subsequent court martial in Kingston the prisoners were tried, and ten of their leaders executed, including the commander, "a remarkably clever talented man & a good soldier," named Von Schoultz. He was a Pole, recently arrived in the United States, who had been misled regarding the situation in the province, as he freely admitted, and there was much sympathy for him.[20] Several prisoners were transported, and the remainder set free.

Other expeditions planned for points along Lakes Ontario and Erie failed to materialize, but on December 4 some thousand "vagabonds" (as Arthur not unfairly called them)[21] crossed into the province from Detroit. Again they were quickly scattered by the militia, and a large number of them captured. In this engagement a notorious incident took place when Colonel John Prince ordered four of the prisoners summarily shot. This incident greatly offended Sir George Arthur's soldierly instincts. His whole policy was to repel the invasions with vigour, but to leave the disposition of prisoners to the processes of the law. He had no wish to give the Patriots "a handle . . . for making more proselytes to their cause."[22]

The failure of these two invasions and the punishment meted out to those taken prisoner went a long way to discourage further Patriot incursions during the remainder of the winter. The people along the frontier were reported to be "quite sick of patriotism" and to be "exclaiming they would not try to assist the cowardly Canadians any more."[23] American authorities tightened their surveillance of the border. Nevertheless, it was an anxious time for the people of the province. The Hunters Lodges were still in full operation in many nearby American centres, and there could be no certainty that new invasions would not be attempted. Conservative newspapers did their best, as one editor put it, "to inspire our fellow Canadian subjects with the hatred of Yankees, which their grasping, cunning, unprincipled and bloody proceedings have taught us ourselves to feel."[24] The invasions had played into the hands of the conservatives, and they tried hard to retain the advantage. Yet it was not long before the conservatives felt themselves to be beset by a new, and as it turned out, far more formidable, adversary. Early in April 1839 the first selections from Lord Durham's *Report* began to appear in the *Christian Guardian*, later to be widely reprinted in provincial newspapers. Within a short time the whole political tone of the province changed profoundly.

Except for his brief visit in July 1838 the people of Upper Canada had seen nothing of Lord Durham, but they had followed the dramatic events leading up to the issuance of his *Report* with the closest attention.

The course of these events had been determined, almost at the outset, by one of Durham's first acts after arriving at Quebec. Finding many scores of prisoners in jail still awaiting judgement for their part in the late Rebellion, he had issued an ordinance banishing eight of them to Bermuda, accompanied by a proclamation pardoning the rest. There had seemed to him to be no other solution to the problem, since a fair jury trial was impossible. French-speaking juries would have set all the men free. English-speaking juries would have been ready to see them all hanged, despite the government's intention that there should be no executions. The ordinance went on to state that if these eight, or sixteen other named leaders (including Papineau) who had escaped to the United States, should return to Lower Canada, they would be put to death. The net result was that, despite the greater magnitude of the Rebellion in the lower province, the punishment of its leaders was more lenient than in Upper Canada.

While dealing with this problem, Durham was already engaged in the main business of his mission: gathering information on which to make recommendations regarding the government of the Canadas. He had appointed a commission to investigate Crown lands and emigration, in the work of which Edward Gibbon Wakefield was the main figure, and later on he appointed sub-commissions to look into education and municipal institutions in Lower Canada. He and his staff were busy that summer collecting information on all aspects of the Canadian and, indeed, the British North American situation.

While he was in the midst of this work Durham learned, early in September, that Lord Brougham, a former friend and now a political enemy, had strongly attacked the legality of his ordinance regarding the prisoners. Although this news did not greatly disturb him, he discovered less than two weeks later not only that Melbourne's government had failed to support him to the full, but that it had disallowed his ordinance ! An impetuous and a proud man, Durham at once concluded that he could not perform his mission without the full confidence of the government, and he determined to resign. When his decision became known there was a great outpouring of sentiment from all groups in both provinces urging him to stay, but he remained adamant. Before he left, he issued a remarkable proclamation (on October 9), in which he flayed the British government for undermining his authority and asserted that he could now be of most use to the provinces by carrying

> into the Imperial Parliament a knowledge derived from personal inspection and experience of their interests, upon which some persons there are too apt to legislate in ignorance or indifference, and [by aiding] in laying the foundations of a system of general government which, while it strengthens your permanent connexion with Great Britain, shall save you from the evils to which you are now subjected by every change in the fluctuating policy of distant and successive administrations.[25]

The reformers of Upper Canada greeted this proclamation enthusiastically, as endorsing "responsibility to the people of the Province and efficient control over their internal affairs."[26] In England, however, it was widely criticized, The Times dubbing Durham "the Lord High Seditioner."

Durham sailed from Quebec on November 1, three days before the second rebellion broke out in Lower Canada. He and his staff worked hard on the Report during December and January, and it was ready by the end of the latter month. As we have seen, its text was available in North America early in April.

Durham had stayed in Canada for only a short time, but in compensation he wrote a long report. Avoiding the stilted and guarded language of official documents, he produced an outspoken and often eloquent state paper, which made no attempt to spare the feelings either of officials and people in the provinces or of the government at home. It was meant to be widely read, as it was, and it became at once the focus of political controversy. Not only did it seek to analyse the causes of political breakdown in the Canadas, but it made sweeping recommendations for the future. It proved to be a prophetic utterance, foretelling the Canadian nation to come and the modern Commonwealth of Nations, but at the same time it gave in many respects a fallible and inaccurate account of the Canadian scene.

Lord Durham stated that, before he reached Quebec, he had believed the bitter conflict in Lower Canada to be the result of defective political institutions and that it might be ended by "a reform of the constitution," or even by sounder administrative practices.[27] It was not long, however, before he concluded that the root of the trouble lay much deeper. In his famous phrases, "I expected to find a contest between a government and a people:

I found two nations warring in the bosom of a single state: I found a struggle, not of principles, but of races."[28] No improvement of political institutions would be effective until the "deadly animosity" separating English and French should be ended. After giving an elaborate account of this animosity, he stated that "the present generation of French Canadians [would never again] yield a loyal submission to a British Government"; nor would the English population of Lower Canada ever again "tolerate the authority of a House of Assembly, in which the French shall possess or even approximate to a majority."[29] Durham saw but one way out of this impasse: there must be an end of "the vain endeavour to preserve a French Canadian nationality in the midst of Anglo-American colonies and states."[30] An unprogressive and unenterprising people, the French Canadians were destined in any event to be overwhelmed; far better that the transition should be planned and orderly.

Turning to Upper Canada, Durham painted a very dark picture of the Family Compact's irresponsible rule. Its selfish and narrow policies had impeded the development of the province, and produced widespread dissatisfaction. On the other hand he referred favourably to "the great body of Reformers," whose only wish was to see "the administration of affairs [entrusted] to men possessing the confidence of the Assembly."[31] Among particular causes of dispute, he gave special attention to the Clergy Reserves, arguing that any attempt to set up an ecclesiastical establishment "in the immediate vicinity of the United States"[32] was bound to fail. He also laid great stress on backward economic conditions which led many, including those who were quite satisfied with "the present political state of the Province," to believe that "there must have been something wrong to have caused so striking a difference in progress and wealth between Upper Canada and the neighbouring states of the Union."[33]

In subsequent sections of the *Report* Durham devoted a few pages to the maritime colonies, and then provided a scathing criticism of land and emigration policies. The material on these subjects reflected the views of Edward Gibbon Wakefield.

In summing up his review of conditions in the several provinces, Durham asserted that the practical mismanagement of their affairs had reached the stage where the very integrity of the British Empire in North America was in jeopardy. Irresponsible rule in the colonies and erratic control from Downing Street had combined to bring about this state of affairs, and it could not be allowed to continue. With the "melancholy contrast" between their own backwardness and the progress and prosperity of the United States always before their eyes, the British population of the provinces could not be expected to remain indefinitely loyal to the connection with the mother country, if they saw no prospect of improvement in their condition.

The two Canadas had reached the stage of crisis, but so might the maritime provinces in time.

In turning to solutions, Durham argued that there was only one answer: to end collision and to restore harmony in the conduct of the provincial governments. Once harmony was restored, it could be assumed that administrative incompetence would rapidly diminish, and the provinces begin to realize their possibilities. And he went on to state the core of his argument:

> It is not by weakening, but strengthening the influence of the people on its Government; by confining within much narrower bounds than those hitherto allotted to it, and not by extending the interference of the imperial authorities in the details of colonial affairs, that I believe that harmony is to be restored, where dissension has so long prevailed; and a regularity and vigour hitherto unknown, introduced into the administration of these Provinces. It needs no change in the principles of government, no invention of a new constitutional theory. . . . It needs but to follow out consistently the principles of the British constitution . . . by administering the Government on those principles which have been found perfectly efficacious in Great Britain.[34]

In short, Durham was arguing for a responsible executive council, as Robert Baldwin and other Upper Canadian reformers had been doing for several years, and he had undoubtedly got the idea from them. He made one important distinction, however, which the reformers had never clearly made. Although he would "place the internal government of the colony in the hands of the colonists themselves," he would reserve to the mother country the control of a few matters of imperial concern: "The constitution of the form of government – the regulation of foreign relations, and of trade with the mother country, the other British Colonies, and foreign nations, – and the disposal of the public lands."[35] By making this distinction Durham sought to show that the grant of local self-government would not harm essential imperial interests.

The introduction of effective popular government in most provincial matters was, therefore, Durham's remedy for the "disorders common to all the North American Colonies."[36] Nevertheless this remedy in itself provided no answer to the most immediate problem of all, the "fatal feud" between the races in Lower Canada. As already indicated, Durham believed that this feud could be terminated only by impressing an English character on Lower Canada, both by renewed immigration and by anglicizing the French Canadians. In the meantime, its government could be entrusted to "none but a decidedly English Legislature."[37] Hence, he recommended the union of Upper and Lower Canada. The 400,000 inhabitants of the upper province when combined with the 150,000 English-speaking residents of Lower

Canada would "give a clear English majority" over the 450,000 French Canadians, "one which would be increased every year by the influence of English emigration." Durham had no doubt that the French Canadians, "when once placed, by the legitimate course of events and the working of natural causes, in a minority, would abandon their vain hopes of nationality."[38]

Durham had come reluctantly to the recommendation of a dual union. His original preference had been for a federal union of all the British North American provinces, and during the previous summer he had held talks with officials from New Brunswick and Nova Scotia and with many individuals in the Canadas, looking to such a plan. He had thought that as part of a large federal union the French Canadians would gradually but surely lose their national character. But the outbreak of the second rebellion, in November 1838, convinced him that a more direct and more immediate overawing of the French Canadians was essential.

After abandoning federal union he had given earnest consideration to the idea of a legislative union embracing the Canadas and the maritime provinces, and this was his favourite plan of all. Even more than a dual union, a legislative union of all the colonies would "at once decisively settle the question of races." More than that, he saw large and attractive gains coming from such a union. The people of the provinces would be able "to cooperate for all common purposes," and their increased power "might in some measure counterbalance the preponderant influence of the United States on the American continent."[39] Of even greater weight in Durham's mind was the need of "raising up for the North American colonist some nationality of his own"[40] as the only way of resisting the all-pervasive influence of the United States which surrounded the colonist on every side. He could see many other advantages in such a union, but reluctantly concluded once again that speed was of the essence. It could not be put into operation without gaining the consent of the maritime provinces, which would take time. The problems of Lower Canada would not wait. Once again he was driven back to the scheme for a dual union, but he recommended that a bill for uniting the Canadas "should contain provisions by which any or all of the other North American Colonies may, on the application of the Legislature be, with the consent of the two Canadas, or their united Legislature, admitted into the union. . . ."[41]

Such in barest outline was the argument of Lord Durham's *Report*: the reunion of the Canadas, hoping that it would be the first step toward a larger union, and provincial governments responsible to legislatures which had English-speaking majorities. Both a perceptive and a naïve argument, it provided one of the many examples of the way in which Anglo-American relationships could impinge on Canadian development. The shadow of the

United States hovered over nearly every page of the Report, and it provided Durham with both insights and blindspots. It helped him to see that the British colonists must have the opportunity to develop their country, as Americans were doing, that they must see the prospect of a national future, and that they must have effective and growing control over their political institutions. But as an Englishman who rejoiced in the progress of his American cousins Durham fell into the trap of believing that there was only one road into the future: the submerging of all other cultures and outlooks by the dominant Anglo-Saxon way of life. The Canadian people had to grasp what they could use in the Report, and reject or ignore the rest.

Certainly the Report was provocative. It became at once a storm centre of provincial debate.

III

In the spring and summer of 1839 the people of Upper Canada were not poised to give Lord Durham's Report a calm and reflective reception. Nerve ends were frayed after a tense winter of crisis along the border. Normal political debate was still scarcely possible, more than a year after the Rebellion. Conservatives, in control not only of the government but of the legislature, believed that the very future of the province hung in the balance; they felt strongly that the province could be saved only if British authority gave determined and unwavering support to its loyal elements. On the other hand, there was a growing sentiment among reformers that the party in power had turned the crisis to partisan purposes. Not only had the tories sought to proscribe their opponents but they had revived the Clergy Reserves question hoping to achieve their old objectives before public opinion could make itself felt. Each side was girding for renewed conflict when the text of the Report became known.

Although men who shared the views of the Family Compact had always had reservations about Lord Durham, they were genuinely shocked to find that a British peer could write or at least sign such a Report. As it happened, the man who, next to Strachan, best personified the Family Compact was also the first of this group to give his impressions of the High Commissioner's analysis and recommendations. Chief Justice John Beverley Robinson had gone to England on what proved to be a lengthy sick leave, but a perusal of the Report did nothing to improve his health; indeed, he wrote that "It absolutely made me ill, to read it," for he found that "all" that related to Upper Canada was "disgraceful and mischievous."[42]

The Upper Canada section of the Report was in fact an easy target for any well-informed resident of the province. It was filled with glaring errors of fact and studded with dubious and often untenable generalizations. As conservatives never tired of pointing out, Durham had spent only "five days on the soil of Upper Canada, one of them at the seat of Government, and the rest at the Falls of Niagara";[43] the kindest explanation was that he had been imposed upon by incompetent or prejudiced advisers. Certainly he wrote this section out of no personal knowledge, and he presented no evidence to support his statements.

In writing to the Colonial Secretary, however, Robinson concentrated his fire on Durham's recommendations. He opposed, as he had always opposed, the reunion of the two Canadas. The conservative Canadian judge differed flatly with the liberal British peer on the subject of the French Canadians. He did not believe that the imperial parliament would legislate upon the assumption of "the hopeless inferiority of the French Canadian Race." "It is not in that spirit that the dominion over half a million of free subjects should be exercised." And from a purely practical point of view the measure would not work since the French-Canadian members would combine "in a close phalanx against the British portion of the Legislature," which would never be as effectively united. He scornfully dismissed Durham's suggestion that the maritime provinces would ever willingly join such a legislative union.

Other recommendations came under Robinson's attacks, but he combatted Durham's proposal for a responsible executive council with particular vehemence. He pointed out that there was in Canada "no Counteracting influence of an ancient Aristocracy, of a great landed interest or even of a wealthy agricultural class; there is little in short but the presumed good sense, and good feeling of an uneducated multitude. . . ." In such a society and with such an electorate, the "new species of responsibility . . . would be nothing more or less than a servile and corrupting dependence upon Party." In comparison with a government so constituted, "the Republican Government of the United States would be strongly conservative." It may be said in passing that Robinson saw quite accurately the implications of responsible government. It would mean party rule, and it would be free of the checks and balances contained in the American framework of government and in the contemporary British system with its influential aristocracy.[44]

Robinson, who spent the next year in England striving to prevent the implementation of Durham's recommendations, had correctly anticipated the views of most conservatives in the province. The issues raised by Lord Durham had, of course, long been under debate there, and positions on them had long been taken.

On the question of uniting the provinces, there were some differences of opinion among conservatives. Recently, the conservative majority in the Assembly had come out for the measure, largely for economic reasons.

Union would mean a great increase of revenue, and an end of French-Canadian resistance to internal improvements. It must, however, be a union in which Upper Canada had a decided majority in the legislature, with English as the only official language and with the capital in the upper province. Representatives of the mercantile outlook, notably William Hamilton Merritt, were consistent advocates of union.

But the inner circles of the Family Compact never liked the measure. Robert Baldwin Sullivan, perhaps its most articulate spokesman in this period, had already, in June 1838, written an extensive criticism of the proposal. Instead of union, he came back to the old suggestion of annexing Montreal and the surrounding country to Upper Canada, leaving the main body of the French Canadians under an appointive government in Lower Canada. Upper Canada would then have a seaport, and there would be no need to harass the French Canadians. "The Government need seldom find itself in opposition to them. They may enjoy bad laws, bad roads bad sleighs, bad food and ignorant legislation in peace and quietness, injuring no others and not being interfered with themselves."[45] About this same time James Fitzgibbon, a veteran soldier of the War of 1812, informed Lord Durham that the Loyalists of Upper Canada were "more averse to connexion with Lower Canada than they are to connexion with the United States."[46] These views were strengthened rather than weakened by the publication of Durham's *Report*.

Each House of the provincial legislature referred Lord Durham's *Report* to select committees, and each committee dealt scathingly with the document. Its factual errors and its inconsistencies were exhaustively exposed, while the recommendation for responsible government would, in the words of the committee of the legislative council, "lead to the overthrow of the great Colonial Empire of England." In a system where the members of the executive council were "the creatures of the prevailing faction or party in the Assembly," there could be no stability or continuity of government. Upper Canada was a small community where political topics were often ephemeral, where there was substantial social and economic equality, where few men of standing enjoyed any personal influence. As in the United States, members of the representative assembly were expected to reflect the views of their constituents. Under these circumstances, the government must be strong enough to resist the whim of the moment if there was to be "consistent legislation on general principles." Yet Lord Durham proposed to make stable government impossible in order to please the reformers, a portion of whose ranks was tainted with disaffection, while he had "not one word of approval" for the loyal men who had saved the province.[47] The report of the Assembly's committee used even stronger language.

For the reformers of Upper Canada, on the other hand, Lord Durham's

Report was a welcome and badly needed weapon. For three years they had been divided and on the defensive. They had seen moderates, both leaders and rank and file, retire from the fray or go over to their opponents. Not only had the party lost control of the Assembly, but it was accused of disloyalty and rebellion. Now, in the spring of 1839, the conservatives were using their control of the legislature to force a solution of the province's bitterest subject of contention, the Clergy Reserves, a solution that flagrantly defied prevailing opinion. After an extremely close vote a bill was passed in May providing that the proceeds from the Reserves should be applied to religious purposes along lines to be determined by the British parliament. This bill was doubly hateful to reformers; not only did they oppose turning the proceeds over to the churches (and they were convinced that the bishops in the House of Lords would ensure that the Church of England received a disproportionate share), but they resented this abandonment to the imperial authority of a matter of internal provincial interest. To conservative assertions that the legislature could not agree on a solution, reformers answered that it could easily do so if the government and legislature were truly responsive to public opinion. It was time to renew the fight for political reform, and Lord Durham's *Report* provided the ground on which to fight.

In consequence, reformers concentrated on one feature of the *Report* – its criticisms of Family Compact rule and its recommendation for responsible government – and ignored nearly everything else in it. They rejoiced in Durham's assertion that responsible government was a truly English solution, and that it was the surest preservative of the connection with the mother country; there was sweet revenge in being able to quote Her Majesty's High Commissioner against tories who had denounced the idea of responsible government as republican and separatist. It should now be clear, as reformers had asserted all along, that the tories clung to the old system for one reason only; to keep a "monopoly of place, profit and power." The tories were the real obstacle to an enduring connection with the mother country, for by clinging to power they forced their opponents into extremist and radical courses. Durham, however, opened the way to a system giving "the colonies the complete control of all their own local affairs," that is, "all the advantages of total independence without any of its disadvantages."[48] The people of Upper Canada wanted the military protection, the trade and the economic assistance afforded by the imperial tie; they also wanted local self-government responsive to provincial public opinion. Lord Durham showed that they could have both.

From the outset, however, reformers realized that the mere publication of Durham's *Report* would not bring change of itself. They must work for it, by coming forward to approve by thousands of Resolutions, their approbation of [Durham's] measures, ... [by holding] meetings in every Township in the Province to establish Durham Clubs, passing Resolutions approving of the Noble Earl's Report, and condemnatory of the machinations of the base and unprincipled Tories."[49] The need for such activity was further emphasized when it became known, early in July, that Lord John Russell speaking for the Melbourne government had informed Parliament on June 3 that he disagreed with Durham's recommendation for responsible government, although he believed that the executive government should be carried on in ways acceptable to the representatives of the people. To some reformers this statement was proof that nothing could be hoped for from the British government; to others, it suggested that Russell would accept responsible government in practice, but boggled at the theory. In either event it called the reformers to action. Upper Canada would no longer "submit to be governed by despatches from Downing Street adopted by an imbecile ministry at the suggestion probably of an under Secretary."[50]

The call to action was answered with enthusiasm. Throughout the summer of 1839 dozens of "Durham Meetings" were held in various parts of the province, all of them adopting resolutions in favour of the Report. Attempts were made to break up some of the meetings, and the conservative press denounced them, but the movement spread and grew. For the first time in three years the reformers were again on the offensive.

Moreover, they were acquiring new and welcome recruits among men who had not acted with the reformers for many years or who had even strongly opposed them in the past. Notable among these men was Egerton Ryerson who had become disillusioned with the tory ascendancy shortly after the Rebellion, and was now in even more open opposition following the passage of the Clergy Reserves Bill. He became an ardent "Durhamite," and defended himself against charges of inconsistency by arguing that there was "as much difference between the 'responsible government' advocated by Mackenzie and his associates in 1835-36 and Lord Durham's 'responsible government,' as there is between an independent democratic Republic and a subordinate Limited Monarchy."[51] Reformers were very glad to have Ryerson, with the influential newspaper which he edited and with the Methodist support which he could muster, once more working with them.

Another valued and significant addition to the ranks was William Hamilton Merritt, a man of conservative instincts and one who had formerly worked closely with the Family Compact. But Merritt had never been concerned with theories of governments, only with getting things done. He was now convinced that a narrow tory oligarchy was inefficient and moribund; only a government responsive to public opinion could generate the energy needed to match the economic progress of the neighbouring states, always Merritt's main concern.[52]

Even stranger converts were won to the new doctrine. One of these was

Ogle R. Gowan, the Provincial Grand Master of the Orangemen. When Sir George Arthur had the temerity to recommend publicly that Orange processions be discontinued, Gowan turned in fury on "the unblushing Compact," "the ungrateful Clique" whom Orangemen had "so long supported," and warned them that "Orangemen can be liberal as well as loyal – that liberality is a game at which two can play." Gowan proceeded to publish a pamphlet endorsing responsible government, and for a time was one of its most vocal advocates. This was going too far for most Orangemen, however, and Gowan had to backpedal in later weeks.[53]

Nevertheless, the rift in the Orange ranks was a good example of the way Durham's *Report* was disrupting the older political alignments. Sir George Arthur bitterly criticized Lord Durham for throwing "a firebrand amongst the People," thereby dividing "the Loyal Party" and giving "a vast preponderance to the Republicans."[54] In a public reply to the resolutions passed by one of the largest Durham meetings the Lieutenant-Governor vigorously denounced the doctrine of responsible government as a scheme that would endanger the connection with Britain and lead to rule by faction.[55]

Despite his opposition to the Durham movement, however, Arthur believed that the government of Upper Canada was in need of drastic overhauling and extensive reform. In fact, from the beginning of his administration he had been dissatisfied with the system or, rather, the lack of system. The executive government was unable to give effective leadership to the Assembly; indeed, its presumed spokesmen, the Attorney General and the Solicitor General, sometimes disagreed openly with one another on the floor. As a result, the members of the Assembly went their own ways, haphazardly concocting legislation without regard to a coherent plan or the cost to the province. Moreover, the executive departments were inefficiently and sloppily conducted: revenue was "not collected as it should be," expenditures were not "at all satisfactorily accounted for," and the landgranting department was the worst conducted of all.[56] Under these circumstances, Arthur could understand the cry for responsible government, and he sought to meet it by introducing and enforcing administrative reforms and by making "all Public Functionaries . . . strictly Responsible in every practical and useful sense of the term."[57] By his "searching investigation" of all the departments of government, begun in the autumn of 1839, Arthur made the first real start at giving Upper Canada a competently run government. He believed that by making these reforms and by conducting the government with a due regard for the wishes of the Assembly he could undercut the popular demand for responsible government. What the loyal people of the province really wanted was good and efficient government, and he would give it to them. He was ready to assist in the transition away from Family Compact rule, which the province had outgrown.

But Arthur was not fated to carry out this policy. Another agent was at hand, with greater authority and with greater political skill, who was ready to break more ruthlessly with the past than Arthur would probably have done. He was the new Governor, Charles Poulett Thomson, who arrived at Quebec in October 1839.

After some uncertainty, the Melbourne government had finally decided on a policy for the Canadas, which to a considerable degree followed Lord Durham's recommendations. The two provinces were to be united, but only after their legislatures consented to the measure. Obtaining this consent would be a simple matter in Lower Canada, where legislative authority was embodied in the appointed Special Council, to be continued if necessary until 1842. The task would be much more formidable in Upper Canada, however, since there was much anti-union sentiment in the Assembly. In addition, many of the particular reforms in the *Report* were to be implemented without, however, conceding the full measure of responsible government proposed by Lord Durham. And to carry out these delicate and difficult tasks, the government turned to one of its best men. Poulett Thomson was a member of the cabinet and one of the rising men in British politics. He was a politician to his fingertips, and at the same time he had a broad and specialized knowledge of economic affairs. A friend and a political follower of Lord Durham, a sanguine and an immensely energetic man, he was a new kind of governor for the Canadas and an excellent choice for guiding them toward a new political era.

But in the autumn of 1839 he did not appear in this light to Sir George Arthur and the conservative leaders of Upper Canada. Arthur thought it most unwise to replace Sir John Colborne[58] by a civilian when there were still signs of unrest along the border which might lead to renewed invasions. The executive council was still strongly opposed to the union; after its leading members had seen the proposed bill, in July, they wrote lengthy and vehement objections to nearly every one of its clauses.[59] Worst of all, however, Arthur and his advisers feared that Thomson meant "to change the current of political feeling in the Province," "to bring down the Conservative party & to raise the American party, for such in fact are the Reformers of Upper Canada." If this were done, Arthur was quite convinced that the Canadas would be lost.[60]

Nevertheless, it was Arthur's duty to co-operate with the new Governor, and like the good soldier he was he prepared to execute his orders. He soon learned from the Colonial Secretary that Thomson was to come personally to Toronto, and to assume the government of the province for the purpose of carrying through the union. After painting a dark picture of the state of parties and stressing that few of the reformers could be relied upon, he surrendered the reins of government to his superior on November 23. He then became a mere assistant to the Governor, with the somewhat humiliating task of working for a measure which he had hitherto openly opposed.

For some three months the spotlight now shifted to the brisk and efficient Governor, and under his energetic leadership the province passed finally and irrevocably out of the political era symbolized by the phrase "Family Compact rule." When he returned to Lower Canada in February 1840, no one could be sure how the new system would work, but everyone was agreed that the old system had been fatally weakened.

Thomson had not been in the province more than a few days before he was convinced that "great changes" were needed at once. "The country was split into factions animated with the most deadly hatred to each other." Finances were "more deranged than we believed even in England." The government was riddled with inefficiency, "all Public works were suspended – & emigration going on fast *from* the Province," and property was worth half what it had been.[61] He was more convinced than ever that Upper Canada must have the benefits that union would bring, and he turned at once to the task of gaining the Assembly's consent to this measure.

It proved to be no easy task. The conservative majority in the Assembly had grown increasingly suspicious of the project following the appearance of Durham's *Report*, and were ready to hold out for the most exacting, indeed impossible, conditions. They wanted a guarantee that Upper Canada would be given a majority in the new legislature, despite the fact that the province had a smaller population than Lower Canada. They wanted the capital to be in Upper Canada, and they wanted assurances that English would be the only official language of the united legislature. Indeed, some of them sought to revive the old alien controversy by demanding that the American-born population should be discriminated against.[62] They wanted no part in a union which did not clearly provide for the predominance of the loyal element.

But Thomson could not accept binding conditions. Instead, he set out to divide and break down his opposition. In an intensive series of personal interviews he won over the reform minority in the Assembly and, with the useful assistance of Sir George Arthur, detached many of the less rigid conservatives from an anti-union stand. The two men were able to promise that Upper Canada would have equal representation in the united legislature, even if not a majority, and to hold out the strong hope, if not the certainty, that it would have the capital. Most persuasive of all was the assurance that the public debt of Upper Canada would be a charge upon the united province. The prospect that union would bring relief from this overwhelming debt, and that it might lead to a resumption of work on the canals and other internal improvements was too powerful to be resisted. When Thomson agreed that the earlier-mentioned conditions might be turned into recommendations all effective opposition collapsed, and a majority was won for the union.

Thomson had done more than get his measure through the Assembly. He had quickened the formation of a new political party of moderates, by winning over the leading reformers, and by detaching men from both the radical and tory extremes. Sir George Arthur sadly remarked that "The Constitutional party wh. supported Sir P. Maitland—Sir J. Colborne—Sir F. Head—& myself, are, as a body, so thoroughly undermined, that I would not on any acct. remain in the Province to witness their utter prostration."[63]

Thomson accomplished this apparent political miracle not only by holding out the hope of renewed economic progress under the union but by meeting head on "the cry for 'Responsible Govt.' "[64] that had been before the province for months past.

He believed that the demand for political change was entirely justified, but he also believed that it was practical rather than theoretical in origin. In even stronger terms than Sir George Arthur had earlier used he denounced the inefficiency and the lack of system in the provincial government. He was soon convinced that by correcting the administrative evils that had grown up and by introducing order and method he could readily calm the prevailing discontent. These improvements and corrections could only be effected by an efficient and vigorous executive that would lead the Assembly and that would proclaim and carry out a coherent policy.

But how "responsible" should the executive be to the Assembly? As he carried on his discussions with politicians in Toronto, Thomson had in his pocket a recent dispatch from the Colonial Secretary, Lord John Russell, stating authoritatively that the practice of responsible government could not possibly exist in a colony.[65] A governor could not serve two masters: he could not obey orders from the British government and at the same time act on the advice of his executive council. Therefore, there were "insuperable objections" to the principle. Nevertheless, Russell saw no objection to the "practical views of Colonial Government recommended by Lord Durham." The British government had "no desire to thwart the Representative Assemblies of British North America" and had every wish for harmony between executive and legislature. Thomson also had a second dispatch, sent two days later, announcing a fundamental change in the practice governing the tenure of office of members of the executive council and of heads of departments.[66] Although officially held during pleasure, by custom these posts had come to be regarded as life appointments. From now on, Russell stated, the governor was to be free to ask for resignations from these offices whenever public policy made changes expedient, and he was particularly free to do so at the beginning of his administration.

Armed with these two dispatches, Thomson proceeded to sketch the outlines of future practice to his many visitors among the provincial politicians.[67] He would resist any scheme that would make the "power of the Governor subordinate to that of a Council," but at the same time he stated "no less forcibly" that the British government intended "to govern the Colony in accordance with the wishes and feelings of the People, and that, whilst the Governor could not shift any portion of his own responsibility upon the Council, it would of course be his best policy to select as members of that Body . . . men whose principles & feelings were in accordance with the majority," and "in all merely local matters . . . to administer the affairs of the colony in accordance with the wishes of the Legislature." And he was able to point to Russell's second dispatch as proof that he, or any governor, would have discretionary authority to change his advisers whenever it was necessary or wise to do so.

These persuasive assurances of the Governor proved to be very convincing to the reform leaders who listened to them. While he did not concede much in the way of theory, he did hold out the prospect that the little group that had so long held power would soon be superseded. Without giving up their intention of continuing to work for a provincial administration that would be directly responsible to the Assembly, the reform leaders agreed to work with the Governor in the task of broadening and modernizing the provincial government. Thomson made his "greatest possible *coup*" when, in February, Robert Baldwin agreed to accept office as Solicitor General.[68] The policy of quietly breaking up "the Exclusive power of the Compact on the one hand," and of repressing "the violent radicals on the other" was beginning to bear fruit, although the full implications of the policy would not be clear for several years and would prove to be very different from what Thomson intended.

Thomson's last great accomplishment during his short stay in Upper Canada was to push a Clergy Reserves bill through the legislature. The British government had refused to accept the reinvestment bill, passed in 1839, because of constitutional defects in its drafting, and the perennial question was again before the provincial parliament. Thomson regarded it as "the one great overwhelming grievance – the root of all the troubles of the Province – the cause of the Rebellion – the never failing watchword at the hustings – the perpetual source of discord, strife and hatred."[69] He was anxious to get this question settled before the union came into operation, and so avoid entangling Lower Canada in the controversy, and he was determined to resist the extreme claims of the Church of England. As he warned Russell later, "five sixths of the province" would never submit to "any attempt to give the Church of England a superiority in point of station, or title, or tenure of property."[70]

Searching for a solution that might satisfy the emerging moderate party, Thomson proposed that after honouring existing obligations, and when the income from future sales was adequate, one half of the income should be divided between the Church of England and the Church of Scotland, according to their numbers, and the other half should be divided among all the other denominations, again according to their numbers. It was a skilfully designed plan. Anglicans who remained loyal to Bishop Strachan (as he now was) bitterly resisted this "spoliation," while the more unbending reformers were equally opposed to any division among religious bodies. But in the middle was a substantial group, drawing off support from both extremes, which was thoroughly tired of the issue and ready to support the bill. It passed the Assembly by a nearly three-to-two majority.

No reasonable person, least of all Thomson, really believed that this settlement represented majority opinion in the province, which was as strong as ever for devoting the proceeds to education and internal improvements. Still, it was the only possible way of disposing of the question in advance of the union, given the political complexion of the Assembly.[71]

In February Thomson returned to Montreal, making a remarkable trip by sleigh which took him just thirty-six hours – a whirlwind end to his whirlwind visit. He left behind him a province that was more optimistic and more united than it had been in many a year. The people, as Arthur presently reported, were "sickened of discord and strife" and ready to "turn their attention to more profitable subjects."[72] Some of the die-hard leaders of the Family Compact toyed with the idea of sulking in their tents, but not for long. Reluctantly, but inevitably, they began to make their adjustment to a more flexible political system. Hagerman joined Robinson on the bench. Strachan, although always ready to enter the public stage in the interests of his church, was increasingly busy with the duties of a growing diocese. Meanwhile, new conservative leaders, such as William Henry Draper, were taking control of the party, and they were very much at home in the new political atmosphere.

As for the reformers, they looked forward cheerfully to the union. They knew that Thomson had no intention of relinquishing his personal direction of the government, but they were equally convinced that, with the political co-operation of the French-Canadian members (an alliance which Francis Hincks had been carefully fostering for several months), they would be strong enough to have their way. To be sure, they were strongly opposed to many clauses of the Union Bill, when its terms became known in the early summer of 1840, but they believed that anything would be possible for the *"overwhelming Reform majority"* which they confidently anticipated.[73]

Yet the prevailing tone continued to be the moderate one that Thomson (Lord Sydenham, after August 1840) had helped to set at the beginning of the year. Editors continued to announce that "the extremes of Toryism and Radicalism" were "equally injurious to the well being of the country" and to advise that "all parties should agree to bury the hatchet, to forget and forgive as much as possible former political animosity, and to unite heart and hand in promoting the prosperity of our common country – the country of our birth or of our adoption."[74] There was a remarkable demonstration of this kind of feeling, which had overtones of incipient nationalism, after Brock's monument at Queenston Heights had been partially destroyed by a charge of gun powder placed in it by a ruffian who came across the Niagara River for the purpose. Men of all parties came together to plan for the reconstruction of the monument and to revive memories now more than a quarter-century old. Sir George Arthur, who had sometimes believed that as many as one-third of the population was disaffected, wrote that he had "never expected to have seen such a scene in the Province."[75]

By the beginning of the new year, and about a month before the union was proclaimed, Arthur could report that the prospects for the future were cheering.[76] The economic scene was noticeably brightening. Agriculture was reviving and exports had risen markedly in the previous year. Both in the towns and in the country people were again busy improving their properties. The union gave promise of lifting Upper Canada's crushing financial burden. The province still lacked men with capital, but there was the prospect of a British loan, and more money would come in with the building of railways. Society still appeared to be unformed and heterogeneous, following the heavy immigration of the previous fifteen years. Yet not long afterward an observer noted that the people of Upper Canada were neither British nor American, and that "a national character [was] in process of formation."[77] A half-century of back-breaking pioneer work, the impact of war and invasion, and prolonged and often bitter debate over forms of government, over economic and social policies, and over the nature of its relations with the American states and with Great Britain had given the province more distinctive contours than most contemporaries realized. In the political realm moderate men were at last gaining at the expense of extremists, and would soon help to release and quicken the constructive energies of the population. No one could tell how the experiment of yoking English-speaking and French-speaking Canadians under a common government would work out, but now it must be tried. For the tasks of the future required that the two peoples must learn to live and work together more closely than in the past, and if legislative union was not the way another would have to be found.

ABBREVIATIONS

The following abbreviations are used in the Notes and the Bibliography:
C.H.A.R.: *Annual Report of the Canadian Historical Association.*
C.H.R.: *Canadian Historical Review.*
C.O.: Colonial Office.
L.L.: Legislative Library, Parliament Buildings, Toronto.
O.A.: Ontario Department of Public Records and Archives, Toronto.
O.H.: *Ontario History.*
O.H.S.P.R.: *Ontario Historical Society, Papers and Records.*
P.A.C.: Public Archives of Canada, Ottawa.
P.A.C.R.: *Annual Report of the Public Archives of Canada.*
R.S.C., P. & T.: *Royal Society of Canada, Proceedings and Transactions.*
T.P.L.: Toronto Public Library.
U.C.: Upper Canada.
U. of T.: University of Toronto.

NOTES TO CHAPTER ONE

1. E. J. Lajeunesse, ed., *The Windsor Border Region* (Toronto, 1960), p. iii ff.

2. R. R. Palmer notes that, in proportion to population, there were about five times as many *émigrés* in the American Revolution as in the French Revolution. See his *The Age of the Democratic Revolution: The Challenge* (Princeton, N.J., 1959), p. 188.

3. E. A. Cruikshank, "Ten Years of Niagara, 1780-90," Niagara Historical Society, *Publications*, No. 17 (1908), pp. 4-12. See also G. E. Reaman, *The Trail of the Black Walnut* (Toronto, 1957), p. 65.

4. J. J. Talman, *Loyalist Narratives from Upper Canada* (Toronto, 1946), pp. xxxviii-xxxix.

5. E. A. Cruikshank, *The Settlement of the United Empire Loyalists on the Upper St Lawrence and Bay of Quinte in 1784* (Toronto, 1934), p. 13, Capt. Justus Sherwood to Capt. Robert Mathews, 11 Oct. 1783.

6 C. O. 42/46, p. 7, Haldimand to North, 6 Nov. 1783.

7. *Ibid.*, p. 224, Meeting with the Missisauga Indians, 22 May 1784.

8. Adam Shortt and Arthur G. Doughty, eds., *Documents Relating to the Constitutional History of Canada, 1759-1791* (Ottawa, 1918), pp. 730-32, Additional Instructions to . . . Haldimand . . . 16th day of July 1783.

9. C. O. 42/46, p. 222, General Abstract of Men, Women & Children settled on the New Townships. . . .

10. C. O. 42/47, p. 34.

11. Louis B. Wright and Mabel Tinling, eds., *Quebec to Carolina in 1785-1786: Being the Travel Diary and Observations of Robert Hunter, Jr., a Young Merchant of London* (San Marino, Calif., 1943), pp. 63, 70, 84.

12. C. O. 42/48, p. 215, Hope to Sydney, 5 Nov. 1785.

13. C. O. 42/49, p. 104, Hope to Commissioners of American Claims, 29 Jan. 1786.

14. O.A., *Second Report, 1904* (Toronto, 1905), Part One, p. 22, Col. Dundas to Lord Cornwallis, 3 Oct. 1787.

15. C. O. 42/46, p. 8, Haldimand to North, 6 Nov. 1783.

16. Shortt and Doughty, *Documents*, pp. 773 ff.

17. C. O. 42/49, p. 39, Memorandum by Sir Guy Carleton, 20 Feb. 1786.

18. Shortt and Doughty, *Documents*, pp. 813-15.

19. *Ibid.*, pp. 880-81, 911, 924.

20. *Ibid.*, pp. 940-41.

21. *Ibid.*, pp. 942, 945, 949.

22. *Ibid.*, p. 948.

23. Internal Correspondence, Province of Quebec, Powell and Collins to Dorchester, 18 Aug. 1787. This report is printed in a condensed form in R. A. Preston, ed., *Kingston Before the War of 1812: A Collection of Documents* (The Champlain Society, "Ontario Series," III [Toronto, 1959]) 122-24.

24. Dorchester to Sydney, 8 Nov. 1787. Quoted in E. A. Cruikshank, ed., "Records of Niagara, 1784-7," Niagara Historical Society, *Publications*, No. 39 (Niagara-on-the-Lake, 1928), p. 132.

25. O.A., *Second Report*, p. 296.

26. C. O. 42/67, p. 202, At the Council Chamber at Quebec, 9 Nov. 1789.

27. C. O. 42/61, p. 122, Dorchester to Sydney, 14 Oct. 1788.

28. This exchange between Sydney and Dorchester is printed in Shortt and Doughty, *Documents*, pp. 954-60.

29. A. L. Burt, *The Old Province of Quebec* (Toronto, 1933), p. 487.

30. Shortt and Doughty, *Documents*, p. 969 ff.

31. *Ibid.*, p. 971.

32. *Ibid.*, pp. 1044-46.

33. *Parliamentary Register* (London, 1791), XXIX, 414-15.

34. In 1794 Dundas informed Lord Dorchester that "temporary and discretionary" allowances might be made to Presbyterian ministers, "for your Lordship will recollect, in framing the Canada Act, that the reservation for the Church and the Crown in all Grants of Land, was fixed at a larger proportion than was originally intended, with a view to enable the King to make from those Reservations, such an Allowance to Presbyterian Ministers, Teachers and Schools, as His Majesty should, from time to time, think proper." C. O. 42/98, pp. 77-78, Dundas to Dorchester, 11 May 1794.

35. *Parliamentary Register* (London, 1791), XXIX, 69-77. Fox's remarks, which had included favourable allusions to the French Revolution as well as to republican institutions in the United States, were used by Burke as the occasion for a prolonged onslaught on those who applauded recent events in France. The subsequent exchanges between the two men, which led to the breaking of their long friendship and which had nothing to do with Canada, gave the debates on the "Quebec bill" a fame they would never otherwise have had.

36. Shortt and Doughty, *Documents*, pp. 1031-51.

NOTES TO CHAPTER TWO

1. E. A. Cruikshank, ed., *The Correspondence of Lieut. Governor John Graves Simcoe, with allied documents relating to his administration of the government of Upper Canada* (Toronto, 1923-1931), I, 18.

2. *Ibid.*, I, 27.

3. H. M. Jackson, *The Queen's Rangers in Upper Canada: 1792 and After* (Aylmer East, Quebec, 1955).

4. He was even willing to give up £500 of his salary toward the payment of a bishop's stipend if expense stood in the way of making an appointment. C. O. 42/361, pp. 185-6.

5. Cruikshank, *Simcoe Correspondence*, I, 47.

6. *Ibid.*, I, 49, 50, 53.

7. Arthur G. Doughty and Duncan A. McArthur, eds., *Documents relating to the Constitutional History of Canada, 1791-1818* (Ottawa, 1914), pp. 3 ff.

8. Cruikshank, *Simcoe Correspondence*, I, 71, 73. Soon afterward the new corps was designated The Queen's Rangers, thus carrying on the name of Simcoe's old Loyalist regiment. There was further continuity in the colour of the uniform and in the fact that several of its leading officers had served under Simcoe in America. *Ibid.*, I, 72, 75.

9. Doughty and McArthur, *Documents, 1791-1818*, p. 55.

10. A. L. Burt, *The United States, Great Britain and British North America from the Revolution to the establishment of peace after the War of 1812* (New Haven, 1940), pp. 85-95.

11. Cruikshank, *Simcoe Correspondence*, I, 91-4, 133-37.

12. D. G. Creighton, *The Empire of the St Lawrence* (Toronto, 1956. Originally published in 1937 as *The Commercial Empire of the St Lawrence, 1760-1850*), pp. 87-88, 131-32.

13. Cruikshank, *Simcoe Correspondence*, I, 141.

14. Doughty and McArthur, *Documents, 1791-1818*, pp. 41-43.

15. Cruikshank, *Simcoe Correspondence*, I, 108-9. Lieutenant-Governor Clarke issued a similar proclamation at the same time.

16. *Ibid.*, I, 264.

17. *Ibid.*, I, 151-54.

18. *Ibid.*, I, 144.

19. *Ibid.*, I, 143-44, 179.

20. W. R. Riddell, *The Life of John Graves Simcoe, First Lieutenant-Governor of the Province of Upper Canada, 1792-1796* (Toronto, 1926), p. 144.

21. R. A. Preston, ed., *Kingston Before the War of 1812* (Toronto, 1959), p. cxiii.

22. Doughty and McArthur, *Documents, 1791-1818*, pp. 72-82; Riddell, *Simcoe*, pp. 155-57.

23. Doughty and McArthur, *Documents, 1791-1818*, pp. 83-84.

24. *Ibid.*, p. 85.

25. The District, comprising several counties, was the unit for the administration of justice and for the conduct of local affairs. In each District a court of general quarter sessions of the peace, made up of magistrates appointed by the lieutenant-governor, administered and supervised a variety of municipal activities, such as the financing, building, and inspection of roads, the establishment of markets and the issuing of liquor licences. Except in the towns that were incorporated from time to time, the magistrates, under close supervision by the executive government, controlled municipal and local affairs throughout the province. With the expansion of settlement and the growth of population the number of Districts was increased to eight in 1800; by 1841, there were twenty Districts. The County was the unit for representation in the Assembly and for the registration of land titles. See G. W. Spragge, "The Districts of Upper Canada, 1788-1849," *Ontario History*, XXXIX (1947), 91-100.

26. W. R. Riddell, "The Law of Marriage in Upper Canada," *Canadian Historical Review*, II (September 1921), pp. 226-48.

27. Cruikshank, *Simcoe Correspondence*, I, 231, 250.

28. *Ibid.*, I, 249-50. D. W. Smith, a member of the Assembly and recently appointed acting Surveyor General, detected a "Democratical Party" among his colleagues, and thought them too prone to adduce "patterns & models" from "the neighbouring States." *Ibid.*, I, 232.

29. O.A., *Sixth Report, 1909* (Toronto, 1911), p. 18.

30. *Statutes of Upper Canada, 1793*, 33 Geo. III, Chap. 1.

31. Cruikshank, *Simcoe Correspondence*, II, 268-71; III, 2-3.

32. The leading authority on local government in Upper Canada has described their role as "all pervasive." J. H. Aitchison, "The Development of Local Government in Upper Canada, 1783-1850." Ph.D. Thesis, University of Toronto, 1953.

33. *Ibid.*, pp. 186-91.

34. Riddell, *Simcoe*, p. 212.

35. Cruikshank, *Simcoe Correspondence*, IV, 221-22, 261.

36. *Ibid.*, IV, 310-11.

37. *Ibid.*, II, 265; III, 237.

38. *Ibid.*, II, 55, 265.

39. C. E. Cartwright, ed., *Life and Letters of the Late Hon. Richard Cartwright* (Toronto, 1876), p. 54.

40. P.A.C., W. D. Powell Papers, "First Days in Upper Canada," p. 1744.

41. Cruikshank, *Simcoe Correspondence*, III, 265.

42. E. A. Cruikshank, "An Experiment in Colonization in Upper Canada," *Ontario Historical Society, Papers and Records*, XXV (1929), 32-77; Ontario Department of Planning and Development, *Don Valley Conservation Report* (Toronto, 1950), General Section, pp. 50-53. See also the executive council's retrospect of the experiment in State Books, Upper Canada, vol. C. 31 Oct. 1801, p. 152.

43. United Empire Loyalist grants were, of course, exempt from the payment of fees. For a criticism of the fee system, see Norman Macdonald, *Canada, 1763-1841: Immigration and Settlement. The Administration of the Imperial Land Regulations* (London, 1939), pp. 218-19.

44. See, for example, P.C.T. White, ed., *Lord Selkirk's Diary, 1803-1804: A Journal of His Travels in British North America and the Northeastern United States* (Toronto, 1958), p. 146.

45. Shortt and Doughty, *Documents, 1759-1791*, p. 1045.

46. Cruikshank, *Simcoe Correspondence*, I, 248.

47. *Ibid.*, II, 51; IV, 136-39. See also C. O. 42/317, pp. 214-15.

48. Note that the plan provided for reserving two-sevenths of all the land in each township, whereas the Constitutional Act had required the reservation to the clergy of "a seventh part" of the land granted. That is, the Act actually required that an eighth of the land in a township be reserved to the clergy, while Smith's plan reserved a seventh to the clergy and a seventh to the Crown. In consequence, the Reserves were considerably larger than they had to be.

49. Cruikshank, *Simcoe Correspondence*, III, 266.

50. *Ibid.*, I, 338-40.

51. Joseph Brant later said that Simcoe "Has done a great deal for this province, he has changed the name of every place in it." White, *Selkirk's Diary*, p. 153.

52. The duties of the Indian Department were to maintain close contact with the Indians, to distribute presents to them, and to keep them as loyal to Great Britain as circumstances permitted. Its traditions had been set by Sir William Johnson in the generation before his death in 1774, and were carried on by his son, Sir John Johnson, who became Superintendent General in 1782, with his headquarters in Montreal. At this time Colonel McKee was deputy superintendent in Upper Canada, supervising a number of agents throughout the province. In 1828 the office of Superintendent General was abolished, and after 1830 the lieutenant-governor of Upper Canada supervised Indian affairs through a chief superintendent for the province.

53. Cruikshank, *Simcoe Correspondence*, I, 207-9.

54. On Indian policy in this period see A. L. Burt, *United States, Great Britain*, pp. 128 ff. S. F. Wise, "The Indian Diplomacy of John Graves Simcoe," *Canadian Historical Association Report*, 1953, pp. 36-44, convincingly argues that Simcoe supported the western Indians, and did not seek for a compromise solution.

55. Cruikshank, *Simcoe Correspondence*, III, 185-86, 188-89.

56. The outstanding discussion of Jay's Treaty in relation to British North America is in Burt, *United States, Great Britain*, Chap. VIII.

57. Cruikshank, *Simcoe Correspondence*, IV, 83-87, 163, 211, 258.

58. *Ibid.*, III, 163.

59. *Ibid.*, III, 235.

60. *Ibid.*, IV, 12, 116-17.

61. *Ibid.*, IV, 302.

62. *Ibid.*, IV, 155-58, 272. The troops in the province now consisted mainly of the Queen's Rangers, who had to turn to garrison duty and away from the public projects on which Simcoe wished to occupy them. The regiment was disbanded in 1802.

63. *Ibid.*, I, 143-44, 179.

64. *Ibid.*, IV, 319.

65. *Ibid.*, V, 247.

66. *Ibid.*, I, 251-52.

67. The term Quebec referred not to the town, but to the province so recently divided.

68. Cruikshank, *Simcoe Correspondence*, III, 91-94.

69. *Ibid.*, IV, 318-19. See also T. R. Millman, *Jacob Mountain, First Lord Bishop of Quebec: A Study in Church and State, 1793-1825* ("University of Toronto Studies, History and Economics Series," Vol. X [Toronto, 1947]), Chaps. VI, X.

70. In a somewhat deflating article, S. R. Mealing argues that Simcoe was not a true imperialist, intent on what was best for Britain, but an ambitious zealot, pushing local projects in a helter-skelter manner. "The Enthusiasms of John Graves Simcoe," *Canadian Historical Association Report, 1958*, pp. 50-62.

NOTES TO CHAPTER THREE

1. The Administrator was also commonly called the President, since he was the presiding officer of the executive council.

2. One of the leading Loyalists stated that many of them visited their former homes after "the spirit of party and political Rancour began to cool," and while some remained, "a greater number returned bringing with them their Connections, who could but admire the liberality of that Nation which had converted into a blessing that greatest of all Curses, Expatriation." P.A.C., W. D. Powell Papers, "First Days in Upper Canada," p. 1742.

3. Cruikshank, *Simcoe Correspondence*, II, 109-10; M. L. Hansen and J. B. Brebner, *The Mingling of the Canadian and American Peoples* (New Haven, 1940), pp. 65, 79-82.

4. J. C. Ogden, *A Tour Through Upper and Lower Canada* (Litchfield, Conn., 1799), pp. 106-9.

5. Cruikshank, *Simcoe Correspondence*, I, 154.

6. D. W. Smyth, *A Short Topographical Description of His Majesty's Province of Upper Canada in North America* (London, 1799), p. 166.

7. Elma Gray, *Wilderness Christians* (Toronto, 1956), Chaps. VIII, IX.

8. W. H. Higgins, *The Life and Times of Joseph Gould, ex-Member of the Canadian Parliament* (Toronto, 1887), p. 24.

9. C. O. 42/330, pp. 201-4, Talbot to John Sullivan, 27 Oct. 1802; C. O. 42/331, pp. 30-31, Hobart to Hunter, 15 Feb. 1803; Fred Coyne Hamil, *Lake Erie Baron: The Story of Colonel Thomas Talbot* (Toronto, 1955), Chaps. III, IV; White, ed., *Selkirk's Diary* (Toronto, 1958), p. 141; C. O. 42/333, p. 130, Hunter to Hobart, 10 Dec. 1803; Fred Coyne Hamil, *The Valley of the Lower Thames: 1640 to 1850* (Toronto, 1951), Chap. IV.

10. State Books, U. C., Vol. C, p. 194, Major Graham to the Hon¹ David William Smith, 29 March 1802.

11. U. C. Sundries, William Fortune to Jas. Green, Secretary of the Lieutenant-Governor, 6 June 1803.

12. C. O. 42/342, pp. 5-6, Memorial of the Rev. Alexander Macdonell to Alexander Grant, April 1806.

13. U. C. Sundries, Francis Gore to Sir James Craig, 5 January 1808; C. O. 42/350, p. 149, Gore to Castlereagh, 1 March 1810; Freer Papers, 1786-1810, quoted in *Michigan Pioneer and Historical Collections* XV (Lansing, 1890), p. 20.

14. C. O. 42/342, p. 350, Hunter to John King, 27 October 1799.

15. White, ed., *Selkirk's Diary*, p. 147; Lillian F. Gates, "The Land Policies of Upper Canada" (Ms Ph.D. thesis, Rad-

cliffe College, 1955), pp. 175-77, argues that the purging of the U.E. list and the strict enforcement of land regulations were leading sources of the discontent evident during Grant's and Gore's régimes; Gore's proclamation of 31 Oct. 1806 is printed in O.A., *Fourth Report*, 1906 (Toronto, 1907), pp. 235-36.

16. E. A. Cruikshank, ed., *The Correspondence of the Honourable Peter Russell* (Toronto, 1932-36), I, 301.

17. D'Arcy Boulton, *Sketch of His Majesty's Province of Upper Canada* (London, 1805), pp. 13-14. Many of the land transactions involved "location tickets" rather than deeds, and the question arose as to their validity. See Lillian F. Gates, "The Heir and Devisee Commission of Upper Canada," *Canadian Historical Review*, XXXVIII (March 1957), 21-36, for an account of the means by which this problem was dealt with.

18. R. G. Riddell, "The Policy of Creating Land Reserves in Canada," in R. Flenley, ed., *Essays in Canadian History Presented to George Mackinnon Wrong* (Toronto, 1939), pp. 296-317.

19. Cruikshank, *Simcoe Correspondence*, I, 185-86.

20. *Letters from an American Loyalist* [York, 1810], p. 86.

21. R. L. Jones, "History of Agriculture in Ontario, 1613-1880," *University of Toronto Series, History and Economics*, Vol. XI (Toronto, 1946), Chap. II; W. T. Easterbrook and H. G. J. Aitken, *An Economic History of Canada* (Toronto, 1956), p. 158 ff.

22. An excellent discussion of this question is to be found in Aitchison, "Local Government," p. 319 ff.

23. C. O. 42/317, p. 189, Petition and Remonstrance of members of the Assembly, 9 July 1793; Cruikshank, *Simcoe Correspondence*, III, 66, 152-53; C. O. 42/319, p. 70, Simcoe to Dorchester, 10 Dec. 1794.

24. O.A., *Sixth Report*, 1909 (Toronto, 1911), pp. 66-67, Journals of the Assembly, 1798; Cruikshank, *Russell Correspondence*, III, 2-15, 174-76.

25. O.A., *Sixth Report*, Journals of the Assembly, 1804, pp. 431, 432; 1805, p. 46; 1806, p. 99; U. C. *Statutes*, 1807, Chap. VI; O.A., *Ninth Report*, 1912, Journals of Assembly, 1812, p. 16.

26. Cruikshank, *Russell Correspondence*, III, 199.

27. *Ibid.*, II, 33.

28. For instance, the Methodist preachers belonged to the New York Conference until 1810, when a division made them part of the Genesee Conference.

29. C. O. 42/351, p. 146, Brock to Liverpool, 3 Dec. 1811.

30. Cruikshank, *Russell Correspondence*, II, 33, Elmsley to Russell, 26 Nov. 1797; W. R. Riddell, "The Law of Marriage," *loc. cit.*

31. C. O. 42/324, p. 361, John White to John King, 15 Nov. 1798.

32. Cruikshank, *Russell Correspondence*, III, 72.

33. C. O. 42/334, pp. 21-22, Hunter to Hobart, 10 April 1804.

34. O.A., Joseph Willcocks' Letter Book, *passim.*

35. O.A., *Sixth Report*, 1909, Journals of the Assembly, 1799, p. 123; *ibid.*, 1800, p. 131.

36. Cruikshank, *Russell Correspondence*, III, 217.

37. O.A., *Eighth Report*, 1911, Journals of the Assembly, 1811, pp. 407-8; John Strachan to Dr James Brown, 9 Oct. 1808, Strachan Papers, Ontario Archives.

38. Cartwright, *Life and Letters*, pp. 91-92, 115-18.

39. O.A., *Eighth Report*, 1911, Journals of the Assembly, 1806, p. 107; C. O. 42/341, pp. 13-14, Grant to Castlereagh, 14 March 1806.

40. O.A., *Eighth Report*, 1911, Journals of the Assembly, 1805, pp. 47-48.

41. P.A.C.R., 1892 (Ottawa, 1893), p. 62.

42. C. O. 42/340, p. 155, Thorpe to Cooke, 1 Oct. 1805.

43. P.A.C.R., 1892, pp. 39, 62.

44. P.A.C.R., 1892, pp. 44-46, 53, 61.

45. *Ibid.*, pp. 57, 58.

46. Cartwright, *Life and Letters*, pp. 131-33.

47. C. O. 42/350, p. 76, R. Hamilton to Major Halton, 20 Jan. 1807.

48. C. O. 42/348, p. 3, Gore to Cooke, 14 Jan. 1808.

49. State Papers, Upper Canada, Vol. 89, pp. 1-5, 4 July 1807.

50. C. O. 42/348, p. 19, Gore to Castlereagh, 20 March 1808.

51. C. O. 42/350, pp. 12-19, for Gore's comments in a dispatch dated 1 Feb. 1810.

52. O.A., *Eighth Report*, 1911, Journals of the Assembly, 1810, pp. 369-70.

53. *A Letter To the Right Honorable Lord Castlereagh* . . . (Quebec, 24th October, 1809), *Letters from an American Loyalist* . . . [n.p., 1810].

54. Macaulay Papers, Ontario Archives, Robinson to John Macaulay, 1 Feb. 1809.

55. Rogers Papers, Ontario Archives, Memorandum on the Assembly debate, 4-5 March 1808.

56. C. O. 42/353, p. 11, Firth to Liverpool, 12 Jan. 1812.

57. *A Letter to* . . . *Castlereagh*, p. 12.

NOTES TO CHAPTER FOUR

1. J. W. Pratt, *Expansionists of 1812* (New York, 1925) argued that the War of 1812 would not have come without the expansionist ambitions of westerners and southerners, but this revisionist view has been contested by Burt, *United States, Great Britain*, who reasserts the primacy of maritime causes. Norman K. Risjord, "1812: Conservatives, War Hawks, and the Nation's Honor," *William and Mary Quarterly*, XVIII (1961), 196-210, stresses the concern for national honour and integrity.

2. E. A. Cruikshank, "The Chesapeake Crisis," Ontario Historical Society, *Papers and Records*, XXIV (1927), 322.

3. P.A.C.R., 1896 (Ottawa, 1897), p. 65; C. O. 42/352, p. 55; W. Wood, *Select British Documents of the Canadian War of 1812* (3 vols.; Toronto, 1920-28), I, 169-71.

4. Wood, *British Documents*, I, 305.

5. E. A. Cruikshank, ed., *Documentary History of the Campaign on the Niagara Frontier* (9 vols.; Welland, Ontario,

1896-1908), III, 85; Wood, *British Documents*, I, 396-97.

6. Wood, *British Documents*, I, 355-57.

7. *Ibid.*, pp. 358, 361.

8. Council held at Government House, York, 3 Aug. 1812, State Papers, Upper Canada, VII, 114 ff.; Cruikshank, *Documentary History*, I, 5.

9. For Brock's use of water communications, see A. T. Mahan, *Sea Power in its Relation to the War of 1812* (2 vols.; Boston, 1905), I, 353.

10. In fact, the medals were never distributed. They were not ready until 1818, when the directors of the society shrank from the invidious and politically dangerous task of selecting heroes from among the thousands of residents who had seen service. The unspent funds of the society were used to found what eventually became the Toronto General Hospital. On the subsequent history of the medals, see Hamilton Craig, "The Loyal and Patriotic Society of Upper Canada and its Still-Born

Child – The Upper Canada Preserved Medal," *Ontario History*, LII (March 1960), 31-52.

11. *The Report of the Loyal and Patriotic Society of Upper Canada* (Montreal, 1817), pp. 10, 11, 26, 365. See also C. P. Stacey, "The War of 1812 in Canadian History," *Ontario History*, L (1958), 153-59.

12. Michael Smith, *A Geographical View of the Province of Upper Canada, and Promiscuous Remarks upon the Government* (Baltimore, 1814), p. 225.

13. Prevost to Bathurst, 26 May 1813, Cruikshank, *Documentary History*, V, 243.

14. *Ibid.*, VI, 283.

15. C. P. Stacey, "Another Look at the Battle of Lake Erie," *Canadian Historical Review*, XXIX (1), March 1958, 41-51.

16. At the end of the war Sir James Yeo made the following comment on the failure of American invasion attempts: "The experience of two years active service has served to convince me that

tho' much has been done by the mutual exertions of *both Services*, we also owe as much if not more to the perverse stupidity of the Enemy; the Impolicy of their plans; the dissensions of their Commanders, and, lastly between *them* and their *Minister of War*." Quoted in C. P. Stacey, "An American Plan for a Canadian Campaign," *American Historical Review*, XLVI (1941), 348.

17. Cruikshank, *Documentary History*, VIII, 226-27; O.A., *Ninth Report*, 1912, Journals of the Assembly, 1814, p. 158.

18. Although it is usually said that the burning of the President's house and the Capitol was an answer to the burning of the York parliament buildings in May 1813, Sir George Prevost in his letters to Admiral Cochrane, on which the latter based his action, referred to "the wanton destruction of private property on the north shores of Lake Erie" in a raid of May 1814, and to "similar outrages" on the Niagara frontier in July 1814. Cruikshank, *Documentary History*, I-II, 176, 402, 414-15, 436.

19. Burt, *United States, Great Britain*, p. 426.

NOTES TO CHAPTER FIVE

1. John Howison, *Sketches of Upper Canada* (3rd ed.; Edinburgh, 1825), p. 96; *Kingston Chronicle*, 20 Sept. 1822.

2. C. O. 42/358, pp. 17-21, John Beverley Robinson to Lord Bathurst, 15 Feb. 1816.

3. C. O. 42/356, p. 121, Gore to Bathurst, 17 Oct. 1815; E. A. Cruikshank, "A Sketch of the Public Life and Services of Robert Nichol," *O.H.S.P.R.*, XIX (1922), p. 50.

4. C. O. 42/355, pp. 405-7, Colonel Edward Baynes to Prevost, 18 June 1814.

5. *Ibid.*, p. 120, Drummond to Prevost, 19 Feb. 1814; *ibid.*, p. 118, Drummond to Bathurst, 12 July 1814; *ibid.*, p. 69, same to same, 30 April 1814.

6. Bathurst to Prevost, 8 Sept. 1814, in W. Wood, *Select British Documents of*

the Canadian War of 1812, III, 785-87; G57, p. 82, same to same, 10 Jan. 1815.

7. G57, pp. 92 ff., Bathurst to Drummond, 20 March 1815, and Memorandum of November, 1814.

8. C. O. 42/356, p. 123, Gore to Bathurst, 17 Oct. 1815; U. C. State Papers, I, 149.

9. P.A.C., U. C. Sundries, Thomas Smyth to William Halton, 20 Jan. 1816; *ibid.*, Public Notice, Executive Council Office, 27 Jan. 1816.

10. Toronto Public Library, W. D. Powell Papers, Gore to Powell, dated only "Sunday morning."

11. Arthur G. Doughty and Norah Story, eds., *Documents Relating to the Constitutional History of Canada, 1819-1828* (Ottawa, 1935), pp. 3-5.

12. C. O. 42/359, p. 106, Gore to Bathurst, 7 April 1817.

13. Robert Gourlay, *General Introduction to Statistical Account of Upper Canada compiled with a view to a grand system of Emigration in connexion with a reform of the Poor Laws* (London, 1822), clxxxvi-cxcvi; Gourlay, *Statistical Account of Upper Canada* . . (2 vols.; London, 1822), I, 270-74.

14. Gourlay, *Statistical Account*, I, 374 ff., 623.

15. Gourlay, *Statistical Account*, II, 471-83; Gourlay, *An Appeal to the Common Sense, Mind and Manhood of the British Nation* (London, 1826), p. 77.

16. On March 14, 1818. See O.A., *Ninth Report*, 1912, Journals of the Assembly, 1818, p. 532.

17. Gourlay, *Statistical Account*, II, 650-51.

18. The Third Address of 2 April 1818, is given in the *Statistical Account*, II, 581-87.

19. P.A.C., U. C. Sundries, Robinson to Smith, 29 June and 4 July 1818.

20. C. O. 42/377, p. 56, Address to Sir Peregrine Maitland, 9 July 1818.

21. G. W. Spragge, ed., *The John Strachan Letter Book: 1812-1834* (Toronto, 1946), p. 182.

22. *Ibid.*, p. 185.

23. W. R. Riddell, "Robert (Fleming) Gourlay," Ontario Historical Society, *Papers and Records* (Toronto, 1916), XIV, 42, 61.

24. *Ibid.*, p. 54; O.A., Macaulay Papers, Strachan to Macaulay, 8 Dec. 1818, 25 Jan., 30 Jan., 11 Feb. 1819; O.A., *Tenth Report*, 1813 (Toronto, 1914), Journals of the Assembly, 1819, p. 99.

25. Gourlay, *General Introduction*, cccclxix, ccccxlvi.

26. O.A., *Tenth Report*, 1913, Journals of the Assembly, 1820, pp. 260, 261; D. McLeod, *A Brief Review of the Settlement of Upper Canada* . . . (Cleveland, 1841), p. 76; C. O. 42/366, p. 113, Maitland to Bathurst, 7 May 1821.

27. O.A., *Eleventh Report*, 1914 (Toronto, 1915), Journals of the Assembly, 1821-22, pp. 102-3.

28. O.A., Strachan Papers, John Richardson to John Strachan, 14 April 1823.

29. Doughty and Story, *Documents, 1819-1828*, pp. 131-36, Petition from the Eastern Townships for Union.

30. W. G. Ormsby, "The Problem of Canadian Union, 1822-1828," *Canadian Historical Review*, XXIX, December 1958, 285-86; Doughty and Story, pp. 106-20.

31. O.A., *Eleventh Report*, 1914, Journals of the Assembly, 1823, p. 257, Robinson to Hillier, 27 Aug. 1822.

32. Doughty and Story, pp. 140, 142, Petitions from Kingston and Wentworth County; Journals of the Assembly, 1823, *op. cit.*, p. 295.

33. O.A., Macaulay Papers, John Strachan to John Macaulay, 13 Nov. 1822; John Strachan, "Observations on a 'Bill...'" in *Union of the Legislatures of the Provinces of Lower Canada and Upper Canada* (London, 1824), pp. 11-12; O.A., Strachan Papers, John Strachan to John Beverley Robinson, 27 Feb. 1823.

34. O.A., Strachan Papers, John Strachan to Simon McGillivray, 1 Nov. 1822; John Strachan to John Macaulay, 20 Nov. 1822.

35. *General Union of All the British Provinces of North America* (London, 1824), No. 1, pp. 32, 36, 37, 40.

36. C. O. 42/387, p. 285, W. H. Merritt to Sir George Murray, 21 July 1828.

NOTES TO CHAPTER SIX

1. *Kingston Chronicle*, 18 Dec. 1820, 30 Nov. 1821; *Upper Canada Gazette*, York, 7 July 1825.

2. *U.E. Loyalist*, York, 3 June 1826; Upper Canada Sundries, A. A. Rapelje to J. B. Robinson, 21 March 1826; unsigned, probably to the Surveyor General, 12 April 1822; Macaulay Papers, Nelson Cozens to John Macaulay, 10 April 1824.

3. U.C. Sundries, J. B. Robinson to Major Hillier, 19 May 1824.

4. *Colonial Advocate*, 18 May 1824.

5. O.A., Macaulay Papers, J. B. Robinson to John Macaulay, 12 June 1824.

6. O.A., Lindsey Collection, Mackenzie Section, M. S. Bidwell to W. L. Mackenzie, 19 June, 21 Aug. 1824; *Colonial Advocate*, 30 Sept., 16 Dec., 30 Dec. 1824, 27 March, 18 April 1825, 6 April 1825.

7. *Colonial Advocate*, 18 May 1826.

8. O.A., Macaulay Papers, Robert Stanton to John Macaulay, 10 June 1826.

9. Doughty and Story, *Documents, 1819-1828*, pp. 5-6.

10. *Ibid.*, pp. 6-9.

11. C. O. 42/365, p. 218, Maitland to Lord Dalhousie, 2 Oct. 1820.

12. O.A., Macaulay Papers, J. B. Robinson to John Macaulay, 19 Feb. 1821.

13. *Ibid.*, Strachan to Macaulay, 13 and 26 June 1820, 18 Nov. 1821; Journals of the Assembly, 1821-22, p. 53; Macaulay Papers, Hagerman to Macaulay, 21 Dec. 1821.

14. Journals, 1821-22, pp. 7-9, 37, 152-53.

15. Doughty and Story, *Documents, 1819-1828*, pp. 85-6.

16. Journals, 1823, p. 315.

17. Doughty and Story, *Documents, 1819-1828*, pp. 159-60.

18. *Ibid.*, pp. 234-5.

19. *Ibid.*, pp. 272-73.

20. Journals, 1825-26, pp. 37-38, 50-52; Doughty and Story, *Documents, 1819-1828*, pp. 294-97.

21. U. C. State Papers, Vol. 91, pp. 19-28, Memorandum and Reply, 1 and 3 Feb. 1826.

22. *Colonial Advocate*, 2 Feb. 1826.

23. Journals, 1826-27, Appendix on the Matthews case.

24. Doughty and Story, *Documents, 1819-1828*, pp. 305-07.

25. *Ibid.*, pp. 356-62.

26. W. D. Powell Papers, T.P.L., B82, S. P. Jarvis to W. D. Powell, 12 Sept. 1827, Macaulay Papers, several letters from Robert Stanton to John Macaulay in 1827.

27. Doughty and Story, *Documents, 1819-1828*, pp. 363-66.

28. C. O. 42/381, pp. 370-77, Maitland to Goderich, 2 Oct. 1827.

29. Doughty and Story, *Documents. 1819-1828*, pp. 428-31.

NOTES TO CHAPTER SEVEN

1. Doughty and Story, *Documents, 1819-1828*, p. 298, Address of Assembly, Upper Canada, 18 Jan. 1826.

2. C. O. 42/377, p. 10, Maitland to Bathurst, 7 March 1826.

3. *Kingston Chronicle*, 2 April 1819.

4. C. O. 42/357, p. 316, Buchanan to Gore, 8 July 1816; *ibid.*, p. 318, Gore to Buchanan, 31 July 1816; *ibid.*, Buchanan to Gore, 17 Aug. 1816; C. O. 42/359, p. 146, Gore to Bathurst, 28 April 1817; Q355, pp. 103-5, Buchanan to Sir George Murray, 15 May 1830.

5. He changed his name to Wilmot Horton in 1823.

6. C. O. 42/377, pp. 168-173, Maitland to Bathurst, 31 March 1826.

7. Lillian F. Gates, "The Land Policies of Upper Canada," Ph.D. thesis, Radcliffe College, 1955, p. 507, quoting the Surveyor General's report of 1826.

8. Doughty and Story, Documents, 1819-1828, p. 4.

9. Robert Gourlay, Statistical Account of Upper Canada (London, 1822), I, 623; Gourlay, General Introduction to Statistical Account of Upper Canada (London, 1822), p. ccccxlix.

10. G. C. Paterson, "Land Settlement in Upper Canada, 1783-1840," O.A., Sixteenth Report, 1920 (Toronto, 1921), pp. 123, 128.

11. Ibid., pp. 132-33.

12. U. C. State Papers, III, 46, Lieutenant-Governor to Executive Council, 12 Jan. 1824.

13. Lillian F. Gates, "The Land Policies of Upper Canada," pp. 383-86.

14. Paterson, "Land Settlement," p. 209.

15. C. O. 42/365, p. 214, Sir Peregrine Maitland to Lord Dalhousie, 2 Oct. 1820.

16. R. K. Gordon, John Galt (Toronto, 1920), p. 52.

17. Doughty and Story, Documents, 1819-1828, pp. 253-63, Canada Company, Minutes of the Intended Arrangements. . . .

18. P.A.C.R., 1935 (Ottawa, 1936), pp. 207-9, 213-15.

19. Strachan to Galt, undated, but summer 1820, quoted in Gordon, John Galt, p. 74.

20. John Galt, Autobiography (2 vols.; London, 1833), II, 296.

21. Colonial Advocate, 16 Dec. 1824.

22. E.g., see Patrick Shirreff, A Tour through North America (Edinburgh, 1835), pp. 360 ff., 435; Canadian Freeman, 5 Sept. 1833.

23. Doughty and Story, Documents, 1819-1828, pp. 386-87; G. A. Wilson, "The Political and Administrative History of the Upper Canada Clergy Reserves, 1790-1854" (Ph. D. thesis, University of Toronto, 1959), p. 275.

24. P.A.C.R., 1935 (Ottawa, 1936), pp. 278 ff., Goderich to Colborne, 21 Nov. 1831.

25. James Young, Reminiscences of the Early History of Galt and the Settlement of Dumfries, in the Province of Ontario (Toronto, 1880), pp. 17, 40, 49.

26. F. C. Hamil, Lake Erie Baron, pp. 49, 51.

27. Ibid., p. 62.

28. C. O. Ermatinger, The Talbot Regime or the First Half Century of the Talbot Settlement (St Thomas, 1904), p. 314.

29. Hamil, Lake Erie Baron, p. 229.

30. Ibid., p. 223.

NOTES TO CHAPTER EIGHT

1. E. G. Stanley, afterwards 14th Earl of Derby, Journal of a Tour in America, 1824-1825 (n.p., 1930), pp. 111-13.

2. See, for example, Ontario Department of Planning and Development, Credit Valley Conservation Report (Toronto, 1956), Moira Valley Conservation Report (Toronto, 1950), historical sections of each, and Fred Landon, Western Ontario and the American Frontier (Toronto, 1941), p. 50.

3. Michael S. Cross, "The Lumber Community of Upper Canada, 1815-1867," Ontario History, LII (December, 1960), 213-34.

4. J. J. Talman, "Travel in Ontario Before the Coming of the Railway," O.H.S.P.R., XXIX (1933), 90.

5. William Smith, *The History of the Post Office in British North America, 1639-1870* (Cambridge, 1920), p. 136; Journals of the Assembly, 1825, p. 57; 1825-26, p. 48; P.A.C.R., 1935, pp. 347-50, Spring Rice to Colborne, 5 Oct. 1834.

6. *Kingston Chronicle*, 27 Aug. 1819; Journals of the Assembly, 1823 (Toronto, 1914), pp. 515-16, Paper of J. Baby, Arbitrator for Upper Canada, 13 Aug. 1823; A. R. M. Lower, *The North American Assault on the Canadian Forest* (Toronto, 1938), pp. 428-35.

7. P.A.C.R., 1935, p. 187, Lord Bathurst to Sir Peregrine Maitland, 8 Oct. 1824.

8. C. P. Stacey, "An American Plan for a Canadian Campaign," *loc. cit.*, pp. 348-58.

9. Robert F. Leggett, *Rideau Waterway* (Toronto, 1955), pp. 34-47.

10. *Ibid.*, p. 57; Stacey, *loc. cit.*, p. 356.

11. William Dunlop, *Statistical Sketches of Upper Canada, for the use of emigrants, by a backwoodsman* (London, 1832), pp. 67-68.

12. O.A., *Tenth Report*, 1913, Journals of the Assembly, 1818, p. 50.

13. O.A., Merritt Papers, Package No. 12, W. H. Merritt to J. P. Prendergast, 13 Jan. 1825.

14. J. P. Merritt, *Biography of the Hon. W. H. Merritt, M.P. . . .* (St Catharines, 1875), pp. 63-67.

15. G62, pp. 286-92, Bathurst to Maitland, 30 Sept. 1826; H. G. J. Aitken, *The Welland Canal Company: a Study in Canadian Enterprise* (Cambridge, Mass., 1954), pp. 82-84.

16. Aitken, *The Welland Canal Company*, p. 86.

17. U.C. Sundries, John Macaulay to Sir George Arthur, 10 May 1838, in a survey of the financial history of the company.

18. O.A., Merritt Papers, Package No. 13, John Macaulay to Justice Jones, 5 March 1838.

19. J. W. Watson, "The Changing Industrial Pattern of the Niagara Peninsula," O.H.S.P.R., XXXVII (1945), 53-55.

20. Merritt, *W. H. Merritt*, p. 81.

21. E. C. Guillet, ed., *The Valley of the Trent* (Toronto, 1957), pp. 131-232.

22. *Colonial Advocate*, 27 May 1824.

23. *Ibid.*, 11 Jan., 3 May 1827; 29 June 1828.

24. *Ibid.*, 6 Jan. 1831.

25. O.A., *Ninth Report*, 1911, Journals of the Assembly, 1817, p. 352; C. O. 42/359, p. 148, Gore to Bathurst, 8 May 1817.

26. Journals, 1817, pp. 378-79; C. O. 42/362, p. 185, Maitland to Goulburn, 7 May 1819.

27. Adam Shortt, "Early History of Canadian Banking," *Journal of the Canadian Bankers' Association*, V (1), October 1897, 21.

28. O.A., Macaulay Papers, John Strachan to John Macaulay, 3 May 1831.

29. *Colonial Advocate*, 18 May 1826; 9 Aug. 1827.

30. Shortt, "The History of Canadian Currency, Banking and Exchange," *op. cit.*, VIII (3), 1901, 231; Journals of the Assembly, 1830, Appendix, Report of the Select Committee on the State of the Currency, p. 24.

31. Bray Hammond, *Banks and Politics in America from the Revolution to the Civil War* (Princeton, 1957), pp. 329, 653-54; Lillian F. Gates, "The Decided Policy of William Lyon Mackenzie," *Canadian Historical Review*, XL (3) September 1959, 198.

NOTES TO CHAPTER NINE

1. R. A. Preston, ed., *Kingston Before the War of 1812* (Toronto, 1959), p. 292.

2. C. O. 42/355, p. 70, Drummond to Bathurst, 30 April 1814.

3. P.A.C., U. C. Sundries, Secretaries of the Wesleyan Missionary Society to Henry Goulburn, 3 July 1821.

4. S. Ivison and F. Rosser, *The Baptists in Upper and Lower Canada before 1820* (Toronto, 1956), pp. 9, 62-63; S. D. Clark, *Church and Sect in Canada* (Toronto, 1948), pp. 304-308; D. Wilkie, *Sketches of a Summer Trip to New York and the Canadas* (Edinburgh, 1837), p. 201.

5. F. A. Walker, *Catholic Education and Politics in Upper Canada* (Toronto, 1955), p. 34.

6. G. W. Spragge, "Dr. Strachan's Motives for Becoming a Legislative Councillor," *Canadian Historical Review*, XIX (1938), 397-402.

7. *The Seventh Report from the Select Committee . . . on Grievances* (Toronto, 1835), p. 86, Strachan's testimony.

8. C. O. 42/362, pp. 194-95, Maitland to Bathurst, 17 May 1819.

9. House of Commons, *Parliamentary Papers*, 1840, Vol. 32, No. 205, Correspondence respecting the Clergy Reserves in Canada, 1819-1840, p. 2, Bathurst to Maitland, 6 May 1820.

10. O.A., *Eleventh Report*, 1914, Journals of the Assembly, 1823-24, p. 607, Address to the King, 5 Jan. 1824.

11. House of Commons, *Parliamentary Papers*, 1840, vol. 32, pp. 3-6, Clergy Reserves Correspondence, Petition of the Clergy Reserves Corporation, 23 April 1823, pp. 8-13, Maitland to Bathurst, 27 Dec. 1823; T. R. Millman, *Jacob Mountain*, p. 162.

12. Journals of the Assembly, 1825-26, 27 Jan. 1826.

13. House of Commons, *Parliamentary Papers*, 1840, vol. 32, p. 20, Maitland to Bathurst, 7 March 1826; P.A.C., Morris Papers (Microfilm), William Morris to Dr Mearns, 20 March 1826.

14. Doughty and Story, *Documents, 1819-1828*, pp. 371-76; Spragge, *Strachan Letter Book*, p. 222.

15. C. B. Sissons, *Egerton Ryerson: His Life and Letters* (Toronto, 1937), I, 1-24.

16. *Ibid.*, pp. 24-28; Anson Green, *Life and Times* (Toronto, 1877), pp. 83-84.

17. *A Speech of the Venerable John Strachan, D.D., Archdeacon of York, in the Legislative Council . . . on the subject of the Clergy Reserves* (York, 1828); Sissons, *Ryerson*, I, 85-89.

18. Journals of the Assembly, 1828, Appendix, Report of the Select Committee, to which was referred the petition of Bulkley Waters . . .March 15, 1828, Address of the Assembly, 20 March 1828.

19. Sissons, *Ryerson*, I, 31-36.

20. *Parliamentary Debates*, 2 May 1828, pp. 299-343.

21. House of Commons, *Parliamentary Papers*, 1828, vol. 7, no. 569, Report from the Select Committee on the Civil Government of Canada, pp. 9, 12, and *passim*.

22. T. R. Millman, *The Life and Times of the Right Reverend, the Honourable Charles James Stewart, Second Anglican Bishop of Quebec* (London, Ontario, 1953), p. 78; C. O. 42/388, pp. 76-7, Colborne to Hay, 31 March 1829.

23. House of Commons, *Parliamentary Papers*, 1840, Vol. 32, Colborne to Murray, 11 April, 29 April 1829; C. O. 42/388, p. 78, Colborne to Hay, 31 March 1829.

24. *Christian Guardian*, 18 Sept. 1830, 16 April 1831; Sissons, *Ryerson*, I, 129.

25. G69, pp. 72 ff., Goderich to Colborne, 2 April 1832; *Christian Guardian*, 21 Dec. 1831, contains the Methodist address to the King, Colborne's reply, and Ryerson's rebuttal.

26. *P.A.C.R.*, *1935*, pp. 278-88. Goderich to Colborne, 21 Nov. 1831.

27. *Ibid.*, pp. 295-97, Goderich to Colborne, 5 April 1832.

28. House of Commons, *Parliamentary Papers*, 1840, Vol. 32, Assembly's Addresses, 14 Dec. 1831, 21 Jan. 1832.

29. Quoted in the *Colonial Advocate*, 1 Nov. 1832.

30. Millman, *Stewart*, pp. 114-23.

31. Sissons, *Ryerson*, I, 135-40, George Ryerson to Egerton Ryerson, 6 Aug. 1831.

32. Professor Sissons's chapter on this subject is entitled "Turning the Other Cheek." *Ibid.*, Chap. V.

33. Spragge, *Strachan Letter Book*, pp. 75-80, Report on Education, 26 Feb. 1815.

34. C. O. 42/366, p. 4, Maitland to Bathurst, 4 Jan. 1821.

35. Spragge, *Strachan Letter Book*, p. 212, Strachan to the Lord Bishop, 26 Feb. 1821.

36. John Strachan, *An Appeal to the Friends of Religion and Literature in Behalf of the University of Upper Canada* (London, 1827), p. 12.

37. *P.A.C.R.*, *1935*, pp. 216-17.

38. Journals of the Assembly, 1828, pp. 112-13.

39. Doughty and Story, *Documents, 1819-1828*, p. 475.

40. *P.A.C.R.*, *1935*, pp. 274-77.

41. J. George Hodgins, *Documentary History of Education in Upper Canada* (Ontario), 28 vols. (Toronto, 1894-1910), II, 7, quoting the *Christian Guardian*, April 1831.

42. C. O. 42/395, p. 470, George Ryerson to Lord Goderich, 5 June 1831.

43. Journals of the Assembly, 1829, 1830, 1831, Reports of Committees on Education and School Lands. Eventually, in 1839, an act was passed providing that a portion of the annual revenues of the university endowment should be used to support the grammar schools.

44. Hodgins, *Documentary History*, II, 51, quoting the Assembly's Address of 26 Dec. 1831.

NOTES TO CHAPTER TEN

1. C. O. 42/381, p. 464, Maitland to Huskisson, 31 Dec. 1827; C. O. 42/384, p. 150, Maitland to Murray, 18 Sept. 1828.

2. Cobourg *Reformer*, quoted in the St Thomas *Liberal*, 18 July 1833.

3. O.A., *Eleventh Report*, 1914, pp. 420-22, Journals of the Assembly, 1823; Journals of the Assembly, 1824, p. 101; C. O. 42/381, p. 406, Maitland to Huskisson, 15 Dec. 1827.

4. Journals of the Assembly, 1825-26, p. 76, Address of 14 Jan. 1826.

5. C. O. 42/381, p. 461-62, Maitland to Huskisson, 31 Dec. 1827.

6. T.P.L., W. D. Powell Papers, B82, S. P. Jarvis to W. D. Powell, 12 June 1828.

7. O.A., Macaulay Papers, Robert Stanton to John Macaulay, 18 July 1828. "Baldwin has become a regular, travelling stump Orator—going about the country from place to place—the man is certainly mad and will soon require shaving and blistering."

8. T.P.L., W. W. Baldwin Papers, M. S. Bidwell to W. W. Baldwin, 8 Sept. 1828, John Rolph to W. W. Baldwin, 9 Oct. 1828.

9. *Colonial Advocate*, 31 Jan. 1828.

10. *Ibid.*, 22 May 1828.

11. O.A. Lindsey Collection, Mackenzie Section, B. Bidwell to Mackenzie, 5 Aug. 1828.

12. C. O. 42/390, pp. 98-103, Petition adopted at a "Constitutional Meeting," 15 Aug. 1828.

13. *Ibid.*, pp. 90-2, W. W. Baldwin to the Duke of Wellington, 3 Jan. 1829.

14. C. O. 42/384, pp. 148-162, Maitland to Murray, 18 Sept. 1828.

15. *Parliamentary Debates*, Second Series, vol. 21, 1327-8, 1334, 1768.

16. *Canadian Freeman*, 25 Sept. 1828; *Colonial Advocate*, 25 Sept. 1828.

17. O.A., Macaulay Papers, Robert Stanton to John Macaulay, 22 Sept. 1828.

18. O.A., John Strachan Letter Book, 1827-1839, p. 27, Strachan to W. H. Hale, 29 Dec. 1828.

19. C. O. 42/38, p. 79, Colborne to R. W. Hay, 31 March 1829.

20. P.A.C., Neilson Collection, vol. 6, M. S. Bidwell to John Neilson, 7 Jan. 1829.

21. Doughty and Story, *Documents*, 1819-1828, pp. 464-5, W. L. Mackenzie to John Neilson, 27 Nov. 1828.

22. T.P.L., W. W. Baldwin Papers, B104, John Rolph to W. W. Baldwin, 10 Dec. 1828.

23. P.A.C., Neilson Collection, vol. 6, M. S. Bidwell to John Neilson, 21 Nov. 1829.

24. T.P.L., W. W. Baldwin Papers, B105, John Rolph to W. W. Baldwin, 5 May 1829.

25. York *Courier*, 28 Feb. 1831.

26. O.A., Macaulay Papers, Strachan to Macaulay, 28 Feb. 1831.

27. *Courier*, 28 Feb. 1831.

28. *Christian Guardian*, 8 Jan. 1831.

29. *Colonial Advocate*, 13 Jan., 23 June 1831.

30. O.A., Macaulay Papers, John Kirby to John Macaulay, 4 Dec. 1831.

31. C. O. Ermatinger, *The Talbot Regime*, p. 155, Talbot to Peter Robinson, 2 July 1832.

32. *Canadian Freeman*, 2 Feb. 1832.

33. Cobourg *Reformer*, quoted in the St Thomas *Liberal*, 27 Dec. 1832.

34. *Christian Guardian*, 20 June 1832, quoting the prospectus of the St Thomas *Liberal*.

35. Ermatinger, *Talbot Regime*, pp. 157-8.

36. John Mactaggart, *Three Years in Canada: An Account of the Actual State of the Country in 1826-7-8* (2 vols., London, 1829), I, 207.

37. P.A.C., U. C. Sundries, Thomas Carr to J. Joseph, 1 June 1836.

38. C. R. Sanderson, ed., *The Arthur Papers* (3 vols., Toronto, 1957, 1959), I, 133, Mr Sullivan's Report, 1 June 1838.

39. St Thomas *Liberal*, 10 Jan. 1833.

40. *Ibid.*, 19 Sept. 1833, quoting the Kingston *Spectator*.

41. *The Advocate*, 26 June 1834.

42. Anna Jameson, *Winter Studies and Summer Rambles in Canada* (London, 1838), I, 190.

43. These were the key words of the "radical party," said S. P. Jarvis, and they were repeated "until one becomes sick by hearing them." T.P.L., W. D. Powell Papers, B82, S. P. Jarvis to W. D. Powell, 24 Dec. 1828.

44. E.g., Hamilton *Free Press*, 8 Nov. 1832.

45. O.A., John Strachan Letter Book, 1827-1839, pp. 109-110, Strachan to James Stephen, 18 Jan. 1831.

46. Richard Pares, *King George III and the Politicians* (Oxford, 1953), p. 195.

47. C. O. 42/388, pp. 35-6, Colborne to Murray, 16 Feb. 1829.

48. See Helen Taft Manning, "The Colonial Policy of the Whig Ministers, 1830-37," *C. H. R.*, vol. 33, (1952), 203-36, 341-68.

49. P.A.C., Neilson Collection, vol. 6, W. L. Mackenzie to John Neilson, 23 March 1829; *Colonial Advocate*, 4 Feb., 11 March 1830; O.A., Macaulay Papers, Robt. Stanton to John Macaulay, 17 March 1830; C. O. 42/413, p. 302, Petition to His Majesty, 19 Jan. 1832; *Ibid.*, 430, p. 363, Mackenzie to Hume, Dec. 1835; W. B. Wells, *Canadiana* (London, 1837), p. 105.

50. O.A., Macaulay Papers, John Macaulay to Col. Rowan, 1 June 1835.

51. Wells, *Canadiana*, p. 63.

52. *Ibid.*, p. 147.

53. Robert Davis, *The Canadian Farmer's Travels in the United States of America. . . .* (Buffalo, 1837), p. 93.

54. *Colonial Advocate*, 25 March, 29 April 1830.

55. O.A., *Ninth Report*, 1912, Journals of the Assembly, pp. 35, 59.

56. *Brockville Recorder*, 15 April 1836, Speech of S. C. Frey; *Ibid.*, 17 April 1835, Speech of O. R. Gowan.

57. *Colonial Advocate*, 28 Dec. 1826.

58. Journals of the Assembly, 1835, p. 271.

59. *Christian Guardian*, 15 Feb. 1832.

60. *Mr. Bidwell's Speech on the Intestate Estates Bill in the Provincial Assembly of Upper Canada, January 24, 1831*, 4.

61. *Christian Guardian*, 29 Jan. 1831.

62. Ermatinger, *Talbot Regime*, p. 167.

63. *Colonial Argus*, quoted in *The Advocate*, 25 Sept. 1834.

NOTES TO CHAPTER ELEVEN

1. *The Constitution*, 8 Feb. 1837.

2. *Colonial Advocate*, 5 June 1828.

3. *Ibid.*, 9 July 1829.

4. P.A.C., Neilson Collection, vol. 6, Mackenzie to Neilson, 7 Dec. 1829.

5. *Colonial Advocate*, 16 Sept. 1830.

6. *Ibid.*, 23 Sept. 1830.

7. *Ibid.*, 21 April 1831.

8. J. E. Alexander, *Transatlantic Sketches* (London, 1833), II, 173; *Colonial Advocate*, 18 Aug., 3 Nov. 1831; C. O. 42/411, p. 249, Colborne to Hay, 7 May 1832; W. H. Higgins, *Joseph Gould*, pp. 55, 91-4.

9. *Christian Guardian*, 21 Dec. 1831, quoting M. S. Bidwell's speech in the Assembly.

10. G69, pp. 72 ff., Goderich to Colborne, 2 April 1832.

11. P.A.C.R., 1935, pp. 310-12, Goderich to Colborne, 8 Nov. 1832.

12. Journals of the Legislative Council, 1832-3, pp. 115-20, Address of 2 Feb. 1833; Journals of the Legislative Assembly, 1832-3, p. 131, Address of 9 Feb. 1833.

13. *Courier*, 6 Feb. 1833.

14. *Ibid.*, 1 May 1833.

15. *Colonial Advocate*, 9 May 1833; *Ibid.*, 23 May 1833, quoting the *Liberal* and the *Free Press*.

16. *Ibid.*, 2 May 1833.

17. *Christian Guardian*, 30 Oct. 1833.

18. Mackenzie's reply was contained in a second edition of the *Colonial Advocate* bearing the original date of 26 Oct. 1833.

19. *Christian Guardian*, 6 and 12 Nov. 1833.

20. Sissons, *Ryerson*, I, 190, John Ryerson to Egerton Ryerson, 7 Nov. 1833.

21. *Ibid.*, I, 214-16, David Wright *et al*, to Egerton Ryerson, 21 Nov. 1833.

22. *The Advocate*, 4 Jan. 1834.

23. *Ibid.*, 11 Jan. 1834.

24. *The Patriot*, 10 Jan., 7 Feb. 1834.

25. Journals of the Assembly, 1833-4, p. 140, Amendment moved on 1 March 1834.

26. *The Advocate*, 6 March 1834.

27. *Colonial Advocate*, 28 Nov. 1833.

28. *The Advocate*, 5 Dec. 1833.

29. *A New Almanack for the Canadian True Blues* . . . by Patrick Swift (York, 1834), p. 19.

30. *Colonial Advocate*, 11 April 1833. Both Baldwins had been defeated in 1830, and they refused to run in the elections of 1834.

31. P.A.C., Neilson Coll., vol. 8, Mackenzie to Neilson, 7 Feb. 1834.

32. *The Advocate*, 13 March 1834.

33. *The Canadian Correspondent*, 26 Apr. 1834.

34. *The Advocate*, 22 May 1834, Hume to Mackenzie, 29 March 1834.

35. *The Patriot*, 23 May 1834.

36. *The Advocate*, 25 Sept. 1834.

37. *Christian Guardian*, 21 Jan. 1835.

38. *Journals of the Assembly*, 1835, p. 51, Address of 23 Jan. 1835.

39. *Ibid.*, p. 142, Resolution of 17 Feb. 1835.

40. *Ibid.*, p. 118, Address of 10 Feb. 1835.

41. *Ibid.*, pp. 391-5, Resolution of 15 April 1835.

42. *The Advocate*, 4 Nov. 1834, "A Few Words at Parting."

43. Mackenzie and his friends seem not to have persisted in this idea.

44. O.A., Lindsey Papers, Objects and Rules of the Canadian Alliance Society.

45. *Christian Guardian*, 18 Feb. 1835.

46. O.A., Lindsey Papers, Mackenzie to A. N. Buell, 15 Dec. 1834.

47. *The Seventh Report from the Committee on Grievances* (Toronto, 1835), pp. iii-vi, xliii.

48. *Christian Guardian*, 10 and 20 Feb. 1836.

49. G74, pp. 91 ff., Genelg to Colborne, 1 July 1835; *Ibid.*, pp. 129 ff., same to same, 2 July 1835; G75, pp. 26 ff., same to same, 28 Oct. 1835; *Ibid.*, pp. 151 ff., same to same, 28 Oct. 1835.

50. C. O. 42/430, p. 360, Mackenzie to Hume, Dec. 1835.

51. P.A.C., Neilson Coll., vol. 8, Mackenzie to Neilson, 28 Dec. 1835.

NOTES TO CHAPTER TWELVE

1. O.A., Macaulay Papers, Strachan to John Macaulay, 12 March 1832.

2. *Ibid.*, C. A. Hagerman to John Macaulay, 17 April 1832.

3. C. O. 42/394, pp. 177-78, Colborne to Hay, 25 Nov. 1831.

4. "Proudfoot Papers," *Transactions of the London and Middlesex Historical Society*, VIII (1917), 23; W. A. Langton, ed., *Early Days in Upper Canada* (Toronto, 1926), p. 11.

5. Martin Doyle, *Hints on Emigration* (Dublin, 1831), p. 100; *Emigration: Letters from Sussex Emigrants* (Petworth, 1833), pp. 7, 10, 42, 45.

6. *St Thomas Liberal*, 4 April, 19 Sept. 1833.

7. Quoted in *The Advocate*, 27 March 1834.

8. *Courier*, 15 June 1833.

9. Adam Fergusson, *Practical Notes Made During a Tour in Canada, and a Portion of the United States in MDCCCXXXI* (London, 1833), p. 115, quoting a conversation with Hagerman.

10. C. O. 42/418, p. 135, Colborne to Hay, 7 March 1834; C. O. 42/423, p. 202, Colborne to Spring Rice, 20 Nov. 1834.

11. O.A., *Eleventh Report*, 1914, Journals of the Assembly, 1824, p. 620, Resolution of 7 Jan. 1824; P.A.C., U. C. Sundries, William Morris to Colborne, 27 May 1830, refers to Maitland's statement.

12. *Patriot*, 24 Oct. 1834; Robert Davis, *The Canadian Farmer's Travels*, p. 9.

13. Catherine Parr Traill, *The Backwoods of Canada* (London, 1836), pp. 3-4, 81-2.

14. *Ibid.*, p. 271.

15. *Canada in the Years 1832, 1833, and 1834 . . . By an ex-settler* (Dublin, 1835), p. 23.

16. P.A.C.R., 1935, pp. 381-97, Glenelg to Head, 5 Dec. 1835.

17. C. O. 42/429, pp. 118-20, Head to Glenelg, 5 Feb. 1836.

18. *Report of the Select Committee to which was referred the answer of His Excellency . . .* (Toronto, 1836), Appendix A, pp. 1-4, Executive Council to Sir F. B. Head, 4 March 1836.

19. Journals of the Assembly, 1836, pp. 289, 303.

20. *Report of the Select Committee . . .* pp. 7, 39, 80-1, 87, 99.

21. *Journals of the Assembly*, 1836, pp. 469, 499, 524 ff.

22. F. B. Head, *A Narrative* (London, 1839), p. 65.

23. *The Patriot*, 17 May, 17 June 1836.

24. C. O. 42/430, pp. 92-3, Reply of His Excellency . . . to an Address . . . from the Electors of the Home District.

25. Langton, *Early Days*, pp. 168-70, John Langton to his father, 13 July 1836.

26. Thomas Need, *Six Years in the Bush . . .* (London, 1838), p. 119.

27. W. B. Kerr, "When Orange and Green United, 1832-9," O.H.S.P.R., vol.

34 (1942), 34-42; same, "The Orange Order and W. L. Mackenzie in the 1830's," *The Sentinel*, 1939.

28. Sissons, *Ryerson*, I, Chapter IX, passim, and p. 361, John Ryerson to Egerton Ryerson, 25 Sept. 1836.

29. *Ibid.*, I, 350-3.

30. Quoted in *The Correspondent and Advocate*, 3 Aug. 1836.

31. G78, pp. 39-47, Duncombe's petition to the House of Commons, enclosed in Glenelg to Head, 8 Sept. 1836.

32. Journals of the Assembly, 1836-7, Appendix 5, Report of the Select Committee on Charles Duncombe's Petition, 23 Jan. 1837.

33. T.P.L., Robert Baldwin Papers, A92, M. S. Bidwell to Robert Baldwin, 29 July 1836.

34. P.A.C.R., 1923, p. 332, Robert Baldwin to Glenelg, 13 July 1836.

35. This conservative Assembly, like its predecessor in 1834, protested against the reservation of banking bills that were "purely local in their nature." *Journals*, 1836-7, pp. 321-22, Resolution of 20 Jan. 1837.

36. Anna Jameson, *Winter Studies and Summer Rambles* (London, 1838), I, 76-7.

37. P.A.C., U. C. Sundries, Merritt to Sir George Arthur, 11 Feb. 1839.

38. P.A.C., Durand Papers, vol. III, J. W. Macaulay to Alexander Hamilton, 17 Jan. 1837.

39. *Constitution*, 24 and 31 May, 14 June 1837.

40. *Ibid.*, 11 Jan. 1837.

41. *Ibid.*, 19 April 1837; O.A., Lindsey Collection, Mackenzie section, Wolfred Nelson to Mackenzie, 4 May 1837.

42. *Constitution*, 5 July 1837.

43. *Ibid.*, 19 and 26 July, 2 Aug. 1837.

44. P.A.C., U. C. Sundries, R. Coate to Sir F. B. Head, 17 July 1837.

45. *Constitution*, 2 Aug. 1837.

46. The places of the meetings are conveniently listed in S. D. Clark, *Movements of Political Protest in Canada* (Toronto, 1959), pp. 379-80.

47. *Constitution*, 13 Sept. 1837.

48. *Ibid.*, 2 Aug. 1837.

49. *Ibid.*, 4 Oct. 1837.

50. Charles Lindsey, *The Life and Times of William Lyon Mackenzie* (Philadelphia and Toronto, 1862), II, 53.

51. *Constitution*, 18 Oct. 1837, letter from James Hunter, dated 29 Sept. 1837.

52. John Barnett, "Silas Fletcher: Instigator of the Upper Canadian Rebellion," *Ontario History*, XLI (1949), 7-35.

NOTES TO CHAPTER THIRTEEN

1. Journals of the Legislative Council, 1837-8, Appendix Z, Report of the Select Committee . . . upon the State of the Province; O.A., Macaulay Papers, John Macaulay to Ann Macaulay, 8 Jan. 1838. It probably did not entirely escape conservative attention that the strengthening of provincial defences would involve extensive British expenditures. As long as Upper Canada was a colony war clouds had a silver, even a golden, lining.

2. W. S. Wallace, "The Periodical Literature of Upper Canada," *C.H.R.*, XII (1931), 10.

3. Brockville *Recorder*, 21 Dec. 1837.

4. Dr W. W. Baldwin, quoted in the Toronto *Mirror*, 6 Jan. 1838.

5. Brockville *Recorder*, 1 March 1838, quoting the Niagara *Reporter*.

6. R. S. Longley, "Emigration and the Crisis of 1837 in Upper Canada," *C.H.R.*, XVII (1936), 28-40.

7. Sissons, *Ryerson*, I, 472, John Ryerson to Egerton Ryerson, 22 May 1838.

8. O.A., Macaulay Papers, John Macaulay to Ann Macaulay, 19 March 1838.

9. Lord Durham's Commission is given in C. P. Lucas, ed., *Lord Durham's Report on the Affairs of British North America* (3 vols., Oxford, 1912), II, 3-5.

10. C. O. 42/446, pp. 31-46, Arthur to Glenelg, 14 April 1838.

11. U. C. Sundries, Report of J. B. Robinson, C. J., and J. Jones, J., on the treatment of prisoners, 2 May 1838.

12. *Upper Canada Herald*, 8 May 1838. Head had virtually banished Bidwell from the province.

13. Sissons, *Ryerson*, I, 434, John Ryerson to Egerton Ryerson, 17 March 1838.

14. *The Examiner*, 3 July 1838.

15. *Ibid.*, 18 and 25 July 1838.

16. P.A.C.R., 1923, pp. 326 ff., Robert Baldwin to Lord Durham, 23 Aug. 1838.

17. Quoted in Chester New, *Lord Durham* (Oxford, 1929), pp. 403-4.

18. Many of these reports are scattered through the Upper Canada Sundries for the months of September, October, and November 1838.

19. E.g., P.A.C., U. C. Sundries, deposition of John Mittelberger, 7 Nov. 1838.

20. Sanderson, *The Arthur Papers*, II, 3, Arthur to W. H. Hamilton, 2 Jan. 1839. The young John A. Macdonald assisted Schoultz at the court martial. See D. G. Creighton, *John A. Macdonald: The Young Politician* (Toronto, 1952), pp. 65-68.

21. Sanderson, *Arthur Papers*, II, 4.

22. *Ibid.*, I, 438, Arthur to Colborne, 11 Dec. 1838.

23. U. C. Sundries, Alexander McLeod to Macaulay, 4 Dec. 1838.

24. *Patriot* (Toronto), 19 Feb. 1839. The *Patriot* had been at this task for years, and on the previous July 18 had attempted a grand summing up: "That the Americans want the Canadas, we believe no man in his senses will attempt

to deny.... They have, however, been woefully mistaken. Yet has it not been for want of emissaries and advocates to preach up the excellencies of 'self-government,' 'republicanism,' and 'pure democracy.' All the advantages that such extrinsic aids could give friend Jonathan has had abundantly heaped upon him. Mackenzie has preached, Rolph has preached, and Bidwell has preached; and scores of others have preached in our Legislative Halls and through a licentious, demoralizing Press; Yankee missionaries have preached in the pulpit, at Camp Meetings, in the wigwams of our simple-hearted Indians, and at the family hearths of our unsophisticated yeomanry. Yankee schoolmasters have preached in our common schools; Yankee Doctors have preached at the bedsides of their patients; Yankee tavern-keepers have preached in their bar-rooms; Yankee stage-drivers have preached on the highways, and eke multitudes of Yankee squatters have preached in our backwoods. All these preachings have been for thirty years; and thus has the poison been unsparingly preached, promulgated, punched, poked and pummelled into the people, from the whining schoolboy to the old gray beard; yet do the affection and reverence of the Upper Canadians to their Sovereign remain intact, and we may now say with more confidence than ever, 'Let them come if they dare.' "

25. Quoted in New, Durham, p. 455.

26. Brockville Recorder, 18 Oct. 1838.

27. Lucas, Report, II, 15.

28. Ibid., p. 16.

29. Ibid., p. 53.

30. Ibid., p. 70.

31. Ibid., p. 151.

32. Ibid., pp. 177-8.

33. Ibid., p. 185. In the previous October W. H. Merritt had advised Durham

that on the American side all was "bustle and activity – there public works are being carried into successful operation, full employment for all classes, high wages and everything . . bearing the mark of prosperity – while here the reverse is apparent in every part of both Provinces," and he had argued that the cause was to be found "in our powerless and divided Legislatures." Merritt to Durham, 4 Oct. 1838. P.A.C., Durham Papers, Sec. 6, II, 269.

34. Lucas, Report, II, 277-8.

35. Ibid., pp. 281-2.

36. Ibid., p. 288.

37. Ibid., pp. 288-9.

38. Ibid., p. 307.

39. Ibid., p. 309.

40. Ibid., p. 311.

41. Ibid., p. 323.

42. Sanderson, Arthur Papers, II, 47, J. B. Robinson to Arthur, 19 Feb. 1839.

43. Ibid., II, 52, Robinson to Normanby, 23 Feb. 1839.

44. Ibid., II, 52-65. Other conservatives made the same point. For instance, Henry Ruttan noted that, whereas in England "the House of Commons was always conservative," in Upper Canada "almost every House of Assembly differed from the preceding one, the only effect therefore which could result would be that of a removal perhaps of all the officers of the Govt. every four years." P.A.C., U. C. Sundries, Ruttan to Arthur, 4 June 1839.

45. Sanderson, Arthur Papers, I, 177, 185.

46. P.A.C., Durham Papers, sec. 6, vol. I, James Fitzgibbon to Lord Durham, 26 June 1838.

47. Journals, Legislative Council, 1839, Appendix GG, Report of the Select Committee to whom was referred the Report of the . . . Earl of Durham, 11 May 1839, pp. 119 ff.

48. Upper Canada Herald, 21 May 1839.

49. *Mirror* (Toronto), 21 June 1839.

50. *Examiner*, 10 July 1839; see also *U. C. Herald*, 16 and 23 July 1839, and *British Colonist* (Toronto), 24 July 1839.

51. *Christian Guardian*, 5 June 1839.

52. See Merritt's speech in the Assembly, 11 May 1839, quoted in the *U. C. Herald*, 28 May, 25 June 1839. Earlier, on March 26, this newspaper had made a similar point as follows: "The Imperial Parliament is too much occupied with other affairs to give ours the constant attention which is requisite to manage them well, and in such a neighbourhood. If we sleep, our neighbours are wide awake; if we neglect our interests, they seize the occasion and profit by our neglect; if we make a false step, they instantly turn it to their advantage; and if we choose to plod along at five miles an hour, they rush ahead under a power of steam, and gain the common goal in half our time, though at the imminent risk of being blown into fragments by the way.

"It is absolutely necessary, then, that a vigilant watch be maintained by persons on the spot – by our own Legislators – in order that our laws suit our circumstances."

53. C. O. 42/461, pp. 271-4, Arthur to Normanby, 27 July 1839; *Ibid.*, pp. 460-1, Arthur to Normanby, 27 Sept. 1839; *Ibid.*, pp. 474-6, Resolutions of Orange meetings; *Brockville Recorder*, 3 Oct. 1839; *An Important Letter on Responsible Government from Lieutenant-Colonel Gowan* (Toronto, 1839).

54. Sanderson, *Arthur Papers*, II, 207, Arthur to Colborne, 8 Aug. 1839.

55. C. O. 42/462, pp. 121-132, Arthur's reply, 24 Aug. 1839, to the Committee appointed by the General Meeting, held at Hamilton.

56. Sanderson, *Arthur Papers*, II, 114, Arthur to J. E. Robinson, 11 April 1839.

57. *Ibid.*, II, 364, Arthur to Thomson, 9 Nov. 1839.

58. Colborne had been appointed Commander of the Forces shortly after leaving Upper Canada, and had become Governor-in-Chief when Durham returned to England in October 1838.

59. Sanderson, *Arthur Papers*, II, 238-65.

60. *Ibid.*, II, 308, Arthur to Lord Fitzroy Somerset, 11 Nov. 1839; *Ibid.*, p. 275, Arthur to Colborne, 3 Oct. 1839; *Ibid.*, p. 290, Arthur to Lord Fitzroy Somerset, 18 Oct. 1839.

61. Paul Knaplund, ed., *Letters of Lord Sydenham to Lord John Russell* (London, 1931), p. 36. Thomson to Russell, 25 Nov. 1839.

62. Address of the Corporation of Toronto to Poulett Thomson, 18 Nov. 1839, quoted in *U. C. Herald*, 3 Dec. 1839.

63. Sanderson, *Arthur Papers*, II, 364, Arthur to Lord Fitzroy Somerset, 24 Dec. 1839.

64. *Ibid.*, II, 350, Thomson to Russell, 15 Dec. 1839.

65. P.A.C.R., 1932, pp. 542-4, Russell to Thomson, 14 Oct. 1839.

66. *Ibid.*, pp. 544-5, Russell to Thomson, 16 Oct. 1839.

67. Sanderson, *Arthur Papers*, II, 351, Thomson to Russell, 15 Dec. 1839.

68. Knaplund, *Sydenham Letters*, p. 48, Thomson to Russell, 13 Feb. 1840.

69. *Ibid.*, p. 43, Thomson to Russell, 18 Jan. 1840.

70. *Ibid.*, p. 71, Thomson to Russell, 28 May 1840.

71. As it turned out, the Clergy Reserves issue still had a long history before it. The British Government disallowed Thomson's bill, and, later that year the British parliament passed a bill much more favourable to the Church of England. This measure kept the issue alive under the united province until the Reserves were secularized in 1854.

72. Sanderson, *Arthur Papers*, III, 46, Arthur to Thomson, 2 May 1840.

73. *Examiner*, 13 May 1840; P.A.C., La Fontaine Papers (Transcripts), Hincks to La Fontaine, 17 June 1840.

74. Kingston *Chronicle and Gazette*, 25 Nov. 1840.

75. Sanderson, *Arthur Papers*, III, 111, Arthur to Sir R. D. Jackson, 18 Aug. 1840.

76. *Ibid.*, III, 233, Arthur to Sydenham, 4 Jan. 1841.

77. J. R. Godley, *Letters from America* (2 vols., London, 1844), I, 201-202.

BIBLIOGRAPHY

GUIDES TO MATERIALS

From 1891 down to the middle 1940's P.A.C.R. published several calendars describing its manuscript collections, and from the early 1950's P.A.C. has periodically published Preliminary Inventories listing its manuscript and record collections. P.A.C. has also published: Magdalen Casey, ed., *Catalogue of Pamphlets in the Public Archives of Canada* (2 vols., Ottawa, 1931-32).

Other finding aids and bibliographies include: *Guide to the Manuscript Collection in the Toronto Public Libraries* (Toronto, 1954), F. M. Staton and M. Tremaine, A *Bibliography of Canadiana* (Toronto, 1935), and G. M. Boyle, ed., A *Bibliography of Canadiana, First Supplement* (Toronto, 1959).

MANUSCRIPTS

P.A.C.: C.O. 42: the most important source for the history of Upper Canada, at the Public Record Office, London, dispatches, letters and a vast assortment of enclosures sent by the lieutenant-governors and administrators to the Colonial Office. The volumes relating to British North America are on microfilm at P.A.C. (the volumes relating to U.C. are also available at O.A.), and supersede the hand-copied transcripts known as the Q Series. C. Series: British military records. G. Series: dispatches from London to the provincial government. Minute Books, State Papers and Land Records of the Executive Council (available on microfilm at O.A.). U.C. Sundries: internal correspondence with the lieutenant-governor and his secretary. Other important collections include: Durham Papers, W. L. Mackenzie Papers, W. H. Merritt Papers, Neilson Collection, W. D. Powell Papers, J. B. Robinson Papers, and John Rolph Papers.

O.A.: Canada Company Papers, Crown Lands Papers, Lindsey Papers (relating to W. L. Mackenzie), Macaulay Papers, W. H. Merritt Papers, J. B. Robinson Papers, D. M. Rogers Papers, John Strachan Papers, Simcoe Papers.

T.P.L.: William Allan Papers, Baldwin Papers, W. D. Powell Papers, Peter Russell Papers, Simcoe Papers.

Many other manuscript collections are to be found in these and other libraries and archives.

NEWSPAPERS

Files, usually incomplete, are to be found in many places, especially P.A.C., Parliamentary Library (Ottawa), O.A., L.L., T.P.L., and various university libraries. The best way to consult the newspapers is on the microfilm reels prepared by the Canadian Library Association, which bring together nearly all known issues of the newspapers filmed. The films are available in several libraries and archives. Among the most important are: *Canadian Emigrant* (Sandwich), 1831-36; *Canadian Freeman* (York, Toronto), 1825-34; *Colonial Advocate, Advocate,* and *Correspondent and Advocate* (Queenston, York, Toronto), 1824-37; *Examiner* (Toronto), 1838-41; *Gazette* (Kingston), 1810-18; *Chronicle* (Kingston), 1819-32; *Chronicle and Gazette* (Kingston), 1833-41; *Upper Canada Gazette* (York, Toronto), 1793-1841; *Canadian Correspondent* (York), 1832-34; *Patriot* (York, Toronto), 1828-41; *Constitution* (Toronto), 1836-37; *Liberal* (St Thomas), 1832-37; *Christian Guardian* (York, Toronto), 1829-41. *Upper Canada Herald* (Kingston), 1826-41, is available on microfilm at P.A.C. as C.O. 47, vols. 56-60.

Other newspapers, not yet microfilmed, include: *Courier* (York, Toronto), 1832-30; *British Colonist* (Toronto), 1838-41; *Brockville Recorder*, 1820-41; *Mirror* (Toronto), 1837-41; *Journal* (St. Catharines), 1833-41; *Western Mercury* (Hamilton) 1831-34. One of the most widely read newspapers was published in New York, *The Albion*, a highly conservative, predominantly literary journal, aimed at the British community throughout North America.

On the newspapers, see W. S. Wallace, "The Periodical Literature of Upper Canada," C.H.R., XII (1931), 4-22; J. J. Talman, "The Newspapers of Upper Canada a Century Ago," C.H.R., XIX (1938), 9-23; and Edith G. Firth, *Early Toronto Newspapers, 1793-1867* (Toronto, 1961).

PRINTED SOURCES

Over the years, P.A.C.R. printed extensive selections from the Q. and G. Series and from other collections. P.A.C. also issued several collections of documents, which are listed in their appropriate places in the bibliography. O.A. reprinted the available journals of the Legislative Assembly and the Legislative Council, for the years 1792-1824, in its annual reports for the years 1909-14. On these reprints see Elaine A. Mitchell, "The 'Sessional Papers' of Upper Canada, 1792-1840," C.H.R., XXII (1941), 280-92. Journals for the years after 1824 are to be found in L.L. and other libraries.

O.A. *Report* for 1906 prints the Proclamations by the governors and lieutenant-governors of Quebec and Upper Canada, 1760-1840.

A great deal of information relating to Upper Canada is scattered through the Parliamentary Papers (the so-called "Blue Books") of the British House of Commons, some of which are mentioned below.

O.H.S. has printed many collections of documents, both in separate publications and in its annual *Proceedings and Transactions* (*Ontario History* from 1947). The most important of these are mentioned in connection with particular topics below, as are collections printed by various local historical societies.

The Champlain Society has published some titles relating to Upper Canada, and since 1957, in conjunction with the Government of Ontario, has been issuing a valuable series of documentary volumes on various regions of the province. Again, these are cited in their appropriate places in the bibliography. W. P. M. Kennedy, ed., *Statutes, Treaties and Documents of the Canadian Constitution, 1713-1929*, Toronto, 1930 (first ed., 1918); W. R. Manning, ed., *Diplomatic Correspondence of the United States, Canadian Relations, 1784-1860* (Four vols., Washington, 1940, 1942, 1943, 1945).

TRAVEL ACCOUNTS AND OTHER CONTEMPORARY DESCRIPTIVE WORKS

Extracts from some of the travel books, and an extensive bibliography, may be found in Gerald M. Craig, ed., *Early Travellers in the Canadas, 1791-1867* (Toronto, 1955). Among the more useful works of contemporary description, listed in a roughly chronological order, are:

PATRICK CAMPBELL. *Travels in the Interior Parts of North America. In the years 1791 and 1792.* Edinburgh, 1793. (Reprinted by The Champlain Society, Toronto, 1937.)

JOHN ROSS ROBERTSON, ed. *The Diary of Mrs. John Graves Simcoe. Wife of the First Lieutenant-Governor of the Province of Upper Canada, 1792-6.* Toronto, 1911. (Revised edition, 1934.)

DUKE DE LA ROCHEFOUCAULD LIANCOURT. *Travels Through the United States of North America, the Country of the Iroquois, and Upper Canada, in the Years 1795, 1796, and 1797.* 2 vols. London, 1799. (See also O.A., Thir-

teenth Report, 1916, Toronto, 1917.)

ISAAC WELD. *Travels through the States of North America, and the Provinces of Upper and Lower Canada, during the years 1795, 1796, and 1797.* London, 1799.

DAVID WILLIAM SMYTH. *A Short Topographical Description of His Majesty's Province of Upper Canada in North America.* London, 1799.

J. C. OGDEN. *A Tour through Upper and Lower Canada. By a citizen of the United States.* Litchfield, [Conn.], 1799.

P. C. T. WHITE, ed. *Lord Selkirk's Diary 1803-1804: A Journal of His Travels in*

British North America and the North-eastern United States. Toronto, The Champlain Society, 1958.

D'ARCY BOULTON. Sketch of His Majesty's Province of Upper Canada. London, 1805. (Reprinted, Toronto, 1962.)

HUGH GRAY. Letters from Canada, written During a Residence There in the Years 1806, 1807 and 1808. London, 1809.

CHRISTIAN SCHULTZ. Travels on an Inland Voyage. 2 vols. New-York, 1810.

MICHAEL SMITH. A Geographical View of the Province of Upper Canada and Promiscuous Remarks on the Government. Hartford, 1813.

JOSEPH BOUCHETTE. A Topographical Description of the Province of Lower Canada, with Remarks upon Upper Canada, and on the Relative Connexion of both Provinces with the United States of America. London, 1815.

C. STUART. The Emigrant's Guide to Upper Canada. London, 1820.

JAMES STRACHAN. A Visit to the Province of Upper Canada in 1819. Aberdeen, 1820.

JOHN HOWISON. Sketches of Upper Canada, Domestic, Local, and Characteristic: To which are added, practical details for the information of emigrants of every class: and some recollections of the United States of America. Edinburgh, 1821.

E. A. TALBOT. Five Years' Residence in the Canadas: Including a Tour through Part of the United States of America in the year 1823. 2 vols. London, 1824.

WILLIAM BELL. Hints to Emigrants in a Series of Letters from Upper Canada. Edinburgh, 1824.

HENRY JOHN BOULTON. A Short Sketch of the Province of Upper Canada. London, 1826.

JOHN MACTAGGART. Three Years in Canada: an Account of the Actual State of the Country in 1826-7-8. 2 vols. London, 1829.

BASIL HALL. Travels in North America in the Years 1827 and 1828. 3 vols. Edinburgh, 1829.

SIR GEORGE HEAD. Forest Scenes and Incidents of the Wilds of North America. London, 1829.

JOSEPH PICKERING. Inquiries of an Emigrant: Being the Narrative of an English farmer, from the year 1824 to 1830. London, 1830.

WILLIAM DUNLOP. Statistical Sketches of Upper Canada. London, 1832.

ADAM FERGUSSON. Practical Notes Made During a Tour in Canada, and a portion of the United States in MDCCCXXXI. London, 1833.

ANDREW PICKEN. The Canadas, as they at Present Commend Themselves to the Enterprize of Emigrants, Colonists, and Capitalists. London, 1832.

E. T. COKE. A Subaltern's Furlough: Descriptive of Scenes in Various Parts of the United States, Upper and Lower Canada, New Brunswick and Nova Scotia, during the Summer and Autumn of 1832. London, 1833.

ISAAC FIDLER. Observations on Professions, Literature, Manners, and Emigration in the United States and Canada, Made During a Residence There in 1832. London, 1833.

JOHN M'GREGOR. British America. 2 vols. Edinburgh, 1833.

T. RADCLIFF, ed. Authentic Letters from Upper Canada. Dublin, 1833. (Reprinted, Toronto, 1953, with an introduction by J. J. Talman.)

Canada in the years 1832, 1833, and 1834. By an ex-settler who resided chiefly "in the Bush" for the last two years. Dublin, 1835.

PATRICK SHIRREFF. A Tour through North America. Edinburgh, 1835.

CATHERINE PARR TRAILL. The Backwoods of Canada. London, 1836.

DAVID WILKIE. Sketches of a Summer Trip to New York and the Canadas. Edinburgh, 1837.

THOMAS NEED. Six Years in the Bush; or Extracts from the Journal of a Settler in Upper Canada, 1832-1838. London, 1838.

H. H. LANGTON, ed. A Gentlewoman in Upper Canada: The Journals of Anne Langton. Toronto, 1950.

W. A. LANGTON, ed. Early Days in Upper Canada: Letters of John Langton from the backwoods of Upper Canada and the Audit Office of the Province of Canada. Toronto, 1926.

ANNA JAMESON. Winter Studies and Summer Rambles in Canada. 3 vols. London, 1838.

T. R. PRESTON. Three Years' Residence in

Canada, from 1837 to 1839. 2 vols. London, 1840.

THOMAS ROLPH. *A Descriptive and Statistical Account of Canada: shewing its Great Adaptation for British Emigration.* London, 1841.

WILLIAM THOMSON. *A Tradesman's Travels in the United States and Canada, in the Years 1840, 41, & 42.* Edinburgh, 1842.

SIR RICHARD HENRY BONNYCASTLE. *The Canadas in 1841.* 2 vols. London, 1842.

JAMES SILK BUCKINGHAM. *Canada, Nova Scotia, New Brunswick, and the other British Provinces in North America, with a Plan of National Colonization.* London, 1843.

SUSANNA MOODIE. *Roughing It In the Bush; or, Life in Canada.* 2 vols. London, 1852.

C. M. STRICKLAND. *Twenty-seven Years in Canada West, or the Experiences of an early settler.* London, 1854.

J. CARRUTHERS. *Retrospect; or Thirty-six Years' Residence in Canada West.* Hamilton, 1861.

JAMES CROIL. *Dundas; or, a Sketch of Canadian History.* Montreal, 1861.

GENERAL SECONDARY WORKS

Among early accounts: William Canniff, *History of the Settlement of Upper Canada (Ontario) with Special Reference to the Bay of Quinté*, Toronto, 1869, reissued in 1872 as *History of the Province of Ontario (Upper Canada)*, a highly patriotic account, reflecting the anti-American feeling following the Fenian raids, but containing informative chapters on settlement, pioneer life, education and religion. The first extensive political narrative was given in J. C. Dent, *The Story of the Upper Canadian Rebellion*, 2 vols., Toronto, 1885, which begins with the Gourlay agitation, and has an extremely anti-Family Compact bias. Dent's attempt to magnify John Rolph's role in the reform movement at the expense of Mackenzie was answered in John King, *The Other Side of the Story*, Toronto, 1886. William Kingsford, *The History of Canada*, 10 vols., Toronto, 1887-98, an early multi-volume history, contains chapters on U.C. in vols. 7 to 10, emphasizing military and political events. Other early compilations are D. B. Read, *The Lieutenant-Governors of Upper Canada and Ontario, 1792-1899*, Toronto, 1900, and Alexander Fraser, *A History of Ontario, Its Resources and Development*, 2 vols., Toronto, 1907. Adam Shortt and A. G. Doughty, *Canada and Its Provinces*, 23 vols., Toronto, 1914-17, contains several chapters on U.C., notably in vols. 3, 4, 17 and 18. W. R. Riddell wrote many articles on U.C., mainly on legal themes, e.g., *Upper Canada Sketches*, Toronto, 1922. An early synthesis of constitutional history is found in W. P. M. Kennedy, *The Constitution of Canada, 1534-1937*, London, 1938 (first edition, 1922). J. E. Middleton and F. Landon, *The Province of Ontario: a History*, 4 vols., Toronto, 1927, is a general narrative. Among later works, J. B. Brebner, *North Atlantic Triangle*, New Haven, 1945, helps the reader to place U.C. in a British and American context, while H. L. Keenleyside and G. S. Brown, *Canada and the United States*, New York, 1952 (first edition, 1929) discusses bilateral relations. Chester Martin, *Foundations of Canadian Nationhood*, Toronto, 1955, stresses the importance of the parliamentary tradition. D. G. Creighton, *The Empire of the St Lawrence*, Toronto, 1956 (first published as *The Commercial Empire of the St Lawrence, 1760-1850*, in 1937), while concerned with the extension of Montreal's influence into the interior, has an illuminating analysis of the development of U.C. S. D. Clark, *Movements of Political Protest in Canada, 1640-1840*, Toronto, 1959, studies U.C. and the other British North American colonies in the light of their "frontier experience."

Other general secondary accounts are listed below in connection with particular topics.

LOCAL HISTORY

The eastern section:

H. F. PRINGLE. *Lunenburgh or the Old Eastern District.* Cornwall, 1890.

J. A. MACDONNELL. *Sketches Illustrating the Early Settlement and History of Glengarry in Canada.* Montreal, 1893.

J. L. GOURLAY. *History of the Ottawa Valley.* Ottawa, 1896.

ANDREW HAYDEN. *Pioneer Sketches in the District of Bathurst.* Toronto, 1925.

THAD. W. H. LEAVITT. *History of Leeds and Grenville, Ontario, from 1749 to 1849.* Brockville, 1879.

R. A. PRESTON, ed. *Kingston Before the War of 1812.* Toronto, Ontario Champlain Society, 1959.

JAMES A. ROY. *Kingston: The King's Town.* Toronto, 1952.

WALTER S. HERRINGTON. *History of the County of Lennox and Addington.* Toronto, 1913.

The central section:

EDWIN C. GUILLET, ed. *The Valley of the Trent.* Toronto, Ontario Champlain Society, 1957.

THOMAS W. POOLE. *A Sketch of the Early Settlement and Subsequent Progress of the Town of Peterborough, and of each Township in the County of Peterborough.* Peterborough, 1867. (Reprinted, 1941.)

G. H. NEEDLER. *Otonabee Pioneers: the Story of the Stewarts, the Stricklands, the Traills and the Moodies.* Toronto, 1953.

EDITH G. FIRTH, ed. *The Town of York, 1793-1815.* Toronto, Ontario Champlain Society, 1962.

HENRY SCADDING. *Toronto of Old.* Toronto, 1873.

J. E. MIDDLETON. *The Municipality of Toronto; a History.* 3 vols. Toronto, 1923.

J. ROSS ROBERTSON. *Landmarks of Toronto.* 6 vols. Toronto, 1894-1914.

K. M. LIZARS. *The Valley of the Humber, 1615-1913.*

A. F. HUNTER. *A History of Simcoe County.* 2 vols. Barrie, Ont., 1909. (Reprinted, 1948.)

HAZEL C. MATHEWS. *Oakville and the Sixteen: the History of an Ontario Port.* Toronto, 1953.

C. M. JOHNSTON. *The Head of the Lake. A History of Wentworth County.* Hamilton, 1958.

JOHN H. THOMPSON. *Jubilee History of Thorold Township and Town.* Thorold, 1897-98.

WILLIAM KIRBY. *Annals of Niagara.* Toronto, 1927 (first published in 1896).

JANET CARNOCHAN. *History of Niagara.* Toronto, 1914.

The western section:

HUGH TEMPLIN. *Fergus, The Story of a Little Town.* Fergus, Ontario, 1933.

JAMES YOUNG. *Reminiscences of the Early History of Galt and the Settlement of Dumfries, in the province of Ontario.* Toronto, 1880.

MABEL DUNHAM. *Grand River.* Toronto, 1945.

CHARLES M. JOHNSTON. "An Outline of Early Settlement in the Grand River Valley," *O.H.,* LIV (1962), 43-67.

FRED COYNE HAMIL. *The Valley of the Lower Thames, 1640 to 1850.* Toronto, 1951.

ERNEST J. LAJEUNESSE. *The Windsor Border Region, Canada's Southernmost Frontier; A Collection of Documents.* Toronto, Ontario Champlain Society, 1960.

On local history one may also consult an extensive list of county histories and historical atlases published in the 1870's and 1880's, as well as the proceedings of many local historical societies throughout the province.

LOCAL GOVERNMENT

J. H. Aitchison. *The Development of Local Government in Upper Canada, 1783-1850.* 2 vols. Ph.D. Thesis, U. of T., 1953, the best work on the subject, and containing an extensive bibliography.

SETTLEMENT AND LAND POLICY

General works: M. L. Hansen and J. B. Brebner, *The Mingling of the Canadian and American Peoples*, New Haven, 1940; Helen I. Cowan, *British Emigration to British North America, the First Hundred Years*, Toronto, 1961 (first edition, 1928); J. Spelt, *The Urban Development in South-Central Ontario*, Assen, The Netherlands, 1955; G. C. Paterson, "Land Settlement in Upper Canada, 1783-1840," O.A., *Sixteenth Report*, Toronto, 1921; Norman Macdonald, *Canada, 1763-1841: Immigration and Settlement*, London, 1939. The last two deal also with land policy, as do Lillian F. Gates, "The Land Policies of Upper Canada," Ph.D. Thesis, Radcliffe College, 1955; R. G. Riddell, "A Study in the Land Policy of the Colonial Office, 1763-1855," C.H.R., XVIII (1937), 385-405, and his "The Policy of Creating Land Reserves in Canada," in R. Flenley, ed., *Essays in Canadian History*, Toronto, 1939; G. A. Wilson, "The Political and Administrative History of the Upper Canada Clergy Reserves, 1790-1854," Ph.D. Thesis. U. of T., 1959; and, more briefly, his "The Clergy Reserves: 'Economical Mischiefs' or Sectarian Issue?" C.H.R., XLII (1961), 281-99, and J. H. Richards, "Lands and Policies: Attitudes and Controls in the Alienation of Lands in Ontario During the First Century of Settlement," O.H., L (1958), 193-209. See also "Correspondence respecting the Clergy Reserves in Canada, 1819-40," *Parliamentary Papers*, 1840, vol. 32.

Narratives of local settlement are provided in several Conservation Reports issued by the Department of Planning [now Economics] and Development of the Ontario Government, including the following: Humber (1948), Don (1950), Moira (1950), Upper Holland (1953), Credit (1956), Rouge, Duffin, Highland and Petticoat (1956), Otter Creek (1957) and Napanee (1957).

"The oldest continuous settlement" in the province is described in E. J. Lajeunesse, "The First Four Years of the Settlement on the Canadian Side of the Detroit River," O.H., XLVII (1955), 122-31, and the migration of the "plain folk" in G. E. Reaman, *The Trail of the Black Walnut*, Toronto, 1957.

Works on the Loyalists include: W. H. Nelson, *The American Tory*, New York, 1961, on the American Revolutionary background; W. S. Wallace, *The United Empire Loyalists*, Toronto, 1914; E. Ryerson, *The Loyalists of America and their Times*, 2 vols., Toronto, 1880, is an early work; A. L. Burt, *The Old Province of Quebec*, Toronto, 1933, has an excellent chapter on the 1780's. There are collections of documents in J. J. Talman, ed., *Loyalist Narratives from Upper Canada*, Toronto, Champlain Society, 1946; E. A. Cruikshank, ed., *The Settlement of the United Empire Loyalists on the Upper St Lawrence and Bay of Quinte in 1784*, Toronto, 1934; Cruikshank also published many documents on Loyalist settlement in the Niagara peninsula in the *Publications* of the Niagara Historical Society, especially numbers 17 (1908) and 38-40 (1927-29). See also: E. Rae Stuart, "Jessup's Rangers as a Factor in Loyalist Settlement," in *Three History Theses*, O.A., Toronto, 1961; W. L. Stone, *The Life of Joseph Brant—Thayendanega*, 2 vols., Buffalo, 1851; Harvey Chalmers, *Joseph Brant*, Toronto, 1955.

On the Talbot Settlement: F. C. Hamil, *Lake Erie Baron*, Toronto, 1955; Edward Ermatinger, *Life of Colonel Talbot*, St Thomas, 1859; C. O. Ermatinger, *The Talbot Regime*, St Thomas, 1904; J. H. Coyne, ed., "The Talbot Papers," R.S.C., P. and T., I (1907), sec. II, 15-210, III (1909), sec. II, 67-196.

Other items include: E. A. Cruikshank, "Imigration from the United States into Upper Canada, 1784-1812," *Proceedings of the 39th Convention of the Ontario Educational Association*, Toronto, 1900, pp. 263-83; his "An Experiment in Colonization in Upper Canada," O.H.S.P.R., XXV (1929), 32-77; Lillian F. Gates, "The Heir and Devisee Commission of Upper Canada, 1797-1805," C.H.R., XXVIII (1957), 21-36; A. R. M. Lower, "Immigration and Settlement in Canada, 1812-1820," C.H.R., III (1922), 37-47; "Reports from the Select Committee on Emigration," *Parliamentary Papers*, 1827, vol. 5; H. T. Pammett, "Assisted Emigration from Ireland to Upper Canada under Peter Robinson in 1825," O.H.S.P.R., XXXI (1936), 178-214; J. K.

Johnson, "The Chelsea Pensioners in Upper Canada," *O.H.*, LIII (1961), 273-89. On the Canada Company: John Galt, *Autobiography*, 2 vols., London, 1833; R. K. Gordon, *John Galt*, Toronto, 1920; R. and K. M. Lizars, *In the Days of the Canada Company*, Toronto, 1896.

SOCIAL AND ECONOMIC DEVELOPMENT

Much has been done to assist those who may wish to observe physical survivals from the period before 1841, and to visit historical sites. The Ontario Department of Travel and Publicity provides brochures and other information, and has erected many scores of plaques around the province. Outstanding among restoration projects is "Upper Canada Village," near Morrisburg, conducted by the Ontario-St Lawrence Development Commission, and "Pioneer Village," near Toronto, conducted by the Metropolitan Toronto Conservation Authority.

The best general social history of Canada is A. R. M. Lower, *Canadians in the Making*, Toronto, 1958. S. D. Clark, *The Social Development of Canada*, Toronto, 1942, uses documents to illustrate a sociological approach. Works pertaining particularly to U.C. include J. J. Talman, "Life in the Pioneer Districts of Upper Canada, 1815-1840," Ph.D. Thesis, U. of T., 1930; E. C. Guillet, *Early Life in Upper Canada*, Toronto, 1933; Fred Landon, *Western Ontario and the American Frontier*, Toronto, 1941, which stresses the role of American settlers; Richard B. Splane, "The Development of Social Welfare in Ontario, 1791 to 1893: the Role of the Province," Ph.D. Thesis, U. of T., 1961. See also M. A. Garland and J. J. Talman, "Pioneer Drinking Habits and the Rise of the Temperance Agitation in Upper Canada Prior to 1840," *O.H.S.P.R.*, XXVII (1931), 341-64, and E. C. Guillet, *Pioneer Inns and Taverns*, 4 vols., Toronto, 1954, 1956, 1958.

A good general economic history is W. T. Easterbrook and H. G. J. Aitken, *Canadian Economic History*, Toronto, 1956. See also H. A. Innis and A. R. M. Lower, eds., *Select Documents in Canadian Economic History*, Toronto, 1933; H. A. Innis, "An Introduction to the Economic History of Ontario," *O.H.S.P.R.*, XXX (1934), 111-23; and M. Q. Innis, "Industrial Development of Ontario, 1783-1820," *O.H.S.P.R.*, XXXII (1937), 104-13.

On farming: R. L. Jones, *History of Agriculture in Ontario, 1613-1880*, Toronto, 1946. On lumbering: A. R. M. Lower, *Settlement and the Forest Frontier in Eastern Canada*, Toronto, 1936, and his *The North American Assault on the Canadian Forest*, Toronto, 1938; Michael Cross, "The Lumber Community of Upper Canada, 1815-1867," *O.H.*, LII (1960), 213-33. On roads and canals: G. P. de T. Glazebrook, *A History of Transportation in Canada*, Toronto, 1938; R. F. Leggett, *Rideau Waterway*, Toronto, 1955; "Report from the Select Committee Appointed to Take into Consideration the Accounts and Papers Relating to the Rideau Canal," *Parliamentary Papers*, 1831, vol 3; H. G. J. Aitken, *The Welland Canal Company*, Cambridge, Mass., 1954; J. P. Merritt, *Biography of the Hon. W. H. Merritt*, St Catharines, 1875. On banking: a long series of articles by Adam Shortt on banking and currency in *Journal of the Canadian Bankers' Association*, Toronto, later Montreal, IV-XIV, 1896-1906, and XXX-XXXIII, 1922-25; Bray Hammond, *Banks and Politics in America from the Revolution to the Civil War*, Princeton, N.J., 1957, has a chapter on Canadian banking.

Other items: William Smith, *The History of the Post Office in British North America, 1639-1870*, Cambridge, 1920; J. J. Talman, "Travel in Ontario Before the Coming of the Railway," *O.H.S.P.R.*, XXXIX (1933), 85-102; John Philp, "The Economic and Social Effect of the British Garrisons on the Development of Western Upper Canada," *O.H.*, XLI (1949), 37-48.

RELIGION AND EDUCATION

There is no satisfactory full-scale synthesis of either religious or educational development. Brief treatments may be found in H. H. Walsh, *The Christian Church in Canada*, Toronto, 1956; and C. E. Phillips, *The Development of Education in Canada*,

Toronto, 1957. For a sociological analysis, see S. D. Clark, *Church and Sect in Canada*, Toronto, 1948.

The essential documents on education are in J. G. Hodgins, ed., *Documentary History of Education in Upper Canada . . . 1791 to . . . 1876*, 28 vols., Toronto. 1894-1910. See also G. W. Spragge, "Elementary Education in Upper Canada," O.H., XLIII (1951), 107-22; and his "The Upper Canada Central School," O.H.S.P.R., XXXII (1937), 171-91.

On pioneer religion: Charles A. Johnson, *The Frontier Camp Meeting* (Dallas, 1955), and M. A. Garland, "Some Phases of Pioneer Religious Life in Upper Canada Before 1850," O.H.S.P.R., XXV (1929), 231-47. On the Protestant churches, and especially the Methodists, see several essays in G. W. Brown, *Canada in the Making*, Toronto, 1953.

On the Church of England, the following articles by J. J. Talman: "The Position of the Church of England in Upper Canada, 1791-1840," C.H.R. (1934), 361-75; "Church of England Missionary Effort in Upper Canada, 1815-1840," O.H.S.P.R., XXV (1929), 438-49; "Some Notes on the Clergy of the Church of England in Upper Canada Prior to 1840," R.S.C., P. & T., XXXII (1938), sec. II, 57-66. See also W. J. D. Waddilove, *The Stewart Missions*, London, 1838. T. R. Millman has written biographies of two Anglican bishops: *Jacob Mountain, First Lord Bishop of Quebec: A Study of Church and State, 1793-1825*, Toronto, 1947, and *The Life of the Right Reverend, the Honourable Charles James Stewart, Second Anglican Bishop of Quebec*, London, Ont., 1953.

There is no adequate modern biography of John Strachan; meanwhile, see Henry Scadding, *The First Bishop of Toronto*, Toronto, 1868; A. N. Bethune, *Memoir of the Right Reverend John Strachan*, Toronto, 1870; A. H. Young, "John Strachan," *Queen's Quarterly*, XXXV (1928), 386-407; and J. D. Purdy, "John Strachan and Education in Canada, 1800-1851," Ph.D. Thesis, U. of T., 1962. Two of Strachan's letter books have been transcribed in G. W. Spragge, *The John Strachan Letter Book: 1812-1834* (Toronto, 1946) and R. C. Good, "Letter Book of John Strachan, 1827-1834," (M.A. Thesis, U. of T., 1940). The former is the best introduction to Strachan; by the same author: "Dr. Strachan's Motives for Becoming a Legislative Councillor," C.H.R. (1938), 397-402, and "John Strachan's Contributions to Education, 1800-1823," C.H.R. (1941), 147-58. Strachan's own writings and speeches include the following: *A sermon preached at York . . . 1825 . . . on the death of the late Lord Bishop; Observations on the provision made for the maintenance of a Protestant Clergy, in the provinces of Upper and Lower Canada* (London, 1827); *An appeal to the friends of religion and literature in behalf of the University of Upper Canada* (London, 1827); *A Speech of the Venerable John Strachan, D.D., Archdeacon of York, in the Legislative Council . . . on the Subject of the Clergy Reserves* (York, 1828); *A Letter to the Rev. Thomas Chalmers, D.D. . . . on the Life and Character of the Right Reverend Dr. Hobart* (New-York, 1832).

On the Methodists see G. S. French, *Parsons in Politics*, Toronto, 1962. Earlier works include: George F. Playter, *The History of Methodism in Canada*, Toronto, 1862; Thomas Webster, *History of the Methodist Episcopal Church in Canada*, Hamilton, 1870; John Carroll, *Case and His Cotemporaries; or, the Canadian Itinerants' Memorial: Constituting a Biographical History of Methodism in Canada, from Its Introduction into the Province, till the Death of the Rev. Wm. Case in 1855*, 5 vols., Toronto, 1867-77; Anson Green, *Life and Times*, Toronto, 1877; J. E. Sanderson, *The First Century of Methodism in Canada*, 2 vols., Toronto, 1908; C. B. Sissons, *Egerton Ryerson: His Life and Letters* (2 vols., Toronto, 1937, 1947), an outstanding work and the best introduction to Canadian Methodism. See also: N. Burwash, *Egerton Ryerson* (Toronto, 1903); J. G. Hodgins, ed., *"The Story of My Life"* by the Late Rev. Egerton Ryerson (Toronto, 1883); *Letters from the Reverend Egerton Ryerson to the Hon. and Reverend Doctor Strachan published originally in the Upper Canada Herald* (Kingston, 1828).

On the Presbyterians: William Gregg, *History of the Presbyterian Church in the*

Dominion of Canada, from the earliest times to 1834, Toronto, 1885; M. A. Garland, ed., "The Proudfoot Papers," O.H.S.P.R., XXVI/XXXII (1930-37), various pages. On the Roman Catholics: H. J. Somers, *The Life and Time of the Hon. and Rt. Rev. Alexander Macdonell*, Washington, 1931; F. A. Walker, *Catholic Education and Politics in Upper Canada*, Toronto, 1955. On other denominations and sects: S. Ivison and F. Rosser, *The Baptists in Upper and Lower Canada before 1820*, Toronto, 1956; E. E. Gray, *Wilderness Christians*, Toronto, 1956, on the Moravian missions on the lower Thames; A. G. Dorland, *A History of the Society of Friends (Quakers) in Canada*, Toronto, 1927; Hilary Spooner, "Sharon Temple and the Children of Peace," O.H., L (1958), 219-27.

On the Orange Order: W. B. Kerr, *The Orange Order in Upper Canada in the 1820's* [and] *The Orange Order and W. L. Mackenzie in the 1830's Pamphlet*, reprinted from *The Sentinel*, Toronto, 1939; and his "When Orange and Green United, 1832-9," O.H.S.P.R., XXXIV (1942), 34-42.

Some items on sectarian controversies: W. R. Riddell, "The Law of Marriage in Upper Canada," C.H.R., II (1921), 226-48; A. N. Bethune, *Thoughts upon the lawfulness and expediency of church establishments and suggestions for the appropriation of the Clergy Reserves in Upper Canada, as far as respects the Church of England, in a letter to C. A. Hagerman, esq., M.P.*, Cobourg, 1836; *Speeches of Dr. John Rolph and Christopher A. Hagerman, esq., His Majesty's solicitor general, on the Bill for appropriating the proceeds of the Clergy Reserves to the purposes of general education*, Toronto, 1837; Charles Lindsey, *The Clergy Reserves* (Toronto, 1851).

GOVERNMENT AND POLITICS TO 1812

Documentary collections: Adam Shortt and A. G. Doughty, eds., *Documents Relating to the Constitutional History of Canada, 1759-91*, 2 vols., Ottawa, 1918; A. G. Doughty and D. A. McArthur, eds., *Documents Relating to the Constitutional History of Canada, 1791-1881*, Ottawa, 1914; E. A. Cruikshank, ed., *The Correspondence of Lieut. Governor John Graves Simcoe*, 5 vols., Toronto, 1923-31; E. A. Cruikshank, ed., *The Correspondence of the Honourable Peter Russell*, 3 vols., Toronto, 1932-36.

On the British and American backgrounds: A. L. Burt, *The United States, Great Britain and British North America from the Revolution to the Establishment of Peace after the War of 1812*, New Haven, 1940; and H. T. Manning, *British Colonial Government After the American Revolution, 1783-1820*, New Haven, 1933.

On Simcoe: W. R. Riddell, *The Life of John Graves Simcoe*, Toronto, 1926; D. B. Read, *The Life and Times of Gen. John Graves Simcoe*, Toronto, 1890; S. R. Mealing, "The Enthusiasms of John Graves Simcoe," C.H.A.R., 1958, 50-62; S. F. Wise, "The Indian Diplomacy of John Graves Simcoe," C.H.A.R., 1953, 36-44. On the last subject see also R. Horsman, "The British Indian Department and the Abortive Treaty of Lower Sandusky, 1793," *Ohio Historical Quarterly*, LXX (1961), 189-213. H. M. Jackson, *The Queen's Rangers in Upper Canada: 1792 and After*, Montreal, 1955.

On other political figures and leaders: Jean N. McIlwraith, *Sir Frederick Haldimand*, Toronto, 1926; D. R. Plaunt, "The Honourable Peter Russell," C.H.R., XX (1939), 258-74; Edith G. Firth, "The Administration of Peter Russell, 1796-1799," O.H., XLVIII (1956), 163-81; E. A. Cruikshank, "A Memoir of Lieutenant-General Peter Hunter," O.H.S.P.R., XXX (1934), 5-32; C. E. Cartwright, *Life and Letters of the Late Hon. Richard Cartwright*, Toronto, 1876; Donald C. MacDonald, "Honourable Richard Cartwright, 1759-1815," in *Three History Theses*, O.A., Toronto, 1961; James A. Roy, "The Honourable Richard Cartwright," C.H.A.R., 1950, 64-71; A. H. U. Colquhoun, "The Career of Joseph Willcocks," C.H.R., VII (1926), 287-93; W. R. Riddell, "Joseph Willcocks, Sheriff, Member of Parliament and Traitor," O.H.S.P.R., XXIV (1927), 475-99; and "Mr. Justice Thorpe, the Leader of the First Opposition in Upper Canada," in his *Upper Canada Sketches*, Toronto, 1922; also his *The Life of William Dummer Powell*, Lansing, Mich., 1924.

Some contemporary items: Matilda Edgar, *Ten Years of Upper Canada in Peace and War, 1805-1815; being the Ridout Letters*, Toronto, 1890; J. M. Jackson, *A View of the Political Situation of Upper Canada*, London, 1809; *A Letter To the Right Honourable Lord Castlereagh*, Quebec, 24th October, 1809; *Letters, from an American Loyalist in Upper-Canada, to his Friend in England; on a pamphlet published by John Mills Jackson*, [n.p.], 1810.

WAR OF 1812

Documentary collections: William Wood, ed., *British Documents of the Canadian War of 1812*, 3 vols., Toronto, The Champlain Society, 1920-28; E. A. Cruikshank, ed., *The Documentary History of the Campaign upon the Niagara Frontier, 1812-14*, 9 vols., Welland, Ont., 1896-1908; and his *Documents Relating to the Invasion of Canada and the Surrender of Detroit, 1812*, Ottawa, 1913.

The discussion of the causes of the war is too vast for adequate citation here, but among recent items see: Bradford Perkins, *Prologue to War* (Stanford, 1961); Reginald Horsman, "British Indian Policy in the Northwest, 1807-1812," *Mississippi Valley Historical Review*, XLV (1958), 51-66; and his "Western War Aims, 1811-12," *Indiana Magazine of History*, LIII (1957), 1-18. The two best general accounts are still A. T. Mahan, *Sea Power in its Relations to the War of 1812*, 2 vols., Boston, 1905, and C. P. Lucas, *The Canadian War of 1812*, Oxford, 1906, respectively from American and British viewpoints. A. C. Casselman, ed., *Richardson's War of 1812*, Toronto, 1902, provides an early Canadian account written by a participant, while C. P. Stacey, "The War of 1812 in Canadian History," O.H., L (1958), 153-59, gives a modern assessment of its significance.

On military and naval events: G. F. G. Stanley, *Canada's Soldiers*, Toronto, 1954 (revised ed., 1960), and his "The Indians in the War of 1812," C.H.R., XXXI (1950), 145-65; Glenn Tucker, *Tecumseh*, Indianapolis, 1956; Alec R. Gilpin, *The War of 1812 in the Old Northwest*, East Lansing, Mich., 1958; C. P. Stacey, "Commodore Chauncey's Attack on Kingston Harbour, November 10, 1812," C.H.R., XXXII (1951), 126-38; his "The Ships of the British Squadron on Lake Ontario, 1812-14," C.H.R., XXXIV (1953), 311-23; and his "Another Look at the Battle of Lake Erie," C.H.R., XXXIX (1958), 41-51. On the occupation of York: W. B. Kerr, "The Occupation of York (Toronto), 1813," C.H.R., V (1924), 9-21; M. M. Quaife, *The Yankees Capture York*, Detroit, 1955; and C. W. Humphries, "The Capture of York," O.H., LI (1959), 1-21.

On treason and disaffection: E. A. Cruikshank, "A Study of Disaffection in Upper Canada in 1812-15," R.S.C., P. & T., VI (1912), sec. II, 11-65; and his "John Beverley Robinson and the Trials for Treason in 1814," O.H.S.P.R., XXV (1929), 191-219; W. R. Riddell, "The Ancaster 'Bloody Assize' of 1814," O.H.S.P.R., XX (1923), 107-25; and his "Benajah Mallory, Traitor," O.H.S.P.R., XXVI (1930), 573-78.

On the internal scene: C. W. Humphries, "Upper Canada in 1813," M.A. Thesis, U. of T., 1959; W. W. Weekes, "The War of 1812: Civil Authority and Martial Law in Upper Canada," O.H., XLVIII (1956), 147-61; Adam Shortt, "The Economic Effects of the War of 1812 on Upper Canada," O.H.S.P.R., X (1913), 79-85; and a contemporary volume, *The Report of the Loyal and Patriotic Society of Upper Canada*, Montreal, 1817.

GOVERNMENT AND POLITICS, 1815-36

Printed sources include: A. G. Doughty and Norah Story, eds., *Documents Relating to the Constitutional History of Canada, 1819-1828*, Ottawa, 1935; "Note C—Naturalization Question," *PACR*, 1898, 35-56; "Report from the Select Committee on the Civil Government of Canada," *Parliamentary Papers*, 1828, vol. 7; *Mr Bidwell's Speech on the Intestate Bill in the Provincial Assembly of Upper Canada, January 24, 1831; The Seventh Report from the Select Committee of the House of Assembly of Upper Canada on Grievances*, Toronto, 1835; *Report of the Select Committee to which was referred the answer of His Excellency, the Lieut. Governor, to an Address of the House of Assembly, relative to a Responsible Executive Council*, Toronto, 1836; *Report of a Select Committee of the Legislative Council of Upper Canada upon the* complaints contained in an Address to the King from the House of Assembly, passed 15th April, 1835, of the Rejection by the Legislative Council, of Bills sent from the House of Assembly; and the Address of the Legislative Council to His Majesty, on That Subject, Toronto, 1836; Declaration of the views and objects of the British Constitutional Society on its re-organization, Toronto, 1836; Report of the Select Committee to which was referred the message of His Excellency the Lieutenant-Governor, communicating the copy of a petition of Charles Duncombe, to the British House of Commons, and other documents, Toronto, 1837.

Of secondary works not previously cited, the best analysis is in Aileen Dunham, Political Unrest in Upper Canada, 1815-1836 (London, 1927). On the British and Lower Canada background: Helen T. Manning, The Revolt of French Canada, 1800-1835, Toronto, 1962; her "The Colonial Policy of the Whig Ministers, 1830-37: I, II," C.H.R., XXXIII (1952), 203-36, 341-68, and her "Colonial Crises Before the Cabinet, 1829-1835," The Bulletin of the Institute of Historical Research, XXX (1957), 41-61; D. M. Young, The Colonial Office in the Early Nineteenth Century, London, 1961; Paul Knaplund, James Stephen and the British Colonial System 1813-1847, Madison, Wisc., 1953; Sir Robert Wilmot Horton, Exposition and Defence of Earl Bathurst's Administration of the affairs of Canada, when Colonial Secretary, during the years 1822 to 1827, inclusive, London, 1838. On the American background, Fred Landon, Western Ontario and the American Frontier, Toronto, 1941, and G. M. Craig, "The American Impact on the Upper Canadian Reform Movement before 1837," C.H.R., XXIX (1948), 333-352.

On the Gourlay episode: Robert Gourlay, General Introduction to Statistical Account of Upper Canada, London, 1822; and Statistical Account of Upper Canada, 2 vols., London, 1822; E. A. Cruikshank, "The Government of Upper Canada and Robert Gourlay," O.H.S.P.R., XXIII (1926), 65-179; and his "Post-War Discontent at Niagara in 1818," O.H.S.P.R., XXIX (1933), 14-46; W. R. Riddell, "Robert (Fleming) Gourlay as Shown by his own Records," O.H.S.P.R., XIV (1917), 5-133.

On the Family Compact: W. S. Wallace, The Family Compact (Toronto, 1915); Alison Ewart and Julia Jarvis, "The Personnel of the Family Compact," C.H.R., VII (1926), 209-21; H. G. J. Aitken, "The Family Compact and the Welland Canal Company," Canadian Journal of Economics and Political Science, XVIII (1952), 63-76; and R. E. Saunders, "What Was The Family Compact?" O.H., XLIX (1957), 165-78.

Biographies include: C. W. Robinson, The Life of Sir John Beverley Robinson, Edinburgh, 1904; E. J. Hathaway, Jesse Ketchum and his Times, Toronto, 1929; G. E. Wilson, The Life of Robert Baldwin, Toronto, 1933; G. C. M. Smith, The Life of John Colborne, Field-Marshal Lord Seaton, London, 1903; Chester New, "Marshall Spring Bidwell," and A. R. M. Lower, "William Hamilton Merritt," in R. G. Riddell, ed., Canadian Portraits, Toronto, 1940; and several essays in William Smith, Political Leaders of Upper Canada, Toronto, 1931.

On W. L. Mackenzie: Charles Lindsey, The Life and Times of Wm. Lyon Mackenzie, 2 vols., Toronto, 1862, written by his son-in-law, and William Kilbourn, The Firebrand, William Lyon Mackenzie and the Rebellion in Upper Canada, Toronto, 1956, a perceptive modern portrait; R. A. MacKay, "The Political Ideas of William Lyon Mackenzie," Canadian Journal of Economics and Political Science, III (1937), 1-22; Lillian F. Gates, "The Decided Policy of William Lyon Mackenzie," C.H.R., XL (1959), 185-208. Most of Mackenzie's own writings are to be found in his newspapers; for a selection, Margaret Fairley, ed., The Selected Writings of William Lyon Mackenzie, Toronto, 1960; also his Sketches of Canada and the United States, London, 1833. Other items: E. A. Cruikshank, "A Sketch of the Public Life and Services of Robert Nichol," O.H.S.P.R., XIX (1922), 6-81; W. R. Riddell, "The Bidwell Elections," O.H.S.P.R., XXI (1924), 236-44; William Ormsby, "The Problem of Canadian Union, 1822-1828," C.H.R., XXXIX (1958), 277-95; G. W. Spragge, "John Strachan's Connexion with Early Proposals for Confederation," C.H.R., XXIII (1942), 363-73; K. D. McRae, ed., "An Upper Canada Letter of 1829 on Responsible Government," C.H.R. XXXI (1950), 288-96; W. R. Riddell, ed., "The Constitutional Debate in the Legislative Assembly of 1836," *Lennox and Addington Historical Society* (Napanee, Ontario), VII & VIII (1916), 7-90; R. G. Riddell, ed., "Egerton Ryerson's Views of the Government of Upper Canada in 1836," C.H.R., XIX (1938), 402-410; J. B. Brebner, "Patronage and Parliamentary Government," C.H.A.R., 1938, 22-30.

REBELLION OF 1837 AND ITS AFTERMATH

Some contemporary writings and memoirs relating to the Rebellion: William B. Wells, *Canadiana*, London, 1837; *Mackenzie's Own Narrative of the Late Rebellion*, Toronto, 1838; Charles B. Durand, *Reminiscences*, Toronto 1897; W. H. Higgins, *The Life and Times of Joseph Gould*, Toronto, 1887; Robert Davis, *The Canadian Farmer's Travels in the United States*, Buffalo, 1837; Leslie R. Gray, ed., "Letters of John Talbot," O.H., XLIV (1952), 139-64. On the background and course of the Rebellion: D. G. Creighton, "The Economic Background of the Rebellions of Eighteen Thirty-Seven," *Canadian Journal of Economics and Political Science*, III (1937), 322-34; C. W. New, "The Rebellion of 1837 in its Larger Setting." C.H.A.R., 1937, 5-17; Fred Landon, "The Duncombe Uprising of 1837 and Some of its Consequences," R.S.C., P. & T., XXV (1931), sec. II, 83-98; and his "The Common Man in the Era of the Rebellion in Upper Canada," C.H.A.R., 1937, 79-91; D. B. Read, *The Canadian Rebellion of 1837*, Toronto, 1896; John Barnett, "Silas Fletcher: Instigator of the Upper Canadian Rebellion," O.H., XLI (1949), 7-35; C. B. Sissons, ed., "Dr. John Rolph's Own Account of the Flag of Truce Incident in the Rebellion of 1837," C.H.R., XIX (1938), 56-59; C. B. Sissons, ed., "The Case of Bidwell," C.H.R., XXVII (1946) 368-82; Egerton Ryerson, *Sir F. B. Head and Mr. Bidwell*, Kingston, 1838; R. S. Longley, *Sir Francis Hincks*, Toronto, 1943; and his "Emigration and the Crisis of 1837 in Upper Canada," C.H.R., XVII (1936), 28-40.

On Sir Francis Bond Head: Sydney W. Jackman, *Galloping Head*, London, 1958; James A. Gibson, "The 'Persistent Fallacy' of the Governors Head," C.H.R., XIX (1938), 259-97; H. T. Manning and J. S. Galbraith, "The Appointment of Francis Bond Head: A New Insight," C.H.R., XLII (1961), 50-52; F. B. Head, *A Narrative*, London, 1839. On Sir George Arthur: C. R. Sanderson, ed., *The Arthur Papers*, 3 vols., Toronto, 1957, 1959.

On the border disturbances: E. C. Guillet, *The Lives and Times of the Patriots*, Toronto, 1939; A. B. Corey, *The Crisis of 1830 to 1842 in Canadian-American Relations*, New Haven, 1941; O. A. Kinchen, *The Rise and Fall of the Patriot Hunters*, New York, 1956; F. P. Prucha, "Reports of General Brady on the Patriot War," C.H.R., XXXI (1950), 56-68; O. E. Tiffany, "The Relations of the United States to the Canadian Rebellion of 1837-1838," *Publications of the Buffalo Historical Society*, VIII (1905), 7-147; E. A. Theller, *Canada in 1837-38*, 2 vols., Philadelphia, 1841.

On Lord Durham and the Report: C. P. Lucas, ed., *Lord Durham's Report on the Affairs of British North America*, 3 vols., Oxford, 1912; C. W. New, *Lord Durham*, Oxford, 1929; C. W. New, "Lord Durham and the British Background of His Report," C.H.R., XX (1939), 119-35; G. W. Brown, "The Durham Report and the Upper Canadian Scene," C.H.R., XX (1939), 136-60; Chester Martin, "Lord Durham's Report and its Consequences," C.H.R., XX (1939), 178-94; *Report from the Select Committee of the Legislative Council of Upper Canada on the Report of the Right Honourable the Earl of Durham, Her Majesty's Late Governor-in-Chief of British North America*, Toronto, 1839; *An Important Letter on Responsible Government from Lieutenant-Colonel Gowan, M.P.P. for the County of Leeds in U. Canada*, Toronto 1839.

On the Union: O. A. Kinchen, *Lord Russell's Canadian Policy*, Lubbock, Texas, 1945; J. B. Robinson, *Remarks on the proposed Union of the Provinces*, [n.p.], 1839; and his *Canada and the Canada Bill*, London 1840.

On Lord Sydenham: G. Poulett Scrope, *Memoir of the Life of the Right Honourable Charles Lord Sydenham*, London, 1844; Paul Knaplund, ed., *Letters of Lord Sydenham to Lord John Russell*, London, 1931; Adam Shortt, *Lord Sydenham*, Toronto, 1926; J. L. Morison, *British Supremacy and Canadian Self-Government, 1839-1854*, Glasgow, 1919.

BIBLIOGRAPHICAL SUPPLEMENT FOR THE 1972 EDITION

GENERAL

F. H. ARMSTRONG, ed. Handbook of Upper Canadian Chronology and Territorial Legislation. London, Ont., 1967. (A valuable reference work.)

J. M. S. CARELESS, ed. Colonists and Canadiens, 1760-1867. Toronto, 1971.

Profiles of a Province: Studies in the History of Ontario. A collection of essays commissioned by the Ontario Historical Society to commemorate the centennial of Ontario. Toronto, 1967.

S. F. WISE and R. C. BROWN. Canada Views the United States: Nineteenth Century Political Attitudes. Toronto, 1967.

LOCAL HISTORY AND GOVERNMENT

F. H. ARMSTRONG. "Metropolitanism and Toronto Re-examined, 1825-1850," C.H.A.R. (1966), 29-40.

————. "Reformer as Capitalist: William Lyon Mackenzie and the Printers' Strike of 1836," O.H., LIX (3), Sept. 1967, 187-96.

————. "William Lyon Mackenzie, First Mayor of Toronto: A Study of a Critic in Power," C.H.R., XLVIII (4), Dec. 1967, 309-31.

EDITH G. FIRTH, ed. The Town of York, 1815-1834: A Further Collection of Documents of Early Toronto. Toronto, 1966.

CHARLES M. JOHNSTON, ed. The Valley of the Six Nations: A Collection of Documents of the Indian Lands of the Grand River. Toronto, 1964.

H. V. NELLES. "Loyalism and Local Power: The District of Niagara, 1792-1837," O.H., LVIII (2), June 1966, 99-114.

ELVA M. RICHARDS. "The Joneses of Brockville and the Family Compact," O.H., LX (4), Dec. 1968, 169-84.

S. F. WISE. "Tory Factionalism: Kingston Elections and Upper Canadian Politics, 1820-1836," O.H., LVII (4), Dec. 1965, 205-25.

SOCIAL AND ECONOMIC DEVELOPMENT

MICHAEL S. CROSS, ed. The Frontier Thesis and the Canadas: The Debate on the Impact of the Canadian Environment. Toronto, 1970.

LEO A. JOHNSON. "Land Policy, Population Growth and Social Structure in the Home District, 1793-1851," O.H., LXIII (1), March 1971, 41-60.

LILLIAN F. GATES. Land Policies of Upper Canada. Toronto, 1968.

MARION MACRAE and ANTHONY ADAMSON. The Ancestral Roof: Domestic Architecture of Upper Canada. Toronto, 1963.

ALAN WILSON. The Clergy Reserves of Upper Canada: A Canadian Mortmain. Toronto, 1968.

RELIGION AND EDUCATION

J. L. H. HENDERSON. John Strachan, 1778-1867. Toronto, 1969.

J. L. H. HENDERSON, ed. John Strachan: Documents and Opinions. Toronto, 1969.

JOHN S. MOIR, ed. Church and State in Canada, 1627-1867. Toronto, 1967.

CLARA THOMAS. Ryerson of Upper Canada. Toronto, 1969.

GOVERNMENT AND POLITICS TO 1812

HARRY H. GUEST. "Upper Canada's First Political Party," O.H., LIV (4), Dec. 1962, 275-96. (On Weekes, Wilcox, et al.)

L. F. S. UPTON, ed. The United Empire Loyalists: Men and Myths. Toronto, 1967.

WAR OF 1812

J. MACKAY HITSMAN. The Incredible War of 1812: A Military History. Toronto, 1965.

PHILIP MASON, ed. After Tippecanoe: Some Aspects of the War of 1812. East Lansing and Toronto, 1963.

MORRIS ZASLOW, ed., assisted by Wesley B. Turner. *The Defended Border: Upper Canada and the War of 1812.* Toronto, 1964.

GOVERNMENT AND POLITICS, 1815-36

DAVID W. L. EARL, ed. *The Family Compact: Aristocracy or Oligarchy.* Toronto, 1967.

LOIS DARROCH MILANI. *Robert Gourlay, Gadfly.* Thornhill, Ont., 1971.

HEREWARD SENIOR. "The Genesis of Canadian Orangeism," O.H., LX (2), June 1968, 13-29.

CAROL LAWRIE VAUGHAN. "The Bank of Upper Canada in Politics, 1817-1840," O.H., LX (4), Dec. 1968, 185-205.

REBELLION OF 1837 AND ITS AFTERMATH

G. F. G. STANLEY. "Invasion: 1838," O.H., LIV (4), Dec. 1962, 237-52. (On the battle at Prescott, Nov. 1838.)

THE
CANADIAN
CENTENARY
SERIES

A HISTORY OF CANADA IN EIGHTEEN VOLUMES

The Canadian Centenary Series is a comprehensive history of the peoples and lands which form the Dominion of Canada.

Although the series is designed as a unified whole so that no part of the story is left untold, each volume is complete in itself. Written for the general reader as well as for the scholar, each of the eighteen volumes of *The Canadian Centenary Series* is the work of a leading Canadian historian who is an authority on the period covered in his volume. Their combined efforts have made a new and significant contribution to the understanding of the history of Canada and of Canada today.

W. L. Morton, Vanier Professor of History, Trent University, is the Executive Editor of *The Canadian Centenary Series*. A graduate of the Universities of Manitoba and Oxford, he is the author of *The Kingdom of Canada; Manitoba: A History; The Progressive Party in Canada; The Critical Years: The Union of British North America, 1857-1873;* and other writings. He has also edited *The Journal of Alexander Begg and Other Documents Relevant to the Red River Resistance.* Holder of the honorary degrees of LL.D. and D.LITT., he has been awarded the Tyrrell Medal of the Royal Society of Canada and the Governor General's Award for Non-Fiction.

D. G. Creighton, former Chairman of the Department of History, University of Toronto, is the Advisory Editor of *The Canadian Centenary Series*. A graduate of the Universities of Toronto and Oxford, he is the author of *John A. Macdonald: The Young Politician; John A. Macdonald: The Old Chieftain; Dominion of the North; The Empire of the St. Lawrence* and many other works. Holder of numerous honorary degrees, LL.D. and D.LITT., he has twice won the Governor General's Award for Non-Fiction. He has also been awarded the Tyrrell Medal of the Royal Society of Canada, the University of Alberta National Award in Letters, the University of British Columbia Medal for Popular Biography, and the Molson Prize of the Canada Council.